THE MOBILE STORY

What happens when stories meet mobile media? In this cutting-edge collection, contributors explore digital storytelling in ways that look beyond the desktop to consider how stories can be told through mobile, locative, and pervasive technologies. This book offers dynamic insights about the new nature of narrative in the age of mobile media, studying digital stories that are site-specific, context-aware, and involve the reader in fascinating ways. Addressing important topics for scholars, students, and designers alike, this collection investigates the crucial questions for this emerging area of storytelling and electronic literature. Topics covered include the histories of site-specific narratives, issues in design and practice, space and mapping, mobile games, narrative interfaces, and the interplay between memory, history, and community.

Jason Farman is an Assistant Professor at the University of Maryland, College Park, in the Department of American Studies and a Distinguished Faculty Fellow in the Digital Cultures and Creativity Program. He is the author of Mobile Interface Theory: Embodied Space and Locative Media (Routledge, 2012).

COMPANION WEBSITE

www.TheMobileStory.com

- INSTRUCTOR MATERIALS
- HANDS-ON EXPLORATIONS OF EACH CHAPTER
- SAMPLE CHAPTERS
- EXAMPLES OF CUTTING-EDGE STORYTELLING PROJECTS

THE MOBILE STORY

Narrative Practices with Locative Technologies

Edited by Jason Farman

Routledge
Taylor & Francis Group

NEW YORK AND LONDON

First published 2014
by Routledge
711 Third Avenue, New York, NY 10017

Simultaneously published in the UK
by Routledge
2 Park Square, Milton Park, Abingdon, Oxon OX14 4RN

Routledge is an imprint of the Taylor & Francis Group, an informa business

© 2014 Taylor & Francis

Library of Congress Cataloging-in-Publication Data

The mobile story : narrative practices with locative technologies / edited by
  Jason Farman.
    pages cm
  Includes bibliographical references and index.
  1. Mobile computing—Social aspects. 2. Digital media—
Social aspects. 3. Storytelling. 4. Spatial behavior. 5. Hypertext
literature. 6. Telecommunication—Social aspects. I. Farman, Jason.
  HM851.M629 2013
  302.23'1—dc23
  2013005423

ISBN: 978-0-415-64148-7 (hbk)
ISBN: 978-0-203-08078-8 (ebk)

Typeset in Bembo
by Apex CoVantage, LLC

TABLE OF CONTENTS

LIST OF FIGURES

PART I

Narrative and Site-Specific Authorship

1

SITE-SPECIFICITY, PERVASIVE COMPUTING, AND THE READING INTERFACE

Jason Farman

How do the examples in this chapter help us understand the practice of story-telling in the mobile media age?

This chapter serves, in part, as an introduction to *The Mobile Story* and offers a historical grounding for the projects analyzed throughout the rest of the book (which are discussed in more detail at the very end of this chapter). By linking mobile storytelling projects to the larger history of attaching narratives to specific places, these projects build on practices that have been done for millennia. From stone inscriptions to the stories that accompany religious pilgrimages, from graffiti in early Rome to historic walking tours of cities, the practice of sited narratives has many precedents. The desire to attach story to space is found in the connection between the historical context of a community and the need to determine the character of that space. Around these two points arises a contention over *who* is actually allowed to tell the story of a location. A site's dominant narrative is often told through durable media such as stone inscriptions, while the narratives on the margins are relegated to ephemeral media such as graffiti or the spoken word. These tensions persist in the era of site-specific digital storytelling, as elaborated in the subsequent chapters in this collection.

Keywords

- **Site-specificity:** The emphasis on the unique qualities of a particular location that cannot be transferred onto another place. When practiced in mobile storytelling projects, site-specificity embraces the characteristics of the location, including its histories, cultural conflicts, communities, and architectures (to name only a few) and makes these aspects foundational for the experience of the space.

- **Urban markup:** The various ways that narrative gets attached to a specific place in a city. Urban markup can be done through durable inscriptions (like words carved into the stone façade of a building or a statue) or though ephemeral inscriptions (ranging from banners and billboards to graffiti and stickers).
- **Creative misuse:** Creatively using a technology in a way in which it was never meant to be used, the results of which offer a thoroughly transformed view of the technology, its place in society, and future practices with the technology.

Introduction

As I look at the ways that people use their mobile devices in different regions around the world, one thing becomes obvious: these devices are being used in vastly diverse ways from community to community and from person to person. There is no single way that people use their cell phones, their tablet computers, their laptops, or other mobile media. There is no "correct" way of using mobile media; instead, we see a wide range of uses globally. There are contrasting—and even contradictory—uses of mobile media worldwide. For example, the idea of multiple people sharing a single cell phone, while out of the ordinary in a place like the United States, where the cell phone epitomizes technology designed for individual use, is a much more common feature in certain communities in India, where cell phones are shared even among strangers.[1] Another example of contradictory approaches to the use of mobile media involves location awareness: some people use their mobile devices to broadcast their location throughout the day, yet this might seem like a tremendous invasion of privacy to others. For example, Sam Liang (co-founder of the company Alohar, which designed an application called "Placeme"), leaves the location-aware services and GPS running on his smartphone in order to track his every move throughout the day (and share it with a broad group of people). Others, such as women who seek protection at a domestic abuse shelter, attempt to limit the amount of data that leaves their cell phones. Here, once a woman checks in, the organization takes her old cell phone (that poses a potential threat of exposing her now-secret location) and replaces it with an emergency-only phone that is able to only call the police or the shelter.

The vast number of ways that people use their mobile devices deeply resonated with me on an afternoon this past summer. I was sitting in the audience of a conference on mobile media listening to many international scholars and practitioners describe the ways they (and the people they study) use their devices. I heard about people in agricultural parts of Africa who use their mobile phone as a banking system, sending payments via text message to transfer money from one account to another when they sell their goods. I heard about people in

London who leave the Bluetooth on (and "discoverable" by others) in order to send semi-anonymous flirtatious messages with others while riding the Underground. I heard about artists who create drawings the size of a city by letting the GPS capabilities of their phones create traces of the pathways they journey as they walk out images across a large area. I heard about tourists who hold their phones up to signs in a foreign language and see real-time translations on their screens through augmented reality. From the creation of flash mobs in New York City with thousands of participants to the Red Cross using text messages as a way to track down people in crisis after a natural disaster, our mobile phones are being used in an amazing number of ways.

I had become so comfortable with my own mobile media practices that it hadn't dawned on me that others would see a phone just like the one I own and imagine such vastly different uses for it. The mobile device is, for many of us, one of our most intimate technologies. For me, it's one of the first things I touch in the morning (when my alarm goes off); thus, I often end up touching my cell phone before I even touch another human being! As I get ready for work in the morning, I put the phone in my pocket, and it sits close to my body nearly all day long. When I wait in line during lunch, I pull out my phone and check several social media feeds or my email. The mobile phone is now deeply woven into my everyday life, and I've become so comfortable with the ways I use it that I have gotten to a point where I don't think of my mobile media practices as noteworthy. These practices are so commonplace that I rarely take notice of them. The interface often even disappears into my actions throughout the day.[2]

When our perspectives of our mobile media practices go from being so familiar that they seemingly disappear and instead shift to a perspective where we see entirely new ways of using these devices, the results can be revolutionary. This shift is a transformative one. This book is about such shifts taking place around us. Emerging storytelling projects offer some of the best examples of the transformative potential of mobile media. The projects discussed in this book typically take the mobile device out of the realm of the everyday and insert it into practices that reimagine our relationship to technology, place, and our own sense of self in the spaces through which we move.

However, such shifts in perspective can be challenging to accomplish. Getting people to reimagine a technology they are extremely familiar with (and the places transformed by these technologies) is similar to asking them to get lost in their own homes. The goal, therefore, of some of the storytelling projects detailed in this book is to "defamiliarize" people with their places and the technologies that mediate these places. In order to accomplish this defamiliarization, artists, authors, and scholars often turn to what is called "creative misuse," or finding a way to use mobile media and software, like iPhone apps, in ways that they were never intended for. The result is often a deeper sense of place and a stronger understanding of our own position within that place.

Ultimately, the level of depth and personal engagement offered by defamil-iarization and creative misuse counters much of the contemporary distrust over mobile media. Over the last several years, we have seen a deluge of messages that argue that mobile media are disconnecting us from "real" and genuine interac-tions with our loved ones and with the places we move through. For example, a 2010 commercial for the Windows phone showed a series of short clips in which people were staring at their phones rather than connecting with the people im-mediately around them. A woman getting married walks down the aisle while texting. A man on a rollercoaster is seemingly oblivious to the ride while he browses the Internet. A spouse is unaware of his wife's sexual advances (as she stands next to the bed in lingerie) while he stares at his phone. Joggers who stare at their phones run into each other. People fall down stairs or sit in seats already occupied by someone else—all because they are seemingly somewhere else when they're staring at their phones. What mobile media storytelling projects demonstrate, in contrast, is that someone can be staring at a mobile device and be more deeply connected to the space and to others in that space than other people might perceive. Storytelling with mobile media takes the stories of a place and attaches them to that place, offering an almost infinite number of stories that can be layered onto a single site. Readers of these stories can stand at a location, access the stories about that site, and gain a deep connection to that space (and the various histories of that space). Thus, not everyone staring into a smartphone is disconnected from his or her surroundings and from the other people in those spaces.

The History of Site-Specific Storytelling

People have attempted to tie stories to places for as long as stories have existed. The meaning of a story is affected by the place in which the story is told and, similarly, the meaning of a place tends to be told through stories. Pervasive com-puting scholar Malcolm McCullough has explained these practices by pointing out the various historical ways site-specific stories have been told. McCullough has contrasted "durable" inscriptions—such as those carved into stone or into the side of a building—to "ephemeral" inscriptions like graffiti, banners, and bill-boards that aren't as long-lasting and are characterized by their transitory nature.[3] He categorizes both of these forms of site-specific storytelling as "urban markup." Interestingly, these two forms of site-specific storytelling also demonstrate the power dynamics and hierarchies involved in *who* gets to tell the story of a space. Those with economic wealth and political clout tend to be the ones who are able to place durable inscriptions throughout a city. They can afford the statue of a par-ticular war hero or politician, linking the life of this figure to the place where the statue is located. In contrast, graffiti functions similarly to tell a certain story or life of a place but tends to be done by those without the power or political clout to create durable inscriptions. These inscriptions often serve to stand in opposition to the legal and "authorized" ways of storytelling about a place.

There have been variations on these two forms of site-specific storytelling throughout history. Examples include stories that are intimately tied to the place they describe, such as the Stations of the Cross. Born out of religious pilgrimages (many of which also fall under the category of site-specific narratives), the Stations of the Cross emerged around the late fourteenth century as a practice in which Christian pilgrims would visit Jerusalem and walk the *Via Delarosa*, walking the path that Jesus took on the final days of his life.[4] At each of these sites, pilgrims would recount the story of the site (e.g., the place where Simon of Cyrene was compelled to carry the cross for Jesus) and meditate in prayer about the significance of the events and the fact that these events happened in the very place at which they stood. Eventually, these sites were duplicated in regions around the world in an attempt to allow Christians the experience of the Stations of the Cross without the pilgrimage to Jerusalem (thus removing the site-specificity of this place-based narrative).

There are many examples of site-specific stories in contemporary society. Many of us have experienced the link between narrative and site-specificity when we have taken a historic tour of a city or a building, when we've gone on ghost tours of places like London or New Orleans, or engaged in historic reenactments of events like Civil War battles. Ultimately, these forms of site-specific storytelling aim to capitalize on the idea that there is value in standing at the site where an event took place; far more than simply reading about an event, being in the place where that event happened offers experiential value that gives us a deeper sense of the story and the ways that story affects the meaning of the place.

As McCullough notes, contemporary mobile media narratives fall somewhere along the spectrum between the durable and ephemeral inscriptions that characterize such urban markup. New forms of urban markup that utilize mobile technologies are "neither organized 'media' as the twentieth century knew them, nor random graffiti as all the ages have witnessed." These forms of site-specific markup are seen in the "new practices of mapping, tagging, linking, and sharing [that] expand both possibilities and participation in urban inscription."[5] Thus, while it is vital to situate the digital storytelling projects in this book historically (and understand how they are building on things like stone inscriptions on buildings, graffiti, or the Stations of the Cross), it is also important to ask, "What is unique about storytelling projects that use mobile media?" We must explore how these projects make important advancements on the process of writing, distributing, and reading a story.

The Mobile Device and Medium-Specificity

As has been demonstrated thus far, stories told about a space (and stories that are deeply connected to the space in which they are experienced) have utilized a wide array of urban markup throughout history. Similarly, mobile media have been used to tell the stories of place for millennia, taking shape in mobile media like books, letters, and more recent mobile media, such as portable radios, audio books for personal listening devices, and books for tablet computers. A key feature of *mobile* media is their relationship to space, since they can move across vast geographic distances. They are portable, unlike many of the media that preceded them (such as stone inscription or even a statue that commemorates the story of a site). They are spatial media (and spatially flexible media) and thus are uniquely equipped to engage with the narratives about spaces and places.

Yet, there are specific attributes of *contemporary* mobile technologies that do not have precedent in previous media for storytelling. Tapping into this mode of exploration is called "medium-specific analysis"; such an approach asks us to understand the medium's unique capabilities (and constraints). These affordances and constraints will significantly affect the content of the story and the experience of it.[6] In line with Marshall McLuhan's famous adage that "the medium is the message," a medium-specific analysis understands that the medium will often impact the ways a story is told, distributed, and experienced.[7] This impact is often because of issues like the interface (does an author want to compose a long text on the small keyboard of a mobile phone?) or the cultural expectations (do we read stories on an iPad in very similar ways that we read them on a print book because that is what is culturally accepted?).

Throughout this book, while many authors acknowledge the deep historical roots of digital storytelling with mobile media, they are keenly invested in exploring the emerging medium-specificity of mobile technologies. Since mobile media are becoming the most pervasive technology on the face of the planet right now, how does such pervasiveness change the ways we tell stories and read stories? Is there a difference between reading a story on a mobile phone versus a tablet computer versus a PDF file? The answers that resonate throughout the chapters in this book point to some key attributes of emerging mobile technologies (such as their relationship to the particular spaces we move through, gained through the devices' location awareness). Mobile media are location-aware and context-specific in ways that other media are not. Simultaneously, mobile media offer the possibility to layer multiple—even conflicting—stories onto a single space. Thus, the possibilities for storytelling are expanded because of the medium-specificity of mobile media. For example, unlike previous storytelling media, mobile media narratives can layer countless stories on that single site using digital urban markup. Due to the constraints of physical spaces and media (such as size and conflicting visualizations as when a painting covers up what was underneath), nondigital forms of storytelling are limited in the number of voices that can contribute to the meanings of a location. Thus, the potentials for digital storytelling using mobile media are truly profound.

The Problems of "Narrative" and "Story"

While we can layer multiple stories on a site to tell a range of perspectives about what a place means, the process can involve some challenging hurdles that are inherent in *all* acts of storytelling. Often, the idea of "narrative" itself is rife with problems because it tends to put forth an idea of a cohesive, linear story about a site, an event, or a community. The act of storytelling can be constrained by such challenges and can often be maneuvered into presenting a narrative that has a distinct beginning, middle, and end. Stories also tend to offer the illusion that they present the events in their entirety (and if they leave out anything, the omitted portions are simply not relevant).

If we hold to the adage that "we are the stories we tell" (and as Indian film director Shekhar Kapur has argued, "[A] person without a story does not exist"[8]), then there is an enormous amount of pressure for stories to be foundational elements of our lives. Once they take on this status, stories must live up to often-unrealistic cultural expectations. The results can be narratives that are cleanly linear and tell a very particular story without regard for nuance and multiple perspectives. Certain historical narratives are a good example. Some approaches, as performance studies scholar David Román notes, seek to tell an "official history" of an event (Román cites the origin stories told about the emergence of HIV/AIDS). In Román's example, these "totalizing narratives . . . [present a] genealogy of AIDS [which] overdetermines the arrival of AIDS and obscures the process(es) of AIDS." As such, "AIDS will continue to be understood within the confines of these narratives of origin."[9] For Román, any narrative or history of AIDS needs to be presented as multiple and discontinuous rather than cohesive and linear. Another performance studies theorist, Sue-Ellen Case, echoes these ideas about narratives, feeling that stories themselves can never adequately present the fundamentally fragmented experience that constitutes life today. Case says, "I'm not against stories, but I think they're not speaking to a lot of people who are looking at fragments, at images on devices of various sizes, and finding new ways of putting things together. I don't know if the traditional notion of storytelling really works with new media. So I really don't think storytelling has a great future."[10]

This book is about some possible futures of the story and ways that mobile devices and locative storytelling practices might offer an intervention to Case's concerns about the limitations of story. Therefore, the chapters in this collection present a wide range of storytelling practices, most of which embrace the subjective experiences of the storyteller and reader (and thus offer narrative practices that encourage fragmentation, limited point of view, and the insertion of many voices to help offset the limited perspective of the individual reader or storyteller). As such, the narrative practices in this book work to achieve what William Uricchio notes, in his work analyzing the practice of media history, any narrative must have: "multiple and sometimes contradictory causalities . . .

[which require] an embrace of multiplicity, complexity and even contradiction if sense is to be made of such a pervasive cultural experience."[11]

Structure of This Book

This book brings together scholars and practitioners who each offer a unique perspective on this emerging form of storytelling. While not putting forth a "totalizing narrative" about the landscape of mobile media storytelling today, the chapters offer important inroads to scholarship and practice working at the intersection of mobile media and storytelling. The book begins with a section about "Narrative and Site-Specific Authorship." Building on the histories of urban markup and site-specific storytelling that I've laid out in this chapter, the rest of the section develops and extends existing narrative theories to offer an updated approach that is informed by mobile and pervasive technologies. Chapter 2, "The Interrelationships of Mobile Storytelling: Merging the Physical and the Digital at a National Historic Site," launches the book by offering the perfect glimpse of what's to come. Written by two scholar-practitioners, Brett Oppegaard and Dene Grigar, the chapter offers both a theoretical and practice-based approach to the implementation of a mobile media narrative. Drawing on the example of the Fort Vancouver Mobile storytelling application, a project that both authors developed, the practice of mobile storytelling is studied through the lens of "intermediality." Through this term—which is a companion idea to the notions of media convergence, interconnectedness, and the global process of production—Oppegaard and Grigar point to four relationships in the practice of locative storytelling: the relationship between content and medium; between people, time, and space; between intersubjective participants; and between people and information.

In their chapter "Re-Narrating the City Through the Presentation of Location," Adriana de Souza e Silva and Jordan Frith analyze narrative and storytelling through the various uses of location-based social networks (LBSNs). These networks ask people to "check in" at locations as they move through the city, typically attaching notes, images, or reviews that are broadcast to their network. In so doing, these social networks provide participants with modes of reading and writing the city. By reasserting the importance of location to the act of writing the self into being, the production of space and production of identity are intimately entwined.

Part II of the book offers insights on the "Design and Practice" of mobile stories. The section begins with an important theoretical and practical overview by Jeff Ritchie in his chapter, "The Affordances and Constraints of Mobile Locative Narratives." Drawing on the work of Donald Norman—who notably theorized the ideas of affordances and constraints, or the properties of an object that determine how it may or may not be used—Ritchie discusses the various ways that stories are either enabled or constrained by these emerging mobile devices. Part of his investigation is to ask designers to also consider the affordances and constraints of the spaces of these stories (and how they often demand "really non-trivial effort" on the part of audiences, since these participants have to physically move through various spaces to access the story). Ultimately, Ritchie argues that mobile locative narratives must foster far greater motivation for the audience to take part in the story in order to overcome the value threshold of the story.

Mark Sample's chapter, "Location Is Not Compelling (Until It Is Haunted)," asks some foundational questions for locative storytelling designers: with so many people using locative media to broadcast their location to their social network, *why should anyone care about your location? Why is your location interesting or compelling?* These questions cut to the heart of why particular places and site-specificity are important to locative storytelling projects. His response is that, while your location might not be compelling, *stories are.* Sample thus sets out to discuss possible storytelling projects that seek to reconcile the poor connection between locational tools and narrative.

Chapter 6, "Dancing with Twitter: Mobile Narratives Become Physical Scores," by Susan Kozel, investigates the relationship between performance, narrative, and mobile media. By looking at narrative through the lens of dance, the term "narrative" is questioned: are mobile narratives that emerge through dance practice considered scripts, scores, notations, archives, or simply documents of live interactions? Kozel investigates these terms (and the ways that narrative, mobile media, and dance can be woven together) through an analysis of her mobile dance project, *IntuiTweet,* in which dancers used Twitter to send short messages to each other describing movement or kinesthetic sensations. Performers across several cities then performed the movements described in the tweets. She ultimately points to the embodied nature of asynchronous forms like Twitter and the power of using a social medium in unconventional ways.

The section ends with John Barber's chapter, "Walking-Talking: Soundscapes, *Flâneurs,* and the Creation of Mobile Media Narratives." Walking-Talking is a proposed mobile storytelling project that uses mobile phones to produce a sound narrative focused on a particular urban location. In discussing the possibilities of a locative sound-narrative project, Barber notes that the experience of a story of this kind resembles the practices of the *flâneur,* the nineteenth-century walker whose leisurely strolls in an urban setting became emblematic of modern life. Walking-Talking projects—unlike previous forms of storytelling that transported users away from their location by immersing them in an alternate, imaginative space—transport participants *into* their physical surroundings.

Part III, "Space and Mapping," offers three chapters that analyze the relationship between maps and mobile media (and how stories can be conveyed through these two media). The section begins with Didem Ozkul and David Gauntlett's experiments with the creation of cognitive maps of London. In "Locative Media in the City: Drawing Maps and Telling Stories," Ozkul and Gauntlett discuss their interactions with participants who were asked to draw maps of their city and their experiences of mobility within the city. These "sketch maps" offer a practice of translating knowing into telling: a process of self-narration about memories, spaces, and everyday life in a city increasingly characterized by mobile media use.

In chapter 9, "Paths of Movement: Negotiating Spatial Narratives through GPS Tracking," Lone Koefoed Hansen focuses on the artistic practice of Dutch media artist Esther Polak, especially her work using GPS technologies to map and track spatial movements. Polak's work explores ways of tracking, visualizing, and discussing the many spatial narratives that emerge when location data is overlaid with everyday life. Through an analysis of Polak's works, and with theoretical reference to Dutch architect Rem Koolhaas and French theorist Michel de Certeau, this chapter discusses how mobile media seem to facilitate an informed (re)engagement with space and the spatial narratives that unfold when people and objects disclose the personal, national, and global stories that are expressed through their paths of movement.

The section concludes with Paula Levine's chapter, "On Common Ground: Here as There." In this chapter, Levine looks at several mobile mapping narrative projects to show how these projects can work to build empathy in participants. Empathy is fostered in these projects by bringing the "distant" into direct relationship with the "local." The projects analyzed—which include Levine's own work *San Francisco-Baghdad* and *The Wall-The World*, Paul Rademacher's *The Gulf Oil Spill*, and *The Transborder Immigrant Tool*—each offer participants a sense of layering and juxtaposition, resulting in what Levine terms "spatial dissonance." By bringing the distant/foreign to bear on the local and immediate surroundings, new narratives emerge and produce experiences in which empathy plays a key role.

Part IV, "Mobile Games," discusses a range of mobile storygames that utilize both locative technologies and nonlocative media. Ben Bunting's chapter, "The Geocacher as Placemaker: Remapping Reality through Location-Based Mobile Gameplay," discusses the link between players' movements in the physical world and the goals of the gameworld as offering a new dimension to in-game storytelling. Bunting looks specifically at geocaching (and his co-authored storygame project, *University of Death*) to show how gameworlds and physical spaces can merge to create engaging in-game narratives that utilize the site-specificity of the player as the immersive backdrop.

Rowan Wilken's chapter, "Proximity and Alterity: Narratives of City, Self, and Other in the Locative Games of Blast Theory," further develops this dynamic by looking at specific instances in locative games where players had to make connections with strangers. Looking at the work of Blast Theory, Wilken argues that such moments in locative games allow players to reimagine the city as a place that encourages connections with "the Other" (or those who are extremely different than we are). What emerges out of Wilken's analysis is an interrogation of the idea of community: locative games can encourage interactions with diversity to such an extent that community becomes defined not through commonality, but through ongoing interactions with difference in the spaces we move through.

Chapter 13, "Playing Stories on the Worldboard: How Game-Based Storytelling Changes in the World of Mobile Connectivity," by Bryan Alexander, traces the longer history of these storygames, noting how changes in gaming platforms have radically transformed the kinds of stories that these games can tell. The specific affordances and constraints of mobile games (from the Game Boy to immersive alternate reality games) offer unique advantages for storygames. Mobile storygames take advantage of the medium by allowing players to play interstitially, or in small pieces throughout the day. Similarly, emerging mobile storygames utilize the medium to incorporate the ability to capture and share content, as well as augment the space of the game with constantly transforming data.

The Mobile Games section ends with chapter 14, "'I Heard It Faintly Whispering': Mobile Technology and Nonlocative Transmedia Practices," by Marc Ruppel. While much of this book thus far has focused on *locative technologies* (and the book itself is primarily concerned with this affordance of mobile media as noted in the subtitle, "Narrative Practices with Locative Technologies"), Ruppel's chapter importantly expands this scope to note how mobile devices can be utilized for narrative and play in *nonlocative ways*. Focusing primarily on transmedia narratives, that utilize a wide range of media to tell their stories (mobile technologies being just one of them), Ruppel shows how mobile media become embedded in the transmedia stories while simultaneously becoming functional tools for the story to progress. In many of the stories he focuses on, such as the alternate reality game for the television series *Heroes*, the mobile phone becomes part of the characters' interactions; however, at the same time, the phone is used by readers to engage with those characters. These uses greatly expand how mobile media is theorized for storygames. They must be understood within a larger media ecology that includes a wide range of technologies. They must also be understood as media that help extend the perceptions and sensory engagements of participants in these transmedia narratives.

Part V, "Narrative Interfaces," begins with Gerard Goggin and Caroline Hamilton's co-written chapter, "Narrative Fiction and Mobile Media after the Text-Message Novel." This chapter aims to situate emerging reading practices among the various platforms for reading. Goggin and Hamilton look back at the history of reading from the novel to the cell-phone novel and, eventually, the e-reader and the location-aware device. Tracing the development of reading, writing, and distributing narratives through these platforms, Goggin and Hamilton show that reading platforms throughout history have encouraged several forms of "discontinuous reading" that extend beyond linear and enclosed models of reading. This form of reading has now dominated the emerging mobile media narratives and has subsequently opened up opportunities for much deeper engagements with narrative dynamics from a wider range of producers, consumers, co-creators and distributors.

Larissa Hjorth's chapter, "Stories of the Mobile: Women, Micronarratives, and Mobile Novels in Japan," builds on the previous chapter to further analyze the specifics of the cell-phone novel. The Japanese *keitai shôsetsu*, sales of which far exceed the sale of print-text books in the West, sends out "micronarratives" in installments to readers. These novels are often written on cell phones and are designed to be read on cell phones. These cellphone novels, the majority of which are written by women and for women through "user-created content," demonstrate how mobile media is undoubtedly transforming what it means to be creative and intimate. Through *keitai shôsetsu*, women can bring intimate and private stories into the public space, proffering new ways to experience storytelling in public places.

Chapter 17, "Telling Their Stories through iPad Art: Narratives of Adults with Intellectual Disabilities," concludes the section on Narrative Interfaces. Co-authored by Jennifer Chatsick, Rhonda McEwen, and Anne Zbitnew, this chapter looks at the practices of the Visual Storytelling Club in Toronto, a group of college students with intellectual disabilities who use iPads as devices for nonlinear storytelling. Prompted by various scenarios, the students use the mobile devices to draw responses about their lives. These drawings, which serve as a means to work around their limited literacy skills, take particular shape when done on a tablet computer rather than on other media like desktop computers or even pen and paper. This chapter explores this medium-specificity to understand how different interfaces can foster certain kinds of narratives, especially in the context of students with disabilities.

Part VI concludes the book, looking at the topics of "Memory, History, and Community." Alberto S. Galindo's chapter, "Mobile Media after 9/11: The September 11 Memorial & Museum App," uses as its main object of study the app released for people to tour Ground Zero and engage with the oral narratives recorded about the events of 9/11. The chapter is motivated by the question, "When considering how such national traumas like 9/11 are told—through oral histories, photographs, visualizations like timelines, to name a few—how might the mobile phone as a narrative interface transform our relationship to these stories and these memorializations?" The narratives of the "Explore 9/11" app take place across several spaces: the site-specific locations related to 9/11 experienced in tandem with images on the phone's screen, the audio space of the oral narratives that are unlocked when walking by certain locations, and space of the archive of eyewitness accounts of the events. An analysis of the app thus shows that acts of memorialization, especially when experienced through emerging storytelling interfaces like the mobile phone, must be read through the lens of narrative—narratives that simultaneously interrogate these traumas as intensely public and private, in the past and ever-evolving.

Chapter 19, "Enhancing Museum Narratives: Tales of Things and UCL's Grant Museum," was co-written by scholars, curators, and designers at University College London and its Grant Museum of Zoology. The authors—Claire Ross, Mark Carnall, Andrew Hudson-Smith, Claire Warwick, Melissa Terras, and Steven Gray—discuss their design and implementation of QRator, a project that utilizes mobile media and QR codes to encourage museum visitors to interact with specific objects. Visitors offer their own interpretations and thoughts about museum objects, connecting their ideas to the broader conversations about these objects. These "narrative engagements," which stem from personal preconceptions (and how those preconceptions may have been challenged in the museum) subsequently become part of the object's history through the interactive label generated by such interactions. Comparing the QRator project to other mobile museum projects, this chapter demonstrates the emerging trend to incorporate the "Internet of Things" into experiences with historical objects. Here, mobile media affords the ability for museum goers to become authors of dynamic content for museum artifacts in a way that was previously unavailable.

The book concludes with Mark Marino's chapter, "Mobilizing Cities: Alternative Community Storytelling." Looking at two mobile story projects that allow people to tell stories about the city of Los Angeles (as citizen journalists documenting stories and as fiction writers imagining possible futures), Marino looks at how mobile media can tell stories that often go untold. Through the main examples of *Mobile Voices* (*VozMob*) and *The LA Flood Project*, this chapter notes how mobile media can offer storytellers unparalleled ways of creating spaces of polyvocality, in which *many voices* are heard equally and marginalized stories are given voice. As with many of the projects discussed throughout this book, the examples in Marino's chapter point to the importance of narratives that disrupt traditional notions of narrative creation and distribution. These emerging mobile stories are multivoiced, layered, situated, and tell important (and often contradictory) narratives about a place and what it means to live in that space.

Notes

1. Molly Wright Steenson and Jonathan Donner, "Beyond the Personal and Private: Modes of Mobile Phone Sharing in Urban India," in *The Reconstruction of Space and Time*, ed. Rich Ling and Scott W. Campbell (New Brunswick, NJ: Transaction Press, 2009), 231–250.
2. For ubiquitous computing researcher Mark Weiser, this mode of interaction is the most powerful. He writes, "The most profound technologies are those that disappear. They weave themselves into the fabric of everyday life until they are indistinguishable from it." See Mark Weiser, "The Computer for the 21st Century," http://www.ubiq.com/hypertext/weiser/SciAmDraft3.html.
3. Malcolm McCullough, "Epigraphy and the Public Library," in *Augmented Urban Spaces: Articulating the Physical and Electronic City*, ed. Alessandro Aurigi and Fiorella de Cindio (Burlington, VT: Ashgate Publishing, 2008), 64.
4. Herbert Thurston, S.J., *The Stations of the Cross: An Account of their History and Devotional Purpose* (London: Burns and Oates, 1914), 21–23.
5. Ibid., 69.
6. See N. Katherine Hayles, "Print Is Flat, Code Is Deep: The Importance of Media-Specific Analysis," *Poetics Today* 25, no. 1 (2004): 67–90.

7. Marshall McLuhan, *Understanding Media: The Extensions of Man* (New York: New American Library, 1964).

8. Shekhar Kapur, "We Are the Stories We Tell Ourselves," *TEDIndia* www.ted.com/talks/shekhar_kapur_we_are_the_stories_we_tell_ourselves.html.

9. David Román, *Acts of Intervention: Performance, Gay Culture, and AIDS* (Bloomington: Indiana University Press, 1998), xviii–xix.

10. Sue-Ellen Case, "Interview: Sue-Ellen Case on Her A.T.H.E. Career Achievement Award," *UCLA School of Theater, Film, and Television*, http://www.tft.ucla.edu/2012/04/interview-sue-ellen-case-on-her-upcoming-a-t-h-e-career-achievement-award/.

11. William Uricchio, "Historicizing Media in Transition," in *Rethinking Media Change: The Aesthetics of Transition*, ed. David Thorburn and Henry Jenkins (Cambridge, MA: The MIT Press, 2003), 23–24.

2

THE INTERRELATIONSHIPS OF MOBILE STORYTELLING

Merging the Physical and the Digital at a National Historic Site

Brett Oppegaard and Dene Grigar

How do the examples in this chapter help us understand the practice of story-telling in the mobile media age?

This chapter focuses on the production of a mobile history platform used to explore Fort Vancouver, a historic site located on the banks of the Columbia River in the Portland–Vancouver metropolitan area. Fort Vancouver, once dubbed the "New York of the Pacific," is a major archaeological resource, with more than two million artifacts in its collection. Most of those pieces, gathered from more than fifty years of excavations, are kept in warehouses, along with the boxes of documents, drawings, and other assorted historical records in storage that, because of severely limited access, obscure the fascinating and multicultural history of the place. It is a goal of the Fort Vancouver Mobile project to make these materials available through a direct experience with the site with the aid of mobile phones. By drawing from this example of a mobile storytelling platform, the chapter points toward ways that mobile stories utilize "intermediality," a term with expansive edges that helps us understand that a wide range of media should work together to transform the ways we experience space.

Keywords

- **Intermediality:** Action that takes place between the media, like an adhesive binding together the swirling mix of ideas inherent in an environment that includes otherwise unconnected media, delivered through mobile devices as well as the physical sensations of the place.
- **Mobile media storytelling:** A mode of storytelling that blends digital media on mobile devices with physical environments.
- **Fort Vancouver National Historic Site:** A National Park Service attraction based in Vancouver, Washington, that served in the nineteenth century

as the early end of the Oregon Trail. It later became the hub of the Hudson's Bay Company's fur-trading empire and the first U.S. Army Post.

Introduction

Paul Kane could sense a story that needed to be told. The self-taught painter, reared in Toronto around "hundreds of Indians," realized in the mid-1800s that the "noble savages" he had befriended as a child had essentially vanished from his region. Inspired to document the indigenous groups before they were eradicated or assimilated in the rest of North America, Kane started exploring the Canadian frontiers and the ways in which he could tell this compelling tale. He used the mobile media of the period: paper and pencils as well as oil and watercolor paints. Those journeys eventually led him thousands of miles west into uncharted wilderness, where he drew sketches of chiefs, women, children, costumes, natural landscapes, and scenes depicting manners and customs of all sorts.[1] Kane then took those hundreds of drawings and detailed journals back with him to Toronto. He translated many of them into romanticized oil paintings. He hosted several popular exhibitions of the material. More than 150 years later, though, these irreplaceable interfaces into the past have become materially irrelevant: Kane's images and stories, extracted from their native homes, simply became disconnected from time and space. No longer tethered to a place, no longer new, the images and observations sank back into their containers, drifted deeper into the library shelves, were placed into storage, and then gradually faded from general concern and consciousness.

While that data has stagnated in a nether space, modern mobile devices—smartphones, tablet computers, portable technology of all sorts—have emerged with unprecedented power to reconnect worlds, recombine media, reconstruct images, recount observations, and reverse the alienation and separation epidemic of contemporary life. These devices also represent an opportunity to forage through our past, to find the stories, like Kane's, that matter and to give them relevance again. So swiftly is society shifting due to this technological innovation that wireless penetration in the United States surged from 34% to 93% during the past decade, with many American adults now carrying around information-rich mobile devices. Meanwhile, wireless data revenue grew over that same period from $140 million to $47 billion.[2] The epoch of pervasive media has begun, just as Kane in his time recognized the sudden ubiquity of European culture in wild northeast Canadian terrain. During Kane's life, Native Americans were almost annihilated; America fought in its deadliest conflict, the Civil War; colonialism, slavery, Manifest Destiny, and other monumental crises of humanity were experienced and debated in real time. While mobile stories need further examination in all forms—from fiction to nonfiction, from narrative to expositional, per the many examples in this book—the core of this chapter is inspired by George

Santayana's prescient yet still widely unheeded mantra, "Those who cannot remember the past are condemned to repeat it."[3]

Mobile devices undeniably are changing the ways in which we view the world. They are affecting our projections of tomorrow and our remembrances of yesterday. These new tools, in turn, are creating unprecedented opportunities for digital authors. When composing mobile stories, a creator can now know where his or her users are (location awareness), what is physically around those users (spatial awareness), and even what the users have been doing before the moment of connection, all while crunching data to predict what they likely will be doing afterward (contextual awareness). These devices can level out the hierarchy of composition between author and audience as much as desired, creating the potential for a high level of collaboration and direct feedback to the story space. They also allow for creative expression by the audience to be incorporated into the content. These devices can even create tangible displays of social connectedness. In essence, mobile storytelling fosters interrelationships between four distinct entities—between content and medium; people and space/time; people and information; and people and other people. Mobile devices open new portals for rediscovering the forgotten, yet illuminating, stories of our shared history, including stories like Kane's on the American frontier.

This perspective has galvanized a team of academics, historians, archaeologists, curators, new media practitioners, and mobile developers who want to further explore this fertile mediascape. The collective effort, dubbed the "Fort Van couver Mobile project," focuses on research into the field of mobile storytelling at a principal historical hub in the Pacific Northwest, the Fort Vancouver National Historic Site, where Kane spent the winter of 1847 and today more than one million people visit each year. This essay, then, looks at one aspect of its theoretical underpinning: the interrelationships made possible by digital media storytelling.

Ideas expressed in this essay are born out of the experiences of developing digital content and a mobile app at the historic site. Fort Vancouver originally served as the early end of the Oregon Trail, and later as the regional headquarters of the British Hudson's Bay Company's fur empire, a hub of a 700,000-square-mile dynasty called the "Columbia Department," located on the north bank of the Columbia River. Later, the site served as the first U.S. Army post in the Northwest. The Fort Vancouver National Historic Site is now home to two million artifacts, most of which are kept in warehouses. These archaeological items, gathered from more than fifty years of excavations, only begin to tell the story of the place, once dubbed the "New York of the Pacific." Countless other boxes of documents, drawings, and assorted historical records add to the complexity of this multicultural mosaic. Because of its vast and diverse history, the site is representative of a long and thick narrative spine, one that materializes as more of a richly detailed realm, stuffed with intriguing characters and plots, rather than a straightforward and narrow string of pearls. It is the kind of story that demands a medium capable of handling its many facets in a way that makes sense geographically, historically, and technologically. National Park Service staff members at the fort understand the potential that digital technology offers across those layers of experience and began, themselves, exploring options, such as on-demand podcasts and social media streams, as a way to augment traditional interpretation efforts like kiosks and printed materials. Yet the storytelling opportunities of a mobile app were thought to offer such a richer and deeper environment for site visitors that the Fort Vancouver Mobile team was formed to explore such melded space, mashing together the physical and the digital, while bringing together scholars and artists from Washington State University Vancouver, Texas Tech University, Portland State University, and the Center for Columbia River History, as well as regional experts in new media production, to conduct experiments in the field. All of us sensed something special emerging, but one of the first tasks was to try to pinpoint exactly what that was.

The Affordances and Challenges of Mobile Media for Storytelling

The handheld mobile phone has been around commercially since the early 1980s, but its secondary use as a device for composing and distributing stories is relatively new. As a point of reference, the first cell-phone novel, *Deep Love*, was created in 2003 in Japan. Other forms of digital stories also have been emerging, with more recent examples drawing on the improved connectivity and robust features made possible by smart technologies. In 2006, Henry Jenkins recognized that modern storytelling, in turn, had become more about world building, as evolving authors began to create compelling digital environments "that cannot be fully explored or exhausted within a single work or even a single medium" because only a world can support the next developmental phase of storytelling in which multiple characters and multiple stories cross into multiple media.[4] The affordances for storytelling as "world building" means that Fort Vancouver can be told as a biography of its founder, John McLoughlin, or from the perspective of any number of the characters who inhabited the place and later became important nationally and internationally, including Ulysses S. Grant, George C. Marshall, and O.O. Howard. Or it can be told from the viewpoint of any of the hundreds of uncelebrated and undocumented workers, or from the perspective of women who kept the semblance of Western civility, replete with Spode china, in the rough and ready frontier. The Fort Vancouver story can be set at the time of the founding of the fort, when the location was part of the Oregon Trail, or during its heyday, when the fort ruled the region as the hub of the Hudson's Bay Company's fur-trading empire, or afterward, when the U.S. Army pushed the Canadians north and created the first American military outpost in the region. Or it could show the time before the Europeans arrived, or even the moment of first contact, à la the settling of Jamestown. The same relatively small piece of land supported all of that narrative activity. Yet people generally come to Fort Vancouver today and want to learn "the" story. History, in this respect, is closer to art and literature than science. Verónica Tozzi refers to the phrase "impositionalist narrativism" as a way to describe the coexistence of multiple interpretations of the same event, dependent upon the storyteller's perspective.[5] This idea presents a picture, of sorts, of the complex intertwining of the personalities and beliefs of the interface, or interpreter, with the individual and personalized interests of the user. The ultimate goal of mobile storytelling from this perspective is, then, as Mei Yii Lim and Ruth Aylett note, to provide ways for visitors to the site to navigate among this interconnected mass of information and gain access to free-choice learning.[6]

Historic sites inherently attempt to connect story and place, for without that tether, such sites have no clearly recognizable spatial or physical purpose, and therefore the community has no logical reason to devote space and resources to maintain them. In Western culture, at least, such a place provides a tangible link to the past, and the historical storytelling makes explicit what is implicitly embedded in the local landscape.[7] Such sites have incorporated various technologies to make such connections for as long as they have existed, and they continue to try to find new ways to make their stories relevant to new generations, including a wide range of techniques such as physical exhibitions, outdoor panels, and audio tours.[8] Despite such alluring affordances, mobile storytelling has been slow to attract architects of narrative realms. These essential producers, who place the portals and filter the noise, rarely are venturing into these types of interactive and immersive forms. With a few exceptions—such as Evan Young's *The Carrier*,[9] the *Tracking Agama* team,[10] and the Neighborhood Narratives projects[11]—it seems odd that arguably one of the most potentially powerful storytelling devices for connecting story and place instead has been relegated to the relatively narrow transmissions of text messages or as a platform for puzzle games. Yet, as this book testifies, those in the digital humanities and media arts are beginning to realize the enormous potential of mobile devices as storytelling tools.

Technical issues right now make authoring in any mobile space a frustrating and time-consuming endeavor. These devices tend to have a highly restricted energy capacity, relatively low computing power, and relatively small amounts of memory and storage space, plus limited color and font support. The keyboards typically are small and hard to use, and limited bandwidth makes downloads typically slow, causing lag.[12] Theoretically, mobile devices eventually will adapt universal standards and gain intuitive features and functionality. These standardizations will increase and allow for presentations that are more complex.[13] Improved technology, higher-speed transfer rates, and more standardization eventually should solve many of the technical issues. Typical users of interactive technologies, though, tend to be less interested in the technologies themselves and more interested in the story or purpose of the interaction.[14] Blank pieces of paper—like

Kane had—might even seem preferable at times. His worst technical glitch was more than likely a broken lead on his pencil, and the toughest medial decision he had to make was between pencil and paint. But the field of mobile storytelling cannot afford to wait this one out. There are no indications that such technological problems will be solved any time soon, and some of the significant theoretical issues within the field already are within reach.

Theoretical Underpinning: Intermediality and Its Interrelationships

When a broad society-changing technological advancement appears, as mobile "smart" phones have in the last few years, extremists typically are the first to measure in, offering polarizing and opposing dystopian or utopian views about how life as we know it is ending or how a new era is beginning. Many of us may remember that when digital writing (replete with hypertext linking) was introduced, Sven Birkerts lamented the end of wisdom and intellectual depth,[15] and Robert Coover predicted "the end of books."[16] Few technologies actually live up to these bold assertions. It takes full mainstream adoption and many years of exposure to a technology, after a general calming and settling, before a true calibration finally can take place. Only then, can we more clearly see what has changed us in significant ways, and what hasn't, as we emerge from the shroud of something different having taken place and having been adopted into society. This general understanding of knowledge stratification parallels and reflects the logic typically applied to the creation of academic theories and the herding of vast realms of decentralized—yet seemingly related—knowledge, such as "new media," into an orderly model. In this model, virtually every step, or new layer of thought, comes directly from, or is an extension of, another. Among the many advancements that spring forth and the continual mashing and remashing of ideas, the intellectual lineage is much more difficult to separate and trace, with the effects also similarly swirling and slipping out of reach.[17]

After a decade of exposure to mobile phones, we still are not even sure what to call this phenomenon of storytelling with these devices. Mobile storytelling? Ambient storytelling? Geostories? Interreality? Mixed reality? Locative narrative? Ubiquitous media? Consistent terminology has become a concern within this field, a barrier keeping us all from talking about what we think we are talking about. Intermedial communication, as bland as that may sound, at least provides an extremely broad umbrella under which the fundamental discussions can begin, for it draws on the notion of, as Robin Nelson has written, "co-relations . . . that result in a redefinition of the media that are influencing each other, which in turn leads to a fresh perception." It suggests a "both-and approach" to understanding information rather than an either-or perspective.[18] The prefix "inter," Irina Rajewsky writes, denotes that intermedial action takes place between the media, like an adhesive that binds together the swirling mix of ideas. That helps to distinguish it from kin theories such as intramedial (within a particular medium) and transmedia or transmedial (a motif, aesthetic, or discourse spread across different media).[19] "Intermedial" has become a term with expansive edges, including referring to the ways in which, as Nelson notes, media "work together in digital culture to challenge established modalities of experience. . . . In some instances, they collide and create a frisson. In other instances, one medium is imbricated within another so that they are almost dissolved into each other but the form of one remains just visible in the solution of the other."[20] Intermediality embraces ideas of media convergence, or, as Klaus Bruhn Jensen describes, "the interconnectedness of modern media of communication. As means of expression and exchange, the different media depend on and refer to each other, both explicitly and implicitly; they interact as elements of particular communicative strategies; and they are constituents of a wider cultural environment."[21] Intermediality also, in its most general sense, André Gaudreault and Philippe Marion argue, covers any process of cultural production.[22] Lars Ellestrom claims in the introduction to his *Media Borders: Multimodality and Intermediality* that "[i]f all media were fundamentally different, it would be hard to find any interrelations at all . . . [and] if they were fundamentally similar, it would be equally hard to find something that is not already interrelated. Media, however, are both different and similar, and intermediality must be understood as a bridge between medial differences that is founded on medial similarities."[23] A story like that of Fort Vancouver, with its innumerable nooks and angles and mysteries, needs such a malleable theory at its base to match the technological flexibility of mobile devices in order to bring clarity and wholeness to the informational chaos. Thus for us, intermediality serves as a theoretical given underpinning our views of the four types of interrelationships of mobile storytelling.

1. *Interrelationship between Content and Medium*

The interrelationship that this unifying approach enables between content and medium is empowering. *Majestic*, credited by many as the first "alternate reality game,"[24] incorporated telephone calls, faxes, emails, instant messages, and web pages to deliver a government conspiracy tale, all of which today could have been handled by a single device.[25] Mobile devices have absorbed the specialties of just about every medium—newspapers, television, radio, books, movies, telephones, Walkie Talkies, watches, cameras, audio recorders, calendars, video games, pagers, address books, and desktop and notebook computers, among others. Fields of specialization have been obliterated, and McLuhan's mantra of the "medium is the message" grows once again in ramifications.[26] Authors suddenly are in control of virtually all media at once, from video to sound files to words, shaping discourse through convergent technologies. In the context of composition, this sudden sense of freedom, potential, and optimism contrasts with the opposite emotions created by a lack of focus and operating outside a clear niche, creating yet another paradox of these devices. Sirkka Jarvenpaa and Karl Lang identify others as well, including the empowerment/enslavement principle, in which mobile users today have access to content at all times, every moment of every day, all year long, wherever they might happen to be, creating unparalleled knowledge access.[27] That is, until the battery dies, leaving the user as helpless as Superman holding Kryptonite.

The modern user, though, also remains in control of a ubiquitous and personal access point, creating just one of the complications for authors. This situation reflects or extends the parallels problematic in the twenty-four-hour news cycle in which increments of information can gain unbalanced importance related to distribution goals rather than quality concerns. If the emphasis for the writer always is on "new" or "first," then the more substantial and worthwhile core of the discourse can get lost in the rapid distribution churn. Meanwhile, as the information changes with the times, the content inherently changes, as if composed on shifting sand, deadening or enriching nuances, shaping and reshaping the work, which could lead to the endless polishing of every piece, or more likely, abandonment that causes irrelevance, like the fading importance of Kane's sketches. Bringing it all together, through an intermedial paradigm, into oneness, accepting rather than separating the interrelationships, creates a new kind of focus for storytellers. But it also creates new problems. Creators of mobile stories not only will need to choose and balance medial forms along with such narrative cornerstones as character and plot, but the fluidity of digital information and the growing expectations of the relevance of such information delivered through mobile devices, breeds rapidly rising quality considerations as well as sustainability concerns.

2. Interrelationship between People, Time, and Space

Jarvenpaa and Lang reference Martin Heidegger, noting that technology destroys distance by destroying closeness, creating a condition in which everyone simultaneously is close and far, independent of geographical distance.[28] Yet physical location also is the primary tether we have left to physical experience, and geographical and organizational proximity tend to naturally increase information flow about a physical location as well as interest in it.[29] In other words, our thoughts may be elsewhere, but our bodies can never be. And we inherently care where our bodies are. So, instead of trying to force a separation that can never truly happen, an intermedial approach to mobile storytelling integrates tangible space with virtual environments. A participant's foot is in both worlds (worlds, it should be noted, that are never completely separate). The user is cognizant of that sensation, and so is the storyteller, with great compositional precision. Location awareness of mobile devices, meanwhile, offers some of the most promising and solid distinctions of mobile composition in which content can be positioned at a particular site, an extremely specific place if desired, and that "mobile" information only can be released to people who go into that physical space and actually commune with the surroundings.

In the Fort Vancouver Mobile project, for example, the story of a Hawaiian pastor is featured in the first module. This man, William Kaulehelehe, is emblematic of the importance of "Sandwich Islanders" to the establishment and development of the fort, but he also illustrates larger themes comparing and contrasting British imperialism with American expansionism. Kaulehelehe gets caught in the middle between these two enormous forces, and the final piece of the mobile narrative shows a video reenactment of an incident in which American soldiers raid his home and burn it down as a way to rid the region of the British. However, this video is not being played in the sanitized and detached theater space of the visitors center or accessible from a comfortable home office; instead, this video is only available when digitally pushed to visitors via their mobile devices after they have experienced several segments of Kaulehelehe's tale, and as they stand at the actual site of the incident, with the empty reconstructed Kaulehelehe home in the background. During beta testing of this narrative, visitors were highly engaged by such alignment of the digital environment with the physical environment, indicating the potential of such intermedial space, when a user feels magically anchored to both worlds. In *Electronic Literature: New Horizons for the Literary*, N. Katherine Hayles outlines the history of what she calls a "three-dimensions interactivity"—that is, the physical relationship between user and object in 3D space—noting Janet Cardiff's locative story "The Missing Voice (Case Study B)" as a primary example of this mobile phenomenon.[30] Cardiff describes her piece as an "audio walk," which begins with the user being physically connected to the content about to be shared through audio delivered in a precise spot matching the visual situation being described. In a similar fashion, users of the Paul Kane narrative module for the Fort Vancouver Mobile project are led through the storyline to actual places where Kane created his images. They then are shown the images on their mobile devices, such as a painting of Native Americans on the banks of the Columbia River near their camp. Users can align geographic landmarks in the picture and reality, such as Mount Hood and the Columbia River, and they also can witness how dramatically the scene has changed since Kane's era, with a highway interchange, railroad tracks, and condos replacing the rural landscape. This experience of exploring spatially placed multimedia, even asynchronously with others, could be one of the ways that mobile technology can start to bring people physically back together in the same space. The question that appears on the phone interface—"Where are you?"—in this sense, helps a user come out of the clouds of technology and back into a situated context, a place, where other people are, or have been, instead of existing as a disembodied voice floating around within the wires of the network.[31]

With a dystopian bent, much of the early research on mobile devices initially focused on tendencies to disconnect users from surrounding spaces. Discussions, such as those by Janet Murray about nontrivial activities that interfere with immersion, prevailed until recently.[32] The general idea has been that deliberative movement and thought related to interacting with an interface would gain the user's attention and, so, move it away from the story itself. This disconnection, this break from the state of immersion, has been seen as a negative aspect of born-digital stories. But what if immersion into the object is *not* the holy grail of storytelling and, instead, the goal is to unite the user with a particular space? Could we not find a new quality unique to storytelling that is not beholden to print sensibilities?

Adriana de Souza e Silva and Daniel Sutko contend that interactive mobile experiences actually reconnect users in new ways.[33] While printed books and landline telephones transport users away from physical surroundings, by immersing users in their own imagination or in the focused interchange of audio conversation, the geolocative feature of smart phones takes users into their physical surroundings. A printed book can take a reader to Mars, back in time to King Arthur's Camelot, or simply inside another human's perspective, but it can never know where he or she is making that mental leap from, or who the reader is (and who other readers encountering the same piece at the same time are), or what other books of this genre the reader has enjoyed or disliked, and then respond accordingly when the reader is finished by offering other likely-to-please titles to explore. This "demassification" of media,[34] without losing amplification attributes, such as enormous reach across innumerable barriers, radically changes the approaches that authors can consider when composing for such devices, connecting them to other users, information, and space in potent ways.

3. Interrelationships among People

Various studies of users at parks, science centers, and museums have shown not only that the competition for time and interest is great but that visitors also are under no obligation to pay attention. They typically do not even look at a majority of the exhibits, and when they do, they often spend far less time with them than designers project or even hope (see, for example, chapter 19 of this book, "Enhancing Museum Narratives: Tales of Things and UCL's Grant Museum"). In turn, many people are unwilling to devote sustained attention to media and messages that are not entertaining. Multimedia exhibits, such as audio tours, though, have shown to be more attractive to visitors and hold their attention longer.[35] Taking the multimedia allure a step further, using the site as a metaphorical game board merges the story space with the unpredictability of the site, including interactions with people inside and outside of the game, such as bystanders.[36] Random encounters with real people are what fuels gameplay in location-based situations, and discussion forums that connect players outside of the game, allowing them to share game experiences, help to build a community of players.[37] The success of connecting players to one another, as seen in Blast Theory's *Uncle Roy All Around You*—where street players using geolocative technologies interact with online players—is a case in point (this topic is discussed in detail by Rowan Wilken in the "Mobile Games" section of this book).[38] On the dystopian side, Mary Flanagan warns that this physical-virtual blend can become a new form of "entertainment colonization" as well, in which unaware bystanders are unwillingly commoditized by the players.[39]

Location also can work as an initiator that can evolve into much richer communication transcending the original place.[40] But it is not a factor that authors traditionally have considered. From the intermedial paradigm, stories can be open to interlopers and unpredictable tangents. In another example, Jeremy Hight describes a city spot as "a collection of data and subtext to be read in the context of ethnography, history, semiotics, architectural patterns and forms, physical form and rhythm, juxtaposition, city planning, land usage shifts and other ways of interpretation and analysis."[41] His coauthored ground-breaking mobile narrative, *34 North, 118 West*, which chronicles the stories surrounding a particular GPS coordinate, demonstrated that "context and subtext can be formulated as much in what is present and in juxtaposition as in what one learns was there and remains in faint traces."[42] He characterized such storytelling efforts as "narrative archeology."[43] Another mobile narrative pioneer, Michael Epstein, offers a different perspective, envisioning mobile media as a way to bring audiences closer to issues and locales through a narrative overlay on maps that also can be consulted for geographic orientation and other data. He pictures these "terratives," as stories delivered through mobile devices "in tandem with real places and people."[44] Maybe the clearest perspective from here is the broadest view, one that expands even media ecology. Mobile devices can provide the full spectrum between physical and virtual environments, and they can flip the passive nature of experiencing most media around into an active proposition. Intermediality works between media, but it also absorbs its surroundings by making connections. Without the nails and glue, a house is nothing more than a big pile of sticks.

4. Interrelationship between People and Information

Interactivity, flexibility, and cohesiveness are the new cornerstones of such collaborative multimedia composition efforts, according to David Fono and Scott Counts.[45] From this perspective, interactivity means giving users multiple opportunities to engage with the shared media artifacts in a variety of ways, as opposed to the traditional model of transmission and consumption. Flexibility is an organizational mantra, in that structures of organization may be encouraged but also disregarded by users. Cohesiveness is the key connection to the traditional paradigm of authorship, in that users should be able to build a cohesive product out of the shared objects, enabled to make a variety of connections and associations. While the behaviors in isolation might not be significantly different than those entrenched in media traditions—such as taking a photograph with a mobile device and publishing it, akin to using a single lens reflex camera and a mass media distribution channel—the complexity involved in those behaviors increases with the choices now afforded.[46] As part of such complex interactions, mobile devices begin to take on traits more like shared objects than individualized terminals, another sign of this process fostering communal coagulation.[47]

Moreover, mobile communication technologies clearly alter our experiences with physical space, particularly in the creation of hybrid realms that incorporate physical, digital, and represented spaces. In these mobile "games," players physically move around the space. They collaborate with other users. They expand the game environment outside of the traditional game space, by merging different physical and virtual spaces, and perhaps the most distinguishing feature, these activities take place simultaneously in at least two different types of spaces. These spaces do not directly overlap, instead being superimposed and connected through social actions.[48] As part of this new blend of place—between the Internet's connectivity, stacks of digital information, and the users—related services typically either embed information in space or foster social mobile networks and interpersonal communication related to proximity and geographical orientation. Meanwhile, in almost every situation, storytelling predominates as a means of sharing experiences and knowledge.

Narrative structure functions as a basic cognitive means of organizing human experience and making sense of it, and that form, compared to exposition or other informational structures, is thought to be easier to read, summarize, and remember.[49] Interactive narratives respond to deeper fissures and generate negotiations of authorship, authenticity, veracity, and the authority to tell stories. Mobile narratives, with their emphasis on real experiences and direct engagement with new articulations of relationships between space, time, and postmodern patterns, provide a salient example of a modern art form that is negotiating, patterning, and understanding our changing nature.[50] Reflective of such social fluidity and bonding, composing for mobile devices may then be considered distinctive in its wide flexibility in which different pieces of information can be accessed and delivered in a variety of ways. This medial evolution increases potential effectiveness by removing the physical or technological barriers of the past, when packages of information typically had to be, for pragmatic reasons, delivered only in one specific medium. Transmedia authoring, as described by Jenkins, may be the ultimate postmodern mobile ideal in which the full narrative can only be ascertained by accessing the distinct parts of this larger discourse puzzle; yet, all of the parts also function individually and completely and satisfy users within the designed medium chunk.[51] With the Fort Vancouver Mobile project, users can listen to an audio clip, watch a video, read digital text, or see images of any number of the site's artifacts—all separate media objects delivered through the same device. Or, users can look at paper brochures, examine tangible objects in the space, or navigate the reconstructed physical surroundings, each of which contributes a complete chunk of the Fort Vancouver story but not the whole story.

The receivers of this array of media generally are absorbing the information outside of classrooms or designated interaction spaces, as in the concept of a situated and lifelong learning environment, conducting tasks that Mike Sharples classifies as "contextual lifelong learning."[52] In that concept, learning does not happen at predetermined times in pre-specified places. It happens whenever a person breaks from routine, reflects on the current situation, and resolves to address a problem, share an idea, or gain an understanding. These environments are dynamically constructed by mobile users in a site-specific way, interacting with their surroundings. The natural alliance of learning as a contextual activity with mobile devices creates a powerful new tool.[53] That combination, in fact, might be the key to understanding how to effectively author for mobile technology.

Authors using mobile devices can have a renewed and expanded sense of audience-awareness, like those in the age of orality, when speakers knew everyone in the crowd. Oral storytellers knew what the audience wanted to hear and intimately understood the context of the communication, including its physical place, its time of day, its season, what came before it, and the pattern being set for what might come after. Only with mobile devices, this sort of precise delivery can be automatically sorted and intricately redesigned as a way to simultaneously tailor messages to the desires of each individual in the crowd, even complete strangers. Mobile devices in this process, then, can collect data from their users that assist authors in continually making better connections to the audience, in real time, and this data allows virtually unlimited on-the-spot calibration, instantaneously, like a built-in usability lab. Unlike most of the technology they can supplant, mobile devices can create a distinctively personalized experience with information, from ringtones and identity-reflecting phone gear to content delivery, ranging across entertainment and services spectrums, individually designed on a mass scale yet with which a single person can interact.[54] This is a long way from pencils and paper, or even the printing press.

Conclusion

Many aspects of mobile media storytelling—delivered through smartphones, computer tablets, and other mobile technologies—feel familiar and like natural extensions of the media that have come before them. The physical act of writing text for a mobile device, for example, is the same as typing for any other digital media. Shooting a video, recording audio, layering animation frames, all of these creative routines have become familiar forms of expression. Just as Lewis and Clark, in essence, merely extended a walk in the woods, modern authors composing in mobile space begin by treading over comfortable compositional ground. The deeper the trip into this mobile media wilderness right now, the more fascinating and bewildering it becomes, and the more surprising fruits and pitfalls it yields.

Mobile media, in turn, are becoming the dominant technologies of human expression, the natural interface through which humans function, yet also a unique instrument of mediating communication between people and the world of inanimate objects.[55] Mobile technology, viewed as this chameleon-like interface, circuitously returns to McLuhan's "medium is the message" mantra,[56] only instead of choosing between media options today, such as a magazine article or radio broadcast, mobile technology adds media choice as a layer of composition, as critical as deciding a protagonist and a plot. Audience awareness with mobile technology goes well beyond typical demographics of age, gender, and social class. Composing with a mobile device means being able to know precisely when and where your message will be delivered, and in what context. This interaction is also not a one-way transmission, of sender and receiver; for mobile technology to truly express itself as a distinct form, a circuit of information (a "feedback loop") should be created among participants. As such circuits cross and interconnect, mobile stories will begin to spread and grow like wildflowers. While the author (or authors) only control a portion of that circuit, he or she does help to put parameters on it, and guide it, ideally keeping it from becoming meaninglessly unfocused, or drifting so far from original intent that the audience loses interest.

The New World, the Wild West, even the most outer reaches of space have been crisscrossed and mapped by our tales. Authors can no longer reach farther away for their frontiers, but, as an apt metaphor, mobile narratives are establishing and developing new territory. The story of Fort Vancouver already is being expressed in wayside signs, brochures, books, videos, podcasts, webpages, social media feeds, online photo galleries, and even through generic mobile applications that track user location and provide social updates and aggregated data, such as the nearest restaurants. Rather than being completely commodified in the digital age, information still can maintain distinct value based on the quality of the interpreter and the interpretation. Paul Kane documented the changing world as he saw it with a sketchpad. He traveled mostly alone, "scarcely meeting a white man or hearing the sound of my own language," for four years.[57] While mobile development is rampant worldwide, composing mobile narratives remains a relatively lonely pursuit, rife with terminological and technological mine fields. Near Fort Vancouver, Kane noted that the "Indians" lived near the river, in "a little village—quite a Babel of languages, as the inhabitants are a mixture of English, French, Iroquois, Sandwich Islanders, Crees and Chinooks."[58] That statement inspired the creators of the Fort Vancouver Mobile stories to find a local speaker of Chinuk wawa, the common language of the village, to give sound to Kane's images of the place. This small step brings the user that much closer to what Kane actually experienced as he was filtering the scene for posterity through his sketches. As the user walks different directions around the site, other characters emerge. Different plotlines converge and diverge. The linear entryway opens into abstraction, in which each user move reveals additional layers of history and other stories. It starts to seem like a hidden world emerging. It starts to feel like new connections are being made and old and broken connections are being mended.

Notes

1. Paul Kane, Wanderings of an Artist among the Indians of North America: From Canada to Vancouver's Island and Oregon and through the Hudson's Bay Company's Territory (Toronto: University of Toronto Press, 2006), vii–x.
2. CTIA Media, "Wireless Quick Facts," http://www.ctia.org/media/industry_info/index.cfm/AID/10323.
3. George Santayana, The Life of Reason (Charleston, SC: BiblioLife, 2009), 217.
4. Henry Jenkins, Convergence Culture: Where Old and New Media Collide (New York: New York University Press, 2006), 114.
5. Verónica Tozzi, "Past Reality and Multiple Interpretations in Historical Investigation," Study of Social Political Thought 2 (2000): 41.
6. Mei Yii Lim and Ruth Aylett, "Narrative Construction in a Mobile Tour Guide," Lecture Notes in Computer Science 4871 (2007): 51.
7. Maoz Azaryahu and Kenneth E. Foote, "Historical Space as Narrative Medium: On the Configuration of Spatial Narratives of Time at Historical Sites," GeoJournal 73, no. 3 (2008): 179.
8. Richard Prentice, Sinbad Guerin, and Stuart McGugan, "Visitor Learning at a Heritage Attraction: A Case Study of Discovery as a Media Product," Tourism Management 19, no. 1 (1998): 5.
9. Evan Young, The Carrier, http://www.carriercomicbook.com.
10. Scott Ruston, Jennifer Stein, et al., Tracking Agama, http://cinema.usc.edu/interactive/research/trackingagama.cfm.
11. Hana Iverson, Neighborhood Narratives, http://www.neighborhoodnarratives.net/.
12. Michael Kenteris, Damianos Gavalas, and Daphne Economou, "An Innovative Mobile Electronic Tourist Guide Application," Personal and Ubiquitous Computing 13, no. 2 (2009): 103–118.
13. Erich Bruns, Benjamin Brombach, et al., "Enabling Mobile Phones to Support Large-Scale Museum Guidance," IEEE Multimedia 14, no. 2 (2007): 16.
14. Loel Kim, "Tracing Visual Narratives: User-Testing Methodology for Developing a Multimedia Museum Show," Technical Communication 52, no. 2 (2005): 121–137.
15. Sven Birkerts, The Gutenberg Elegies: The Fate of Reading in an Electronic Age (New York, NY: Fawcett Columbine, 1994), 74.
16. Robert Coover, "The End of Books," The New York Times on the Web (1992), http://www.nytimes.com/books/98/09/27/specials/coover-end.html.
17. Craig Baehr and Bob Schaller, Writing for the Internet: A Guide to Real Communication in Virtual Space (Santa Barbara, CA: Greenwood Press, 2009), 17.
18. Robin Nelson, "Introduction: Prospective Mapping and Network of Terms," in Mapping Intermediality in Performance, ed. Sarah Bay-Cheng et al. (Amsterdam, NL: Amsterdam University Press, 2010), 13–23.
19. Irina Rajewsky, 2005. "Intermediality, Intertextuality, and Remediation: A Literary Perspective on Intermediality," Intermédialités 6, (2005): 43–64.
20. Nelson, "Introduction," 13–23.
21. Klaus Bruhn Jensen, "Intermediality," in International Encyclopedia of Communication, ed. Wolfgang Donsbach, http://www.communicationencyclopedia.com.
22. André Gaudreault and Philippe Marion, "The Cinema as a Model for the Genealogy of Media," Convergence: The International Journal of Research into New Media Technologies 8, no. 4 (2002): 12.

23. Lars Elleström, *Media Borders, Multimodality and Intermediality* (New York, NY: Palgrave Macmillan, 2010), 12.

24. *Majestic*, Electronic Arts (2001), http://www.pcworld.com/article/48191/majestic_you_dont_just_play_this_game_you_live_it.html.

25. Janelle Brown, "Paranoia for Fun and Profit," *Salon* (2001), http://www.salon.com/technology/feature/2001/08/10/majestic/index.html.

26. Marshall McLuhan and Quentin Fiore, *The Medium Is the Message* (New York, NY: Touchstone Books, 1967), 26.

27. Sirkka Järvenpää and Karl Lang, "Managing the Paradoxes of Mobile Technology," *Information Systems Management* 22, no. 4 (2005): 7–23.

28. Ibid., 7.

29. Andre Torre and Alain Rallet, "Proximity and Localization," *Regional Studies* 39, no. 1 (2005).

30. N. Katherine Hayles, *Electronic Literature: New Horizons for the Literary* (Notre Dame, IN: University of Notre Dame Press, 2008), 11.

31. Sadie Plant, "On the Mobile: The Effects of Mobile Telephones on Social and Individual Life," (2001), http://classes.dma.ucla.edu/Winter03/104/docs/splant.pdf.

32. Janet Murray, *Hamlet on the Holodeck: The Future of Narrative in Cyberspace* (New York, NY: Free Press, 1997), 97–125.

33. Adriana de Souza e Silva and Daniel Sutko, "Playing Life and Living Play: How Hybrid Reality Games Reframe Space, Play, and the Ordinary," *Critical Studies in Media Communication* 25, no. 5 (2008): 447–465.

34. Baehr and Schaller, 15–17.

35. Levi Novey and Troy Hall, "The Effect of Audio Tours on Learning and Social Interaction: An Evaluation at Carlsbad Caverns National Park," *Science Education* 91, no. 2 (2007): 260–277.

36. de Souza e Silva and Sutko, "Playing Life and Living Play," 458.

37. Adriana de Souza e Silva, "Alien Revolt (2005–2007): A Case Study of the First Location-Based Mobile Game in Brazil," *Technology and Society Magazine, IEEE* 27, no. 1 (2008): 18–28.

38. Blast Theory, *Uncle Roy All Around You*, (2003), http://blasttheory.co.uk/bt/work_uncleroy.html.

39. Mary Flanagan, "Locating Play and Politics: Real World Games & Activism," *Leonardo Electronic Almanac* (2007): 6–7.

40. Giulio Jacucci, Antii Oulasvirta, and Antii Salovaara, "Active Construction of Experience through Mobile Media: A Field Study with Implications for Recording and Sharing," *Personal & Ubiquitous Computing* 11, no. 4 (2007): 215–234.

41. Jeremy Hight, "Narrative Archeology," *Media in Transition 4: The Work of Stories* (Cambridge, MA: May 6–8, 2005), http://web.mit.edu/comm-forum/mit4/papers/hight.pdf.

42. Jeff Knowlton, Naomi Spellman, et al., *34 North, 118 West* (2002), http://34n118w.net.

43. Hight, *Narrative Archeology*.

44. Michael Epstein, "Moving Story," *Media in Transition 6: Stone and Papyrus*, (Cambridge, MA: April 24–26, 2009), http://web.mit.edu/comm-forum/mit6/papers/Epstein.pdf, 1.

45. David Fono and Scott Counts, "Sandboxes: Supporting Social Play through Collaborative Multimedia Composition on Mobile Phones," Conference on Computer Supported Cooperative Work (Alberta, Canada, November 4–8, 2006).

46. Ibid.

47. Antii Salovaara, Giulio Jacucci, et al. "Collective Creation and Sense-Making of Mobile Media," SIGCHI Conference on Human Factors in Computing Systems (Montréal, Canada, April 22–27, 2006).

48. de Souza e Silva and Sutko, "Playing Life and Living Play," 449.

49. Kim, "Tracing Visual Narratives," 121–137.

50. Jennifer Stein, Scott Ruston, et al., "Location-Based Mobile Storytelling," *International Journal of Technology and Human Interaction* 5, no. 1 (2009): 41–50.

51. Jenkins, *Convergence Culture*, 20–21.

52. Mike Sharples, "The Design of Personal Mobile Technologies for Lifelong Learning," *Computers & Education* 34, no. 3–4 (2000): 177–193.

53. Mike Sharples et al., "The Design and Implementation of a Mobile Learning Resource," *Personal and Ubiquitous Computing* 6, no. 3 (2002): 234.

54. Harvey May and Greg Hearn, "The Mobile Phone as Media," *International Journal of Cultural Studies* 8, no. 2 (2005): 195.

55. Kristóf Nyíri, "Towards a Philosophy of M-Learning," Proceedings from the IEEE International Workshop on Wireless and Mobile Technologies in Education (Vaxjo, Sweden, August 29–30, 2002).

56. McLuhan, 26.

57. Kane, ix.

58. Ibid., 171

3

RE-NARRATING THE CITY THROUGH THE PRESENTATION OF LOCATION

Adriana de Souza e Silva and Jordan Frith

How do the examples in this chapter help us understand the practice of story-telling in the mobile media age?

Through examples of "location-based social networks" such as Foursquare, this chapter examines how location-aware mobile devices enable new ways for individuals to reshape how they interact with and understand locations. The chapter begins by discussing how adding location-based digital information to physical spaces can impact what we call *the presentation of location*. After detailing the presentation of location, we then move on to how location-aware mobile devices allow people to "read" and "write" space in new ways, linking digital narratives to how people relate to locations. We examine how the location-based information present in location-based services and art works like Textopia allow people to follow others' trajectories through space and examine the stories they tell about places through location-based tips and reviews. With services like Foursquare and projects like Textopia, people not only "read" space, but they also "write" space and contribute to spatial narratives through the paths they take through the city.

Keywords

- **Location-based social networks (LBSNs):** Mobile phone applications that allow users to broadcast their locations to their social network (and also see the locations of their friends as they "check-in" or post reviews of locations). Users have the ability to customize the types of information they are willing to interact with (which friends they would like to see, which coupons they want to receive, and what information they want to access); thus individuals can now use these devices to personalize and control their experiences of public spaces in new ways.

- **The presentation of location:** As places are embedded with location-based information, these places acquire dynamic meanings depending on the types of site-specific information attached them via location-aware mobile interfaces.
- **Spatial trajectories:** The paths people take through physical space. With applications like Foursquare and projects like Textopia, people are able to share these trajectories with others through location-based social networks.

Introduction[1]

One of the most interesting ways the Internet has affected social life has been by enabling new forms of self-presentation. People construct their digital selves through blogs, article comments, personal websites, and a range of social networking sites. The conscious construction of one's digital self involves choosing what type of information one wants to present to the world, and that information can represent everything from political views to a favorite bar. The development of location-based mobile phones added a new layer to one's digital presentation of self: location. This layer is enacted through location-based social networks (LBSNs) like Loopt and Gowalla, and location-based mobile games (LBMGs) like Foursquare, Mogi, and Botfighters. By choosing to check in to some places and not others, LBSN participants show their social network some aspects of their lives and not others. Those locations, then, become part of their "presentation of self," a term made famous by Erving Goffman.[2]

However, LBSNs and LBMGs are not only important interfaces to social relationships among peers—they are also interfaces to public spaces. By checking in to some locations and not others, LBSN users also validate places. By checking in, they are telling their friends which locations are worth going to and which are not. By writing reviews on specific restaurants and "attaching" them to the location of a venue, location-based service (LBS) users also attribute different meanings to places. Interfaced through location-aware mobile interfaces, individuals can also access other people's interpretations of those locations and interact with digital information that has become part of that location. For example, a user equipped with a GPS-enabled cell phone at Times Square who opens the application WikiMe on her cell phone is able to read *Wikipedia* articles about Times Square. She can then have a personalized experience of that public space through the manipulation of digital information. Ultimately, people are able to control public spaces by making some locations more visible than others (e.g., showing some visited places to friends and not others), by modifying the information about a location (e.g., adding or removing digital information that is attached to them), or by attributing meaning to locations (e.g., reading reviews and other texts attached to that location). Through users' ability to access different location-based information, locations are presented differently to different people. This, as we will argue later, constitutes what we call "the presentation of location."

Locations, however, are not isolated entities. They are relational, and their meaning derives from their ability to develop connections to other locations. Consequently, locations will be understood differently depending on which other locations are perceived as connected to them. For example, imagine two people having a conversation, and one telling the other about her recent trip to Europe, during which she visited Lisbon, Madrid, and Oslo, respectively. For the listener, Madrid and Oslo may have been places that shared no association, but from then on may be connected in her mind. This connection can also happen through an LBSN interface. Most LBSNs such as Foursquare, Latitude, and the now-defunct Brightkite, Loopt, and Whrll record users' location history. By accessing the profile of a user who makes that history available, one is able to see a list of all the previous locations a user has been since joining the application. This list, rather than only displaying isolated locations, can be seen as a particular way of influencing people's mobility through space—a user's personal mode of reading the city. Furthermore, if a user checks in to a particular location, that might be a way of saying, "Hey, I'm here. Is there anybody around?" Users might intend to gather friends in a specific location, and as a consequence, this might influence their way of moving through the city by providing them with new ways to "read" the city. With LBSs, however, users are not only able to read spaces—they "write" spaces as well. Instead of following someone's spatial trail, people might choose to create trails for others to follow. By attaching meaning (in the form of text, images, and other media) to locations, they might also connect formerly unrelated locations. Either through LBMG play or by participating in LBSNs, people are able to create narratives as paths in public spaces.

In this chapter, we examine how location-aware interfaces enable new ways for individuals to reshape the way they interact with and understand location. We do so by examining how individuals use LBSNs and LBSs to personalize and manipulate public spaces, altering the meanings of specific locations. Through the combination of physical place and location-specific digital information, locations are presented in new ways. As these locations are presented to the user through location-aware interfaces, users then compile locations to "read" a personalized urban narrative of the city. In the final section of this chapter, we explore how users might also write and narrate the city by examining early forms of location-based media artworks and newer forms of location-based commercial services. With this, we explore how individuals can use location-aware interfaces to both read and write the city in new ways.

The Presentation of Location

Locations are important pieces of people's identity, but the identity of locations derives from the people in them. The geographic location of a place has often been considered the basis for the development of local identities through local cultures and local communities.[3] Geographical location has also been a relevant factor that determined the identity and meaning of that place, which can be seen in communities ranging from the mountains of Appalachia to the coastal cities of California. It is also true, however, that identities are developed in relation to other peoples, other cultures, and other places—established by mutual difference. As Goffman describes, an individual's presentation of self is a relational social process because the expressions given off by people depend on who and what is around them.[4] The same happens with places. Cities and settlements on the paths of trading routes have always experienced this relationality; their identity was constituted primarily by how their citizens saw themselves as different from others. Exchange of goods, communication among diverse peoples and cultures, and media representations of places have thus influenced the construction of local identities.

While geographical features play a role in the construction of spatial identity, places do not construct their identity on their own. Their identities are instead constructed by people. People attribute meanings to places. These meanings are created by the elements that exist in a place, such as physical elements (e.g., buildings, public plazas, streets), social elements (e.g., the people who live in them), cultural elements (e.g., historical traditions, folklore, etc.), and the various ways that these categories converge. The interaction of these elements is what gives spaces their identity. As Henri Lefebvre argued, spaces are not merely containers.[5] They are constructed by social relationships, but those social relationships are not limited to the people who live in a specific place; instead, places are also influenced by other people who live elsewhere. With globalization and the increasing adoption of communication technologies, these external influences become more obvious.[6]

Throughout most of history, contact with what was not physically close was very limited. Consequently, the identity of a place was mostly developed in relation to its internal elements. However, the development of communication and transportation technologies, such as the train and the telegraph, enabled connections with distant people and places.[7] This connection contributed to the development of relational identities, that is, a way of seeing one place in contrast to other different (and similar) places.

But even with the development of new transportation and communication technologies in the nineteenth century, many of the world's cities and settlements were not reachable by the railway or the telegraph. Thus, for most of the world, local identities were still mostly rooted in local practices. In the twentieth century, however, newly developed electronic media, such as the radio and television brought distant actors into people's private homes, contributing to a much greater awareness of what was happening outside the local village or community. As a consequence, people gained awareness of distant places. Rather than just erasing local cultures and local identities, as many globalization scholars suggested,[8] Joshua Meyrowitz observed that these mass communication media actually helped people foster greater emotional attachments to places, through what he calls the "generalized elsewhere."[9] According to Meyrowitz, the generalized elsewhere works as a mirror in which to view and judge our localities. The generalized elsewhere makes us more aware of our local spaces because they acquire relationality. The comparison to other localities adds meaning to places.

The popularity of the Internet, however, complicated the idea of the "generalized elsewhere" because, unlike with the television and radio, individuals could directly communicate with distant others in chat rooms and other social platforms. The possibility of connecting and socializing with distant others without the need to physically travel led many to believe that physical space would lose importance because people could now create online communities and develop identities independent of geographic location. As a consequence, the importance of physical location in the construction of sociability and identity online was often dismissed in scholarly discourse during the 1990s and early 2000s.[10] According to this line of thinking, people could live in places without fully integrating into place-defined communities because they could create their own "community" in an online chat or virtual world. As Meyrowitz pointed out, "we can exit places psychologically without ever leaving them physically."[11]

The idea that physical location and mobility would become unimportant as we spend more time online, however, has more or less been proven false. People still drive and take public transportation to work, they still frequent cafes and restaurants and meet face-to-face, and they actually engage in corporeal travel at unprecedented rates.[12] With the development of new interfaces to connect to the Internet in the first decade of the twenty-first century, such as mobile, location-aware technologies and mapping software, it became clear that physical location has always been important to the construction of people's identities and to the development of sociability.

The development of location-specific digital information does not just represent the links between location and identity; it also suggests new ways people relate to and construct location. Increasingly, our physical spaces are embedded with networked connections and digital information, constituting what Eric Gordon and Adriana de Souza e Silva call "net-localities."[13] Locations now do not only acquire meanings through their relationality to other places, the people, and architecture in them, but also through the digital information embedded in them. For example, the LBS Socialight allows users to attach blog posts to the places they move through. A first-time visitor to a location who uses Socialight is then able to read about how others relate to that place through the posts of the other users. She may then experience that location differently than if she just had a brochure offered by the tourist office nearby. The experience is shaped by the social nature of the Socialight information that is produced by a member of the community rather than the depersonalized broadcast/mass media forms of information that have traditionally been disseminated about locations. These new forms of community-constructed location information are one of the most important affordances of LBSs and contribute to the presentation of location.

The presentation of self, according to Goffman, is composed of expressions given and given off.[14] The way people physically and discursively construct places means places also give off meanings through human action. For example, the owner of a restaurant might advertise the place in a specific way to a particular group of people, or design the restaurant to target certain customers. But then "eventually, word of mouth gets around, and places develop recognizable character based on frequent customers," which is often outside the control of the owner of that place.[15] Similarly, a location that is unfamiliar might also gain familiarity by the use of an LBSN or a LBMG. For example, if an individual has never been to a certain restaurant but sees on Facebook Places that many of his friends check in to that location, he might be more willing to trust that the restaurant is a good one. So, a location might gain familiarity by the appearance (on the map on the cell phone screen) of one or more friends. The presence of certain types of people might contribute different meanings to a specific location. Daniel M. Sutko and Adriana de Souza e Silva called this ongoing shift in the meaning and identity of locations through the use of LBSs and LBSNs (either by a conscious decision of the designer/owner of the place, or by the reviews and comments of people) *the presentation of place* (as a play on Goffman's presentation of self).[16] We would like to move a step forward and suggest that in fact what is happening through the interface of location-aware mobile devices is the *presentation of location*: the presentation of location is the new potentiality that locations (as places embedded with location-based information) have in acquiring dynamic meanings depending on the types of location-based information attached to them via location-aware mobile interfaces.

The concept of place has been defined in several and often conflicting ways, but four of the characteristics often attributed to places are particularly useful to help us understand the idea of location: their networked aspects, their social aspects, their meaningfulness, and their dynamic nature. There is a large body of literature debating the meaning of place,[17] but rather than engaging with that long and ongoing debate, we offer instead the term *location* to refer specifically to a particular geographical location (measurable by longitude and latitude coordinates) embedded with location-based information (e.g., texts, pictures, videos, and people). We depart from the above-mentioned four-faceted definition of place in order to suggest that *locations* are places, and therefore composed of networked interactions, social interactions, and meaning. Their meaning, however, is dynamic, constantly shifting, and constructed by the increasing amount of location-based information that is "attached" to that place via location-aware mobile interfaces. Through the production of location-based information, individuals are able to shape how locations are presented in ways that were not possible before.

For example, when using an LBS like Yelp, an individual is able to read nearby restaurant reviews, but if another person opens the application from a different location, different restaurants will appear on the screen. Both people are using the same application, but because they are in different locations, they are able to access different information from the database of reviews—but never the whole database.[18] Another example would be two people in the same location, one looking for budget meals and the other looking for expensive restaurants using an LBS like UrbanSpoon. Even though both are in the same location, they access different information through the location-aware interface. Locations present themselves differently depending on each user's preferences.

Another example of the presentation of location happens with the use of LBSNs. When LBSN users constantly check in to a location, it encourages friends to go to that location and might attract or repel other people depending on the context. The presence of certain people in certain locations might make people feel more familiar with them because they feel they can trust that location. Sociability in urban environments is strongly dependent on trust.[19] Even though people may not interact with others in a shared space, they still take comfort from knowing they are surrounded by others who are similar to them. LBSNs, by helping users find similar "friends," can also contribute to people's feelings of familiarity with their environment: if people are able to access information about the types of people inhabiting a location, they might be able to trust those locations and feel more comfortable in them.

A direct implication of the presentation of location is that users are able to "control" locations in ways that were not possible before. By being able to attach information to locations and to select nearby people and information they see on their mobile phone screen, individuals select aspects of locations with which they would like to interact. For example, with the LBS WikiMe, users can not only read *Wikipedia* articles about a location depending on their physical position, but can also contribute to how other users will perceive that location by writing articles. By participating in a LBSN like LooptMix, people can set preferences in order to be alerted when others with similar characteristics come in the range of their mobile phone. The ability to control and therefore personalize locations can thus be seen as a type of technological filter to public spaces.

Filtering the information one accesses about location functions as a type of personalized "reading" of location. It is also important to remember that, depending on the LBS being used, people can also "write" the space by contributing the information that will then be filtered by later users. By writing a location-based blog post, publishing reviews about locations, or participating in an LBMG, people are able to collectively construct locations in ways that were not possible before. They are also able to collectively share that new experience of location. But the use of location-aware interfaces does not only change the meaning of specific locations. By attaching information to places, participating in a LBSN, or playing a LBMG, people are also able to connect locations in new and unprecedented ways. Through their mobility in space (and in between locations), individuals can reread and re-narrate urban spaces.

Urban Narratives

In his book *Consumers and Citizens*, cultural studies theorist Néstor García Canclini writes,

> Walking though the city [Mexico City] is like a video clip in which diverse musics and stories are mixed. . . . One alternates passing by seventeenth-century churches with nineteenth-century buildings and constructions from every decade of the twentieth, interrupted by gigantic billboards layered with models' phony bodies, new cars, and newly imported computers. Everything is dense and fragmentary. . . . The city has been created by plundering images from everywhere, in any order whatsoever. Good readers of urban life must adapt themselves to the rhythm and bliss out of the ephemeral visions.
>
> I end up asking myself if we will be able to narrate the city again. Can there be stories in our cities, dominated as they are by disconnection, atomization, and insignificance?[20]

Canclini's quote points to the fragmentation of the urban landscape, both through the influences of history and globalization. He argues that though local cultural and social characteristics were influenced by the globalization process, they nevertheless did not disappear. They instead were incorporated with other influences, leading to an urban landscape that refuses narrative form. He asks whether, in the face of all these influences fighting for space in the city, it is possible to construct a coherent narrative. To Canclini's question, we suggest, "Yes, it is possible to narrate the city again." And location-aware interfaces play a critical role in helping us to construct these urban narratives.

Canclini observed that narrating the city at the end of the twentieth century meant knowing that it was no longer possible to have the experience of order that Baudelaire's *flâneur* expected to find in his nineteenth-century strolls through the city. (For a full discussion of the relationship between the *flâneur* and mobile storytelling projects, see chapter 7 of this book by John Barber, "Walking-Talking: Soundscapes, *Flâneurs*, and the Creation of Mobile Media Narratives.") Because of the fragmentation of the contemporary mega-cities, the city becomes "like a video clip, an effervescent montage of discontinuous images."[21] Finally, Canclini adds that "it is no longer possible to imagine a story from the purview of a historical or modern center that would permit us to draw the only possible map of a compact city that has ceased to exist."[22]

We agree with Canclini in that it is no longer feasible, if it ever was, to draw only one map of a city. Rather, urban spaces might be represented and narrated in many different ways, producing multiple maps, each of which contains different elements and perspectives of the urban environment. One might ask, as Valentina Nisi, Ian Oakley, and Mads Haahr do, "[H]ow can stories be distributed and fragmented but remain meaningful?"[23] Increasingly, location-aware mobile interfaces are important tools for constructing meaning *through* this fragmentation. These interfaces enable us to connect fragmented locations in the urban landscape, and in doing so, they create new forms of mobility within the city.

Reading Space

As explained earlier, when people talk about different locations in a coherent narrative, these locations may become connected in the listener's mind. The production of location-based information also has the power to link disparate locations. Either through a user's location history or through a pattern of similar information embedded in different locations, users create connections among previously disconnected locations in the city; they suggest patterns of mobility through urban spaces. Other users may follow these patterns and therefore "read" urban spaces in ways that were not previously intended. The act of embedding location-based information leads to a new way of narrating urban spaces. The LBSN Whrrl was initially marketed as a tool to help users create their own stories and narratives as a way of socializing with other users: "Twitter asks, 'what are you doing?' Facebook wants to know, 'What's on your mind?', instead, Whrrl asks, 'What's your story?'"[24] By focusing on personal stories, user feeds from Whrrl read like a narrative. They included not only descriptions of locations, but also stories about what users were doing, and pictures of the locations in which they were present. Needless to say, location played a prominent role in the construction of these narratives because these stories were automatically attached to wherever the user created the information.

Similar to Whrrl, other LBSNs allow users to publish stories about locations. As we saw in the last section, LBSs like Socialight and Yelp enable people to write posts and reviews about locations and imbue those locations with new meanings. That is what we called the presentation of location. While writing about specific locations, people are also able to create their own connections among locations. For example, a Loopt user who checked in at home and posted "going to Central Park" as a status update created a link between formerly unrelated locations—in this case, Central Park and his or her home. Similarly, a group of Foursquare users might go barhopping one night, checking in at every bar they visit. Each check-in creates a new link among previously disconnected locations. The combination of these links represents a new possible path through the city for other users. Other Foursquare users then might decide to follow the trail their friends left, validating that trajectory.

The experience of reading the city is even stronger other with LBMGs like *Botfighters* or *Mogi*, in which players are required to actively move through the city.[25] Additionally, because games already have narratives, players experience a double sense of narrative: the one created by the game designer and the one created by moving through the city. For example, when playing *Alien Revolt*, players had to embody an alien or a human as their character and engage in a role-playing adventure in order to save (or dominate) Earth.[26] Because it was an LBMG, players had to search for other players in public spaces in order to engage in combat. The narrative of the game became intrinsically merged with their mobility through the city. Players, therefore, create many different paths through the city and, in so doing, create a multilayered narrative through locations and the LBMG interfaces.

Following a path through urban spaces can be compared to hypertextual reading. The origins of hypertext trace back to Vannevar Bush's memex, though it was Ted Nelson in the 1960s who actually coined the term. Bush's idea with the memex was to create an associative database that allowed for a new mode of reading that precluded a pre-established textual order. As a consequence, the person who linked the available information created a narrative. The memex was envisioned to help users filter information stored in a huge database made of microfilm. The Web, although comprised of digital information and undoubtedly larger, can also be thought of as a series of databases.[27] Building on that idea, Lev Manovich suggested that the Web is composed of two main characters: interfaces and databases. While databases are collections of elements, subdivided into categories, interfaces are ways of accessing databases and of rearranging their elements in a linear, humanlike way. Interfaces allow users to "read" information in different ways.

As individuals began to access texts through the computer screen, the linear narratives that had dominated print culture were challenged by the ways users could construct their paths through hypertext. Manovich argued that with the Web, the database had replaced narrative, but the Web can also be read as a huge database that allows the construction of countless reader-produced narratives. With hypertext, the concept of authorship is challenged because readers compose narratives from the disparate pieces of the database they draw from to construct their path through information.

With location-aware mobile interfaces and the ability to attach information to locations, urban spaces are now transformed into databases. As Canclini argued, the modern city has always been a collection of disparate items, such as different types of buildings, and outdoor advertising. Location-specific information adds even more to the already information-rich environment of the city, and location-aware technologies become the interfaces that enable people not only to filter this information but also to connect to it in multiple ways. The hypertextual mode of reading is thus transferred into urban spaces.

The ability to read physical spaces by connecting information as one moves through space existed before the development of location-aware technologies. Artist Janet Cardiff has been developing audio walks since the early 1990s. Cardiff did not use any type of location-aware technology in her walks. Instead, a person would listen to a recording with instructions about how to move in space. For example, her 1997 *Chiaroscuro* walk, created for an exhibition at the San Francisco Museum of Modern Art, was her first walk to be experienced inside a museum. At the beginning, the person experiencing the audio installation listened to her voice: "Push the elevator button. We'll go down to the first floor." Then a bit later, "Let's go up. Go around the corner to the front of the main stairs. Walk up the stairs. I'll walk slowly so we can stay together."[28] By giving the museum visitor instructions on how to move through the space, Cardiff was allowing the listener to share her connections among the museum's different rooms. The narrative created by Cardiff works as an audio layer on top of physical space that influenced how people experienced both the museum and their personal mobility.

Cardiff's audio walks, however, are different from a hypertextual experience because the spatial narrative was not location-aware; that is, it was not triggered by the location of the user. For the participants to experience Cardiff's narrative, they had to proceed in the order dictated by the audio narration. If they did not, they could still hear the narrative, but they would not be in the physical location it was describing. Thus, there was only one possible way of connecting the narrative chunks: the one chosen by the artist. Cardiff's design was likely influenced by the technical limitations of mid-1990s location technologies. However, with the removal of the Global Positioning System (GPS) signal degradation in 2000, media artists started employing GPS devices as interfaces to create location-based audio walks. One of the first was *34 North, 118 West*—discussed in the previous chapter—which was developed in 2001 and launched in 2002 by Jeff Knowlton, Naomi Spellman, and Jeremy Hight.[29] *34 North, 118 West* tells a story about the railway industry in downtown Los Angeles at the turn of the century. As people navigate the city streets, they hear the voices and activities of people who lived and worked in the area. In order to experience the narrative, people were given a tablet PC and headphones. On a map on a tablet PC, individuals could see the location of hotspots. Approaching a hotspot would trigger the story attached to that location. Each individual who experienced the piece created a new narrative by following different hotspots in different orders on the map.

Audio walks began to point to the hypertextual nature of paths through space, in which individuals construct narratives through the locations they visit and the stories they access and string together. Marie-Laure Ryan, addressing electronic textuality, suggests an interesting spatial metaphor to think about hypertextual narratives. She says,

> In this mapping, the text as a whole is a territory, the links are roads, the textual units are destinations, the reader is a traveler or navigator, clicking is a mode of transportation, and the itinerary selected by the traveler is a "story." Since every reader follows a different itinerary, every reading session "writes" a different narrative, and through her own agency the reader becomes the "author" of her own adventures.[30]

With the movement enabled by location-aware technologies, the spatial metaphor of hypertext stops being metaphorical because individuals experience the information as spatially distributed throughout a physical location and the narrative as constructed by their personal spatial trajectory.

These personal spatial trajectories using location-aware technologies interweave physical and digital spaces, creating different experience of hybrid spaces. According to de Souza e Silva, hybrid spaces are social spaces created by the mobility of users equipped with location-aware interfaces.[31] For example, *Mogi* required Tokyo residents to complete a collection of virtual objects and creatures that were "attached" to specific locations. Christian Licoppe and Yoriko Inada found that some *Mogi* players changed their route from home to work—for example, going by bus rather than by subway—so that they could find and collect more objects.[32] Once downloaded to their mobile phones, these objects could then be exchanged with other players. Other players decided to go out at night in groups in order to collect particular objects. Players constructed their own trajectory through physical and digital spaces, and so "read" the city in different ways. LBMGs, LBSs, and audio walks allow users to link different locations, and therefore follow their own narrative throughout the city.

However, in these early audio walks and many LBSs, individuals are only reading space. Like the hypertextual reader, they are following chunks of information that somebody else created. Mostly, users "follow" trails left by somebody else— the artist who designed the walk, the user who uploaded the restaurant review, or the person who wrote the short location-based blog post. But when people start contributing to create the information that is attached to a location, they actively create the links among these locations. As we discuss in the next section, people are then transformed from readers into writers of urban spaces.

Writing Space

Almost all LBSNs and many LBSs allow users to attach information to locations. As we discussed in the last section, embedding information in locations contributes to change their intrinsic meaning (the presentation of location), but it also influences new patterns of mobility through the city by the linking of locations. We can trace the origins of location-based narratives to digital annotation projects that allowed users to create their own content, instead of just following content created by others. For example, Proboscis' *Urban Tapestries* was perhaps the first mobile annotation project.[33] The project aimed at allowing users to "author" the environment around them by uploading location-specific information, such as stories, sounds, and videos. The real innovation of *Urban Tapestries* was to develop a location-aware platform that challenged the common top-down approach of location-based experiences at that time. *Urban Tapestries* enabled users to share knowledge and create a series of "threads" that consisted of information about local resources that linked locations to people.

More recently, Anders Sundnes Løvlie developed a project named *Textopia*.[34] *Textopia* allowed users to walk through the city of Oslo and listen to location-based texts via their mobile phones. However, because one of the artist's aims was to make it easy for users to also contribute their own texts to the piece, he created a wiki to serve as a database of texts. To populate the wiki, Løvlie then organized a competition in which users could create their own location-based texts and submit to the system. One of the interesting findings of this experiment was that there were three main categories of texts uploaded by users: *placetexts*, *voice sculptures*, and *stray voices*. While *placetexts* and *voice sculptures* were mostly stories and descriptions of locations (something similar to what users do when writing a Socialight post or a location-based review on Yelp), *stray voices* had a distinct character. According to Løvlie, these were a "series of texts which form stories that move from place to place, requiring the user to physically traverse the landscape of the story in order to traverse the text of the story (though not necessarily in linear sequence)."[35] *Stray voices* are types of texts that truly constitute a location-based narrative because they explicitly engage people in connecting locations by requiring them to move through public spaces. For example, one text series that belonged to his original project required participants (readers) to physically follow the narrator as she walks home from a night out with her friends. We suggest that *stray texts* encourage specific spatial trajectories,[36] but these are spatial trajectories created by common users, rather than by artists. Through *stray texts*, people can narrate the city again, and locations acquire different meanings dependent on people's mobility through the city. In addition, those who write urban narratives are actively contributing not only to add new meanings to locations (presentation of location), but also to "write" and narrate urban spaces in a very specific way.

Not all urban narratives are structured and organized as spatial trajectories. Nonetheless, they are ways of writing space. LBSNs and LBMGs show this quite well. There are different ways of engaging with LBSNs: checking in, putting up status updates, acquiring coupons, gaining points, engaging with a game narrative, and sharing location. Lee Humphreys noted that Dodgeball enabled users to "catalog" their lives by recording each past location, which could later be visualized on a Google map.[37] Even if unintentionally, cataloging also creates new connections and links among locations that now can be clearly visualized on a map of the city. Each person, with their movement, creates their own threads and maps through their mobility through the urban space, and each set of combined locations constitutes a different narrative. These different threads can all be thought of as different texts, written over the physical space of the city.

Conclusion

In this chapter, we have shown how the growth of hybrid spaces through the use of location-aware mobile interfaces creates new ways to read and write the city. With location-aware interfaces, individuals are able to access place-specific information about a location and either add to the location, in a sense "building" the location on the fly, or read the traces left by others. Locations then begin to present themselves in new ways, which we called the *presentation of location*. These new forms of presentation are closely linked to the urban narratives that users construct when using both LBSs and LBSNs, urban narratives that can be read by others or added to while moving through the city. Through access to someone's location history, a user can read the city as a culmination of spatial practices and spatial trajectories, analyzing how places have been woven together by a specific person in the form of a sort of physical hypertext. Users can also write the city by adding to the traces that are scrawled on the longitude and latitude coordinate of a specific location.

Through these new practices, the identity of location is constructed in new ways. Going forward, scholars should investigate how locations act to shape their identity in hybrid spaces and observe how the conflict between the self-expression of a location and the impressions of its inhabitants plays out through mobile interfaces. One thing we can be sure of is that the presentation of location will continue to be more and more dynamic, never fully fixed on the interface of a mobile device.

Notes

1. This chapter is a shortened version of one of the chapter in our book: Adriana de Souza e Silva and Jordan Frith, *Mobile Interfaces in Public Spaces: Locational Privacy, Control and Urban Sociability* (New York: Routledge, 2012).
2. Erving Goffman, *Behavior in Public Places: Notes on the Social Organization of Gatherings* (New York: Free Press of Glencoe, 1963).
3. Mike Featherstone, "Global and Local Cultures," in *Mapping the Futures: Local Cultures, Global Change*, ed. Jon Bird, et al. (London, New York: Routledge, 1993).
4. Erving Goffman, *The Presentation of Self in Everyday Life*, (New York: Doubleday, 1990), 73–74.
5. Henri Lefebvre, *The Production of Space* (Malden, MA: Blackwell Publishers, 1991), 170.
6. Joshua Meyrowitz, "The Rise of Glocality: New Senses of Place and Identity in the Global Village," in *A Sense of Place: The Global and the Local in Mobile Communication*, ed. Kristof Nyíri (Vienna: Passagen Verlag, 2005).
7. See Wolfgang Schivelbusch, *The Railway Journey: The Industrialization of Time and Space in the 19th Century* (Berkeley & Los Angeles, CA: University of California Press, 1986); Tom Standage, *The Victorian Internet: The Remarkable Story of the Telegraph and the Nineteenth Century's on-Line Pioneers* (New York: Walker & Company, 2007); James Carey, *Communication as Culture* (Boston: Unwin Human, 1988).
8. See Thomas L. Friedman, The World Is Flat 3.0: A Brief History of the 21st Century (New York: Picador, 2007); David Harvey, The Condition of Postmodernity: An Enquiry into the Origins of Cultural Change (Malden, MA: Blackwell, 1992); Paul Virilio, The Art of the Motor (University of Minnesota Press, 1995).
9. Meyrowitz, "The Rise of Glocality: New Senses of Place and Identity in the Global Village," 23.

10. See Howard Rheingold, The Virtual Community: Homestead on the Electronic Frontier (Cambridge, MA: The MIT Press, 1993); Margareth Wertheim, The Pearly Gates of Cyberspace: A History of Space from Dante to the Internet (New York: W.W. Norton & Company, 1999).

11. Meyrowitz, "The Rise of Glocality," 27.

12. Helen Couclelis, "Misses, Near-Misses and Surprises in Forecasting the Informational City," in Societies and Cities in the Age of Instant Access, ed. Harvey J. Miller (Dordrecht, The Netherlands: Springer, 2007).

13. Eric Gordon and Adriana de Souza e Silva, Net Locality: Why Location Matters in a Networked World (Boston: Blackwell Publishers, 2011).

14. Goffman, The Presentation of Self in Everyday Life.

15. Daniel M. Sutko and Adriana de Souza e Silva, "Location Aware Mobile Media and Urban Sociability," New Media & Society 13, no. 5 (2011).

16. Ibid.

17. See Shaun Moores, "The Doubling of Place: Electronic Media, Time-Space Arrangements and Social Relationships," in Media/Space: Place, Scale and Culture in a Media Age, ed. B. Couldry and A. McCarthy (London: Routledge Comedia Series, 2004); Manuel Castells, The Rise of the Network Society (Oxford: Blackwell, 2000); Doreen Massey, "Power-Geometry and a Progressive Sense of Place," in Mapping the Futures: Local Cultures, Global Change, ed. Jon Bird et al. (London and New York: Routledge, 1993); Meyrowitz, "The Rise of Glocality: New Senses of Place and Identity in the Global Village"; Lefebvre, The Production of Space.

18. Sutko and de Souza e Silva, "Location Aware Mobile Media and Urban Sociability."

19. Ibid., 90–91; Gordon and de Souza e Silva, Net Locality: Why Location Matters in a Networked World.

20. Néstor García Canclini, Consumers and Citizens: Globalization and Multicultural Conflicts (Minneapolis: University of Minnesota Press, 2001), 85.

21. Ibid., 84.

22. Ibid., 85.

23. Valentina Nisi, Ian Oakley, and Mads Haahr, "Location-Aware Multimedia Stories: Turning Spaces into Places," in Proceedings of ArTech 2008 (Porto, Portugal 2008), 4.

24. Derek Walter, "Whrrl Wants to Know Your Story," AppCraver: iPhone App News and Reviews: http://www.appcraver.com/whrrl/.

25. See Adriana de Souza e Silva, "Hybrid Reality and Location-Based Gaming: Redefining Mobility and Game Spaces in Urban Environments," Simulation & Gaming 40, no. 3 (2009): 404–424; Christian Licoppe and Romain Guillot, "Icts and the Engineering of Encounters: A Case Study of the Development of a Mobile Game Based on the Geolocation of Terminals," in Mobile Technologies of the City, ed. John Urry and Mimi Sheller (New York: Routledge, 2006); Christian Licoppe and Yoriko Inada, "Emergent Uses of a Multiplayer Location-Aware Mobile Game: The Interactional Consequences of Mediated Encounters," Mobilities 1, no. 1 (2006): 39–61; Olli Sotamaa, "All the World's a Botfighters Stage: Notes on Location-Based Multiuser Gaming." Paper presented at the Computer Games and Digital Cultures Conference (Tampere, Finland, June 6–8 2002).

26. Adriana de Souza e Silva, "Alien Revolt: A Case-Study of the First Location-Based Mobile Game in Brazil," IEEE Technology and Society Magazine 27, no. 1 (2008): 18–28.

27. See Lev Manovich, The Language of New Media (Cambridge, MA: The MIT Press, 2002); Janet Murray, Hamlet on the Holodeck: The Future of Narrative in Cyberspace (Cambridge, MA: The MIT Press, 1997).

28. Janet Cardiff and George Bures Miller, "Chiaroscuro, 1997," http://www.cardiffmiller. com/artworks/walks/chiaroscuro.html.

29. Jeff Knowlton, Naomi Spellman, and Jeremy Hight, *34 North, 118 West* (Los Angeles, 2002): http://34n118w.net/.

30. Marie-Laure Ryan, *Narrative as Virtual Reality: Immersion and Interactivity in Literature and Electronic Media* (Baltimore, MD: The Johns Hopkins University Press, 2003), 218.

31. Adriana de Souza e Silva, "From Cyber to Hybrid: Mobile Technologies as Interfaces of Hybrid Spaces," *Space and Culture* 3 (2006): 261–278.

32. Christian Licoppe and Yoriko Inada, "Mediated Co-Proximity and Its Dangers in a Location-Aware Community: A Case of Stalking," in *Digital Cityscapes: Merging Digital and Urban Playspaces*, ed. Adriana de Souza e Silva and Daniel M. Sutko (New York: Peter Lang, 2009); ———, "Emergent Uses of a Multiplayer Location-Aware Mobile Game: The Interactional Consequences of Mediated Encounters."

33. Proboscis, "Urban Tapestries," (2002–2004), http://research.urbantapestries.net/.

34. Anders Sundnes Løvlie, "Poetic Augmented Reality: Place-Bound Literature in Locative Media," in *Proceedings of the 13th International MindTrek Conference: Everyday Life in the Ubiquitous Era* (Tampere, Finland: ACM, 2009).

35. Ibid., 22.

36. Steve Benford et al., "From Interaction to Trajectories: Designing Coherent Journeys through User Experiences," in *Proceedings of the 27th International Conference on Human Factors in Computing Systems* (Boston, MA: ACM, 2009).

37. Lee Humphreys, "Mobile Social Networks and Social Practice: A Case Study of Dodgeball," *Journal of Computer-Mediated Communication* 13, no. 1 (2007): http://jcmc. indiana.edu/vol13/issue1/humphreys.html.

PART II

Design and Practice

4

THE AFFORDANCES AND CONSTRAINTS OF MOBILE LOCATIVE NARRATIVES

Jeff Ritchie

How do the examples in this chapter help us understand the practice of storytelling in the mobile media age?

Mobile locative narratives, as "transmedia" stories, blur the line between storyworld and physical world, requiring that authors tell stories across a variety of media, including architectural space and the physical environment. As an intensely open, interactive, transmedia form, mobile locative narratives take advantage of the perceived affordances and constraints of digital, interactive narratives and the spaces in which these stories are told. Stories told via mobile locative devices require "really nontrivial effort" on the part of audiences because they have to physically move through various spaces to access the story. The result is that mobile locative narratives must foster far greater motivation for the audience to take part in the story in order to overcome the value threshold of the story. This chapter outlines the design considerations that make mobile locative narratives successful, including ways of taking advantage of the medium, interactivity, spatial storytelling, wayfinding, and narrative bridges.

Keywords

- **Affordances and constraints:** An affordance is both the perceived and actual properties of a system or object that determine *how it may possibly be used*. Conversely, a constraint is the actual and perceived attributes of an object or system that *limits its possible uses*. There are four types of constraints: physical, semantic, cultural, and logical.
- **Transmedia narrative:** A story told across a number of a different media, all of which are coherent and set within the same storyworld. The story is thus an expansive creation of a fictional world composed through multiple

media platforms and multiple modes of engagement (e.g., gaming, reading, listening, and web browsing, among others).

- **Narrative value threshold:** For a reader to be willing to expend the perceived effort necessary to continue "reading" a story, the reader must perceive the rewards of that narrative to exceed the perceived efforts required. This threshold is particularly relevant given the "really nontrivial effort" necessary to "read" mobile locative narratives.

Introduction

All media tend to privilege some narrative approaches and elements over others. For instance, narrative-driven, mimetically told first-person games like *Myst*[1] privilege the exploration of setting. This formative influence of media means that a mobile locative narrative is more than simply relating a story to another person on a phone, as this conversation doesn't realize the medium's potential. A phone call is as much a mobile locative narrative as televising a radio drama without moving images is a television show; a radio-drama-as-television-show fails to avail itself of the possibilities of television as a medium, and the mobile locative narrative doesn't realize its narrative potential because it fails to take full advantage of the narrative possibilities of both media used to communicate the story—the mobile device and physical space. As a medium,[2] physical space is used by architects, urban planners, civil engineers, and interior designers to carve out those spaces in which we live our lives. We all unwittingly "read" the fabric of physical space, our corresponding reactions conversing with it. If we're unversed in the vocabulary of physical space, we respond to spaces without the benefit of knowing how or why we react as we do to them.

This chapter examines how the media of physical spaces and mobile locative devices, in interplay with user(s), affords and constrains the narrative possibilities of mobile locative narratives as transmedia narrative forms. Henry Jenkins describes transmedia storytelling as a form of narrative that is purposefully conveyed through multiple media channels that essentially allow the audience to view multiple glimpses of a larger world in which the stories are set (the storyworld) whose scope exceeds the bounds of one work in one medium. Multiple narratives published across a variety of media give a fuller sense of the storyworld in which the narratives take place. As Jenkins explains:

> A transmedia story unfolds across multiple media platforms, with each new text making a distinctive and valuable contribution to the whole. In the ideal form of transmedia storytelling, each medium does what it does best—so that a story might be introduced in a film, expanded through television, novels, and comics; its world might be explored through game play or experienced as an amusement park attraction.[3]

Each text needs to be self-contained to provide multiple entries into the storyworld, and each entry should distinctively contribute to audiences' understanding of the storyworld. The example that Jenkins uses is *Star Wars*, told through seven movies, a television show, multiple video games, countless books, and action figures.[4] Such a means of storytelling often provides a richer exploration of the different elements of the storyworld than traditional stories mediated in one medium; however, doing so often requires more effort on the part of audiences in order to get at the narrative. As acts of transmedia storytelling, mobile locative narratives require specific apparatuses (cues, links, or referents) to bridge the digitally and physically mediated story spaces formed by digital media and the environment, and in so doing, blur the line between storyworld and the physical world and affect the immersive nature of the story thus mediated. (For a detailed example of transmedia narrative using mobile media, see chapter 14 of this book, "'I Heard It Faintly Whispering': Nonlocative Transmedia Design and Mobile Technology.")

Affordances and Constraints

Donald Norman's *The Design of Everyday Things*[5] explains how design choices and materials of everyday things afford and constrain the behaviors of users. An affordance "refers to the perceived and actual properties of the thing, primarily those fundamental properties that determine just how the thing could possibly be used."[6] Essentially, the potential and actual uses of a thing depend on all of the design decisions that make up that thing. Glass affords seeing through—and breaking. A mobile phone affords communicating with others and mobility. There are four different types of constraint. Physical constraints are "[t]he physical limitations [that] constrain possible operations,"[7] such as the shape of Lego blocks only allowing specific configurations. A semantic constraint relies "upon the meaning of the situation to control the set of possible actions."[8] In building a Lego police motorcycle, for instance, the meaning of the object (a motorcycle as a means of conveyance for the police) limits possible actions of the model builder. Given the meaning of the object, the rider should sit on top and face forward if the model is to conform to its meaning. Cultural and logical constraints also create a set of allowable actions for social situations and the expectations of those situations.[9] These ideas of affordances and constraints affect the creation, distribution, and consumption of interactive narratives that use mobile media.[10]

Of Stories and Interfaces

While there is considerable debate about whether emergent narratives are stories, whether "recounting" is required for an act to be a narrative,[11] or whether the implied author exists in post-postmodernism, for this chapter's purposes, a narrative is a mediated act that contains characters and setting, conveys a sequence of events that are causally or chronologically linked, involves a degree of struggle (or *agon*), requires an implied author, and requires an act of mediation while not being specific to any one medium.[12]

Stories "told" or mediated via digital media present new challenges for story-tellers, as digital/interactive media require an interface. I choose to define *interface* in the broadest possible sense—as the point at which two independent systems meet and interact. In this instance, a human user interacts with a digital narrative through an interface mediated on a mobile device, both of which are varyingly aware of and interact with the environment in which the mobile device is used. This multimodal definition (allowing for haptic or even olfactory interfaces) extends the idea of interface beyond merely the auditory and visual interactions of graphical user interfaces. Furthermore, mobile locative narratives afford far more environmental influence over this interaction than in traditional human computer interaction models due to networked and locative features.

While the author facilitates this interactivity in designing and developing the interface, the audience helps create the narrative they experience and actually brings the story's discourse into being. Interfaces offer a selection economy, where the choices afforded to the users by the interface determine those behaviors available to audiences and constrain other behaviors through omission or design.[13] The more open the interactivity of the device's interface, as an object designed by an author or authors, the more the interface affords the user choice and behavior in interacting with digital objects mediated through the device. For instance, by providing a menu of possible actions from which users can select, interfaces afford those specific behaviors that they include and prioritize in the interface and constrain other possible behaviors, through omission or design. Interfaces allowing for user input (such as text entry or photo submissions) afford more choice to the audience; however, the interface still constrains their behaviors (for instance, by placing limitations on text length or file size and format). The audience essentially co-authors the "sjuzet" (i.e., the ordering of a story—or "fabula"—how each telling of that story is a different representation of that story) through interaction with an interface that affords and constrains their behaviors (and is in turn molded by the possibilities afforded by the code of the work—or the "digi-fabula"). Until that interaction with the interface, the particular instance of the story experienced doesn't exist—it is only a potential existing in code. The networked nature of digital media and the new opportunities provided by Web 2.0 technologies further enable this co-authoring, allowing multiple users/authors to add to the story. However, unless those co-authors meet in physical proximity to one another, the interface will mediate, and thereby influence and constrain, their interactions.

Narratives, Interactivity, and Framing

Given cultural and semantic constraints placed on how audiences "consume" narratives in traditional media such as books and television, digitally mediated stories afford greater interactivity, requiring of the audience a degree of "nontrivial effort"[14] to bring these stories (the fabula) into being (sjuzet). Interactive narratives (such as hypertext and video games) have frequently used spatial metaphors to understand the nature of this interactivity. Jay David Bolter's *Writing Space* uses the metaphor of space, and Mark Stephen Meadows's *Pause and Effect* uses architectural space to describe how audience members interact with hypertextual and interactive narratives (and to a lesser extent writing in general).[15] The more open the interactivity built into a work, the more space the work provides its audience to globally or locally affect the narrative or explore outside of the work's narrative arc, in what would have been considered the backstory of the narrative. Take, for instance, the mobile locative narrative *[murmur]*, which allows participants to record stories at a specific location in a city using their mobile phones. Prompted by a large green sign shaped like an ear (with a phone number and location code to dial), users listen to stories recorded about that particular location and can contribute their own. *[murmur]* allows participants to tell their own stories at specific nodes in the space of the city—essentially adding a lexia to the story. If audiences could add their own nodes as well, *[murmur]* would afford even more open interaction.

As an affordance of the form, digitally mediated and interactive narratives are remarkably open regarding the sequence in which the narrative is experienced. While mediated through the interface and device, the order in which the audience interacts/views these elements is determined by the audience's interactions with the interface. Because narratives that branch in many directions depend on audience choices, such narratives need not necessarily have a specific beginning or a necessary end. This absence of beginning or end is increasingly important given the openness of the physical environment. Mobile locative narratives can now be boundless across two media. This characteristic affords that the order in which the audience interacts with the story elements can change with the user, thereby allowing for a branching storyline that changes the audience's reception of the narrative.[16]

Mobile Locative Narratives Require "Really Nontrivial Effort"

The desire for closure in these branching story lines is an essential element of transmedia narratives such as mobile locative narratives. Given that achieving this closure in mobile locative narratives usually requires that the audience successfully navigate two different spaces (digital and physical), negotiating these two systems in order to gather together and then make sense of these different elements requires considerably more effort than in traditional linear narratives or even hypertext narratives. This "really nontrivial effort"—to pun Espen Aarseth's "nontrivial effort"[17]—is necessary because the story space has the possibility of being harder to understand, due to its existing across two different media spaces to be explored, being potentially bigger than other types of narratives, and requiring audiences to constantly discern what does or doesn't belong within the storyworld. Turning a page or clicking a link takes far less perceived effort than moving through physical space and attempting to identify a narrative element or narrative bridge.

As such, mobile locative narratives composed of narrative elements that are geographically dispersed must, to varying degrees, both instill in their audiences a desire for closure that warrants them to take the extra effort to "read" the mobile locative narrative and provide digital and physical wayfinding systems that allow audiences to successfully navigate the narratives. The narrative must offer a reward perceived to be greater than the effort required of the audience. This difference between perceived effort and perceived reward is what I call the "narrative value threshold." Once the audience perceives that the value offered by the mobile locative work exceeds the threshold of "really nontrivial effort" necessary to enact the work, the audience will be willing to expend those efforts necessary to navigate the storyworld and come to identify and understand the story itself. As such, to understand and navigate these spaces, let alone arrive at any degree of narrative closure, requires "really nontrivial effort."

Spatial Storytelling

Which brings us to spatial storytelling. Michel de Certeau describes the cityscape—and by extension the physical environment—as a medium through which a story can be told through the actions of its inhabitants in the spaces themselves. "The ordinary practitioners of the city live 'down below,' below the thresholds at which visibility begins. They walk—an elementary form of this experience of the city; they are walkers, *Wandersmänner*, whose bodies follow the thicks and thins of an urban 'text' they write without being able to read it."[18]

De Certeau's walker describes merely one of four types of spatial story cataloged by Henry Jenkins: evoked, embedded, enacted, and emergent. *Evoked* narratives are narratives that remediate story spaces and element from other narratives, usually relying on the audience's knowledge of this story for the evoked narrative to have an effect.[19] A good example of a spatial narrative (that is not digitally mediated) is the Wizarding World of Harry Potter theme park in Orlando that recreates Hogwarts. Mobile locative narratives often rely on evocative narrative practices, such as situating a well-known story in a physical space.

Embedded narratives are spaces within which narrative elements are placed. Audiences gather together narrative elements and actively assemble them into a story.[20] Once again, the spatially organized nature of mobile locative narratives, and the fragmenting of large narrative units by the constraints of the mobile device's form factor, affords what can be loosely termed a type of narratological *bricolage* (a creation using a diverse range of objects on hand).

What Jenkins describes as *enacted* narratives, which occur in spaces that serve as stages on which audiences perform or witness narrative events, mirrors what de Certeau describes as spatial storytelling, the telling of a story through the

The Affordances and Constraints of Mobile Locative Narratives   **59**

actions of the pedestrian.[21] What audiences do and see forms the story. Again, the performative aspects of mobile locative narratives—requiring participants to perform specific actions, to move along a prescribed path, or to view a structure or perspective in the physical world—all afford enacted narratives. In *emergent* narratives, the space provides resources for audiences to create their own narratives. These narratives are not prestructured or preprogrammed but take shape through game play or exploration.[22]

How spaces actually tell stories depends on both controlling perception and movement and also conveying evoked, embedded, enacted, and emergent narratives through architectural and spatial languages. Walls, spaces, perspectives, and paths—all can be used for narrative purposes by affording or constraining movement and revealing or concealing information. A change in physical location or in point of view can physically reveal information or reinforce a feeling that influences the reception of the story. Architects and city planners have long manipulated pedestrians' movements and perspectives to impart a view or tell a story through a spatial "vocabulary" of entrances/exits, circulation paths, districts, decision points (or nodes), vertical circulation (stairs, elevators), and landmarks, as is seen in the roving point of reference incorporated into the design of the Athenian Acropolis.[23] And while the physical environment can potentially constrain narrative pacing in that travel across space requires a passage of time perhaps inconsistent with narrative purposes, movement through space can also be used to frame enacted narratives.

Narratives in physical spaces afford both simultaneous and successive experiences. Built environments afford simultaneous experiences in that discrete elements of the *mise-en-scène* of a particular place do not singularly unfold over time as in a novel. In a novel, the physiology of the eye[23] and the nature of print media result in the act of reading successively revealing information (a, then b, then c). Physical spaces, however, reveal information in a series of simultaneous events (abcdefghijklmnopqrstuvwxyz), such as what occurs in plays, circuses, or other forms of visual storytelling. For narrative purposes, the effects of simultaneous storytelling pose problems in that not all elements conveyed are important to the unfolding of the narrative, yet it's difficult to edit the physical environment or strictly control the views of the audience. That being said, built environments afford successive experiences in that experience and movement are both a function of time and distance and therefore unfold over time in a linear, successive manner. Regardless of the number of "narrative elements" occurring simultaneously, selective attention on the part of the audience means that only a few objects can be focused on at once. The same could be said of a printed page; however, cultural constraints govern our reading process (we usually don't start anywhere on the page but rather at the top left). Consequently, signage and directions must draw attention to those elements important to furthering the narrative.

While mobile locative narratives can attempt to guide audience movement and perception, controlling perspective and/or point of view in mobile locative narratives is difficult. One manner of controlling perception and behavior is through the creation of a semantic constraint. As per the Kuleshov effect, the order in which we see or experience narrative elements influences the perception of later narrative elements. Thus, the perception of a playground would be altered were we to know that a horrible crime had been committed at that place, just as providing directions to move through a slaughterhouse and into a cow pasture would change the interpretation of the pasture. If the participant would visit the cow pasture first, their impressions would be slightly altered. So, narrative elements mediated via space or device can influence the perception of later narrative elements.

Point of view and perspective can also be influenced either through actively providing precise directions/signage to look at environmental details or relying on a previously established strong or prominent visual hierarchy in the physical environment to draw the attention of the participant. That being said, directions and the existing visual hierarchy of the physical environment can prompt an audience's point of view to move across the *mise-en-scène* in a predefined manner for a desired effect. For instance, Cirque du Soleil unfolds a number of "events" at the same time—we are free to view whatever part is visible. A clever designer manipulates the visual hierarchy to draw the participants' attention (or "pull focus") to one specific area and thereby drawing attention away from other areas, through lighting, for instance. Or the ringmaster could announce that someone will be performing in the central ring, and in so doing, the designer is attempting to actively control participant perspective/point of view and, through a succession of such efforts, effectively guide most of the audience through a predetermined sequence of views. However, to emphasize narrative elements, designers must either control the design and construction of the narrative's physical environment or rely on instructions/signage and/or existing visual hierarchies.

By influencing the perception and movement of the audience through the physical world, embedded narrative elements can be emphasized and consequently chronologically connected to convey a narrative. Likewise, the experience and changing perspective of moving through a space is an enacted narrative. Like the classic detective stories, embedded narratives can be experienced through the audience searching for the different narrative elements found in physical space. The audience's movement through space and its attempts to navigate or find narrative elements convey a sense of struggle or *agon* that either constitutes or augments the narrative constructed.

The act of physical spaces evoking narratives also involves virtually and/or physically building narrative elements into physical spaces and the audience subsequently recognizing this evoked or embedded narrative meaning. The geographer Yi-Fu Tuan describes how architectural space evokes and embeds narratives:

> In the Middle Ages a great cathedral instructs on several levels. There is the direct appeal to the senses, to feeling and the subconscious mind. The building's centrality and commanding presence are immediately registered.

Here is mass—the weight of stone and of authority—and yet the towers soar. . . . Inside the cathedral there is the level of explicit teaching. Pictures in the stained glass windows are texts expounding the lessons of the Bible to illiterate worshippers. There are the countless signs pointing to Christian doctrine, practice, and mystery. . . . Finally the cathedral as a whole and in its details is a symbol of paradise.[24]

The architectural languages used evoke religious contemplation and celebration through the design of the space and rely on the audience to recognize those embedded and evoked symbols and languages that convey religious meaning—such as how knowledge of the story of the cross informs the "story" of a cathedral.

In addition to controlling/affording perspective and movement, evoked spatial storytelling space can be used to carry meaning through denotation, metaphor, mediated references, and association.[25] The Sydney Opera House denotes sails. A gothic cathedral's soaring vaults, arches, and walls built of glass metaphorically evoke a sense of the spiritual and draw the eye upward—ostensibly toward heaven. Mediated references are those like the Disney headquarters, whose design evokes the high culture of the Athenians through the classical Greek architectural style, yet, by creating columns resembling the seven dwarves, creates a tension between opposing ideas of high and low culture. On a more literal level, signage and symbolic ornamentation is another means by which space mediates meaning. Lastly, consider the associations that are linked to the White House—or the space formerly occupied by the World Trade Center. The meanings associated with both spaces rely on audience being aware of the backstory associated with that space.

Perception and Point of View in Spatial Storytelling

A mobile locative narrative capitalizes on the medium of the physical environment for the purposes of spatial storytelling through locating the narrative in strategic physical places—or nodes.[26] Tying a narrative to a location is nothing new, given loco-meditative works, installation art, and public history installations. Loco-meditative literary works are those that reflect and/or meditate on a specific location. For instance, William Wordsworth's loco-meditative poem "Lines Composed a Few Miles above Tintern Abbey on Revisiting the Banks of the Wye during a Tour, 13 July 1798" (more manageably abridged as "Tintern Abbey") tells an allegedly autobiographical story of the poet's experiences along the River Wye.[27] Works of public art such as the Oklahoma City Bombing Memorial document the story of a terrorist attack that had taken place at the location. Plaques usually tell a story of a place, often historical. In architecture, we have the writing of the Koran decorating the walls of the Umayyad Mosque in Damascus and the statuary and stained glass of gothic architecture. All of these are narratives tied to a specific location; however, mobile locative narratives combine the digitally mediated with the spatially/environmentally mediated and as such are fairly new in that they collapse the boundary between the digitally mediated storyworld and physical worlds.

What affords the marriage of digitally mediated content, or lexia, and physical spaces, or nodes, is the mobility and locative affordances of current mobile devices. Rita Raley defines this technology as "'unframed' media practice, unframed in the sense of unbound from the desktop, detached from the singular screen and thus a fixed spectatorial perspective, dependent on signals rather than cords for data transfer in one's immediate vicinity."[28] By being detached from "landlines," mobile devices afford movement as an integral part of the narrative experience, which creates an opportunity for performance[29] and enacted narratives on gestural and spatial levels. Accelerometers and compasses can inform a narrative of gestures, allowing for new forms of interaction with both the physical and the digitally mediated story worlds. Mobile device features such as GPS afford the interplay between digital and physical/built environments. While most designers of mobile locative narratives are constrained in their ability to create the architecture or details of the spaces within which they unfold their narratives, storytellers can still take advantage of the opportunities afforded by the language of physical space and the interplay between digitally mediated and physically mediated story elements. The *mise-en-scène* of nodes in the physical (built and natural) environments, augmented as they are through the addition of digitally meditated narrative elements or lexia, affords rich opportunities for framing the perspective and point of view of the participant/reader. In addition to story elements incorporated into the environment—such as the signs or placards one might see near historic places, spatial and environmental elements can also afford the "telling" of the mobile locative story through metaphoric/semiotic evocation and audience interactions.[30]

For instance, movement's influence on point of view/perception can further be augmented through digitally linking layers of meaning to a space, thus framing how audiences perceive subsequent spaces and elements. Digitally guiding the movement of audiences so that the physical spaces experienced unfold in a dramatically compelling sequence, and framing these experiences through prior exposure to digitally mediated narrative elements, allows audiences to chronologically connect this series of physical and digital spaces to create a narrative. Conversely, the perception of and movement through the physical world can influence the movement through and interpretation of the digitally mediated storyworld. The nature of this transmedia storytelling affords the potential to collapse the boundary between narrative worlds and the environment in which they are told, creating truly immersive narrative experiences. It blurs the lines between storyworld and "physical world." The movement and tension between the physical and digitally mediated storyworlds can be used to support or disrupt the narrative, calling into question the mediation or disrupting the verisimilitude of the storyworld.

Wayfinding and Narrative Bridges

As a means of negotiating the tension stemming from the storyworld of mobile locative narratives being mediated through both physical nodes and digital lexia, and helping audiences to successfully navigate these spaces, mobile locative storytelling requires "wayfinding" and "narrative bridges."

As story elements are located in space, the audience must be able to find and recognize those nodes important to the telling of the story. Unlike a book, which is discrete and has a clear beginning and end,[31] hypertexts or physical spaces are not always so and often have, for all intents and purposes, arbitrary and unacknowledged boundaries. For instance, while walls and barriers can define different spaces within a city, such as Rittenhouse Square in Philadelphia, exactly where this square actually ends is open to interpretation. Absent of physically defining such spaces, such as a white picket fence around a yard, the physical environment often has no clear beginning or end. If a crime occurred in a place, where does that place end? Without a map or clear signage, few individuals would be able to identify the line that divides Michigan from Indiana or the different places of note on the battlefield of Gettysburg.

Consequently, mobile locative narratives require physical or digital wayfinding to delineate these spaces significant to the narrative, to change or direct audience perspective, to inform audience movement, and to draw the audience's attention to important narrative elements in the built environment. Wayfinding is both signage (simply those cues external to audiences that allow subjects to locate themselves in space and help them reach their intended goals) and those psychological and physiological functions related to subjects navigating space.[32]

For example, in creating their mobile locative project, *The Mystery of the Red Avenger*[33] (a historical campus figure on Lebanon Valley College's campus), my students' audiences ran into wayfinding problems. The story involved a fairly standard plot structure relying on an embedded narrative that required the audience to sequentially engage the elements and find clues in specific locations around campus. As a detective story, solving the identity of the red avenger was thought enough incentive for the audience to move through campus and further the story. Yet audiences struggled to find those spaces relevant to the narrative. As a result, the authors had to rely on the campus's existing signage and digitally provide directions, a map, and locative elements to further the storyline.

While wayfinding elements such as signage can play a part in conveying narrative or wayfinding information, the nature of mobile locative narratives also requires some means of having the story, as it is experienced by the audience, bridge the two media through which the story is told and experienced. These "narrative bridges" serve as links that further the story by signaling or allowing narrative progress across the different media involved. Narrative bridges can be embedded in the interface (for instance, a digital map with the audience's location on it) or in the environment. All bridges have a degree of *agency* attached to them, making them either active (e.g., the *[murmur]* signs in Toronto or Quick Response codes (QR codes) that require audiences actively take part) or passive (e.g., a device cued to respond to GPS coordinates). Narrative bridges don't necessarily signify anything; instead, they help move the audience's experience of the storyworld between media. While they are similar to both the gutter in comics,[34] and a hyperlink,[35] they are more a transmedia link between digitally and physically mediated narrative elements.

If audience perceptions are influenced by what they've seen and the order in which they've seen it, the narrative bridges frame the perception of contents in the other medium through the associations formed. For example, another student mobile locative narrative, *A Tale of Two Roommates*,[36] followed the lives of two roommates on Lebanon Valley College's campus. Different buildings on campus contained different stories about these characters and the dramas that they faced. As part of the story, the students struggled to make audiences aware of locations that were important to the narrative and then connect the audience to digitally mediated narrative elements that would frame the story. Where the QR code bridges were placed became important. Because these bridges were often placed at the entrance to most physical spaces, the possibility of the initial experience of that physical space framing the digital story was lost. Also, bridges in the physical environment occupy space and compete with other environmental stimuli for the attention of the audience. If ten discrete QR codes are provided at a location, these bridges must stand out from their background to be noticed, and the audience must understand which code to use and whether the bridges are sequenced. Clearly communicating the subject, purpose, and usage of each bridge becomes necessary.

There are three types of narrative bridges. Mimetic narrative bridges are folded into the story and appear to be part of the storyworld. For instance, in Blast Theory's game/narrative *Uncle Roy All Around You*, a mobile device prompts the audience with the following message: "Meet me in the park by the lake. I've marked your map with the location. Click on the 'I'm here' button to confirm you've arrived and I'll come to meet you." The map mediated by the device indicates where they are to go.[37] In this instance, the digitally mediated bridge is folded into the action of the story and provides wayfinding information that furthers the narrative. (For a detailed discussion of *Uncle Roy All Around You*, see chapter 12 of this book, "Proximity and Alterity: Narratives of City, Self, and Other in the Locative Games of Blast Theory.") Diegetic narrative bridges are narrated, rather than represented, and while slightly disruptive, are still part of the storyworld. Disruptive narrative bridges are self-reflexive; they point out the mediation of the story—they disrupt the verisimilitude or immersion of the narrative—either purposefully or as a result of a poorly conceived and told story. For instance, *A Tale of Two Roommates* requires that audiences scan QR codes. This action is not explained by the logic of the storyworld and, by falling outside the actions of the story, disrupts the verisimilitude of the narrative.

The lack of authorial control over the physical environment and the behaviors of the audience are both affordances and constraints, lending the physical environment agency over the narrative and affording a far greater degree of openness to the story's narrative arc. Much like the digital environment, the physical environment is ephemeral, multivocal, and aggregative.[39] Everyday life and experience in the built environment affords nearly limitless agency, albeit constrained by culture, law, and the reality of physics (e.g., most people can't kick down buildings). From the standpoint of a narrative, even telling a story about a particular space defines it. The events of the story influence the audience's understanding of different spaces in which the story takes place and, due to the meaning imposed, form a semantic constraint that often governs those actions available to the audience.

Conclusion

As acts of transmedia storytelling, mobile locative narratives depend upon the affordances and constraints of the media used to convey stories. As interactive works, mobile locative narratives only come into being through the decisions and efforts of audiences. These works require that audiences navigate across digital and physical spaces, attempt to identify in these spaces the elements relevant to the story (and ignore elements outside the story), to understand these narrative elements, and through their actions and decisions, to co-author a narrative. This is a really nontrivial effort. To more readily afford these interactions, mobile locative narratives must provide audiences with wayfinding information and narrative bridges. Ultimately, the exchange between digital and physical is, to some extent, a realization of the tension between competing narratives. Both digital and physical media provide counternarratives to the other, through which the place or digitally mediated objects are semantically constrained or "held" down and labeled or defined through an implicit or explicit act of chronologically or causally creating a sequence of events. To impose a single narrative or multiple narratives on the other is a form of control—a constraint on the narrative possibility of built and digital environments.

Notes

1. *Myst.* CD-ROM. Cyan, 1997.
2. For discussions of space as a medium, see the following: Jane Jacobs, *The Death and Life of Great American Cities* (New York: Modern Library, 1993); Bryan Lawson, *The Language of Space* (Oxford: Architectural Press, 2001); *The Structure of the Ordinary, Form and Control in the Built Environment*, ed. Jonathan Teicher (Cambridge, MA: MIT Press, 1998); Michel de Certeau, *The Practice of Everyday Life* (Los Angeles: University of California Press, 1988); Yi Fu Tuan, *Space and Place: The Perspective of Experience* (Minneapolis: University of Minnesota Press, 1977); and Gaston Bachelard, *The Poetics of Space* (New York: Beacon Press, 1994).

3. Henry Jenkins, *Convergence Culture: Where Old and New Media Collide* (New York: NYU Press, 2006), 95–96.

4. Ibid., 106.

5. Donald A. Norman, *The Design of Everyday Things* (New York: Basic Books, 2002).

6. Ibid., 9.

7. Ibid., 84.

8. Ibid., 85.

9. For instance, culture determines the color and position of the police lights on the Lego model. Logical constraints rely on the assumptions we make based on acknowledged or unacknowledged premises. For instance, an often unacknowledged premise is that all of the parts in a Lego model would be used. Any uses of this set would be limited to some extent by this premise. See Norman, *The Design of Everyday Things*, 85.

10. For further discussion, see: Chris Crawford, *On Interactive Storytelling* (Berkeley: New Riders Games, 2005); Espen Aarseth, *Cybertext: Perspectives on Ergodic Literature* (Baltimore: The Johns Hopkins University Press, 1997); Matthew Mateas and Andrew Stern, "Interaction and Narrative," in *Game Design Reader*, ed. Katie Salen and Eric Zimmerman (Cambridge, MA: The MIT Press, 2005).

11. Jesper Juul, "Games Telling Stories?" *Game Studies*, 1, no. 1 (July 2001), http://www.gamestudies.org/0101/juul-gts/.

12. See Marie-Laure Ryan's idea of "narrativity," in her "Introduction," in *Narrative Across Media: The Languages of Storytelling*, ed. Marie-Laure Ryan (Lincoln, NE: University of Nebraska Press, 2004), 4.

13. Jay David Bolter, *Writing Space: Computers, Hypertext, and the Remediation of Print* (Mahwah, NJ: Lawrence Erlbaum Associates, 2001), 43.

14. What Espen Aarseth calls *ergodic*, in his book, *Cybertext: Perspectives on Ergodic Literature* (Baltimore: The Johns Hopkins University Press, 1997), 1.

15. Mark Stephen Meadows, *Pause and Effect: The Art of Interactive Narrative* (Indianapolis: New Riders Press, 2003).

16. How the story unfolds in turn frames the audience's reception of the work. This idea, in film termed the Kuleshov effect, was illustrated by early twentieth-century film experiments demonstrating that the order in which elements are perceived frames the interpretation of later elements. In the Kuleshov effect, the audience viewed the same picture of a man, yet interpreted his expression differently depending on whether they saw a coffin or a bowl of soup, and in so doing, created a chronological or causal relationship between the elements. Framing also demonstrates a deep-seated desire for narrative closure, which forms a cultural constraint.

17. Aarseth, *Cybertext*, 1.

18. de Certeau, *The Practice of Everyday Life*, 93.

19. Henry Jenkins, "Game Design as Narrative Architecture," in *Game Design Reader*, ed. Katie Salen and Eric Zimmerman (Cambridge, MA: The MIT Press, 2005), 677.

20. Ibid., 681.

21. Ibid., 678.

22. Ibid., 682.

23. Spiro Kostof, *A History of Architecture: Settings and Rituals* (Oxford: Oxford University Press, 1995), 151–155.

24. See Meadows's discussion of foveal vision in *Pause and Effect*, 57–58.

25. Yi-Fu Tuan, *Space and Place: The Perspective of Experience*, (Minneapolis: University of Minnesota Press, 1987), 114.

26. Lawson, *The Language of Space*, 85–86.

27. I've coopted this term from Lynch's study of wayfinding. Kevin Lynch, *The Image of the City*, (Cambridge, MA: The MIT Press, 1960), 47.
28. William Wordsworth, "Tintern Abbey," in *Selected Poems*, ed. Stephen Gill (New York: Penguin Books Limited, 2004).
29. As noted by Rita Raley, "Walk this Way," in *Beyond the Screen: Transformations of Literary Structures, Interfaces and Genres*, eds. Jörgen Schäffer and Peter Gendolia (Bielefeld, Germany: Transcript Verlag, 2010), 299–316.
30. Raley, "Walk this Way," 303.
31. See Jeremy Hight, "Locative Narrative, Literature and Form," in *Beyond the Screen: Transformations of Literary Structures, Interfaces and Genres*, eds. Jörgen Schäffer and Peter Gendolia (Bielefeld, Germany: Transcript Verlag, 2010), 317–329.
32. Due to intertextuality and a number of books in a series sharing the same backstory, even this claim may be disputed.
33. See Paul Arthur and Passini Romedi, *Wayfinding: People, Signs, and Architecture* (New York: McGraw-Hill, 1992). Further discussions of wayfinding include: Craig Berger, *Wayfinding: Designing and Implementing Graphic Navigational Systems* (Mies, Switzerland: RotoVision, 2005); David Gibson, *The Wayfinding Handbook: Information Design for Public Spaces* (Princeton, NJ: Princeton Architectural Press, 2009); Per Mollerup, *Wayshowing: A Guide to Environmental Signage Principles and Practices* (Baden: Lars Müller, 2005).
34. Holland Pintarch, Cody Shepp, and Abigail Tomlinson, *The Mystery of the Red Avenger*, 2011.
35. Scott McCloud, *Understanding Comics: The Invisible Art* (Amherst, MA: Kitchen Sink Press, 1993), 90.
36. Jeff Parker, "A Poetics of the Link." *ebr* 12 (2001), http://www.electronicbookreview.com/thread/electropoetics/linkletters.
37. Kayla Fulfer, Emily Gertenbach, Lauren Lange, and Allison McFadden. *A Tale of Two Roommates*, 2011.
38. Blast Theory, *Uncle Roy All Around You*, http://www.blasttheory.co.uk/bt/work_uncleroy.html.
39. See N. J. Habraken, *The Structure of the Ordinary: Form and Control in the Built Environment*, ed. Jonathan Teicher (Cambridge, MA: The MIT Press, 2000), 6.

5

LOCATION IS NOT COMPELLING (UNTIL IT IS HAUNTED)

Mark Sample

How do the examples in this chapter help us understand the practice of story-telling in the mobile media age?

Looking at the emerging practices of "checking in" to a location using location-based social media, this chapter argues that such platforms for social interactivity tell us very little about our network, our interactions, and our places. Location is not compelling. To state it more accurately: *your* location is not compelling. While location may not be compelling, stories are, and this chapter explores various ways to "misuse" existing locative social networks for narrative purposes. Beginning with the thought that GPS receivers are made for storytelling (yet predominately offer only an impoverished notion of place), this chapter seeks to reconcile the poor connection between locational tools and narrative. The connection between these categories is explored by discussing a storytelling practice called "Haunts," which uses existing locative social media to tell stories.

Keywords

- **Haunts:** A game in which teams work to leave fragments of a narrative around various spaces using existing locative social media.
- **Ubiquitous media:** A postdesktop paradigm for computing, in which the technologies we interact with weave themselves into everyday life. These media are seemingly everywhere but often become so incorporated into our actions that we rarely notice them.
- **Heterotopias:** Drawn from the theories of Michel Foucault, heterotopias are a single "real" place that is layered with incompatible counter-sites. These counter-sites are juxtaposed against one another, often telling very different stories about the same location.

Introduction

I am strangely drawn to the power of GPS, to the possibility of knowing my precise location on the face of the planet. This aspect of the Global Positioning System, of pinpointing myself on a map, has always been more fascinating to me than navigation or turn-by-turn directions. I don't want to know to where I'm going or how to get there. I want to know where I am. There's something magical, something mystical about seeing myself as a little pushpin in a map right there on the screen of my phone. I'm reminded of a scene in Don DeLillo's uncannily prescient *White Noise*, when the narrator Jack Gladney checks the balance of his bank account on an ATM. "The figure on the screen roughly corresponded to my independent estimate," Jack says with wonder. An "estimate," he continues, "feebly arrived at after long searches through documents, tormented arithmetic. Waves of relief and gratitude flowed over me. The system had blessed my life. I felt its support and approval."[1] In the early days of GPS, I felt a similar sort of blessing when I saw my position on a map. Spiritual validation: the satellite gods in the sky have deemed me to be exactly where I think I am.

White Noise was published in 1985, which incidentally was the year that the tenth and final BLOCK-I GPS—in those days known as NAVSTAR—satellite was placed into orbit on an Atlas E/F rocket, launched from Vandenberg Air Force Base. Developed by Rockwell International in the 1970s, the BLOCK-I satellites were 1,700-pound proof-of-concept orbiters, designed to test the idea of a global-scale geographic positioning system.[2] Such a system had been a dream of the U.S. military since the 1950s, when it became crucial for the Navy to know the precise locations of its Polaris missile submarines.[3] While the Department of Defense built a system of low orbiting satellites called TRANSIT in the 1960s for this purpose, it was primitive compared to NAVSTAR; for example, TRANSIT offered only two-dimensional fixes (latitude and longitude) instead of three-dimensional fixes (which would also include elevation). Not only did NAVSTAR work, but the BLOCK-I satellites lasted far longer than their projected three-year lifespan. In 1989 the United States began updating the system with BLOCK-II satellites, and by 1995, modern GPS was fully operational, with twenty-four satellites orbiting the planet. For the first few years, only the U.S. military and other government entities had full access to GPS signals; the military intentionally reduced the system's accuracy for everyone else under a program called Selective Availability.[4] On May 2, 2000, Selective Availability was shut down, and the system was entirely opened up for nonmilitary use.[5]

Ubiquitous GPS

GPS as we know it is less than two decades old. Yet consider this astonishing fact: by May 2012, nearly half of all American adults—46% to be precise—owned a GPS-enabled smartphone, an incredible adoption rate for a technology that has only been available to civilians for twelve or so years. These smartphone owners use the GPS on their phones too. Almost three-quarters of them (74%) access location-based information on their phones, such as directions or restaurant recommendations.[6] GPS is so ubiquitous that it's difficult to imagine a world without it.

But of course, many of us can. Almost everyone born before 1985 has a GPS origin story, a narrative about their first experience with GPS, similar to the stories their parents or grandparents might tell about their first television set. My own is earlier than most, but later than some. In between the opening up of GPS in 2000 and the debut of YouTube five years later, I received my first GPS device. It was an all-black peripheral made by Magellan, roughly the size of a paperback book, and it snapped onto my silver Palm Tungsten T PDA. In hindsight, what I liked about this pairing is how explicitly peripheral GPS receivers used to be. Called the Magellan Companion, it was an add-on accessory, an afterthought even. The maps on this Palm-Magellan combo were crudely rendered, blocky vector graphics against a white background. Nevertheless, using this piggybacked GPS receiver was a powerful engagement with what Edward Soja calls a "secondspace perspective."[7] While a firstspace perspective is rooted in the material world, the secondspace perspective is conceptual, a kind of a cognitive map, externalized in this case onto a GPS receiver screen. Unlike Jorge Luis Borges's map of the empire, there was no danger that this 320 × 320 pixelated map would ever replace the territory it represents. Yet at the time it was engrossing and immersive, perhaps precisely because it was confined to such a small space. It shrunk the whole world into the Palm in the palm of my hand. I vividly remember the day my Magellan GPS receiver arrived. It was May 2003. I was still a graduate student, and I was supposed to be working on my dissertation. Instead I was checking the progress of the package on the UPS website all day. In an ironic twist, UPS delivered it to the wrong address. When I saw it had been delivered, but not to me, I panicked. I called UPS, and because I called within minutes of the misdelivery, UPS was able to retrieve my package and get it to me that day. As soon as I had unboxed the device, I ran outside and stood in a wide open field, arms held high, waiting for my Palm to detect signals from space. That moment is when I first felt that validation, that approval that Jack Gladney felt. But mine was even more essential. The ATM simply told Gladney how much money he had. My GPS told me my worth. It told me my place in the universe.

A few years later I received as a gift a PDA with the GPS receiver built right in, an iQue 3600 made by Garmin. Hyperbolically named, the 360 degrees of a compass elevated by a power of ten, the iQue automatically switched to GPS mode when a small antenna was flipped up. In a matter of two years, GPS had gone from a clunky accessory for my PDA to a component integrated into the device—which, of course, I should add, itself was an accessory, something I carried along with my MP3 player and my cell phone. And now, a few years later, for many, if not most of us, GPS is a hidden part of that single accessory we never leave home without, that accessory so seemingly necessary that it's more of an appendage than an accessory. The phone. It's a prosthetic, not a peripheral.

The progression from an obviously external GPS receiver to an invisible element of the most take-it-for-granted device of the twenty-first century reminds me of something the science fiction author Bruce Sterling once wrote: that the difference between the technology of modernism and the technology of postmodernism is a matter of size and intimacy. The technology of modernism culminated in breathtakingly tall steel skyscrapers and gargantuan concrete dams, what David Nye calls the "technological sublime."[8] The most advanced technologies today are the opposite—small and personal. The technology of postmodernism is technology that, as Sterling puts it, "sticks to the skin, responds to the touch."[9]

Sterling wrote that in 1986.

Nearly thirty years later, and a decade into my own GPS narrative, I still feel a thrill when my location on Earth is validated by satellites in space. GPS is not merely for finding one's self on the map anymore, though. Nor is GPS limited to directions and wayfinding. Over the past few years, a number of location-aware mobile services—the most popular is Foursquare—have emerged. The focus of these social media services is "checking in" to venues and sharing those check-ins with a circle of friends or, in some cases, strangers. Most of these mobile apps let you tag your check-in with a note or a photo, and some of them incorporate game-like elements, such as the coupons and badges Foursquare offers for repeated check-ins. I've experimented with most of these geosocial services, and I've reached a conclusion at odds with my own history with GPS.

Location Is Not Compelling

Location is not compelling. Or, perhaps, to state it more accurately: *your* location is not compelling. I still enjoy having my own location verified by satellites in the sky. But I'm too busy with my own life to care about your exact location. Especially when most of the people I know are either students or professors, and the only places they ever seem to check in to are coffee shops, classrooms, or bars.

Research suggests that I'm not alone in thinking that sharing one's location is not compelling. In November 2010, when interest in geosocial services had reached a fevered pitch and the field was crowded with many competing—and now defunct—services (Gowalla, Loopt, Brightkite, and MyTown among them), the Pew Research Center's Internet & American Life Project found that only 4% of adults who were online used check-in services. That figure was actually a decrease from May 2010, when 5% of online adults reported using check-in services.[10] The numbers have grown steadily since 2010, but users of geosocial services are still relatively rare. By May 2012, when 74% of smartphone owners were regularly relying on the location services on their phones for directions or recommendations, the Pew Research Center found that only 18% of these smart-phone owners checked in to locations or shared their locations.[11]

Why?

Pew doesn't say. But I'll restate my own theory: because your location is not compelling. Check-ins are not compelling. They offer an impoverished sense of place. Borrowing from Clifford Geertz, we might say that a check-in is a "thin" description of a place. Under the check-in model, every location becomes a point-of-sale and little else. Check in to a California Tortilla on Foursquare, and you earn free chips and salsa. But do you learn anything about the place itself? Do the friends with whom you've shared the check-in learn anything either? Your check-in, from their point of view, is simply an advertisement for California Tortilla. While I have, I admit, availed myself of Foursquare's special offers, they do nothing to sell me on the promise of geolocation. It is also true that some of the benefits of geolocation have been seized upon by museums and historians. For example, Foursquare and the History Channel have partnered up to provide historical tidbits if you check in near a historic locale.[12] In practice this version of pop-up history is history "lite," lacking any kind of creative or pedagogical imagination, little different from a Fodor's guidebook. In general, check-ins are a consumer-based, trivial use of technology, and most smartphone owners recognize this.

The world is a rich and a complicated place, with layers of hidden experiences embedded in the most mundane of spaces, and these experiences do not deserve to be reduced to a badge on a screen. The social geographer E.V. Walter highlights what he calls the expressive intelligibility of places by noting that the ancient Greeks' oldest word for place was *chora*, which referred to the "spirit of a place." *Chora* is distinct from the other ancient Greek word for place, *topos*, which referred to the geographic location itself or the "objective features" of a place. Walter recalls that the opening chapter of Geographia, Ptolemy's second-century A.D. masterpiece, retains this distinction between chorography and geography. Ptolemy saw these two modes of mapping as separate disciplines. Geography, as Walter explains it, "pictorially represented the earth as a whole, describing its nature, position, and general features," while chorography "set off a part of the world, exhibiting it separately, representing exactly and in minute detail nearly everything contained within it."[13] Maps over the centuries came to favor the former mode of representing the world, though this was not always the case, as expressive features—say a sea serpent or some other evocative beast—were once common features on classical and medieval maps.

Beyond Location

Like most modern maps, geosocial apps are bereft of any chorographic sensibility. They do not provoke the imagination or convey the spirit of a place. They do not express what folklorist Kent Ryden calls "the invisible landscape" of a place. By "invisible landscape," Ryden means the stories about a place that cannot be reduced to a Cartesian grid. The invisible landscape is comprised of lived history, both tangible and intangible. "While the modern map is a marvel of efficient geographical communication," Ryden writes, "in other important ways it does not tell us very much at all."[14] Maps convey a limited range of geographic experiences: distance, elevation, vegetation, rivers, and buildings. But maps fail to convey the *meaning* of these geographic elements, how they impact both the broad history of a place and the daily life of the people who live there. Ryden's phrase "modern map" might easily be replaced by "modern app." Ryden calls for a reawakening of the discipline of chorography. "If geographers," Ryden observes, "make maps and formulate interpretations of the physical landscape, chorographers are mappers and interpreters of the invisible landscape."[15] Location-aware apps could prove to be the means to create such maps of the invisible landscape. I have a vision of infusing geosocial applications with a sense of depth, with meaning that goes beyond the check-in. We ought to repurpose Foursquare and similar geolocative apps in order to foster critical and creative misuse of technology, and to encourage serious yet playful (or, playfully serious) chorographic thinking. Let's turn locative media from gimmicky entertainment coupon books and glorified historical guidebooks into platforms for renegotiating space and telling stories about places.

Many of the mobile apps themselves contain the raw material for such chorographic work. Mappers need only play with the way they use these apps. When I say "play," I have in mind the game designers Eric Zimmerman and Katie Salen's concept of play: "free movement within a more rigid structure."[16] In the case of geolocation, the rigid structure comes from the core mechanics of the different geolocation apps: checking in and tagging specific places with tips or comments. What's supposed to happen is that users visit bars or restaurants and then post tips on the best drinks or bargains. But what can happen, given the free movement within this structure, is that users can define their own places and add tips that range from lewd to absurd. For example, within my dully named building at George Mason University, Robinson A, I've created my own space, The Office of Incandescent Light and Industrial Runoff. Likewise, when I'm home, I often check in to the Treehouse of Sighs. I have an actual tree house in my yard, but the Treehouse of Sighs is not that one. The Treehouse of Sighs exists only in my mind, part of the invisible landscape.

Not all geosocial services allow users to create new locations. Some, like Google Latitude, only allow users to check in to verified places. In this case, it can be just as evocative to tag existing venues with virtual graffiti, which you can use to create a counterfactual history of a place. Anyone who checks into the Starbucks on my campus can see my advice regarding the fireplace there ("The fireplace isn't real but if you close your eyes really tight and think about Bambi fleeing a forest fire you can almost smell smoke"). Also on my campus I've uncovered the research library's powerful secret ("Probably the best place to read tacos on campus"). I've left surrealist epigrams in other public places, like the enigmatic tip in the claustrophobic Z terminal of Washington-Dulles International Airport ("The clocks in the walls of the hulls of the plane are bent, broken, and hard to wind").

All of this play has led me to consider teaching students to evaluate geosocial media by *using* geosocial media. My initial idea was to have students add new venues to Foursquare's database, with the stipulation that these new venues be Foucauldian "Other Spaces"[17]—parking decks, overpasses, bus depots, and so on—that stand in sharp contrast to the officially sanctioned places on Foursquare (coffee shops, restaurants, bars, parks). One of the points I'd like to make is that much of our lives are actually spent in these nether-places that are neither here nor there. Tracking our movements in these unglamorous but not unimportant unplaces could be a revelation to my students. It might actually be one of the best uses of geolocation—to defamiliarize our daily surroundings.

But let's take this idea further. Why not combine the various elements of my playful approach to geosocial media: other spaces, other stories, an invisible landscape both written and excavated by visitors to those spaces? This is how my idea for an alternate reality game called *Haunts* developed. *Haunts* is part game, part story, a kind of game about stories.

Haunts: Narrative Play as Creative Misuse

> *HAUNT, v.—from the French hante-r (12th century), "of uncertain origin . . . it is not clear whether the earliest sense in French and English was to practise habitually (an action, etc.) or to frequent habitually (a place)."*
> —*Oxford English Dictionary, Second Edition*[18]

The word "haunt," as its origins in French make clear, refers to both a practice and a place. No ghosts are necessary. Any living soul can haunt a place, making that place a haunt. The ghosts appear only when those living souls have departed, making a haunt *haunted*, a physical space permeated with spectral traces. In other words, a physical space written over with stories, a chorographic space.

Haunts is about the secret stories of spaces.

Haunts is about the production of what Foucault calls "heterotopias"—a single real place in which incompatible counter-sites are layered upon or juxtaposed against one another.[19]

The essence of *Haunts* is this: players (in my case, I imagine students) work in teams, visiting various public places and tagging them with fragments of a fictional story. This story explores the various "traumas" of a space. I'm using "trauma" in the most open-ended way possible here, in the same way that trauma itself is open—any open wound, any unassimilated experience. As a narrative framework, trauma is especially fitting for *Haunts*. Trauma is often connected to a place in a way that it is never quite connected to a time.[20] Because trauma is enduring, what Cathy Caruth calls an "unclaimed experience," it is nearly timeless for the traumatized victim, but it is not placeless.[21] Individual and collective traumas are part of nearly every inhabited place's invisible landscape. If chorography seeks to uncover the spirit of a place, *Haunts* seeks to imagine the unknown trauma witnessed by a place. Just as posttraumatic stress disorder (PTSD) is characterized by intrusive, repetitive memories, *Haunts* imagines the same traumatic kernel, being told again and again, from different points of view.[22] Each team will work from an overarching traumatic narrative that they've created, but because the place-based tips are limited to text-message-sized bits, the story will emerge only in glimpses and traces, across a series of spaces. But emerge for whom? For the other teams, of course, but also for random strangers using the geosocial apps, who have no idea that they've stumbled upon a fictional world augmenting the real one—a fictional world haunting the real one.

Haunts is influenced by Augusto Boal's *Theater of the Oppressed*, particularly Boal's concept of "invisible theater," in which a scene is acted out—Boal uses the term "erupts"—in some public place, in front of people who are not spectators. As Boal puts it, "The people who witness the scene are those who are there by chance. . . . All the people who are near become involved in the eruption and the effects of it last long after the skit is ended."[23] *Haunts* goes beyond invisible theater because the story or stories take place across a number of spaces. Most narratives do not require any kind of breadcrumb trail more complicated than sequential page numbers. In *Haunts*, however, players would need to create clues that act as what Marc Ruppel calls migratory cues—nudging participants from one locale to the next, from one medium to the next.[24] These cues might be suggestive references left in a check-in note, or perhaps obliquely embedded in a photograph taken at the check-in point.

Another twist of *Haunts* subverts the tendency of geolocation apps to reward repeat visits to a single locale. As I've described, check in enough times at your coffee shop or Shell station with Foursquare and you become "mayor" of the place. *Haunts* disincentivizes multiple visits. Check in too many times at the same place and you become a "ghost." No longer among the living, you are stuck in a single place, barred from leaving tips anywhere else. Like a ghost, you haunt that space for the rest of the game. It's a fate players would probably want to avoid, yet players will nonetheless be compelled to revisit destinations, in order to fill in narrative gaps as either writers or readers.

The final twist of *Haunts* is that it does not rely on any single geosocial platform. Most geolocative apps have the same core functionality. This means players can use competing services, weaving parallel yet diverging stories across the same series of spaces. Each haunt hosts a number of haunts. The narrative and geographic path of a single team's story could alone be engaging enough to follow, but even more promising is a kind of cross-pollination between haunts, in which each team builds upon one or two shared narrative events, exquisite-corpse style. The trouble with building a haunt with multiple platforms, however, is that the platforms themselves are not necessarily reliable or long-lasting. The geosocial landscape has changed dramatically since I first conceived *Haunts* in 2010. Bright-kite is no more; neither is Loopt. Gowalla shut down in 2012, after Facebook acquired the company in 2011. Facebook itself dialed back its aggressive push into check-ins, removing the "Places" button from its apps in 2011 as well.[25] In some cases (for example, Loopt), users were provided a temporary way to down-load their check-in history as an XML file. Other services (for example, Gowalla) promised an "easy way to export your Passport data . . . and your photos as well," but such capabilities never materialized.[26] The result in the case of Gowalla is an entire history of geosocial activity that has become irretrievable, a literalization of the invisible landscape *Haunts* seeks to evoke. Given the inherent instability of social media, the history of geolocative apps oddly mirrors the kind of storytelling I had wanted *Haunts* to tell. The apps themselves become invisible, haunted places.

Position/Navigation/Timing

I have said that location is not compelling, but that stories about location are. There are in fact suggestive correspondences between GPS and stories, between location and storytelling. Nearly everyone knows that GPS stands for *global posi-tioning system*, and many know it was originally developed by the military, but few know what government organization actually coordinates GPS. It is the cumber-somely named National Executive Committee on Space-Based PNT, established by a presidential directive in 2004 and made up of various cabinet secretaries, the Joint Chiefs of Staff, and NASA.[27] And what does *PNT* stand for?

1. Positioning
2. Navigation
3. Timing

These sound to me a lot like storytelling terms. Isn't positioning analogous to perspective, the vantage point from which we witness a story? Navigation recalls the nontrivial choices readers make in what Espen Aarseth has coined "ergodic" narratives.[28] And timing is the heartbeat of narrative—chronology, plot, the se-quence of events unfolding across time.

PNT: positioning, navigation, timing.

GPS is made for storytelling. It simply hasn't been understood this way. *Haunts*—and other mobile media narratives discussed in this collection—attempt to shift the focus of location-aware platforms away from geography and into the expressive realm of chorography. Perhaps *Haunts* will only ever work as a concep-tual game, a thought experiment, but I find its project compelling, and even nec-essary. The endeavor turns a consumer-based model of mobile computing into an authorship-based model. It is a uniquely collaborative activity, but also one that invites individual introspection. It imagines trauma as both private and public, deeply personal yet situated within shared semiotic domains. It operates at the intersection between game and story, between reading and writing, between the *topos* and *choro*. And it might finally make geolocation worth paying attention to.

Notes

1. Don DeLillo, *White Noise* (New York: Penguin, 1985), 46.
2. United States Naval Observatory, "Block I Satellite Information," ftp://tycho.usno.navy.mil/pub/gps/gpsb1.txt.
3. Norman Bonnor, "A Brief History of Global Navigation Satellite Systems," *Journal of Navigation* 65, no. 1 (January 2012): 3.
4. Ibid., 1–5.
5. United States Naval Observatory, "GPS Constellation Status," ftp://tycho.usno.navy.mil/pub/gps/gpstd.txt.
6. Kathryn Zickurh, "Three-Quarters of Smartphone Owners Use Location-Based Services," Pew Internet & American Life Project, http://pewinternet.org/Reports/2012/Location-based-services.aspx, 2.
7. Edward W. Soja, *Thirdspace: Journeys to Los Angeles and Other Real-and-Imagined Places* (Oxford: Wiley-Blackwell, 1996).
8. David E. Nye, *American Technological Sublime* (Cambridge, MA: The MIT Press, 1996).
9. *Mirrorshades: The Cyberpunk Anthology*, ed. Bruce Sterling (New York: Arbor House, 1986), xi.
10. Kathryn Zickurh and Aaron Smith, "4% of Online Americans Use Location-Based Services," Pew Internet & American Life Project, http://www.pewinternet.org/~/media//Files/Reports/2010/PIP-Location%20based%20services.pdf, 2.
11. Zickurh, *Three-Quarters of Smartphone Owners*, 2.
12. Jolie O'Dell, "History Channel Launches Foursquare Campaign and a New Badge," *Mashable*, April 13, 2010, http://mashable.com/2010/04/13/history-channel-foursquare/.
13. E.V. Walter, *Placeways: A Theory of the Human Environment* (Chapel Hill, NC: University of North Carolina Press, 1988), 116–119.
14. Kent Ryden, *Mapping the Invisible Landscape: Folklore, Writing, and the Sense of Place* (Iowa City: University of Iowa Press, 1993), 20.
15. Ibid., 50.
16. Katie Salen and Eric Zimmerman, *Rules of Play: Game Design Fundamentals* (Cambridge, MA: The MIT Press, 2004), 304.
17. Michel Foucault, "Of Other Spaces," trans. Jay Miskowiec, *Diacritics* 16, no. 1 (Spring 1986): 22–27.
18. "Haunt, v.," *Oxford English Dictionary* (Oxford: Oxford University Press, 1989), http://www.oed.com/view/Entry/84641.
19. Foucault, "Of Other Spaces," 24.
20. Brian Croxall, "Comment on Haunts: Place, Play, and Trauma," *SAMPLE REALITY*, June 1, 2010, http://www.samplereality.com/2010/06/01/haunts-place-play-and-trauma/#comment-4540.
21. Cathy Caruth, "Unclaimed Experience: Trauma and the Possibility of History," *Yale French Studies*, no. 79 (1991): 181–192.
22. For more on PTSD, see Bessel A. Van der Kolk and Alexander C. McFarlane, "The Black Hole of Trauma," in *Traumatic Stress: The Effects of Overwhelming Experience on Mind, Body, and Society*, ed. Lars Weisaeth, Bessel A. van der Kolk, and Alexander C. McFarlane (New York: Guilford Press, 1996), 3–23.

23. Augusto Boal, "Theatre of the Oppressed," in *The New Media Reader*, ed. Noah Wardrip-Fruin and Nick Montfort (Cambridge, MA: The MIT Press, 2003), 347.

24. Marc Ruppel, "Learning to Speak Braille," Ph.D. qualifying exam paper (College Park: University of Maryland, 2005).

25. Leslie Horn, "Gowalla Shuts Down Following Facebook Acquisition," *PCMag.com*, March 12, 2012, http://www.pcmag.com/article2/0,2817,2401433,00.asp.

26. Josh Williams. "Gowalla Is Going to Facebook," *Gowalla*, December 5, 2011, http://gowalla.tumblr.com/post/13782997303/gowalla-going-to-facebook.

27. See http://www.pnt.gov/.

28. Espen J. Aarseth, *Cybertext: Perspectives on Ergodic Literature* (Baltimore: Johns Hopkins University Press, 1997).

6

DANCING WITH TWITTER

Mobile Narratives Become Physical Scores

Susan Kozel with Mia Keinänen and Leena Rouhiainen

How do the examples in this chapter help us understand the practice of storytelling in the mobile media age?

This chapter expands the reflections on narrative in this collection by considering Twitter, SMS, and dance. At the heart of it is a project called *IntuiTweet*, where dancers used Twitter to send short messages to each other describing movement or kinesthetic sensations. Performers across several cities then performed the movements described in the tweets. The focus of this chapter is structured around two questions: "Why consider mobile media narratives through a project based in dance?" and "Why consider dance through the lens of mobile media narratives?" The term "narrative" is questioned, and several alternatives are evaluated: script, score, notation, archive, or documentation. *Score* fits the qualities of these "bodily tweets" best because it relies on listening, with implications for preservation as well as reenactment. Finally, the relevance of bodily tweets is expanded to a context wider than art, suggesting that social media is not significant simply because multiple connections are made between people, but because the intention to use a media platform in an unconventional way can be a transformative act.

Keywords

- **Choreography:** The composition of a dance, a form of art based on bodily movement, rhythm, and gesture.
- **Score:** The translation of music or dance into words or symbols so that it can be recorded, preserved, and performed once again.
- **Kinesthetic:** Pertaining to the sense of motion; the faculty of being aware of the position and movement of parts of the body.

Glancing Touches

These tweets were little touches.
They followed me around, they came in and out of my awareness, of my consciousness.
They were on my skin, then digested, then they came out of me . . . I witnessed the
*   movement in an improvisatory mode . . . and I sent them off again.*
Like birds landing on me and taking off again.
The people closest to me, to my bodily movement, were not the ones in my immediate
*   vicinity.*
Vicinity and proximity became separated.
As if I carried a secret with me;
the invisible in daily life.
I was dancing, and few around me knew it.
I saw less, I sensed. I listened.

Introduction

This chapter expands the reflections on narrative in this collection by considering Twitter, SMS, and movement improvisation. At the heart of it is a project called *IntuiTweet* that used Twitter as a platform for dance improvisation: tweets were written by small group of dancers to promote kinesthetic and corporeal exchanges in public spaces. The basic qualities of this project are that the bodies were in motion and they were geographically distant; further, they were linked only by a set of improvisatory practices and by Twitter on their mobile devices. The improvisations left traces in the form of words.

Making sense of this project in the context of mobile media narratives, two questions fold back on each other: why consider mobile media narratives through a project based in dance? And why consider dance through the lens of mobile media narratives? In pursuing these parallel but inverse lines of questioning, both the sense of narrative and the understanding of the movement practices are transformed. Yet the scope of this chapter extends beyond narrative and dance: in exploring the qualities of these embodied micro-narratives and what happens when they are exchanged, we can learn more about how we live in the world with our mobile media. Saying that our media practices reveal how we exist in the world is like calling them an ontological mirror; in other words, they reveal our states of being. This deeper layer of reflection is accomplished by drawing upon Jean Luc Nancy, a contemporary French phenomenologist who is rarely integrated into considerations of culture and media outside of Europe. His phenomenological writings are valuable for exploring mobile media used in the context of dance or movement because for him, thinking deeply about sensory engagement with the world and with other people is a valid way to understand experience. He can also help us understand the multiplicity, or many overlapping layers, of narrative and bodies that arise through mobile media. Finally, he reveals the importance of receptivity, or listening when we create and distribute shared narratives.

Body Tweets

The *IntuiTweet* project began from a desire to explore intuition in daily life from the perspectives of dance and design combined with the intention to respond to the characterization of social networking, Twitter in particular, as banal and superficial.[1] The three main dancer-researchers (Mia Keinänen, Leena Rouhiainen, and myself) adopted the starting point that any technology that is networked, mobile, and carried around on bodies is not necessarily superficial: with the intent to use a system differently, new expressive modes can emerge. In other words, we intended to shift the social choreographies associated with Twitter. We initiated a series of improvisations using the SMS function of Twitter following a few simple rules:

a)   take a moment to listen to your body and notice a movement intuition or sensation;
b)   code it into a Tweet of 140 characters or less;
c)   send it to other participants by SMS through Twitter;
d)   when a Tweet is received, improvise it immediately or with a time lag (hours or days);
e)   notice how it has morphed in your own body over time and through space;
f)   recode it into a fresh Tweet and resend it to be received and improvised once more.

The physical response was triggered by few characters—we rarely filled the full 140-character range—but the link between words and motion was kinesthetically direct, rather than intellectually filtered. This made the experience akin to contact improvisation with the peculiar side product of a written residue in the form of our archive of tweets. Contact improvisation is a form of exploratory dance where movement is initiated by contact with another person, an object, another part of his own body, or something in the environment such as bumpy ground, wind, or music. The dancer receives the contact (it can be a very light touch or a strong push) and lets her body move in response to this until she contacts someone or something else. The movement continues, contact after contact, across people and objects. Often there is no overall pattern or choreography for the dancer to follow; the movement creates its own momentum. With *IntuiTweet*, we were accustomed to the movement of contact improvisation disappearing after being performed: it was at first almost a surprise to notice that we were left with the traces of the movement saved in words on the Twitter platform and held in our mobile phones. These traces felt different from performances that were captured on video for archiving or broadcast. They seemed more personal and strangely closer to the movement, but they were also very incomplete. There were huge gaps in the sequence of what actually happened in real time (see Figure 6.1).

These micro-narratives seem to defy categorization.[2] Are they traces? Definitely. An archive? In a loose way. Documentation? Evocative but flawed.

Leenamaar Disorientation: after seeing my face in the mirror stepped out of the toilet, did not know where I was. My body lost itself.
2:14 PM May 14th from web

Leenamaar Handshake did soften and saw it repeated on stage today at Hilde Rustad performance: future, past, present. . repetition
2:12 PM May 14th from web

susankozel it's all about feet today. slight humidity makes my bare feet stick slightly to the floor, like frog feet. wish my toes could spread further
6:14 AM May 14th from web

miaorvokki angry handshake repeated until it softens
4:14 AM May 14th from web

Leenamaar Burnt my fingers on a hot tea cup a second ago. . . tired me went into an angry handshake
9:19 AM May 12th from web

Leenamaar The thought of bubbles make my body yearn for easy bubbly support of a jacuzzi – passive flow and float
9:17 AM May 12th from web

miaorvokki Leena's dusk setting induces Susan's relief in me. I want to try bubbles tomorrow morning.
9:08 AM May 12th from web

susankozel mia's mini-me imprinting in my core: small spirals. and bubbles. a relief.
6:45 AM May 12th from web

susankozel feeling stiffness associated with nurturing: gardening, baby holding, wall painting, upper back & chest stronger but tired at the same time
6:44 AM May 12th from web

Figure 6.1 *IntuiTweet* exchange between Keinänen, Kozel, and Rouhiainen using SMS and Twitter. This is to be read from the bottom up if there is an interest in preserving chronological sequencing. Image courtesy of the artists.

Notation? If so, a very imprecise form. A script? Yes, but one written after the performance rather than prepared in advance by a playwright or choreographer. Or are they scores? (Pause for a moment; take a breath, or let a beat pass.) The idea that these mobile tweets are scores reaches out to a sense of musicality and rhythm. These five variations on narrative point to different artistic fields: *notation* has a home in dance and music; *scripts* occur in theater and film, while *scores* are generally thought of as musical. *Archiving* and *documentation* cut across fields and are motivated by the desire to preserve or promote, calling to mind libraries, databases, and press kits. As such, each suggests different roles for bodies and recollection, not to mention the scope for reenactment. Notation makes a leap from movement to symbols, and attempts to preserve with as much specificity as possible the presence of the fleeting moment of dance. Script is a powerful analogy for its translation of action, poetry, affect, and motion into words and for close proximity with improvisatory practices. Scripts can be detailed or very, very sparse. The obvious way to consider these tweets is as scripts, but something about producing and revisiting these words evades scripting. Score makes a leap to music and the practices of composition and listening, with implications for preservation and repetition. Before settling on which of these is most relevant to the narratives of *IntuiTweet*—notation, script, archive, documentation, or score—it is best to examine more deeply the exchanges—in particular, their mobility.

Asynchronous Mobility

Mobility pervaded these dance improvisations. For four of the improvisations, we used the SMS function of Twitter (one improvisation relied on the Web interface for logging tweets accessed by means of desktop computers).

The phenomenon of receiving a tweet while moving in the world differed from the more intentional mode of opening a browser and checking for tweets: the tweets were powerful for being both immediate and asynchronous. This is paradoxical because it is often assumed that immediacy is associated with the synchronicity of a shared here and now, but in this case the immediacy of receiving the SMS touch, or nudge, was given poignancy rather than diluted by the many layers of other daily movement or by the network. Further, there was an awareness that by the time I responded to the person who sent the tweet, their motion was already transformed by other stimuli, affects, constraints, and freedoms: they had moved on, but this did not make interaction with them less tangible or meaningful. These were glancing touches: they arrived obliquely from different time zones, emanated from other bodies, and lived through the ripples of a network of exchange. They were palpable. The gestural vocabulary generated by the tweets was mediated by the surrounding world, the movement flows, and patterns of the urban life around us.

At times, the narrative contained recognizable references to movement in such a way that a clear sequence could be constructed. For example, the exchange below between Rouhiainen and me leads to the specific movement transition from "bad pedestrian" to falling on "all fours" (see Figure 6.2). After receiving the second message while driving—when I could not respond immediately—I reached my home, and I fell to my hands and knees in my kitchen.

Direct exchanges like this provided a sort of continuity, but it was also compelling to be liberated from the need to respond to a specific movement with a similar movement. This was another dimension of asynchronicity; it was possible

Figure 6.2 *IntuiTweet* exchange between Rouhiainen and Kozel using Twitter. The performers set up Twitter to have all messages related to the *IntuiTweet* project pushed to their phones as SMS messages. Image courtesy of the artists.

to let a particular gesture or movement quality enter one's body and morph into something else over time, to be transformed and sent off once again. It was also possible to let a tweet pass without an obvious response, knowing it would somehow resonate in further exchanges. These moments were like letting the tweet sink into our bodies; they were inherently mobile and dispersed. They revealed that, unlike being in a dance studio, as we went about our lives, we rarely had the chance to bracket out the noise of living in order to contemplate how to respond. Our narratives emerged through our bodies and on the fly. Above all, these narratives were of shared corporeality because the tweets evoked a bizarrely strong sense of touch and proximity with those who were moving in concert, but far away.

Between Duration and Instant Connection

Sometimes life intervened heavily and rendered active participation, or at least response through SMS, impossible (heavy workload, travel, exhaustion). One improvisation took place and I simply could not respond even though I knew it was happening. Messages arrived, and I received what the others were doing, but the narrative was backgrounded rather than foregrounded as I moved through my life. Mobility implies generosity: acceptance of different corporeal rhythms. Mobile temporality is a combination of *duration* and the *instant*, where duration

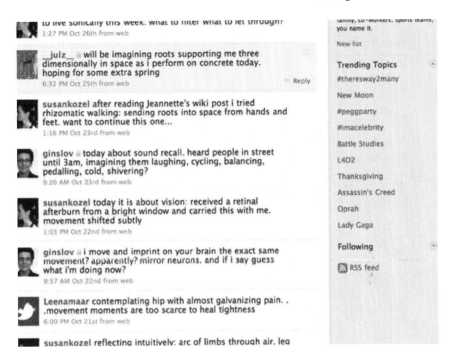

to live sonically this week: what to filter what to let through?
1:27 PM Oct 26th from web

julz will be imagining roots supporting me three
dimensionally in space as i perform on concrete today.
hoping for some extra spring
6:32 PM Oct 25th from web   Reply

susankozel after reading Jeannette's wiki post i tried
rhizomatic walking: sending roots into space from hands and
feet. want to continue this one...
1:16 PM Oct 23rd from web

ginslov today about sound recall. heard people in street
until 3am, imagining them laughing, cycling, balancing,
pedalling, cold, shivering?
9:20 AM Oct 23rd from web

susankozel today it is about vision: received a retinal
afterburn from a bright window and carried this with me.
movement shifted subtly
1:03 PM Oct 22nd from web

ginslov i move and imprint on your brain the exact same
movement? apparently? mirror neurons. and if i say guess
what i'm doing now?
9:57 AM Oct 22nd from web

Leenamaar contemplating hip with almost galvanizing pain. .
.movement moments are too scarce to heal tightness
6:00 PM Oct 21st from web

susankozel reflecting intuitively: arc of limbs through air, leg

family, co-workers, sports teams,
you name it.

New list

Trending Topics

#theresway2many

New Moon

#peggparty

#imacelebrity

Battle Studies

L4D2

Thanksgiving

Assassin's Creed

Oprah

Lady Gaga

Following

RSS feed

Figure 6.3 *IntuiTweet* improvisation using web browser access. Tweets posted by Cruz, Ginslov, Keinänen, Kozel, and Rouhiainen in October 2009. Image courtesy of the artists.

is a more continuous flow of time, and the instant is a sharp plunge into this very moment. Announced by the alert tone, or vibration, the instant the message received is frozen in time and pinpointed by my personal spatial coordinates. I may not have a chance to read the message immediately because I am on my bicycle, but I know it arrived precisely at the corner where this street meets that park. The temporal quality of the instant is when mobile communication punctures the flow and makes us aware of the moment a text arrives, makes us aware of what we are thinking, feeling, and doing precisely then. The temporal quality of duration is folded in with the flow of life: as I weave through my daily existence, the movement trace stays with me, fading or embedding itself in my imagination, to be forgotten or transformed into another message.

Our third improvisation was not mobile but was orchestrated through the Twitter interface (see Figure 6.3).[3] It differed in terms of style, voice, conceptual elaboration, and movement qualities. It felt heavier, less spontaneous, more cerebral. A sense of connection was produced, but the movement was filtered conceptually to a greater degree, and the words were crafted with greater care. Corporeality was there, but it was less raw, less immediate. The exchange was more deliberate in that the improviser had to decide to leave the flux of life, sit down at a computer, and write the tweets using a standard keyboard. The words felt composed, the thoughts deeper; references to the ideas of others were introduced almost like academic writing, and the posts were longer. There was a sense of being removed from the process, like looking in on movement rather than participating in it. In some respects the timing of the improvisation was off. It was all duration and no instant. I missed the highly kinesthetic moment of receiving the tweet on my mobile phone, that point of contact causing an acceleration of time and a "heightened experience of the moment."[4]

A further example of extension and snapping, or duration and the instant, is useful to deepen the understanding of mobility and exchange in these improvisations. A strange thing happened: due to an unreliable Internet connection I did not receive a full update of all messages for close to five days. I sent my messages one by one and received very few responses that seemed to bear no direct reference to my own. Perhaps they are busy, I thought. The process was meaningful for me, but I felt a little isolated, unreciprocated. Misunderstood even. My implicit social contract was being challenged, stretched to a temporal limit. Suddenly all of the missing posts arrived at once, like a deluge, and my familiar, if lonely, space was flooded with posts. My reaction was the disorientation of waking from sleep, akin to someone who thought she was alone and suddenly realized the room was full all along. Too many people arrived all at once, and I could not move due to excessive stimulation. I experienced sensory overload, and a series of affective qualities arose: first, the desire to run or jump as a reaction to a kinesthetic or auditory surge. Opening the dimension of listening, the flood of tweets felt loud. This was followed by a bizarre ethical imperative to respond to everything at once, combined with a strange guilt that I did not respond to the offerings of others when my implicit improvisatory contract was to do so. I also noticed a sense of loss at having missed out on living with the richness of all of these posts, and I could not possibly digest them all at once. This experience points to a realization that all forms of social media have implicit temporalities and a wide affective range: delicate balances between the instant and duration that can only be pushed so far before the delight of exchange becomes the bombardment of noise.

Script or Score?

The messages we sent using SMS from our phones in the midst of our lives were words squeezed out of the intervals of motion. Negotiating the slowness of the interface (those tiny buttons) as a way of capturing a fleeting movement or half-formed kinesthetic sensations caused frustration at times. It was deeply constraining—a painful reminder that making a dance using networked or responsive computer systems of any sort is always about dealing creatively with constraint.[5] In an exchange from a rare co-located improvisation in Helsinki, where we separated in the city for one hour of *IntuiTweet* exchanges in minus-15-degree centigrade weather, our cold fingers stumbled out short messages (see Figure 6.4).

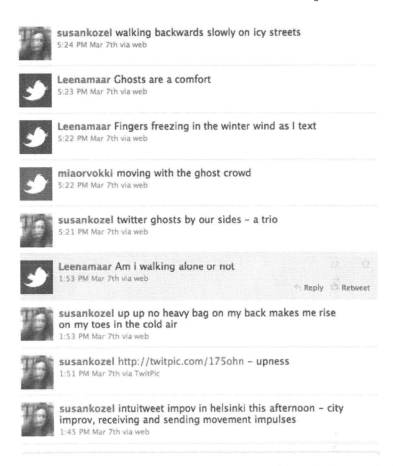

Figure 6.4 *IntuiTweet* improvisation on Twitter during a cold March day in Helsinki, 2010. The brevity of the tweets reflect the temperature outside. Tweets posted by Keinänen, Kozel, and Rouhiainen. Image courtesy of the artists.

The climate could be read so strongly through the words that we wondered what would happen if we presented these tweets to improvisers in another season and another place—a hot place for example. This transposition invited the use of the tweet traces as scripts or a score, the way a script is given to actors in the context of theater or a musical score given to musicians.

A related project by British theater director Tim Etchells helps to reflect upon the notion of a mobile script and to refine distinctions between reception and response. In 2001, his SMS project *Surrender Control* used text as a tool for, in his words, "summoning presence." People were invited to sign up to receive text messages conveying instructions over a specified period of days. "Responding to the intimate context of the mobile phone and of SMS as a form of communication,

Surrender Control invites the user into an evolving game of textual suggestions, provocations and dares."[6] The messages Etchells sent to participants exhibited his characteristic writing qualities of poetry—viscerality, and, at the same time, humor: "Take your pulse," "Change your plans," and "Make things symmetrical" were some of the instructions. Others were more kinesthetic: "Glide," "Float," "Be clumsy," and some implicitly invited social choreographies: "Include another person," "Give something away." These were, according to Etchells, "slight and small interventions in the space of people's lives."[7] There was mobility and responsivity, but these were different from *IntuiTweet*, for Etchells's script was prewritten and sent to a group whose members then responded in their own undocumented ways. In contrast, *IntuiTweet*'s script was generated by the improvisers themselves, and there was an obligation to respond to the group in order to keep the movement flowing. Our media platform permitted the feedback loop of responses; in fact, the project utterly relied on this.

It is clear that these mobile narratives have qualities of traces, archives, and documentation—the more challenging question posed in the first part of this chapter is whether they are more akin to notation, scripts, or scores. While there exist poetic approaches to dance notation such as that offered by Laurence Louppe, who writes of dance drawings and notation as intimate and secret activities with expressive force and visual energy,[8] for the most part, notation requires gestural precision and an explicit intention to preserve the improvised dances for posterity. This pulls in a different direction than our mobile tweets do. Also, the Twitter platform does not make a reliable archive: tweets are no longer "searchable" after a very short window of time; the API for Twitter only offers developers 6–9 days of tweets from which to draw.[9] Despite "scripting the body" being such an evocative and apt metaphor, and the dancers' tendency to refer to the collective tweets as "tweet scripts," they are more than scripts. These tweets have a different corporeal existence than scripted actions because of the necessity to respond and the openness in response—the response could be simple or strange, immediate or delayed, but a response was essential to keep the movement rolling. This leads me to suggest that these mobile tweets are not scripts, but scores. This allows for their slippery and multiple qualities: they need to be considered not just by what remains but also by what they are in the moment of collective improvisation. As such, they benefit from a musical approach that considers not just composition but also the act of listening. They benefit from thinking of multiple voices (polyphony) and multiple bodies (polymorphy).[10] Such an approach to listening is provided by Jean Luc Nancy. In his writing on listening, he offers ways of understanding the mobility of the shared physical expression at the heart of *IntuiTweet*. He can also shed light on what it means to be in a mode of receptivity through our social media.

Listening to Jean Luc Nancy

Jean Luc Nancy asks the question: "What does it mean for a being to be immersed entirely in listening, formed by listening or in listening, listening with all his being?"[11] His question of listening enacts a profound shift in the ways we consider being: not just *listening to* something, rather *being in a state of* listening with your whole body. Mapping this onto a discussion of narrative and mobile media, the focus is no longer on the nature of narratives or the ways in which mobility and media transform narratives. Instead, attention is directed to the embodied and ontological transformations that occur as we spin and share our narratives from the mobility of our lives, and as we create conditions for collective listening.

It is worth situating Nancy briefly and indicating the project of his book *Listening*. As a contemporary French philosopher writing from embodied and sensory experience, he is located in the tradition of phenomenology that explores lived experience. He believes that it makes "no sense to talk about the body and thought separate from one another;"[12] but, at the same time as being a phenomenologist, he frequently refers to qualities of being that are beyond phenomenology.[13] The result is that he shakes free from the tradition while at the same time preserving some of its most valuable elements, such as corporeality, sensibility, displacement, multiplicity, and the deep entwinement between art and philosophy.[14] His book on music is as much a commentary on philosophical thinking as it is subtle, and in some ways relentless, phenomenological writing about how one listens to music by letting it permeate one's entire being. Truly listening plunges us into the domain of the uncertain, the multiple, and the resonant. A piece of music becomes a myriad of echoes and reverberations but, even more significantly, our bodies ripple and extend as we listen.

Listening is closer to the spacing and rhythm of touch than it is to seeing, and touch is extremely important to Nancy: not just the obvious contact of hands stroking, but touch that is enacted through machines, eyes, objects, "the infinitesimal dust of a contact, everywhere interrupted and pursued."[15] Touch is also a significant point of contact between his thought and the experience of *IntuiTweet* because the paradox of these little tweets is that they were more like touches than they were snippets of information. The tweet arrived, and it acted like a nudge or a caress. Even prior to the receipt of the tweet, the performer was in a state of waiting or listening.

Each *IntuiTweet* improvisation was carefully framed to last a specific length of time (a week, a day, an afternoon), which caused me to enter into a different or almost split state: I went about my life but knew the movement flow was happening somewhere and would draw me in at any moment. As such, I lived through my mobile device with a strong sense of potentiality. I did not know when I would receive a message, and I did not know what movement qualities it would contain. I waited, poised and listening. My attention was stretched toward the others, and my intention was to receive and respond. For Nancy, this quality of stretching is innate to listening and is mobile within the context of the senses, if not exactly in the sense of mobile bodies. "To listen," he writes, "is *tendre l'oreille*—literally, to stretch the ear—an expression that evokes a singular mobility, among the sensory apparatuses."[16] This is the state of receptivity that is required for most improvisation in dance and music, and it is a form of listening that is not focused on the ears: we listened with our bodies. As such, the other dancers were present for me, yet mediated. The mediated presence of the others was not inferior or brittle; they were simply with me, and they expected from me a willingness to listen and to respond. This state of waiting, of a willingness to receive and respond, is an important but overlooked state afforded by social media.

Mobile Narratives as Social Choreographies

Having pursued in the previous sections the question "why consider mobile social media from the perspective of dance?" the final section of this chapter addresses the second question folded into this chapter: "why consider dance through the narratives of mobile media?" These two questions balance each other. It is not enough to say that the corporeal qualities of dance can expand mobile narratives and reveal their limitations; equally there is something about mobile media narratives that can expand or challenge approaches to dance and choreography.

Exploring the topic of narrative in dance usually leads to asking what story the choreography tells, or what each dance movement might mean as if it were a piece of narrative or a unit of language. Considering dance through the narratives of mobile media reveals that dance can exist in the translation across movement, words, and media networks, and that a dance can be choreographed in fragments by many people. The movement of the dancers provides the shape of the choreography rather than the choreography shaping the movement of the dancers. Further, it is not only trained dancers who dance. The dancer can be replaced by someone who simply moves in daily life. The result is that dance becomes located in the wider field of social choreographies. If choreographers traditionally set patterns, shapes, steps, rhythms, and gestures upon bodies, then social choreographies are those where the dance is shaped, mixed, and produced by a wide range of bodies with reference to the dances of daily life.[17]

Speaking from the experience of *IntuiTweet*, many expectations concerning dance, or its wider choreographic patterns, are unfulfilled. There are no set patterns to a dance coming from mobile media. The rhythm of the movement is not known in advance. The content or affective qualities cannot be predicted. There is no way of knowing how many dancing bodies will take part. There is no predictable time length. The choreography does not take place on a stage nor in any location we can know in advance. There might be no movement or participation at all. From the perspective of the wider economy of dance as an art form, it is impossible to sell tickets to performances like *IntuiTweet*. Despite all of these factors that seem to eliminate dance, this does not mean that choreographers and dancers have nothing to do. Their roles are transformed. Choreographers who work with mobile social media create spaces, frameworks, or even bubbles of potential; then they step back to watch and wait.[18] Above all, they have to accept movement that they might not like: nonmovement. Nonparticipation. They experience a sort of unraveling of the intended patterns for the dance. Dancers, instead of being told what to do by choreographers, receive movement impulses or fragments of narrative from others and embody these into more movement, yielding a corporeal depth to the narratives. The freedom to respond intuitively in any way to what is received can be daunting, or the sense that one might be revealing one's inner self can be intimidating.

The choreography begins to reveal itself in the midst of the flow of movement, and once the improvisation period has closed, it is possible to look back on it. The mobile quality of the actions means that the movement pattern or narrative structure of the whole can never fully be grasped: much of the movement is partial, private, not recorded in words, or occurs deep within the participants in the form of intuition, affect, or memory. One of Nancy's "constant and rudimentary" assumptions that "people are strange (*les gens sont bizarres*)"[19] helps us to understand that we can predict neither the narratives coming from one person, nor the overall narrative or choreographic structure. Moments of unexpected insight, collective shifts in attitude, or unusual actions may be identified in the Twitter scores. Or nothing may be seen or understood clearly. The dancers are choreographers *and* participants; they can never fully know the extent of the movement work that they create.

Change and Critique

There is an additional significance to kinesthetic exchange, to the moment of dipping into one's body in daily life to receive, transform, and send off once more a gift of motion. It might help to disrupt the tension of daily life, perhaps providing relief or well-needed distraction from overwhelming cares or concerns, but there is more to it. Comedian Trevor Griffiths refers to humor, a different social convention existing through repeated exchanges, when he says:

> A joke releases the tension, says the unsayable, any joke pretty well. But a true joke, a comedian's joke, has to do more than release tension, it has to *liberate* the will and the desire, it has to *change the situation*."[20]

And therein lies the depth of social media, why we celebrated the use of Twitter and Facebook in the political uprisings in the Arab world in 2011: not just because social media was used or because grass roots connections between people correspond to a political ideal, but because the deliberate and intentional use of a media platform can change a situation. It can launch new narratives, politically or corporeally. The approach to social media illustrated by *IntuiTweet* is not overtly political, but it is a circumvention of technological determinism—one that also reveals much about our social and embodied selves.[21]

This points to a critical component of social choreographies just beneath the surface of the discussion above. The micro-narratives of everyday life produced by *IntuiTweet* both converge and diverge from the events and stories of our exchanges with others: they might reveal the dance where we least expect it—a pleasing event—or they might reveal a lack or distortion that we had not noticed before—a disturbing event. In other words, a social choreographic approach to the corporeality of daily life sees and respects existing choreographies; it emphasizes the dance and the strange beauty of the patterns of life. The opposite is also true: a social choreographic perspective affords a critical view on how bodies might be constrained, contained, limited, distorted, or in pain and fear. Mobile narratives from the midst of life reveal what they reveal.

> *We resonate.*
> *We rebound.*
> *Our personal narratives are always emanated and returned to us by others,*
> *by the world,*
> *or by our own senses which themselves are always in a state of emission and rebounding.*
> *Listening is not just what we do with another in order to live ethically,*
> *it is how we live.*
> *And it is mobile, kinesthetic, and fluid.*
> *Yet, despite its fluidity, listening does not leave us untransformed.*

Returning to the suggestion that the micro-narratives of *IntuiTweet* are scores, it is possible to consider an additional sense of the word score: social media may reflect and shape the scores of people's lives, their pathways and affective journeys, but to score is also to leave a groove or pattern in the material composition of a place, person, or object. We score each other.

Acknowledgments

This chapter was developed out of the collaborative efforts between the author, Mia Keinänen, and Leena Rouhiainen.

Notes

1. *IntuiTweet* (2009–2010) was part of an initiative called "Intuition in Creative Processes," a Helsinki-based collaboration between dance researchers associated with the Theatre Academy (Leena Rouhiainen, Mia Keinänen, Susan Kozel) and designers from the Media Lab of the University of Arts and Design (Asta Raami and Samu Mielonen). This project has been considered from several angles: for a pedagogic approach (Samu Mielonen et al., "Intuitive Knowledge Processes among Design Students, Professional Designers and Expert Intuitive Practitioners," *Proceedings of the Communicating (by) Design Conference* [Brussels, 2009]); from the perspective of improvisation and social aesthetics (Susan Kozel, "Devices of Existence: Contact Improvisation, Mobile Performances and Dancing with Twitter," *Improvisation and Social Aesthetics*, eds. Georgina Born and Eric Lewis [Durham, NC: Duke University Press, forthcoming]); and addressing design and method (Susan Kozel, "Intuitive Improvisation: A Phenomenological Method for

Dance Experimentation with Mobile Digital Media," *Studia Philosophia, Universitatis Babes-Bolyai* 3 [2010]: 71–80). *IntuiTweet* received support from the Academy of Finland and La Chartreuse National Center for Performance Writing (Avignon, France) with the A.C.C.R. (Association des Centres Culturelles de Rencontres, France). I am grateful to my collaborators for permission to reproduce and discuss our exchanges.

2. I will sidestep the wider debate over whether these are or are not narratives in conventional literary or narratological senses because in limited space I wish to address the more pertinent question of what sort of narratives they are. I see them as micronarratives of everyday life, both converging and diverging with the events and stories that sustain and emerge from our exchanges with others.

3. In October 2009, the three primary researchers Mia Keinänen (in Russia), Susan Kozel (in France), and Leena Rouhiainen (in Finland) were joined by dancer/choreographers Jeannette Ginslov (in Denmark) and Julie Cruz (in the United States).

4. For a discussion of the play between the instant and duration, resulting in a "snapping" of the moment that releases duration into the instant, see Simon Critchley's description of how we react to hearing a joke. Simon Critchley, *On Humour* (New York: Routledge, 2002), 7.

5. I discuss constraint in creating dance using an Augmented Reality application in Susan Kozel, "AffeXity: Performing Affect with Augmented Reality," Fibreculture 3.0 (2012).

6. Tim Etchells, "Surrender Control," http://www.timetchells.com/projects/works/surrender-control/.

7. These words are from Etchells's panel presentation at the Transmediale conference (Berlin, 2011).

8. Laurence Louppe, "Les Imperfections du Papier," in *Dances Tracées: Dessins et Notation des Chorégraphes*, ed. Laurence Louppe. (Paris: Editions DisVoir, 1991), 3.

9. "Using the Twitter Search API," https://dev.twitter.com/docs/using-search.

10. I am suggesting an unstructured and experiential notion of the score in order to evoke qualities of musicality and listening in movement that may not conform to the standard understanding of the score in musicology or music practice. An interdisciplinary use of the word *score* has precedence in the landscape architecture of Lawrence Halprin who, inspired by collaborations with choreographer Anna Halprin, amongst others, devised a graphic "motation" system of movement through space and ways of creating a score for people's spatial activities. See Lawrence Halprin, *Changing Places* (San Francisco: San Francisco Museum of Modern Art, 1986), 41–42. (Thanks to Maria Hellstrom Reimer for calling this work to my attention.) Scores also have an open source or do-it-yourself quality, see *Everybodys Performance Scores* from www.everybodystoolbox.net.

11. Jean Luc Nancy, *Listening*, trans. Charlotte Mandell (New York: Fordham University Press, 2007), 4.

12. Jean Luc Nancy, *Corpus*, trans Richard A. Rand (New York: Fordham University Press, 2008), 37.

13. Nancy, *Listening*, 20–21.

14. Jacques Derrida in his careful reading of Nancy considers his divergence from Edmund Husserl and suggests consistencies with Maurice Merleau-Ponty. See Jacques Derrida, *On Touching—Jean Luc Nancy* (Stanford, CA: Stanford University Press, 2005). I read Nancy as offering convincing extrapolations of Merleau-Ponty's last writings, in particular *The Visible and the Invisible* (left incomplete when he died in 1961). See Maurice Merleau-Ponty, *The Visible and the Invisible*, trans. Alphonso Lingis (Evanston: Northwestern University Press, 1987).

15. Nancy, *Corpus*, 51.

16. Nancy, *Listening*, 5.

17. Susan Kozel, "Mobile Social Choreographies: Choreographic Insight as a Basis for Research into Mobile Networked Communications," *The International Journal of Performance and Digital Media* 6, no. 2 (2010): 137–150.

18. I appreciate Michael Klein and Steve Volk's work on cybernetic choreography, which offers the term "framemakers" as a way of considering social choreographies. Daghdha Dance Company and Jeffrey Gormley, *Framemakers: Choreography as an Aesthetics of Change* (Limerick, Ireland: Daghdha Dance Company, 2008).

19. Jean Luc Nancy, *Being Singular Plural*, trans. Robert D. Richardson and Anne E. O'Byrne (Stanford, CA: Stanford University Press, 2000), 6.

20. Trevor Griffiths, cited in Critchley, *On Humour*, 10.

21. Nicola Dibben in her study of Björk provides a clear definition of technological determinism relevant to digital music practices that, like *IntuiTweet*, emphasize intimacy and nonhierarchical structures. Technological determinism sees "technology as an oppressive and controlling force dominating culture and forcing a set of values, practices and hierarchies that shape the individual." Nicola Dibben, *Björk*. (Bloomington, IN: Indiana University Press, 2009), 85.

7

WALKING-TALKING

Soundscapes, *Flâneurs*, and the Creation of Mobile Media Narratives

John F. Barber

How do the examples in this chapter help us understand the practice of story-telling in the mobile media age?

This chapter imagines a project called "Walking-Talking" that utilizes digital/mobile telephony to produce a sound narrative focused on a particular urban location. While there are previous examples of locative narrative using mobile telephony, Walking-Talking seeks an alternative approach by actively engaging participants in the production as well as the consumption of historical and personal narratives. In that regard, this chapter explores the concepts of soundscape, *flâneur*, and mobile telephony. The chapter defines and links each of these concepts to the theoretical exploration of hands-on design for narrative engagement with place and community. The mobile telephone becomes a portal between the *flâneur*/participant and the narratives of the sound environment through which he or she travels. The desired outcome is to provide those wanting to theorize, design, and undertake such a project with a better understanding of narrative in a digital/mobile age and its utilization.

Keywords

- **Soundscape:** All the sounds that might be heard in a particular environment. Digital/mobile telephones increase opportunities to produce, interpret, and interact with sounds associated with particular places. These participatory soundscapes, as they create auditory narratives, speak to the ways that the sounds of a place relate to the identities and communities in a specific location.
- **Flâneur:** Most often associated with nineteenth-century Paris, the *flâneur* is someone who leisurely strolls about an urban setting where others are likely

to gather, conduct life activities, and consume the latest cultural artifacts. The *flâneur* watches these activities, hoping to draw knowledge and understanding from them, and so becomes both a witness and a reporter. For many poets and scholars like Charles Baudelaire and Walter Benjamin, the *flâneur* was the embodiment of modernity.

- **Narrative archaeology:** The discovery and recreation of locative narratives that have been lost over time or buried in archives and thus forgotten. These narratives might be in the form of maps, written documents, or audio sound files. Reclaimed and utilized, these forgotten narratives speak to a personal/community history of that place, the people who lived there, and their experiences.

Introduction

In his essay, "Narrative Archaeology," Jeremy Hight explores recreating narratives of places lost in time or buried in archival depositories. These narratives consist of maps, written information placed as guideposts at key locations, or audio files triggered by proximity to specific GPS coordinates—Hight calls them "triggers" or "hot spots." One discovers the artifacts of a place, Hight argues, not by digging vertically in the ground as in traditional archaeology, but rather navigating horizontally through the ground-level context of a particular space. One reads existing and discoverable narratives that, taken together, speak to an overall narrative history of the particular location and the peoples who lived there.[1]

Hight, a pioneer of this combined material and virtual reading, calls the result "locative narrative," which he defines as literature "experientially driven literally and figuratively as a person moves through a space on Earth."[2] With locative narrative, says Hight, physical and narrative spaces can be integrated. Actual and/or metaphorical narratives can be written and placed ("woven into" or juxtaposed) at specific geographic coordinates locatable using GPS technology. The result is to see history return to the site of its origin as an accessible narrative that otherwise would be lost, known only to a few individuals, or hidden in distant books or other archives.[3]

Putting his thoughts and theories into practice, Hight—with Jeff Knowlton and Naomi Spellman—focused on a former industrial area in downtown Los Angeles, California, for their locative narrative project *34 North, 118 West* (2002). Imagine walking through an urban area surrounding the former railroad Freight Depot with a tablet computer equipped with a GPS card and headphones. Physical maps are also available. GPS tracks your position in the neighborhood and triggers audiovisual narratives when you enter hot spots created by Hight, Knowlton, and Spellman. Physical elements/details at each location augment the narrative, providing metaphors and symbols for your interaction(s) with the characters and history of this place. By wandering about the area and evoking multiple narratives, many lost or forgotten, you can uncover the hidden history of this once thriving part of downtown Los Angeles. The streets, the buildings, the ghosts of former residents, all provide fragments that, taken together, offer a deep and rich narrative of this place.[4]

Hight sees locative narrative as a new form of literature, connected to a physical place and interwoven into any experience of that place. As a result, he says, the mobile locative narrative will be a more immediate and compelling experience for participants.[5] Given this vision, what types of narratives might be created and shared, and how, are very interesting questions. This chapter imagines one answer: utilizing digital/mobile telephony to produce a sound narrative focused on a particular urban location. Called "Walking-Talking" for its focus on these two modalities, this vision combines Hight's ideas about locative narrative, the concepts of soundscape, *flâneur*, and mobile telephony (each defined and described below), and a theoretical and hands-on practice of narrative engagement to produce and consume digital/mobile narratives. The desired result is to facilitate a more personal interaction between the participants and the narrative location.

Specifically, "Walking-Talking" envisions mobile narratives geotagged to particular locations and positioned as components of the locative soundscape(s), the *flâneur* as a participant-observer involved in the creation and experience of these narratives, and mobile telephony as a portal to engender and enhance interaction. "Walking-Talking" seeks to engage *flâneurs*/participants in a narrative that is both historical and immediately personal. The mobile telephone becomes a portal between the *flâneur*/participant and the potential narratives of the sound environment through which he or she travels. Those wanting to design and undertake a similar project should have a better understanding of narrative in a digital/mobile age and its utilization at the end of this chapter.

I will begin by detailing the "Walking-Talking" project. "Participants"—a term promoted by Rita Raley—geolocate sites of historic or cultural interest using their mobile telephones.[6] They listen to recorded audio narratives, oral histories, and commentaries. If they desire, they can interact with these narratives by preparing and publishing audio responses through freely available mobile telephony technologies. Locative narratives will no longer be crafted by a single author, as in Hight's pioneering work. Instead, they may emerge, in the moment, from multiple authors. This will expand Hight's notion of an invisible layer of single-author vertical locative narratives to include collaborative authorship. These new narratives will be accessible from different places, through multiple channels. This will provide additional details and immersive experiences, increasing the sense of presence and participation.

The Walking-Talking project hinges on the interactions between the soundscape, the concept of the *flâneur*, and the mobile technologies that serve as the primary technology for the project. The soundscape, with its many aural attributes, particularly the human voice, speaks to the fundamental interactivity and immersion afforded by the oral narrative tradition, even in a multimedia context heavily aligned with the visual. The *flâneur* is seen as the wandering but engaged participant-observer involved in the creation of narrative experiences/interactions within sites of historical or cultural interest. The mobile telephone, a device of convergence, engenders this interaction by prompting the creation and sharing of narratives that are at once site-specific, mobile, and aurally focused, thus leaving the visual and tactile senses free to provide additional, layered, sensory input. This approach positions the seemingly ubiquitous mobile telephone as a portal between the participant/*flâneur* (as creator and observer of the mobile narrative) and the soundscape (narrative environment) through which he or she travels.

The desired upshot is, following Hight's vision, to expand mobile narrative in two distinct yet intricately intertwined ways: first, by positing a methodology for collaborative authorship of mobile narratives, and second, by acknowledging and incorporating the importance of sound as their basis. The emphasis on sound is both important and interesting. Sound increases opportunities for immersion and interactivity. Also, in a multimedia context that is arguably overly invested in the visual, a shift to the aural allows a focus on different sensory input and how it contributes to the creation and consumption of narratives. This shift revisits the primacy of the human voice in the narrative tradition and the technology of the telephone for sharing voice over distance to preserve and transfer memory, history, and culture.[7] Finally, Paul Levinson argues that the voice, as the most fundamental realm of human communication, provides an abstract, symbolic language by which we can express anything we please, to anyone we please, even if they are physically distant.[8]

Walking-Talking: Project Vision

The Walking-Talking project envisions a walking, mobile narrative experience of discovery and connection at locations of historic and/or cultural interest. At each location, participants listen to and/or create audio recordings (and other online, digital media content) playable via a mobile telephone app. As Hight suggests, this will provide potential for a deeper, richer mobile locative narratives comprised of multiple voices, moments, and elements of a shared place.[9]

In addition to Hight's work, antecedents for Walking-Talking include a plethora of mobile-phone–based museum tours and audio travel/tour guides. For example, DIY Tourguide offers GPS-triggered audio tour apps for Outback Australia that include menus, a zoomable map, image galleries, and narratives about the area surrounding the particular tour. HearPlanet provides audio recordings of *Wikipedia* entries regarding points of interest surrounding one's current location. Lonely Planet, an international publisher of independent travel guides, offers a series of audio walking tours featuring audio content provided by company authors and the BBC Archive. These tours follow a location map and can be downloaded and used offline. Rick Steves Audio Europe offers self-guided audio tours of Europe's top museums, sights, and historic walks, as well as audio travel tips and insights taken from his radio shows. These audio tours, as well as images, can be downloaded and utilized offline. The Broadcastr app streams narratives about particular locations to mobile telephone users. An additional layer of social media is prompted by the ability of participants to create and share their own narratives via an interactive map. The catalog of user-generated narratives can be searched from several directions: location, category, creator, rating, or creation date.

Finally, Woices allows participants with mobile telephones to create, share, and listen to location-based audio narratives as well as view text and video both on location or from a distance via a web browser. Each audio recording is associated with a specific geolocation and indicated on an interactive map provided by the Woices app. Using this map and GPS technology embedded in their mobile telephones, participants can navigate to a desired geolocation where, again using their mobile telephones, they can listen to an audio recording while standing at the location about which that recording speaks. Recordings can be started on demand by the participant, rather than by triggering a hot spot through proximity as is the case with examples noted earlier. In addition to listening, participants can record an audio response, called an "echo," using the in-app recorder. These echoes can be uploaded to the Woices server where they are freely available to anyone interested. Similar experiences are available through the Woices website, and are useful for those without appropriately enabled mobile telephones. Using a mobile or desktop browser, one can search for audio recordings at desired locations around the world, note their positions on a map of the target location, and listen to desired recordings. For all these reasons, Woices provides an excellent test app for Walking-Talking and the creation and sharing of mobile locative narratives.

As noted, using web browsers rather than mobile telephones, distant participants can experience site-specificity from the recorded narratives. Additionally, they can participate in those narratives through the creation of their own responses (echoes). It is, therefore, fair to ask whether one needs to be physically present to participate in/with such locative narratives, and whether mobile telephones are necessary for their production and sharing. It is perhaps more interesting to ask, however, what additional details, experiences, and opportunities are afforded by being present. What does being present at the site of the narrative change? What can be done with mobile telephones to enhance the envisioned narrative experience of Walking-Talking that is not otherwise possible, or as immersive?

Rob Kitchin and Martin Dodge, responding to such questions, argue that computer code is increasingly written to produce space, which in turn, is increasingly dependent on code. As a result of this dyadic relationship with space, computer code increasingly determines human interaction with economic, social, cultural, and personal space(s), more so than the technologies it enables.[10] More fundamentally, we have an increased opportunity for immersion within, and interaction with, the narrative. This includes the ability to overlay additional content—textual, visual, and aural—in support of the narrative. There is simply more content and context with which the participant can interact, thus helping to make the experience more believable and rewarding. The ability of the participant(s) to move within the narrative context, seeing and touching its various attributes, while hearing the historical/hidden/personal soundscape(s) associated with that context, provides an opportunity for increased information/experiential overlay. This realizes Hight's call for mobile narratives that are at once composed and experienced in conjunction with the physical environment.

By providing a portal into another, virtual, environment, while at the same time allowing the participant to experience the sensory stimuli of the material world, mobile telephones utilize what is already present (both current and historical) to collect and share narratives that visualize a location in multiple, new, participatory ways. Raley suggests that these narratives are unbound from the fixed spectatorial perspective of a singular screen.[11] As a result, participants become avatars, capable of assuming roles in the narratives. Locative mobile narratives are attractive by their ability to draw participants into different materialities through suggestion and participation. Beyond choosing predetermined, often linear, narrative paths, participants can shape the narratives through their immediate participation and response, thus contributing to the building of even more complex narrative structures for subsequent participants.

In this sense, mobile telephones promote scaffolding around Hight's contention that the key to locative narrative is the use of sound. Through direct participation in creating and sharing the aural narrative, Walking-Talking promotes the inclusion of a wide variety of sounds representing soundscapes both past and present. For example, in addition to (or instead of) spoken voice recordings, participants may create and share audio files of environmental, industrial, commercial, and personal sounds. Such sounds provide authors a way of combining sensory input in order to guide experience and fuse critical analysis and creative response. The author of a locative narrative, says Hight, establishes an experience (augmented by sound, my overlay) through which participants navigate and from which they derive experience or insight.[12]

The Woices program encourages Walking-Talking to expand and explore mobile locative narrative in another way. Photographic images and textual descriptions, created using participants' mobile telephones or via other means, can be connected to individual audio files. As a result, audio recordings, their "echoes," and any ancillary visual or textual materials draw participants into personal, immediate reactions to life experiences associated with contexts for mobile locative narrative.

In short, where other locative narratives provide a unidirectional push of information—the participant positions him- or herself near enough to a predetermined hot spot to trigger a sound file to which he or she may react but probably not respond—Walking-Talking seeks to promote bidirectional narrative exchange between participants. This overlay or embedding seeks to reinstate that which has already happened, or has been forgotten, into mobile locative narratives. Additionally, Walking-Talking encourages site-specificity through physical exploration, by walking the various locations associated with the mobile narrative environment. This *flâneur*/participant experience promotes the firsthand acquisition of knowledge. And, with its focus on personal narratives shared via mobile telephones, participants are encouraged to produce collaborative location-based narrative environments that are simultaneously inviting, believable, and responsive.

The engaging experience of these narrative environments is accomplished by more than just the auditory elements. Embodiment is never a single-sense experience. Instead, it is a combination, an overlay of different sensory inputs so as to promote the belief in materiality, immersion, and interactivity within a unique space or community. Arguably, however, emergent sites for mobile locative narratives are predominately influenced by, even given over to, the visual. Walking-Talking does not negate, replace, or supersede the visual. Rather, it foregrounds the aural and its abilities to convey important narrative information. Attributes of the narrative soundscape, particularly the human voice (as in oral tradition), may promote a unique sense of place and community connection. When combined with the information-carrying capacity of other senses, the aural provides the ability to attach multiple narratives, in multiple forms, to a specific location, thus providing a more engaging sense of embodiment. This narrative development of an embodied experience will be ongoing; one can enter at any time and add additional insights, responses, or concerns.

By promoting a public forum for the preservation of essential community knowledge and experience through mobile telephones, Walking-Talking encourages a broad-based critical participation in open-ended narratives about experiences associated with specific locations. Additionally, Walking-Talking engages participants in shared concerns while providing a balance of individual ideas and approaches.

Walking-Talking: Theoretical Underpinning

As noted earlier, concepts of soundscape, the *flâneur*, and mobile telephony provide theoretical underpinning for Walking-Talking and will help promote construction of a collaborative mobile locative narrative experience. A brief discussion of these concepts follows.

Soundscape

The term "soundscape" (also "sonic environment," "sonic universe," and "universal orchestra"), introduced by Canadian composer and environmentalist R. Murray Schafer, denotes all the sounds that might be heard in a particular place.[13] As Bruce R. Smith notes, "[M]ost of us live immersed in a world of sound."[14] The sound events in any soundscape, therefore, may be quite numerous. Schafer says we can experience the elements of any soundscape by actively listening to the sound sources, "openly attentive to whatever is vibrating."[15] Following on

Schafer, Michael Bull and Les Beck advocate "deep listening," or "agile listening," to carefully determine the multiple layers of meaning potentially embedded in any sound. Deep listening, they say, involves investigation and interpretation of the sounds we hear."[16] Barry Blesser and Linda-Ruth Salter call this practice "attentive listening," the intense focus on "the sounds of life in the immediate environment." Attentive listening, they say, is important because it creates a link between the participant and the activities of life, both human and natural. Specifically, attentive listening promotes propagation of cultural symbols, stimulation of emotions, experience of the movement of time, building social relationships, retaining memories of experience, and communicating aural information.[17]

These ideas about listening suggest that we live in a world surrounded by sounds, many of which we choose not to privilege to the extent that they are often ignored. Those sounds that we privilege, understand, and extract information from must be carefully considered through deep, agile, or attentive listening. Such engaged listening promotes dynamic connections between our lives, those of others, and the material (or virtual) world in which the sounds originate. The soundscape can be broad and narrow; broad as the city in which we live, narrow as the particular street down which we walk. In both cases, digital mobile technologies allow us to produce and consume aural narratives associated with specific locations. These mobile locative narratives speak to lived cultural and/or historical experiences directly associated with a particular soundscape. As Hight notes, echoes of such aural interactions can provide both a sense of identity and community directly connected to specific locations, interactions that otherwise would be lost or difficult to access. The soundscape then becomes both repository and creative site for narratives. A mutable collage is created where multiple sounds can be selected, sampled, mixed, and rearranged to create unique and personal dialogues. Traces of these narratives can be found and listened to by others.

The Flâneur

Into the soundscape comes the *flâneur* as "earwitness" (testament to what is heard) seeking to experience his or her multiple personal narratives.[18] The term "*flâneur*" has etymological associations with the Greek word *planasthai*, to wander. Nominalized from the Norman French verb "to stroll," and with no English equivalent, *flâneur* has the multiple meanings of "stroller," "lounger," "saunterer," and "loafer." Use and theorization of the term by French poet Charles Baudelaire (1821–1867), German critic Walter Benjamin (1892–1940), and others has centered the *flâneur*'s activities in or around urban settings, the arcades, shop-lined streets, and avenues—the places where residents are likely to gather, conduct their life activities, and consume the latest cultural artifacts. In general, the *flâneur* exists because of capitalism, either as a witness to the theater of consumption, or in resistance by being a wanderer rather than a consumer.

In either case, the *flâneur* interacts personally with a physical space, not once removed by virtuality, as does the so-called "cyber*flâneur*" noted by Evgeny Morozov[19] (and by John Hendel in his response to Morozov).[20] It is the *flâneur*'s quest to draw knowledge and understanding from a physical community endeavor that is at the heart of Walking-Talking. The *flâneur* is both witness and wanderer—one who, through participant observation, simultaneously detached but aesthetically perceptive, experiences and appreciates the idiosyncratic modernity of an urban environment by strolling through, carefully observing, and interacting with components of that environment. Baudelaire and Benjamin center this understanding with the visual gaze. Walking-Talking argues for at least equal understanding through aural attention, drawing support from Smith, who says that knowing the world through sound is essentially different from knowing it through vision, in that "sound is at once the most forceful stimulus that human beings experience, and the most evanescent."[21]

Additionally, as Fran Tonkiss notes, "[C]ities provide a soundstage for the dramas of modern life."[22] But both Tonkiss and Schafer note that contemporary city environments can be confusing with their many sounds. More specifically, Schafer says urban soundscapes, with their multiple sound elements and events, can be overwhelming, especially with "noise"—any undesired sound signal.[23] As a result, Tonkiss says an "individuals' relation to sound in the everyday spaces of the city tends to be one of distraction rather than attention."[24] As a defense against an overwhelming soundscape, one becomes indifferent to all but the most essential sounds.

Mobile Telephony

One solution to such sonic overload (the ears, after all, cannot be shut, like the eyes), according to Bull, is the use of personal stereos and iPods to construct personal narratives that will resist the overwhelming and fragmented soundscape inherent in urban experience. More specifically, Tonkiss says personal media players and mobile telephones allow their users (or *flâneurs* in Walking-Talking) to orchestrate the sounds that will occupy their primary aural attention as they move through the city. Tonkiss argues that one can use both technologies to create private, personal soundscapes that are "smaller, tamer, more predictable."[25] Iain Chambers argues that a personal listening device provides one with a portable soundtrack that can be used to mediate their public experience. Says Chambers, one can impose "your soundtrack on the surrounding aural environment," thereby domesticating the external world, and, even if only briefly, transposing the experience from passive to active.[26]

On the other hand, Schafer argues that the personal worlds constructed with these devices are anesthetized and thus become whatever the user wants them to be. This kind of personal sound management transforms public space into private property while providing a background for personal activity.[27] Jean-Paul Thibaud suggests the term "sonic bridge" for this phenomenon.[28] Concluding on a positive, if not cryptic, note, Schafer says, "[B]eyond what fascinates your ear today is something else, incessantly and obdurately present, although you cannot or do not hear it yet—but whoever hears it first has a good chance of inheriting the future."[29] This "something else" may be interactive capabilities engendered by mobile telephony through which, Tonkiss suggests, we can create and share "sound souvenirs," audio events where "the past comes to us in its most unbidden, immediate and sensuous forms." Unlike travel photographs, which seem fully formed and carry forward all their details, Tonkiss says that sounds, especially those only half-remembered, have a quality and texture similar to memory.[30]

These arguments by Tonkiss, Chambers, and Schafer might be construed to mean that personal listening devices detach the listener from the soundscape, thus removing the *flâneur* from the community rather than promoting active engagement. It is more useful, however, to redirect Thibaud's term "sonic bridge." Instead of a personal aural background for activity in a larger soundscape, a sonic bridge might suggest the ability to build outward from the isolated observational status of the *flâneur* to a position more engaged in the collaborative community narrative. Caroline Bassett argues this point when she says users of mobile telephony, walking about in a city, are "no longer embedded in [their] immediate locality or environment." Instead, these *flâneurs* are connected simultaneously to other people in remote locations. As a result, rather than being detached, they are more connected because they can both be reached and reach out via their mobile telephones and are thus more likely to discover new perspectives.[31]

The mobile telephone thus offers, different from the personal stereo device, "the possibility of remote intervention."[32] Bassett goes on to say that use of mobile telephony creates/facilitates a sense of location different from the physical space occupied by the user. Echoing Kitchin and Dodge, Bassett says, "Regarded as a practice of space, and as a practice that makes space, the mobile phone draws up the cultural conditions under which it itself is made—all the species of space—unto itself: like a map, a dream, or even like a prayer might do."[33] These spaces are neither individual nor private, but rather are socially collective constructions that offer a sense of "being there" of "being live."[34] For the mobile telephone user, travel/discovery is no longer a broken connection, a separation between the mode of travel and the environment in which one travels. There is no dislocation between the traveler/*flâneur* and the world beyond. Instead of a boundary, mobile telephones provide an interface.[35]

Levinson elaborates on this point when he notes the ability for people to talk with distant others and share information on demand. This is facilitated by the technological ability to make information available to large, disperse audiences; the reduction in size of devices that can send and receive this information; and the rise of the Internet as an information repository and distribution technology. In short, people can "communicate on their own terms and equipment."[36]

Building on these concepts, Walking-Talking will be, in Schafer's term, a soundwalk, "the exploration of the soundscape of a given area using a score as a guide. The score consists of a map, drawing the listener's attention to unusual sounds and ambiances to be heard along the way....When the soundwalker is instructed to listen to the soundscape, he is audience; when he is asked to participate with it, he becomes composer-performer."[37] (For further discussion of mobile narratives as scores, see chapter 6 of this collection by Susan Kozel.)

For Walking-Talking, the mobile telephone provides both the map (through its built-in GPS location technology) and the listening device (through its audio playback technology). Following Levinson, the mobile telephone will allow both reception and production, both immediately or over long distance—in both cases, interactively.[38]

This dual participant/performer role acknowledges what Francisco J. Ricardo calls the fundamental strategy of locative art, or "a shift between the presentation of place as a physical entity and its representation as a site of alternative significa-tion, something stimulated by rhetorical and sensory trigger."[39] Such interpreta-tions of stimulation and triggering draw from Roland Barthes, who argues in "The Death of the Author" that any narrative lays dormant, awaiting the reader to bring it to life through movement, processing, and interpretation.[40] By exten-sion, the *flâneur*, as witness-wanderer, participant-observer, using location-aware digital multimedia mobile telephony, evokes the narrative by completing a circuit of functionality, interaction, and involvement. The *flâneur*'s gaze evokes accessible aural, as well as visual, narratives written, read, embedded, woven/juxtaposed into specific locations—narratives that otherwise would be lost, forgotten, or made difficult to access.

Walking-Talking: Results

The Walking-Talking *flâneur* is both an observer and participant through his or her engagement with a mobile locative narrative. Such participation, as argued by Raley, prompts the application of play and performance metaphors to mobile narrative, and suggests the term "participant" rather than "reader" or "user."[41] The result is the ability to deliver multimedia or other content directly to a mobile device, "unbound from the desktop," according to Raley, and "detached from the singular screen and thus a fixed spectatorial perspective, dependent on signals rather than cords for data transfer in one's immediate vicinity."[42]

Mobile narrative becomes, according to Hight, "a literature of action, of move-ment, of moment and of place. . . . Publication now can be a signal, air, a spot of land. It can be maps, and it can be only transcribed by a person as they move."[43] Hight's own work, *34 North, 118 West* (with Naomi Spellman and Jeff Knowlton), demonstrates "a possible new way to lay literature across places and to see [or perhaps hear] history move into where it was written of."[44] (Another interest-ing example is Mark Marino's chapter on the *LA Flood Project*, chapter 20 in this book.) As a result, says Hight, "places could be their own literal storytellers and history could be given a new breath and breadth as much as location." Artifacts, sound files recorded from "works that came before" could be placed for those moving throughout the narrative location (*flâneurs*/participants), layered for discovery and reading, and written with the world itself, providing renewed access to "what was lost in time."[45]

Walking-Talking: Conclusion

An underlying theme of this collection is that digital media is increasingly mobile with regard to both its delivery and access. The need to access media regardless of location has been, according to Levinson, prevalent for centuries, since the "first time someone thought to write on a tablet that could be lifted and hauled— rather than a cave wall, a cliff face, a monument that usually was stuck in place, more or less forever." This need, along with changing media capabilities, has "led logically and eventually to telephones that we carry in our pockets."[46] The present-day handheld mobile telephone shows high promise and potential for converging access and delivery of multimedia content. Such content can create new kinds of places that merge the infrastructures of geography and technology. The result is a new set of capabilities to solve problems, present information, teach processes, persuade points, entertain, or share narratives.

This chapter presents a design for promoting bidirectional and collaborative authorship of digital mobile locative narratives through the use of mobile telephones. Using these technologies facilitates the capture and communication of sensory input to provide a sense of historical and current presence both in the material location of the narrative(s), as well as distant and/or more virtual locations.

Simply put, a project like Walking-Talking can provide opportunities for disbursed participants to create and share collaborative storytelling without the need, or necessity, for a centralized structure. As Hight and Barthes remind us, such collaborative narratives are all around us all the time, always being created, often without our awareness. Finding ways to make sense of these narratives and search through them to find the connected story is a goal of Walking-Talking. The central component of Walking-Talking, as facilitated by mobile telephony, will be, as Levinson notes, "the most fundamental realm of human communication: the voice."[47] Speech he says, provides an abstract, symbolic language by which we can express anything we please, to anyone we please, even if they are physically distant.

These theoretical concepts will play out in Walking-Talking in the following ways. First, the project is envisioned to feature a deep and rich vein of recorded personal narratives, oral histories, and commentaries, as well as other aural representations geolocated to specific locations of historic, community, and cultural interest. Second, participants, here *flâneurs*, can, in addition to listening to these recordings, prepare and submit personal audio responses. Third, Walking-Talking seeks to foreground direct interaction between the participant and the sound-scape that explores and speaks to a situated collaborative engagement with ideas of place, community, and common humanity.

As a result, as Adriana de Souza e Silva and Daniel Sutko contend, unlike printed books and landline telephones that transport users *away* from physical surroundings by immersing them in their own imagination or in the focused and directed interchange of defined content, interactive, mobile, geolocative narra-tive experiences, like Walking-Talking, transport participants *into* their physical surroundings.[48] The Walking-Talking participant, more than simply a sightseer or a casual observer, will be expected to be a critical and aesthetical participant/ inspector of the soundscape, not merely seeing, but hearing, and responding as well, bridging the divide between participant and the narrative.

Walking-Talking can provide sensory access to sites of alternative signification that are experiential rather than ontological. Such instantiations alter our concep-tions of reading, storytelling, and the dissemination of narratives. They speak to the nature of space and place in mobile narratives. And they challenge our think-ing regarding mapping and mobile storytelling, immersion and locative narrative, and virtual community developed through digital mobile narrative/storytelling.

In conclusion, Walking-Talking envisions new kinds of narrative contexts that merge the infrastructures of geography, technology, and techno-social practices. The upshot can be the thoughtful creation and consumption of social collabora-tive mobile narratives that consider historical, social, and cultural issues. Follow-ing this vision, Walking-Talking can enhance the ability of participants to think imaginatively and critically about the world in which they live, and to share their thoughts through a new range of mobile locative narrative possibilities.

Notes

1. Jeremy Hight, "Narrative Archaeology," http://www.neme.org/1556/narrative-archaeology.
2. Jeremy Hight, "Locative Narrative, Literature and Form," in *Beyond the Screen: Transfor-mations of Literary Structures, Interfaces and Genres*, ed. Jörgen Schäffer and Peter Gendolia (New Brunswick, NJ: Transition, 2010), 303–309.
3. Ibid., 327–328.
4. Jeff Knowlton, Naomi Spellman, and Jeremy Hight, *34 North, 118 West*, http://34n118w. net/34N.
5. Hight, "Locative Narrative," 323.
6. Rita Raley, "Walk this Way," in *Beyond the Screen: Transformations of Literary Structures, Interfaces and Genres*, ed. Jörgen Schäffer and Peter Gendolia (New Brunswick, NJ: Transition, 2010), 301.
7. See Jason Farman, "Site-Specific Storytelling and Reading Interfaces," in *Mobile In-terface Theory: Embodied Space and Locative Media* (New York: Routledge Press, 2012), 113–130.
8. Paul Levinson, Cellphone: The Story of the World's Most Mobile Medium and How It Has Transformed Everything (New York: Palgrave Macmillan, 2004), 129.
9. Hight, "Locative Narrative," 328.

10. Rob Kitchin and Martin Dodge, *Code/Space: Software and Everyday Life* (Cambridge, MA: The MIT Press, 2011).
11. Raley, "Walk this Way," 301, 303.
12. Hight, "Narrative Archaeology."
13. R. Murray Schafer, *The Tuning of the World* (New York: Alfred A. Knopf, 1977), 274–275.
14. Bruce R. Smith, "Tuning into London c. 1600," in *The Auditory Culture Reader*, ed. Michael Bull and Les Beck (Oxford, UK: Berg, 2003), 127–128.
15. R. Murray Schafer, *The New Soundscape: A Handbook for the Modern Music Teacher* (Scarborough, Canada: Berandol Music Limited, 1969), 5.
16. Michael Bull and Les Beck, eds., "Introduction," in *The Auditory Culture Reader* (Oxford, UK: Berg, 2003), 3–4.
17. Barry Blesser and Linda-Ruth Slater, *Spaces Speak, Are You Listening? Experiencing Aural Architecture* (Cambridge, MA: The MIT Press, 2007), 4, 15.
18. R. Murray Schafer, *The Tuning of the World*, 8–9, 272.
19. Evgeny Morozov, "The Death of the Cyberflâneur," *The New York Times*, February 4, 2012, http://www.nytimes.com/2012/02/05/opinion/sunday/the-death-of-the-cyberflaneur.html?pagewanted=all&_r=0.
20. John Hendel, "The Life of the Cyberflâneur," *The Atlantic*, February 8, 2012, http://www.theatlantic.com/technology/archive/2012/02/the-life-of-the-cyberfl-neur/252687/.
21. Bruce R. Smith, "Tuning into London c. 1600," in *The Auditory Culture Reader*, ed. Michael Bull and Les Beck (Oxford, UK: Berg, 2003), 127–128.
22. Fran Tonkiss, "Aural Postcards: Sound, Memory and the City," in *The Auditory Culture Reader*, ed. Michael Bull and Les Beck (Oxford, UK: Berg, 2003), 304.
23. Schafer, *The New Soundscape*, 17.
24. Tonkiss, "Aural Postcards," 304.
25. Ibid., 305.
26. Iain Chambers, "The Aural Walk," in *Audio Culture: Readings in Modern Music*, ed. Christoph Cox and Daniel Warner (New York: Continuum, 2004), 98, 100.
27. R. Murray Schafer, "Open Ears," in *The Auditory Culture Reader*, ed. Michael Bull and Les Beck (Oxford, UK: Berg, 2003), 38.
28. Jean-Paul Thibaud, "The Sonic Composition of the City," in *The Auditory Culture Reader*, ed. Michael Bull and Les Beck (Oxford, UK: Berg, 2003), 9.
29. Schafer, "Open Ears," 39.
30. Tonkiss, "Aural Postcards," 307.
31. Caroline Bassett, "How Many Movements?" in *The Auditory Culture Reader*, ed. Michael Bull and Les Beck (Oxford, UK: Berg, 2003), 344–345.
32. Ibid., 344–345.
33. Ibid., 354.
34. Ibid., 351, 354.
35. Ibid., 346.
36. Levinson, *Cellphone*, 129.
37. Schafer, *The Tuning of the World*, 212–213.
38. Levinson, *Cellphone*, 52.
39. Francisco J. Ricardo, "Framing Locative Consciousness," in *Beyond the Screen: Transformations of Literary Structures, Interfaces and Genres*, ed. Jörgen Schäffer and Peter Gendolia (New Brunswick, NJ: Transition, 2010), 261.
40. Roland Barthes, "The Death of the Author," in *The Rustle of Language*, trans. Richard Howard (Berkeley, CA: University of California Press, 1989), 49–55.
41. Raley, "Walk this Way," 301.

42. Ibid., 301, 303.

43. Hight, "Locative Narrative," 321, 322.

44. Ibid., 326–327.

45. Ibid, 327, 328.

46. Levinson, *Cellphone*, 16.

47. Ibid., 152.

48. Adriana de Souza e Silva and Daniel M. Sutko, "Playing Life and Living Play: How Hybrid Reality Games Reframe Space, Play, and the Ordinary," in *Critical Studies in Media Communication* 25, no. 5 (2008): 447–465. Emphasis mine.

PART III
Space and Mapping

8

LOCATIVE MEDIA IN THE CITY

Drawing Maps and Telling Stories

Didem Ozkul and David Gauntlett

How do the examples in this chapter help us understand the practice of story-telling in the mobile media age?

This chapter explores how users of locative media experience urban spaces through "cognitive maps" that they create. Rather than asking them to consider this in relation to predefined geographical maps, we wondered what it would be like if participants were asked to create their own maps, from scratch, of the city that they live in, and share their stories accordingly. As a mental process, cognitive maps consist of collecting, organizing, storing, recalling, and manipulating spatial information. With the help of those maps, our "*knowing* is translated into *telling*"—as Hayden White has put it—where experiences of places as well as memories are narrated.[1] Within this process of representation and creating a self-narrative of one's everyday life through location information, a tool commonly used for identifying routes—the map—comes to be used as an interface, where users can create their own geotagged stories of their lives. Here, cognitive mapping is also defined as a storytelling platform, focusing on several examples of participant maps of London. Used in this way, the method offers a fresh extension of creative visual methods, in which people are invited to spend time applying their playful or creative attention to the act of making something, and then reflecting on it. The process offers insights that would otherwise be difficult to access about the lived experience of mediated life in a city.

Keywords

- **Cognitive map:** A person's mental sense of a place, including both a broad and specific sense of its geographical features, as well as memories, emotions, and other associations. As a mental process, cognitive maps consist of collecting, organizing, storing, recalling, and manipulating spatial information.

- **Sketch map:** Freehand drawn maps of a place. They are used for obtaining insights into how people mentally structure a location, and which elements are perceived as important.
- **Emplotment:** A term coined by Hayden White, this is the act of imposing an overarching structure that takes various narrative pieces and creates a coherent plot out of them. While locative stories that utilize large social networks rarely achieve emplotment (due to the large number of authors and the intermittent nature of audience attention), the act of creating a sketch map reintroduces this aspect into the storytelling process.

Introduction

Our experiences, and therefore our memories of those experiences, are located in both time and place. Mobile technologies clearly have the potential to affect this process of memory and meaning making, as they offer new ways to store and share information and reflections. These may take the form of communications addressed to family, friends, and the outside world, and so contribute to the presentation of self-identity to others. At the same time, they are likely to play a more internal role, in the shaping of self-perception and memory, and therefore identity (or, at least, some aspects of identity).

The study discussed in this chapter sought to explore the connections between lived experiences and locative technologies (i.e., mobile Internet-connected devices, primarily smartphones, location awareness, and location-based services). The study, conducted in 2012, involved thirty-eight participants, all of whom lived in London.[2] One approach might have been to show participants a geographical map of London and ask them to think of key memories or activities and plot them on the map. However, building on the model of creative research methods outlined in David Gauntlett's *Creative Explorations*,[3] we wondered what it would be like if participants were asked to create their *own* maps of the city, from scratch, and share their stories accordingly.

The research was conducted in small groups of four to eight people, all of whom were users of a mobile communication device. Each participant was asked to draw a map of London showing "frequently visited places," which they then presented to the group. Then they were asked to add more places that had particular importance for them (in whatever sense they liked) on their map. They were also told that the maps they drew did not need to be geographically accurate but rather should show London as they experienced it in their everyday lives. We were therefore anticipating that they would create a selective representation, a version, of their "cognitive map" of London. As each workshop progressed, after the initial stages of drawing sketch maps, and as the participants started talking about their maps and memories of London, they would typically mention and discuss their use of locative media.

Cognitive Maps and Sketch Maps

In previous literature, the term "cognitive map" has been used to refer to a kind of "mental picture" of a place, including both a broad and specific sense of its geographical features, as well as memories, emotions, and other associations. The pioneering researchers Roger Downs and David Stea distinguish between "cognitive mapping," which they describe as the mental process of thinking about a place or a route, and "cognitive map," which they say is "a person's organized representation of some part of the spatial environment."[4] In other words, they are relatively cautious about separating out concepts "in" the brain from things in the world. However, there is some slippage in this distinction: for example, their examples of cognitive maps—the *representations* of mental models—include a drawn map and a child's painting of their neighborhood, but also "the picture that comes to mind every time you try to cross town on the subway system," which really should be treated as part of cognitive mapping, the process, rather than as a cognitive map, or representation.[5]

More recent studies of neuroscience and consciousness have increasingly challenged the notion of having "a picture in your head"; all we really have, it is suggested, is a fluctuating set of stored knowledge and emotions, which are dynamically compiled into the stuff that we have "in mind" at any given moment.[6] Creating a "representation" of these elements is clearly, therefore, a separate act of creation, as the cognitive map does not exist as a "thing" that you could then hope to draw or reproduce. The collection of memories, feelings, and associations about a place, which are somewhere, somehow, in a person's brain, are not things that could be straightforwardly transferred to paper.

Accordingly, Rob Kitchin and Mark Blades have taken the term "cognitive map" to refer to the mental processes, with other representations described for what they are.[7] This cognitive process, they argue, consists of the encoding and retrieval of spatial information. As a result of this process, we acquire knowledge of spatial and environmental relations, which can be defined as a cognitive map—a somewhat more sophisticated formulation, although it leaves out related emotions and memories. We will follow this terminology, and to ease confusion, will use the term "sketch map" when we talk about the hand drawn maps of London.[8]

Spatial behavior is central to everyday life. Our spatial ability to navigate in a city is usually taken for granted and goes unnoticed. Locative media can complement this, potentially enriching our understanding and use of location information in urban spaces. They serve not only as tools to find and locate things, and to navigate in any given city, but also as multiple platforms of gaming, entertainment, arts, and even of personal narratives and biographies.

Users of mobile technologies can add layers of virtual information to places, which has increased the integration of maps into our everyday lives. Maps are not only used to navigate in contemporary urban life but also to spatialize information. The act of checking in at a place on a service such as Foursquare, for example, creates personal traces on the network—and also, those traces start to define what kind of a place we do check in at and why. This has created—for some users at least—individual storytelling platforms, as these technologies and applications allow users to map their everyday activities and write reviews, insert photos, or add memory notes onto those places visited. (For further discussion of the narratives of self and place written and read through location-based social media, see chapter 3 of this book, "Re-Narrating the City Through the Presentation of Location," by Adriana de Souza e Silva and Jordan Frith.)

With the help of those maps, we are able to find "a solution to a problem of general human concern, namely, the problem of how to translate *knowing* into *telling*"—as Hayden White has put it—where experiences of places as well as memories are narrated.[9] Within this process of representation and creating a self-narrative of one's everyday life through location information, a relatively new use of maps has emerged. From being a tool commonly used for identifying routes, the map comes to be used as an interface where users can create geotagged stories of their own lives.

Experiencing an environment helps us to build spatial knowledge about that environment, and on our next visit to the same place, we may somehow retrieve that information and refer to it in order to remember how to navigate. On the other hand, the experience associated with a certain place is not only spatial. There are many other factors that construct a sense of a place, such as our memories associated with a place, our social circles, family and friends with whom we have been to a place, or under which circumstances we can call a place a home. As Henri Lefebvre notes, space is a social product and a "social practice [that] presupposes the use of the body."[10] Accordingly, being or becoming social should not be understood as being inserted into an already existing place; we, as human beings produce and reproduce various spaces and perceive what is produced or reproduced.[11] These elements all feed into the formation of a cognitive map, which occurs through the *process* of traversing space, reflecting on it, and making connections.

As a mental process, cognitive maps consist of collecting, organizing, storing, recalling, and manipulating spatial information.[12] These maps—which have been used as research tools in social science disciplines such as psychology and sociology, looking at "the overall course of a person's life,"[13]—thus have many connections with how we feel and experience a certain navigation experience or place emotionally. So the drawing of sketch maps can be used to explore how a person's self-narration of a place and the representation of that place relate to each other, and in what ways locative technologies have the potential to affect this relationship.

Personal Narratives in Cognitive Maps

We can also define sketch maps as a storytelling platform. Used in this way, the process of making sketch maps, as a method, offers a fresh extension of creative visual methods, in which people are invited to spend time applying their playful or creative attention to the act of making something and then reflecting on it.[14] The process of asking participants to draw maps of the city where they live and to reflect upon their own drawings offers insights into the lived experience of mediated life in a city, which would otherwise be difficult to access.

Defining Space, Place, and Spatial Environment

Space, place, and mobility acquire different meanings as a result of our relationships both with each other and with the spatial environment itself. When we are asked to define or explain sense of place and mobility, we face difficulties in putting our spatial and social experiences into words, and in making clear what those words mean when we talk about certain associations and feelings about different places. Although we have our own experiences, narratives, and depictions of different places, it has always been hard to articulate and verbalize them, as they reflect and represent our *inner spaces*.[15]

Sketch Maps and Narrating Memories

Beginning with Kevin Lynch's pioneering work, *The Image of the City* in 1960, the 1960s and 1970s witnessed a growing interest in developing research designs to better understand how people develop spatial knowledge and how it is used in everyday life. Lynch introduced the concepts of "legibility" and "imageability" of a city. By legibility, he meant "the ease with which [a city's] parts can be recognized and can be organized into a coherent pattern," and he demonstrated how this concept could be used in urban planning in rebuilding cities.[16] Imageability—investigating the relationship among identity, structure, and meaning of a "mental image," and as a quality of a physical object, "which gives it a high probability of evoking a strong image"—can also be understood as "legibility" and "visibility."[17] In other words, if a city was "imageable," it was also likely to be "legible."[18] By asking residents of Boston, Jersey City, and Los Angeles to draw sketch maps, Lynch found that the image of a city is composed of "paths," "edges," "districts," "nodes," and "landmarks." Although his work focused on urban planning, his approach helped researchers in other disciplines struggling with the methodological problem of understanding not only how people navigate in a city but also how they form associations, attach meanings, and establish connections based on the history of a city, or on their own experiences.[19] Lynch "provided insight into citizens' differential knowledge of the urban environment and supplied an accessible methodology by which it might be studied."[20]

Cognitive maps, and the freehand sketch maps that are meant to partially represent them, are unlikely to be geographically accurate. The shapes and sizes are usually distorted, and spatial relationships are altered.[21] In his study of environmental images, Lynch found that "none of the respondents had anything like a comprehensive view of the city in which they had lived for many years."[22] Different people's cognitive maps, visible in the individual differences in sketch maps, can help us to see and understand how memories and meanings attached to certain places have a relationship with how we remember those places and how we establish a sense of those places. Therefore, geographical accuracy is not a significant concern in cognitive mapping.

Downs and Stea categorized the roles of cognitive mapping in our everyday lives according to how they serve our utilitarian needs and our personal worlds.[23] Cognitive maps can help us to find where things are located and how to get to those places quickly, easily, and safely. As we have said, they also contain emotional aspects, including the memories associated with places. Locative media do not *replace* the role of cognitive maps in our everyday lives, of course, but our thinking about places might become different as location-based technologies become more embedded into activities in everyday life.

Besides helping us to navigate in spatial environments (by providing us with sensory cues as well as meanings, memories, and associations), cognitive maps necessarily involve a personal dimension, in which our self-identity and narration play a crucial role. Cognitive maps can help us to establish our memories, to recall them, to place them in time, and to experience the world in different ways.

Mobile Nodes: Mapping London

For the study discussed here, thirty-eight people who were users of at least one mobile communications technology (most typically a smartphone) volunteered to draw sketch maps of London. Participants were selected in an unstructured manner, with no specific age, gender, or ethnicity given priority. The recruitment process started with tweets and Facebook groups and events, as well as email lists. For participants to see what kind of a study they would be taking part in, a research website was established: www.mobilenodes.co.uk. Adapting the work of Lynch,[24] and adjusting his study to locative media, each participant was provided with an A2-size piece of white paper and colorful pens and took part in a 90-minute session, which involved drawing and discussing one sketch map of London each.

As the study was based in London, it is important to look at the participants' maps within the context of how they perceive London in general. There was a common tendency among the research participants to consider London as a *mobile* city. For some, it was hard to mark only the "nodes" of mobility and instead of doing so, they shaded all parts of London to explain its mobility.

My London, My Smartphone: "I am forever forever mobile, forever on 3G!"

One of the basic associations that people make with mobility is based on where and how they can use their smartphones. For example, C.D. (24, male) shaded all of London (with blue), indicating pervasive mobility throughout the whole of London. Mobility, for this participant, was mainly associated with his smartphone. He described why and how he associates London with mobile communication, especially his smartphone and its location-aware features:

> Sometimes it is just by accident. They just pop-up. You know, that I forget to turn off the location. But it is useful if I am going somewhere and like when I'm filming. I geotag where I am, so people, rest of the crew would know where I am at that moment. If I'm meeting somebody, it is handy to share location, using messages or whatever, to people. You know it is literally convenience.

Another respondent, E.F. (22, male) noted that on his map (Figure 8.1) South London is represented by *nothing*. "First thing I've done is that I've pretty much shaded the south of the river. There's nothing there, we don't go south of the river. Because there is nothing there!" When asked what he means by "nothing there," his reply was indicative of both physical mobility and communicative mobility:

> I mean the tube doesn't go down there. . . . I think I'll stick to this shading here, because you can't get good reception on the South of the river either. I'm on T-Mobile, and I go there, I go there and I go to Clapham and the reception is shit as well. So T-Mobile doesn't work south of the river either!

Spatial knowledge is created via primary sources (our ability to remember and think about space such as walking in a city) and secondary sources (external references such as maps).[25] Locative media and map applications on smartphones help people navigate in a city and act as secondary sources; however, at the same time, they bring with them a dependence on those technologies. With the example of the map of London drawn by E.F., even someone who knows how to skillfully navigate a particular city may still wish to make sure that the route he or she knows is correct, short, or safe. Knowing how to get to places *quickly*, *easily*, and *safely* is listed by Downs and Stea as one of the main utilitarian uses of cognitive mapping, but this may be replaced by dependence on locative media, as locative media can have consequences for our everyday spatial cognition, and therefore for our senses of places.[26]

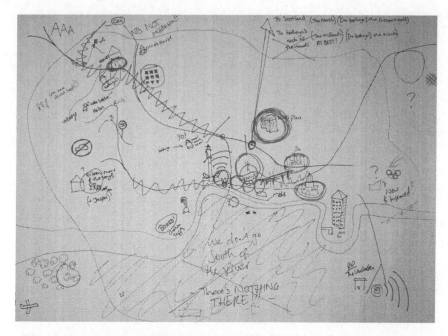

Figure 8.1 A sketch map of London by a respondent who decided to highlight that there's "nothing" in South London. This represented a lack of mobility (i.e., public transportation) to this area and also a lack of mobile connectivity on his smartphone. Image courtesy of Didem Ozkul.

Personal Narratives: Where? Who? What?

In an urban space, it is almost impossible to imagine the city's inhabitants without considering their regular social interactions. The meaning that is attributed to and constructed by space and spatial relations defines that space in each individual's mind. Lefebvre defined social space as "the space of society, of social life."[27] In the study, social construction of space was a common theme that emerged from the sketch maps.

Participants usually referred to their social circles when explaining their maps. For example, in her map, O.P. (21, female) drew Hampstead Heath and Leicester Square and recalled some memories associated with those places (see Figure 8.2):

> Basically that's me, my boyfriend, Mark and another person, we went to Hampstead Heath and watched the fireworks on New Year's Eve. Also, I spend a lot of time going to King's Cross, going into London and out of London. And that's where I went ice-skating.

As Downs and Stea observe, "An image of 'where' brings back a recollection of 'who' and 'what.'"[28] So, by drawing Hampstead Heath and Leicester Square, O.P. recalled the memories with her friends and boyfriend (the "who" of the social

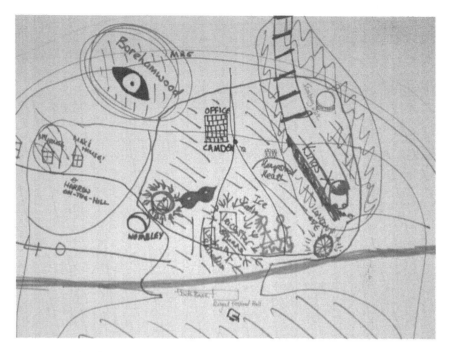

Figure 8.2 The sketch map of a participant who connected the space of the city with her various social groups and the activities associated with those groups. Image courtesy of Didem Ozkul.

interaction) while watching the fireworks and ice-skating (the "what" of the social interaction). She has shaded and circled railways and train stations as nodes of mobility.

From those genuine social relations that one establishes within a city, the place acquires a different meaning. This sense of place provides the individual with a sense of belonging to the community. This sense of belonging is believed to construct personal identities, and in turn, communities.[29]

Locative media mean that people can visualize their own location in a different way, as well as communicating it to others. When we talk or think about our own experiences of a place, we refer back to our personal biographies, our stories that have been created socially and somehow inscribed on our mental maps. Thus, there is an element of nostalgia in cognitive mapping, as it involves recalling and recollecting.[30]

Recall and Recollect: When?

Feelings about certain places are shaped by past events, and mobile communication devices can be used to keep a record, a form of biography or diary. Participants in this study stated that they go back to their photos, mobile Facebook status updates, or Foursquare check-ins to remember those places and recall those memories. One of the main uses of locative media, especially smartphones, in these situations is taking pictures, geotagging them, and uploading them to Facebook or Foursquare. For instance, S.T. (21, female) said that she uses her smartphone to take pictures either in order to remember places and memories associated with those places, or to share those moments with loved ones.

While observing the process of participants' drawing sketch maps and using them for telling stories, we saw that people recalled memories associated with places and inserted them on their maps as iconic images. For instance, W.X. (25, female) drew a pipe representing Sherlock Holmes just by Baker Street, his fictional home (Figure 8.3).

She then added King's Cross St. Pancras Station, location of Platform $9^{3/4}$ in the Harry Potter novels and films:

> Sherlock Holmes is, I think, the first memory of the UK, *because my father bought the book for me when I was 7*, so Baker Street . . . I think it is a dream place. I think the second most important memory about London is Harry Potter. So King's Cross, the station for Harry Potter is the second one.

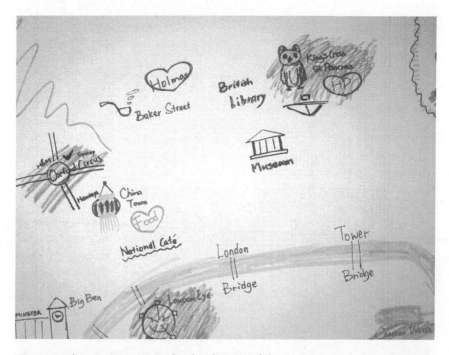

Figure 8.3 As was common in the sketch maps of the participants, the sites depicted recalled memories associated with places, as seen here in the choice to draw a pipe next to the site associated with fictional home of Sherlock Holmes. Image courtesy of Didem Ozkul.

These examples suggest that places, even if they are ordinary and taken for granted by some people, can acquire a special meaning not only through social events that took place there but also with associations that we recall from books, other people's stories, movies, and media in general. Of course, we should note that "special meanings" are not necessarily positive ones. Some participants marked places on their maps as the site of traumatic or upsetting experiences—usually with dark colors. These remind us that individual meanings are not always sweet, or charming, or cause for warm nostalgia.

Sketch Maps as a Storytelling Platform

We would expect that sketch maps "provide insights into the relationship between people's environmental representation and their behavior in the environment," as Kitchin and Blades argue.[31] They serve as platforms where people can spend time creating their own representations of places, and telling their stories based on those representations. The maps typically capture the crucial characteristics of a sense of place—where things happen, and with whom—mixed with emotions and associations, blending the sense of a place with aspects of time. The sketch maps, used as storytelling platforms, can therefore be infused with nostalgia, a way of trying to preserve the past.[32]

The notion of rapid change and the need to hang onto a moment is closely related to modern urban lifestyles and their struggles with mobility. It is not only the location of things and people that matter to us but also the meanings of the relationships hidden under each of those locations. We may sometimes bypass the importance of those memories and associations just by *remembering* to check in or sharing memories about places with our social networks, but in the end not only what we tell and share but also how we remember becomes important. Sketch maps, therefore, can suggest the ways in which locations are turned into meaningful places and memories, which also have a close relation not only to how we perceive and (re)present places but also to how we tell stories about our lives.

Paul Ricoeur's three-volume study of how narratives are made meaningful, *Time and Narrative*,[33] and his discussion of these ideas in relation to personal identity, in *Oneself as Another*,[34] acquire new value when we consider lives in the city mediated by today's communications technologies. For Ricoeur, understandings are achieved through storytelling, a process that takes place across time; also, therefore, self-understandings are acquired by the same route. We tell stories—in other words, narrative accounts (to call the account a "story" doesn't mean that it is untrue)—in order to share ideas about the world or other people or ourselves. Storytelling selects a number of particular elements and arranges them into an order to suggest a particular meaning.

The electronic mobile communications which people engage daily within a city—status updates and location check-ins—can be seen as an ongoing weaving of narrative; the elements are certainly *selected*, for consumption by some kind of audience. However, these ongoing stories are a continuous "middle"—most readers would never look for the "beginning," and there is usually no "ending." The transitory nature of social media—where we turn our attention to the fast-flowing river of information when we choose to but do not even *hope* to attend to it all in the way that one is meant to examine every item in one's pile of email—also means that many bits of the "story" will be missed by most members of the "audience." Both of these factors—the continuous middle, and the scatter-gun relationship with an audience—mean that these stories typically lack *emplotment*, an overall meaning that configures and makes sense of all the individual bits. The process of drawing and talking about sketch maps, however, tends to drive that element back in: implicitly, if not explicitly, the process requires that stories are told, based on experiences of the city and mobile technologies.

Therefore, we are really talking about two modes of storytelling. First, there is the continuous narrative of the self shared in social media—a self that is often quite abstract in its positioning and sometimes is located in specified places. (Some users, of course, are more likely to report physical locations than others, and some kinds of social media take location as the starting point of all interaction.) Second, there is the narrative created in the process of making and talking about a sketch map. Obviously, the first happens all the time for many people; the second occurs rarely, as part of a research process. But the latter gives us insights into what is happening in the former. If memories and self-identities are already stored and shared through a kind of storytelling process—which is heightened and made more apparent by the use of social media, and especially locative media—then our sketch map research process involves a second pass through the storytelling process: not just a telling, but a compact *retelling*, of stories about self and identity in the city.

Ricoeur suggests that there is a playfulness in all narratives, a testing-out of ideas regarding the stories that it is possible to tell. "In this sense," he writes, "literature proves to consist in a vast laboratory for thought experiments in which the resources of variation encompassed by narrative identity are put to the test of narration."[35] We might similarly view people's everyday performances in social media as experiments in self-representation.

Parallel to the dialectic of "sameness" and "selfhood," which Ricoeur identifies as central to personal identity, we can see that mobile social media stories are often about the dialectic of the ordinary and the extraordinary: stories of life being played out between the poles of "Here I am, doing this, *again*," and "Wow! I'm doing *this*!" Locative media adds a layer of illustrative realism by confirming the mundaneness ("I'm waiting for my train") or excitement ("I'm *inside* the BBC!") of moving between places in everyday life.

Leaving these traces in the online space has a parallel with another earlier sociological study, which studied identity and the connection to meaningful objects. Tony Whincup considered the physical objects that people keep and display in their homes, seeing them as attempts to preserve feelings and memories that otherwise would be intangible and become forgotten. He writes that the nature of memory is of "vital concern" to both individuals and groups:

> Memory, a slippery and fragile thing, is constantly open to subtraction and addition. Inevitably, people have searched for strategies through which to restore the memory of these otherwise tenuous and transitory life events and socially agreed values.[36]

Writing a decade ago, Whincup was not thinking of mobile and locative social media, but his approach is fruitful in this realm. Tweets, shared photographs, and Foursquare check-ins here take the role of the "mnemonic objects," which Whincup says "generally encapsulate the best of people's reflections about themselves," enabling an "'advantageous' sense of self" to be sustained.[37] The material "broadcast" in social media is both ostensibly and actually for an external audience, then, but perhaps is most significant in constructing a narrative identity for *oneself.* This point is heightened by the fact that the sender is likely to be the only individual in the world who sees all of it (as mentioned above, other members of the "audience" will typically only see the bits that coincide with the times when they happen to turn their attention to that social media service). This is not to suggest that individuals concoct representations of the self based on an insecure or paranoid orientation to the world. As Whincup suggests, drawing on Wilhelm Dilthey, this is part of a social process in which we naturally consider our symbolic output in relation to other people's and tends toward a positive and "identity-affirming" role.[38] Locative media enable users to create a record of the interesting places that they have been to, as well as a cheerful or resigned note of the boring locations that they frequent, and—when used alongside text and images, as they typically are—to build up an illustrated story of a particular identity in the world.

Conclusion

We can argue, then, that encouraging users of mobile communication technologies to draw their own maps of London provided the participants with a platform to tell their stories and the researchers with a tool to better understand the *inner worlds* of the participants. Sketch maps, used this way in understanding spatial behavior in mobile media, and how we make associations with places via locative media, can be seen to offer personal representations of memories and nostalgic feelings. During the process of drawing and recalling, a story—which otherwise might have been buried and forgotten—was often revealed. The stories of everyday life and locative media use are, of course, entwined, with each informing the other. Everyday life is brought into focus though the ways in which bits of it are captured and reflected in electronic media, and the value of locative media becomes apparent when we see its role in telling the stories of everyday lives.

Notes

1. Hayden White, *The Content of the Form: Narrative Discourse and Historical Representation* (Baltimore, MD: Johns Hopkins University Press, 1987), 1.
2. The project is part of Didem Ozkul's Ph.D. research, based at the University of Westminster, with David Gauntlett.
3. David Gauntlett, *Creative Explorations: New Approaches to Identities and Audiences* (London: Routledge, 2007).
4. Roger M. Downs and David Stea, *Maps in Minds: Reflections on Cognitive Mapping* (New York: Harper & Row Publishers, 1977), 6.
5. Ibid.
6. See: Susan Blackmore, *Consciousness: An Introduction* (London: Hodder Arnold, 2003); Susan Blackmore, ed., *Conversations on Consciousness* (Oxford: Oxford University Press, 2005); David Rose, *Consciousness: Philosophical, Psychological, and Neural Theories* (Oxford: Oxford University Press, 2006); Daniel Dennett, *Consciousness Explained* (London: Penguin, 1991); Daniel Dennett, *Sweet Dreams: Philosophical Obstacles to a Science of Consciousness* (Cambridge, MA: The MIT Press, 2005).
7. Rob Kitchin and Mark Blades, *The Cognition of Geographic Space* (London: I.B. Tauris, 2002), 1.
8. Kevin Lynch, *The Image of the City* (Cambridge, MA: The MIT Press, 1960).
9. Hayden White, "The Value of Narrativity in the Representation of Reality," *Critical Inquiry* 7, no. 1 (1980): 5.
10. Henri Lefebvre, *The Production of Space*, trans. Donald Nicholson-Smith (Oxford: Blackwell, 1991), 40.
11. Ibid.
12. Ibid.
13. Roger M. Downs and David Stea, *Maps in Minds: Reflections on Cognitive Mapping* (New York: Harper & Row Publishers, 1977), 7.
14. Gauntlett, *Creative Explorations*.
15. Downs and Stea, *Maps in Minds*, 4.
16. Kevin Lynch, *The Image of the City* (Cambridge, MA: The MIT Press, 1960), 2–3.
17. Ibid., 9.
18. David Clark, *Urban Geography: An Introductory Guide* (London: Croom Helm Ltd, 1982), 18.
19. Lynch, *The Image of the City*, 92–102.
20. John R. Gold and George Revill, *Representing the Environment* (New York: Routledge, 2004), 294.
21. Downs and Stea, *Maps in Minds*.
22. Lynch, *The Image of the City*, 29.
23. Downs and Stea, *Maps in Minds*.
24. Lynch, *The Image of the City*.
25. Kitchin and Blades, *The Cognition of Geographic Space*.
26. Downs and Stea, *Maps in Minds*.
27. Lefebvre, *The Production of Space*, 35.
28. Downs and Stea, *Maps in Minds*, 27.
29. Edward Relph, *Place and Placelessness* (London: Pion, 1976).
30. John Eyles, *Senses of Place* (Cheshire: Silverbrook Press, 1985).
31. Kitchin and Blades, *The Cognition of Geographic Space*, 7.
32. Yi-Fu Tuan, *Space and Place: The Perspective of Experience* (Minneapolis, MN: University of Minnesota Press, 1977), 188.

33. See: Paul Ricoeur, *Time and Narrative: Volume 1*, trans. Kathleen McLaughlin and David Pellauer (Chicago: University of Chicago Press, 1984); Paul Ricoeur, *Time and Narrative: Volume 2*, trans. Kathleen McLaughlin and David Pellauer (Chicago: University of Chicago Press, 1985); Paul Ricoeur, *Time and Narrative: Volume 3*, trans. Kathleen McLaughlin and David Pellauer (Chicago: University of Chicago Press, 1988).

34. Paul Ricoeur, *Oneself as Another*, trans. Kathleen Blamey (Chicago: University of Chicago Press, 1992).

35. Ibid., 148.

36. Tony Whincup, "Imaging the Intangible," in *Picturing the Social Landscape: Visual Methods and the Sociological Imagination*, ed. Caroline Knowles and Paul Sweetman (London: Routledge, 2004), 80.

37. Ibid., 81.

38. Gauntlett, *Creative Explorations*, 142.

9

PATHS OF MOVEMENT

Negotiating Spatial Narratives through GPS Tracking

Lone Koefoed Hansen

How do the examples in this chapter help us understand the practice of story-telling in the mobile media age?

As GPS technologies are embedded into mobile devices—and thus everyday life—it has become common to track the location and trajectories of humans as well as objects. While knowing where people and things actually are and have actually been can be interesting, by also engaging with the lives and (hi)stories of both "nomad" and location, factual data is transformed into narrative potential. When location data is layered with everyday life, spatial narratives emerge. This chapter analyzes the artistic practice of Dutch media artist Esther Polak, who demonstrates how location data can be brought to life as narrative material and as a storytelling tool. With her GPS receiver, Polak experiments with ways of accessing and discussing the many (spatial) narratives that humans, animals, machines, and goods (e.g., dairy products) create in their everyday trajectories. Through an analysis of Polak's works, and with theoretical reference to Dutch architect Rem Koolhaas and French theorist Michel de Certeau, this chapter discusses how mobile media seem to facilitate an informed (re)engagement with space and the spatial narratives that unfold when people and objects disclose the personal, national, and global stories that are expressed through their paths of movement.

Keywords

- **"The Generic City"**: A text by Dutch architect Rem Koolhaas, "The Generic City" both serves as a manifest and describes an architectural concept of the modern day metropolis: it is newly built, consists of skyscrapers, is populated by global migrants and brands, and could have been built anywhere. In twenty years, it will either be completely different or have disappeared.

- **Tactics and strategies:** As complimentary notions, the *strategic* and *tactical* were coined by French theorist Michel de Certeau. The terms originate from military jargon and describe the plan of the attacker and the countermeasures taken by the attacked, respectively. As metaphors, the strategic describes the position held by entities of power and control (for instance, political entities or agencies of cultural production). Tactics, then, describes the position or actions of those who, in theory, do not hold power but in practice manage to maneuver and circumvent the plans made by the strategic entity (for instance, the way that "ordinary" people avoid bureaucratic measures).
- **Psychogeography:** Coined in the 1960s by the primarily French artist group, Situationist International, psychogeography describes the way that locations are felt and experienced. Where geography produces maps of Euclidean space, psychogeography maps space as it is felt and used by those that inhabit it. One of the most famous maps is "Paris, the Naked City" (1957) by artists Guy Debord and Asger Jorn. In recent years, with the existence of GPS, psychogeography also means making maps by tracking movements, thus visualizing the use-patterns of individuals and/or cities.

> *The key issue to examine with locative media and pervasive games is that many of these new, mediated experiences refer to and appropriate space while divorcing it from its meaning, history, and significance.*
>
> —*Mary Flanagan*[1]

Introduction

Critically discussing locative media projects, digital media theorist Mary Flanagan presents a critique of their tendency to only explore a location superficially. This is especially true, she argues, of projects that mediate or add layers to a location. Such projects often demonstrate little reflection on the particular urban space they are designed for. While they may be "context aware" in a strict technological sense by using position data as design material, they are rarely "aware" of their location in any other sense. Flanagan makes this argument as part of an explicit critique of the many locative media projects that claim to be indebted to the psychogeographic practice of the Situationist International (SI) because this artist group emphasized how every location has a unique way of fostering individual experiences. With this and others of their interventional artistic practices, the SI sought to investigate the myriad of (historical, social, and political) layers, experiences, and narratives imbued in every location in 1960s Paris, France. Understanding the city as a complex historical and political assemblage, the practices and theories of the SI stood in contrast to the then-dominant paradigm of functionalism, where the ideal city would be a well-functioning "machine," built to enable efficient transportation and living as well as maximizing capital gain and spectacular experiences.[2] Reminding readers of the full SI agenda, Flanagan argues that rather than embracing the full potential of psychogeography, most locative media projects simply understand a location as a point on a game board.

Flanagan suggests that one possible way to overcome this is to insist that locative media projects "begin to reflect the contested nature of the lived reality of such spaces" when they seek to reengage site-specificity.[3] In other words, mobile media projects need to take (the often complex) spatial layers into account when they seek to expand the participant's experience of a location in the here and now.

I will argue in this chapter that the narrative potentials of mobile media go beyond expanding the locational experience of the here-and-now participant. Mobile media are also able to make manifest the lived practice(s) of space and thus make spatial narratives available for negotiation. My primary case will be an analysis of Dutch media artist Esther Polak's artistic practice—primarily her two recent GPS tracking projects, *Souvenir* (2008) and *NomadicMILK* (2009). Polak herself states that her interest lies in the way that trajectories are experienced by the people making them.[4] Using the GPS receiver as a storytelling tool, she accesses individual stories about everyday practices and how individuals experience their relationship to the larger structures that are part of their movements. I understand Polak's projects as site-specific narratives that both "write" and "read" a location with the heterogeneous "voices" of those who embody the place. The argument will be supported by two theoretical positions discussing the relationship between the experiencing individual and the larger social, societal, and political structures: French scholar Michel de Certeau and his famous distinction between "writing" and "reading" a city narrative through movement,[5] as well as Dutch architect Rem Koolhaas's ideas about how (living in) a postmodernist city is built on globalized capital's ability to reinvent itself in the same image everywhere.[6] I will discuss how Polak's two projects embody multiple interpretations of de Certeau and Koolhaas in ways that meet Flanagan's critique by renewing the challenge she poses. Of particular relevance is de Certeau's focus on the difference between experiencing ("writing") and tracing ("reading") a city, as he argues that it is impossible to do both at the same time. The questions then obviously become: Must the conclusions arrived at by de Certeau be changed for the mobile media era? Has it become possible to reconstruct an individual narrative with the help of the tracking possibilities offered by mobile devices? When it comes to digital movement data, what is the relation between narrative and tracking?

Polak's Artistic Practice

Esther Polak was one of the first media artists to explore the artistic potential of the GPS receiver. The GPS satellite system, owned by the American military, was unlocked for civil use in 2000 and already in 2002 Polak did her first GPS project, *Amsterdam REALtime*, in collaboration with the Dutch foundation Waag Society.[7] By logging the movements of select citizens of Amsterdam, she explored how the city was used on an everyday basis. Grey and white lines of movement gradually filled a black projection screen in an art gallery, thus mapping the life of Amsterdam; popular places and routes are highly visible, whereas unvisited areas are left as a black void.

MILK project (2003) visualized the traces of people and movements "embedded" in a common Dutch cheese.[8] Again using GPS receivers, she followed a dairy route from the (Latvian) cow, to the (Dutch) consumer thereby visualizing how the Dutch cheese bought at a Dutch farmer's market was rather a Dutch-type European cheese carrying hidden stories from those who manufactured it. People who played a role in the supply chain from Latvia to the Netherlands were invited to carry a GPS receiver to register their movements for one day, after which Polak's team used custom-made software to visualize and subsequently discuss the tracks with the participants. The result is an online exhibition of pixelated maps, tracks, participant comments, and other elements that shows how the milk's route is part of complex transnational economic transactions and flows.

In the project *Souvenir | the landscape as a place of work*, Polak and her partner Ivar van Bekkum worked (under the joint name PolakVanBekkum) with Dutch farmers working their fields for crops. By tracking tractors, the movements of plowing a field were translated into a series of prints (see Figure 9.1). Knowing

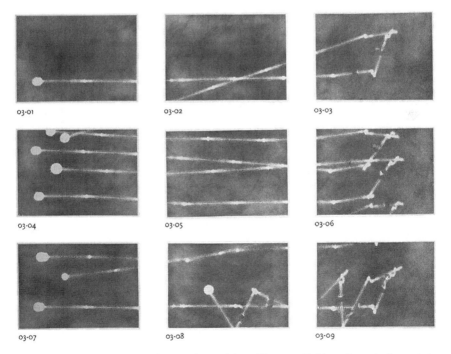

03-01   03-02   03-03

03-04   03-05   03-06

03-07   03-08   03-09

Figure 9.1 A series of prints from Esther Polak and Ivar van Bekkum's work, *Souvenir | the landscape as a place of work*. The white lines show the movements of tractors, which were traced using GPS receivers in the Netherlands. Monoprints Souvenir Zeeland, PolakVanBekkum, © 2008.

that the prints are visualizations of a plowing tractor and recalling a furrowed field's straight lines, the pattern of movement is easily recognizable even if it is a bit distorted. When looking at the prints, it is entirely possible for the inner eye to see the land and visualize the tractor driving up and down the field.

Unlike Polak's own projects, the primary purpose of this project by PolakVan-Bekkum was to get into dialogue with outsiders, to investigate ways of satisfying the often nostalgic idea of farming and the rural landscape by creating artworks for tourists.[9] This is not unlike classic landscape painting, which was also made for those not actually inhabiting them; however, the visualizations in *Souvenir* are different because they depict movements and not vistas. Furthermore, they are made from the perspectives of the working farmer and the satellite instead of the artist looking for picturesque views. Rather than exploring the dynamics between an individual and his or her own tracks, *Souvenir* explores different relationships to the same land.[10] By recording, visualizing, and ultimately selling the movements, PolakVanBekkum investigate the landscape as artistic material when seen from the perspectives rendered by the gazes of the tourist and the farmer, respectively. In *Souvenir*, the paths of movement are detached from the experiences of the tracked individuals and the depiction thus stays an abstraction. As with any other souvenir, it confirms "the idea of farming"—or the stories told about farming by onlookers—instead of challenging the viewer's (often nostalgic) perspective.

Like *Souvenir*, the *NomadicMILK* project is concerned with landscapes and people in the food supply chain. Set in Nigeria, *NomadicMILK* investigates the everyday spatial narratives of contemporary African dairy transports. Two very different, but closely interwoven, dairy production and distribution situations are the project's artistic material: one narrative centers on imported, powdered milk where one brand, the Dutch PEAK, is particularly popular and is available in even the most rural parts of the country. The second narrative centers on Nigerian cultural heritage, as one particular nomadic tribe, the Fulani, has been responsible for herding cows for as long as anyone can remember. Although the Fulani are struggling to maintain their traditions, both cultures are still active; the tribe is still herding cows while PEAK milk is being transported into every corner of the country. Polak realized that these two types of milkmen share space and working conditions: their workspace is the land of Nigeria, and both lead very nomadic lives. With the aim of illustrating and discussing how herdsmen as well as truck drivers embody, understand, and narrate their nomadic practice, *NomadicMILK* shows how the individual stories construct this "shared workspace." Concretely, Polak used her normal procedure of collecting movement data with GPS receivers and discussing the tracks with the participants in order to give them "a new perspective on their own perceptions of place, mobility and economics."[11] Through the participants' relations to—and narrations of—this space of milk transportation, the project investigates how the practices relate to the political and economic structures in Nigeria in general.[12]

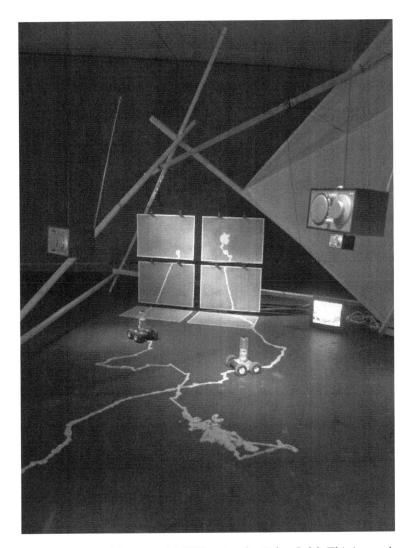

Figure 9.2 Pathways of the *NomadicMILK* project by Esther Polak. This image shows the installation view at the Transmediale, Berlin. © 2009 Esther Polak.

NomadicMILK is exhibited online and in galleries (see Figure 9.2). Both show the abstract paths as well as videos of interviews with the participants whose paths are visualized by a sand-drawing robot that Polak brings to the interview. By using sand as drawing material, participants are able to interact and modify the path with hands, feet, and available tools. (Prints and videos of the project are available on the online exhibition of the project at nomadicmilk.net.) As is evident from the videos, the "hidden narratives" of the abstracted paths materialize in a very concrete and engaging way through the physical relation to the tracks (especially pointing, moving a bit of sand, and moving around the track during the interview). And to the exhibition spectator, the Nigerian locations and practices come to life in a way that is both very close and very abstract. Polak thus manages to make participants aware of their own spatial engagements, but she also makes it possible for spectators to see the many narratives that are embedded in the landscape. With the individual practices of Nigerian land as narrative material, the lived reality that Flanagan seeks is exposed by help of GPS, some sand, and an interested interviewer.

In my analysis below, I will look at some of the issues at stake in *NomadicMILK* while adding *Souvenir* to the mix. Two aspects of these projects are particularly compelling: first, both *Souvenir* and *NomadicMILK* address the difference between the person being tracked and the person trying to make sense of the tracks. Second, both projects show how the tracked participants negotiate and navigate structures of politics, economy, and the concrete landscape through their movements. Through the theories of Koolhaas as well as de Certeau, I will explore how we might understand the way that the two projects expose and discuss the (spatial) narratives that are created and negotiated when someone creates a path of movement that others can explore.

Koolhaas: Generic Cities and Economies

> *All Generic Cities issue from the tabula rasa; if there was nothing, now they are there; if there was something, they have replaced it. They must, otherwise they would be historic.*
>
> —Rem Koolhaas[13]

In his monumental book *S, M, L XL*, Rem Koolhaas (co-founder of OMA: Office for Metropolitan Architecture) introduced the idea of "The Generic City," describing how every modern metropolis is essentially a slightly reconfigured clone of any other hyper-urban area. As an architect, he finds the search for "historic identity" meaningless as the "perpetual quest for 'character,' grinds successful identities down to meaningless dust."[14] What most would bemoan, Koolhaas applauds, because out of this identity stripping rises the Generic, "an endless repetition of the same simple structural module."[15] Koolhaas is concerned with identity and with how the very contemporary city has neither history nor core identity. Nothing refers to what happened "yesterday," and if it is referred to, it is only superficial. Every place is just a placeholder until something new pops up elsewhere:

> [I]t is the city without history. It is big enough for everybody. It is easy. It does not need maintenance. If it gets too small it just expands. If it gets old it just self-destructs and renews. It is equally exciting—or unexciting— everywhere. It is "superficial"—like a Hollywood studio lot, it can produce a new identity every Monday morning.[16]

So according to Koolhaas, contemporary cities have neither character nor history. The "original" cities have already "disappeared," partly through the attempts of conserving them, and Koolhaas finds the idea of bemoaning this loss of identity almost ridiculous. Instead, we see places that have more in common with places elsewhere in the world than with places that are physically closer; Singapore has more in common with Dubai than with a rural village in Malaysia even though the latter is closer. This also means that we see similar patterns of movement, of politics, of capital, and of life everywhere. The differences between life "here" and life "there" are very small, and most places share the same generic narrative about a "proper" way of organizing life.

Following this, Koolhaas does not accept the idea of the layered city but rather argues that the new city is layer-less. If something changes, the changes are visible in the next city that is being built: "The Generic City, like a sketch which is never elaborated, is not improved but abandoned . . . it *has* no layers. Its next layer takes place somewhere else."[17] So if we understand mobile media as something that works with narrative layers of cities and experiences of locations, which is clearly what Flanagan does when she argues for "meaning, history and significance" in the opening quote, Koolhaas's points seem to undermine or contradict the very possibility of making projects that "reflect the contested nature of the lived reality of such places."[18]

However, if we look closer at Koolhaas's understanding of the contemporary city, the generic is also transient. Independent scholar Richard Prouty expounds upon Koolhaas and believes that "the generic city describes a way of seeing as much as it describes a set of objects."[19] So, while Koolhaas seemingly describes the postmodern metropolis, other types of locations—for instance, the countryside—can also be subject to this postmodernist way of looking at the world; always with a distanced look and always ready to move on. The gaze belongs to globalization and to the tourist: every place is understood as a marketplace, and every place can be objectified and subject to preconceived narratives such as "the idea of farming," as Polak addresses in the *Souvenir* project when the farmer's movements are transformed into abstract patterns that please the tourists' gaze.

"A generic city is the humid boomtown you visit on business," Prouty remarks, thus highlighting that the generic space disappears when site-specific narratives emerge as a result of lived practice. Everyday life produces narratives, and also the generic becomes embodied; it is always sensed, understood, and "lived" in relation to the individual—even if it is often generic to someone else. This idea of narrative is aligned with Michele Chang and Elizabeth Goodman's notion that locative projects "consider how player activity constructs 'place' out of data," a practice that can be eye-opening for the person experiencing it.[20]

The idea that the embodiment of a location is what constructs a "place" obviously refers to Michel de Certeau's famous statement, "Space is a practiced place,"[21] where the embodiment of a place is crucial to its space-ness.[22] He clearly distinguishes between experiencing the world (the inside view) and looking from a distance at the person experiencing (the outside view). This qualifies Prouty's points about the fundamental difference between being a tourist and a resident and that (political) structures and (individual) actions co-create complex spatial narratives.

Michel de Certeau: Reading the Embodied City

A city's narrative and history is created by everyday actions of ordinary people, de Certeau argues, using the metaphor of writing. It is the engagement with a place that in itself establishes the "text" or the "narrative" of the location:

> The ordinary practitioners of the city live "down below," below the thresholds of at which visibility begins . . . they are walkers, *Wandersmänner*, whose bodies follow the thicks and thins of the urban "text" they write without being able to read it. . . . The paths that correspond in this intertwining, unrecognized poems in which each body is an element signed by many others, elude legibility. It is as though the practices organizing a bustling city were characterized by their blindness.[23]

Grand narratives do not form a city's narrative; instead, the narrative is formed by the many different voices created by individuals as they navigate between power structures and possibilities. From a de Certeauian point of view, there is a big difference between being engaged in "writing" and being able to "read" this kind of narrative whose broader perspectives are invisible to the individual who lives "below the thresholds of at which visibility begins."

This example of city narratives is part of a bigger argument where de Certeau examines the ways in which people reappropriate—and thus create—culture through everyday actions and in everyday situations. This important discussion serves to argue that many of the formal or statistical approaches in the social sciences fail to capture significant aspects of cultural production. Differentiating between the elevated and the immersed position, de Certeau uses the metaphor of the city's "text" to explain strategic and tactical thinking and/or actions. The strategic is the planned and "elevated" view largely held by those in power positions and control—for instance, political entities or agencies of cultural production—whereas the tactical is the way that "ordinary" people manage and evade these power structures either explicitly or implicitly. On a political level, the embedded walking practices of people "down below" is an image of how power relations between "systems" and "users" are thwarted when individuals transform designed strategies through tactical "operations" on—in this case—space.

While arguing that it is what you do with the opportunities you are given that matters (again echoing the distinction between strategies and tactics), de Certeau strengthens the argument by showing how every experience of a site will always involve some level of embodiment. But if walkers write with their movements within the city's structures (all while questioning and engaging these structures), who reads these narratives? What is possible to "read" from the "writing" done by the walkers, and what is the reader's role? By differentiating between what individuals experience and what distant others see them experience, de Certeau establishes a distinction between structures and operations, between doing and looking, and between engaging in the moment on location and analyzing actions from a distance in time and space.

Interestingly, de Certeau argues, this engagement or narrative cannot be "read" merely by tracking the person traversing the cityscape. Only "the absence of what has passed by" is visible, which is not to be confused with the actions themselves because "surveys of routes miss what was: the act itself of passing by."[24] It is not possible to be strategic and tactical at the same time. Though it is possible to ascertain the routes people take, this will neither capture details nor the reasons for particular behaviors. So, in order to be able to read the narratives of the city, it is necessary to engage instead of trying to decipher general patterns or a bigger picture.

Fast-forwarding to the present time, mobile technologies have led to a renewed interest in facilitating, collecting, and displaying individual tracings and trajectories, often using a map interface. It is well argued that maps and mapping practices are always imbued with power relations and politics.[25] Following this, one might view maps as tracings of performative processes of politics, and one might view the act of tracking and displaying paths of movements as a performance of a particular (and often politically embedded) embodied narrative. Contemporary literature on mapping practices and mobile media suggest that mobile media strengthen the emancipating potentials of these performances; it enables the surfacing of previously concealed insights into how an individual's actions are connected to a bigger picture.[26]

By design, mobile technologies thus seem to be able to simultaneously make explicit the structures of strategy and the traces of tactics. Even if de Certeau regards "tracing" (reading) and "writing" (narrating) as mutually exclusive, it appears that this picture may change with mobile technologies as they enable knowledge on how specific actions are related to other actions and agendas. In many ways, mobile media in general, and Polak's projects in particular, thus seem to facilitate an informed (re)engagement with space and spatial narratives in ways that both echo and resist de Certeau's ideas.

Polak: Negotiating Spatial Narratives and Practices

In the opening quote to this chapter by Mary Flanagan, she argues that the appropriation of space through these kinds of traces often divorces space from its "meaning, history, and significance." However, "the contested nature of the lived reality" of locations is exactly what Polak's artistic practice addresses on at least three levels. First, the projects enact and explore "readings" of locations based on how they are embodied. Second, they enable individuals to discuss their everyday practices from an "outside" perspective through the technology, the software, and the artistic intervention. And third, there is a political dimension where Polak, though often unarticulated, examines the movements of globalized economy and culture. All three levels are concerned with how paths of movement become spatial narratives.

In two ways, *Souvenir* and *NomadicMILK* deal with the relationships between the perspectives of the particular and the generic. First, they show that it is possible to simultaneously hold the inside and the outside view. Second, the visualizations show how the tracked participants negotiate and navigate structures of politics, economy, and the concrete landscape through their movements. In regard to the first issue, both *Souvenir* and *NomadicMILK* install a difference between the person being tracked and the person seeing the tracks. There is clearly an "inside" and an "outside" view; *Souvenir*'s art explicitly expresses two very different perspectives on the landscape—even though one perspective may not see the other (the farmer may not understand the art of the project and the tourist may not see the farmer's efficiency perspective). Furthermore, the abstract prints allow tourists (i.e., outsiders) to maintain their often nostalgic view on the landscape because they are only confronted with a slightly different perspective on what they know: the rhythmic structure of the furrowed field. Had *Souvenir* used the same procedure as *NomadicMILK* of displaying video recordings of Polak interviewing participants about their work and their struggles to maintain their culture, this knowledge of contemporary Dutch farming could probably destroy the nostalgic tourist gaze, which is the one that the project instead seeks to activate. This dynamic is not without irony, though: tourists acquire an abstract artwork of a familiar landscape that for many holds nostalgic narratives about farming the land and about the Netherlands as an agriculture country, but this familiarity is from a perspective that has little to do with the perspective of both contemporary farming and with the person who knows every twist and turn of the land. In this case, the project shows no intention of making viewers ("readers," in de Certeau's terms) engage further, physically or emotionally, with the producers ("writers") of the tracks. This is primarily because the foundation of the project is the difference between "writing" and "reading" the landscape's culturally embedded, spatial narratives, even if the participants themselves do not fully realize it.

The clashing of inside and outside perspectives is also evident in *NomadicMILK*. First of all, the Nigerian participants are able to view, explain, and reflect on their moves from an "outside," or at least distanced, perspective when the robot draws the paths in the sand. By mixing the two perspectives, participants are able to see their own actions and decisions in a larger perspective. As in *Souvenir*, the exhibition-goer meets abstract prints in the exhibition context, but Polak very much aims to let the viewer know as much as possible about how the prints came into being and of the life leading to these kinds of movements. However, the remoteness of context also establishes (or maintains) a distance between the Nigerian participant and the spectator's gaze even though we see both tracings and video, and even though the contemporary life of Nigerian milk industry (including the Fulani herdsmen) is thoroughly explained. In a way, both prints and video are exotic and very hard to relate to for a Western buyer who has never been to Nigeria. In this sense, tracings, prints, and videos become abstractions of a location the viewer will never quite understand—just like the outside spectator will never understand the life on the streets from tracings on a map in de Certeau's theories. Still, just like Prouty's remark on Koolhaas, also the exhibition-goer might get moments of embodied experiences through the exhibition material's ability to immerse the viewer in the gallery's spatial narratives. This is different from being in Nigeria but still an experience that transgresses the generic view.

The participants in the *NomadicMILK* project, however, are given "access" to being outside and inside at the same time. The traces come to life and are no longer only "relic sets" of what once was, as de Certeau stated. From the videos, it is clear that Polak's repeated visits make participants begin to explain and explore the broader perspectives of their particular actions. When they see their movements replayed in the sand drawings, both herdsmen and truck drivers begin telling the stories of their movements in and intertwining with the locations through which they navigate. The contested nature of these locations becomes visible through the stories that they tell Polak. So it seems like de Certeau's assertion that it is impossible to be both a "reader" and a "writer" would have to be rethought in light of the possibilities of seeing one's own actions with the help of mobile media. It is clear from the project and the videos that participants are now reading their own writing.

In this way, *NomadicMILK* has at least three layers of visualization: it shows individual narratives and how they can be discussed by help of mobile media traces; it shows the interpersonal and shared workspace of drivers and herdsmen as well as their different perspectives on this space; and then it has a third—international, perhaps—layer, which creates a particular narrative about how these individual experiences are interwoven with global dynamics.

This third visualization layer has to do with the second of my two primary points of interest, which addresses how both projects show the ways that tracked participants negotiate and navigate structures of politics, economy, and the concrete landscape through their movements. *Souvenir* shows that the farmer's plowing is highly choreographed in order to make the most profit out of the land: the field and its furrows are optimized in order to maximize the amount of crops per field. *NomadicMILK* shows that PEAK truck drivers are part of a centralized distribution system leading them onto even the smallest roads, but also that this system only functions because the driver is able to improvise through the unpredictable landscape. Similarly, the movements of the Fulani herdsmen are affected by structural issues: as nomads, they traditionally go where the cows go, but, for instance, the availability of processed milk has changed the cultural view on nomadic cows. And with the increasing focus on the value of land, herdsmen now also have to navigate between permitted and forbidden routes. Both projects thus address how global structures influence everyday actions and cultures even if the participants are not explicitly aware of this in the moments when they move. In this sense, the milk in Nigeria becomes a carrier of hidden stories about everyday spatial narratives just like *MILK project*'s Dutch-style European cheese shows how everyday movements of people, animals, and goods are the backbone of the globalized economy. But participants are only able to see this pattern and "read" the story when they have access to the full picture, which few people have.

Most of *NomadicMILK*'s audience has no frame of reference to the Nigerian landscape, which is why Polak provides plenty of information on the Nigerian cultural history of milk. But even though we see every detail in the participants' moves, the distance in both culture and miles makes it difficult to understand the movement patterns in any other way than a very generic one. In this way, the project shows how everything is connected through the same exchange flows and, unless you know a place very well, everything can only be understood as part of a generic pattern. Koolhaas's generic view belongs to the tourist. In many ways, this gaze is similar to the tourist's gaze in *Souvenir*: primarily based on distant and distancing preconceptions. A similar dynamic is visible in *NomadicMILK*: even though the maps and stories visualize highly embodied spatial movements, and even if viewers are provided with information about the context, they are left with few references through which they can internalize the movement visualizations if they have had little or no exposure to African reality. In that sense, the participants' movements in *NomadicMILK* are hard to comprehend in other ways than the generic idea of the African land and life. The paths drawn by *NomadicMILK* are hard not to read as paths that could have been made anywhere, anytime, and by anyone.

Lastly, Koolhaas's thoughts of generic globalization provide a framework for understanding what is also at stake in *NomadicMILK*: a story about the impact of globalization on ways of life. In the generic economy, everything is already or is about to become a commodity. This is true for Nigeria's milk culture, as it slowly changes from a local and particular structure to a generic structure where milk is a processed staple being distributed from center to periphery in a preplanned pattern. Nigerian dairy distribution can and should be understood within the framework of dairy distribution in other countries, especially because the PEAK milk is itself "migratory," as it is made from Dutch milk powder transported by boat from the Netherlands to Nigeria. In this way, the nomadic narrative has shifted from describing a certain way of life to describing a particular economic pattern, where goods and capital move freely around the world looking for "greener pastures."

Conclusion

Viewed as a collection of projects, Polak's artistic practice highlights that every movement in space is imbued with private narratives as well as with the influence of global trends, structures, and movements. In every single project, we see a particular pattern of attachment (which directly relates to Teodor Mitew's distinction between different types of mappings),[27] but I have argued that Polak makes different things visible to different types of viewers. The narrative that the GPS receiver makes available for readers depends on whether you are a tracked participant or an outside viewer. Additionally, Polak's artistic practice also shows that the particular and the generic are tightly connected; even though people see different things, it is possible to "read" and "write" simultaneously with mobile tracking technologies (and a fitting artistic approach). In this sense, we can understand generic space—which is also about capitalist patterns making every place accessible to generic goods—as something that is made visible through particular acts of movement.

Projects like *NomadicMILK* thus embrace GPS technology as something that allows for concealed patterns of movement and capital to become explicit and available for public scrutiny. This is one of the aspects that Polak investigates by using mobile GPS receivers to track, store, and later replay the everyday movement patterns of individuals who, in de Certeau's terms, produce space as they make use of it. Also, Polak's artistic practice clearly has a political aspect—even if she understates this by rarely mentioning political motives and by barely bringing it up in the exhibition contexts. I have argued here that all of her projects deal with the political dimensions of how individual actions are always tightly interwoven with larger societal structures, and if we look at her artistic practice in total, we can see that she shows that this pattern is repeated everywhere. Basically, it is possible to see her projects as a way of investigating the spatial narratives of the individual with the help of mobile technologies and subsequently highlighting how each everyday practice is a result of strategic structures and tactical embodiment thereof, be it in Latvia, Nigeria, or the Netherlands.

Notes

1. Mary Flanagan, "Locating Play and Politics: Real World Games & Activism," *Leonardo Electronic Almanac* 16, no. 2–3 (2007): 5.
2. Simon Sadler, *The Situationist City* (Cambridge, MA, and London: MIT Press, 1998).
3. Flanagan, "Locating Play and Politics: Real World Games & Activism," 9.
4. Ibid.
5. Michel de Certeau, *The Practice of Everyday Life*, trans. Steven Rendall (Berkeley, CA: University of California Press, 2002).
6. Rem Koolhaas, "The Generic City," in *S,M,L, XL*, ed. Rem Koolhaas et al. (New York: Monacelli, 1998).
7. Esther Polak and Waag Society, "Amsterdam Realtime," http://realtime.waag.org/.
8. Esther Polak, "MILK project," http://milkproject.net.

9. "In the case of the *Souvenir* project the interaction is more intended to be between the local tourists and the visualization than on the farmers and their own tracks [. . .]" (Polak, 2008).

10. Esther Polak, "*Souvenir*: Explanation and monoprints," http://souvenirzeeland. wordpress.com/explanation-and-monoprints/.

11. Esther Polak, "NomadicMILK: The project," http://nomadicmilk.net/blog/?page_id=2.

12. Ibid.

13. Koolhaas, "The Generic City," 1253.

14. Ibid., 1248.

15. Ibid., 1251.

16. Ibid., 1250.

17. Ibid., 1263.

18. Flanagan, "Locating Play and Politics: Real World Games & Activism."

19. Richard Prouty, "Buying Generic: The Generic City in Dubai," *Static* 8 (2009): 7.

20. Michele Chang and Elizabeth Goodman, "Asphalt Games: Enacting Place Through Locative Media," *Leonardo Electronic Almanac* 14, no. 3/4 (2006).

21. De Certeau, *The Practice of Everyday Life.*

22. As Rowan Wilken notes, the terms "place" and "space" have a "lack of definitional clarity and precision," which is often confusing. In, for instance, Yi-Fu Tuan's distinction between space and place, place is the embodied location, whereas Michel de Certeau uses the same two words in the exact opposite way. For the rest of this chapter, however, I will stick to de Certeau's terms, as he is my primary source, in which case Chang and Goodman's argument in the previous paragraph would have been that living and acting in a location is what constructs a "space." See Rowan Wilken, "From Stabilitas Loci to Mobilitas Loci: Networked Mobility and the Transformation of Place," *Fibreculture Journal* 6 (2005), http://six.fibreculturejournal.org/fcj-036-from-stabilitas-loci-to-mobilitas-loci-networked-mobility-and-the-transformation-of-place/ and Yi-Fu Tuan, *Space and Place: The Perspective of Experience* (London: Edward Arnold Ltd., 1977).

23. De Certeau, The Practice of Everyday Life, 93.

24. Ibid., 97.

25. See e.g., David Pinder, "Subverting Cartography: The Situationists and Maps of the City," *Environment and Planning A* 28, no. 3 (1996): 405–427; Frank Mort, "Cityscapes: Consumption, Masculinities and the Mapping of London since 1950," *Urban Studies* 35, no. 5–6 (1998): 889–907.

26. See e.g., Scott W. Ruston, "Storyworlds on the Move: Mobile Media and Their Implications for Narrative," *StoryWorlds: A Journal of Narrative Studies* 2 (2010): 101–120; Teodor Mitew, "Repopulating the Map: Why Subjects and Things Are Never Alone," *Fibreculture Journal*, no. 13 (2008).

27. Teodor Mitew, "Repopulating the Map."

10

ON COMMON GROUND

Here as There

Paula Levine

> *How do the examples in this chapter help us understand the practice of story-telling in the mobile media age?*

Many mobile and locative media projects testify to the power of these emerging wireless and networked systems to introduce narrative as a way to augment, annotate, or add historical richness to public spaces. These projects transform participants into story bearers who keep the narratives of the unique character, histories, and local experiences of a place alive. But there is also the potential for mobile and locative media to change one's relationship to a place by introducing distant events or circumstances onto local spaces and making events that are happening elsewhere highly relevant to the immediate, local space. This chapter discusses works that map temporal and geospatial shifts to create a spatial layering that offers viewers a distinct sense of juxtaposition and dissonance. These clashes are important opportunities to form new narratives. Ultimately, these narratives can be potentially more expansive experiences where empathy can play a prominent role.

Keywords

- **Empathic narratives:** Empathy, unlike sympathy, allows one to feel a deep connection to a feeling or event as if it was happening to him or her. While sympathy allows a person to feel a sense of mourning or loss for another, empathy puts the person in another person's shoes. Empathic narratives thus develop stories that encourage this level of identification with the experiences and feelings that are happening to someone else.
- **Tactical media:** The artistic practice of producing media that engage with—and ultimately critique—the dominant power structures. Tactical media tend to engage with a politics of disruption, politics that typically "supplement but

[do] not displace other forms, modes, and practices . . . [like] refusal, destructivity, cyberactivism, and hacktivism," as Rita Raley notes.[1]

- **Spatial dissonance:** Drawing from the concept of "cognitive dissonance," spatial dissonance is the experience of two contradictory spaces (or ideas about a space). This juxtaposition of spaces—often the distant mapped onto the local—must be held in mind, for example, when information about that space stands in conflict with the local and personal experiences of that space.

Introduction

Many mobile and locative media projects testify to the power of technology to introduce narrative as a way to augment, annotate, or add historical richness to public spaces. Some important examples have included the following: *34 North, 118 West* (2002), which overlaid audio stories of local histories, bringing life back to a vacant downtown Los Angeles lot near the Freight Depot station;[2] *'Scape the Hood* (2005), which brought to light diverse and unique local characteristics within three blocks in San Francisco's South of Market neighborhood using audio and graphics delivered via Hewlett-Packard's *Ipaq* and *Mscape* platforms;[3] and *[murmur]* (2007), an aural history project that embedded stories within the city, which were accessed via cell phones using phone numbers publicly posted in the places described.[4] These projects are among many others that use mobile media to mix *now* with *then*, bringing hidden histories and stories of a place to the surface. In doing so, these projects transform participants into story bearers who keep the distinctive, local character and collectively shared experiences of place alive.

In addition to reseeding local histories and stories in areas of the city, mobile and locative media can collapse geographies to mix *here* with *there*, introducing events or circumstances into locations they would not normally be. This less common mobile experience inventively collapses geographic spaces, ignoring boundaries, borders, and coordinates that anchor geographies. Projects of this kind rely upon participants to narrate their way between (and through) the dissonances created by the spatial layering of a distant place onto a local space. By narrating pathways among the geospatial-temporal gaps, participants forge links between familiar places and their relationships to events, locations, and circumstances that normally lie outside of the local borders. Like traveling in unfamiliar countries, these experiences can be opportunities to form new cross-cultural, historical, conceptual, or theoretical connections between local and global, in which empathy can emerge and play a more prominent role.

Local and Global, Near and Far

Wireless networks create a radically different kind of world from the one depicted by the seventeenth-century Cartesian coordinate system. Developed by

René Descartes, his system provided the framework of a globe made up of discrete, unique areas of geographical space mapped, measured, and anchored through a grid of x and y coordinates. Unlike the precise and mutually exclusive global space of Descartes system, the world today is a mix of physical space overlaid with digital data from anywhere at anytime, taking up residence in places it does not necessarily belong.[5] What is spatially and temporally far away can be experienced as close at hand; what is foreign can permeate domestic spaces.

In the early 1990s, cultural geographer Doreen Massey wrote of a time and space compression that was the result of a ramped-up world, characterized by transglobal movements and rapid communication.[6] Today, location-based mobile systems and tools combine with these global networks to add the component of geospatial simultaneity to the compression of time and space. The result is the enabling of place to be both local and global at the same time.

Empathy and Space

Our daily spaces, a changing mix of physical and virtual, are radically altering how we live, work, and respond to events and circumstances. These alterations modify our expectations and understandings of both geospatial and personal boundaries, as well as norms of public and private. Jeremy Rifken highlights the phenomena and sensations of living closer and closer to what once was geospatially and culturally distant, noting:

> [We are] brought together in an ever closer embrace and are increasingly exposed to each other in ways that are without precedent. . . . While the backlash of globalization—the xenophobia, political populism, and terrorist activity—is widely reported, far less attention has been paid to the growing empathic extension, as hundreds of millions of people come in contact with diverse others. . . . Hundreds of millions of human beings have become part of a global floating Diaspora as the world transforms into a universal public square.[7]

At the time of this writing, the most recent example of events taking place in this universal public square is the "Youth Revolt," the viral civil disobedience and unrest that began in Tunisia and spread, thanks to social, mobile, and location-based media, through Saudi Arabia, Egypt, Yemen, Iraq, Bahrain, Libya, Syria, and elsewhere. Termed the first networked revolt,[8] this experience of global and local *in proximity* creates an open field in which new directions and possibilities emerge for exploring empathy: the capacity to extend one's connection to another, beyond sympathy, on a global scale. It may be a step toward imagining how, as Susan Sontag described, "in situations of war or murderous politics . . . our privileges [may be] located on the same map as [the] suffering [of others]."[9]

Narrative, Experience, and Knowledge

As we rewrite the spaces in which we live with these new tools, systems, and devices, we are also inventing the language to convey these experiences—speaking and writing our ways through newly forming hybrid territories that combine informational and physical spaces.[10] At the core of this rewriting of space is narrative practice. Hayden White traces the etymological roots threading *narrative* to *experience, knowledge, skill, knowing,* and *expert.* He roots *narrative* in the Sanskrit word *narro,* meaning *to tell,* and *gna,* meaning *to know.*[11]

The connections among *experience, knowledge,* and *telling what one knows* through narrative are profound. White maps the flow from "experiencing something" to "narrative" as the way one navigates through situations presented in the moment, with no overarching, privileged knowledge of what is to come.[12] The best one can do is to tell the story as one goes, making connections in the face of prevailing circumstances, step by step, as each event presents itself. Such was the situation in 2003 while I was facing the unfolding of events that ultimately led to the U.S. invasion of Baghdad, and the news that we had just gone to war in Iraq.

March 20, 2003 . . .

> . . . *It began one night when bombs and missiles were dropping 7,000 miles from where I sat, and yet I could (almost) feel them falling in my backyard.*

The United States was threatening to bomb Iraq. It seemed too preposterous to be true, yet there was a growing fear and panic at the possibility that it would happen. During the night and the following early morning, I searched the Web, read blogs from around the world; emailed friends, colleagues, and others I encountered online; watched events on my computer; and listened to broadcasts on my FM radio. I collected images from online sites of people in Paris, Jerusalem, Baghdad, Washington, New York, Tel Aviv, Toronto, and other cities where they were holding peace vigils, lighting candles, demonstrating, and praying. In spite of distances, we connected, sharing the same moments, waiting, watching, and fearing the worst.

Throughout the long day and night, intensity rose in stark contrast to a calm sky and the still trees outside my window, as two cities—San Francisco and Baghdad—geographically far apart, drew closer together. Flashes of lights from bombs and missiles didn't illuminate the sky outside my studio window, but events taking place over 7,000 miles away felt palpable.

The invasion was local.

I was reminded of a contrasting experience, watching television coverage of the devastation caused by the 1989 Lomo Prieta San Francisco Bay earthquake. Living in San Francisco, I began as a passive observer seeing the evidence through the restricting eye of televised news coverage. In frustration, I became a participating observer. I got on my bicycle and rode through the city to see the damage, and actively witnessed the aftermath of the event.

Fourteen years later, on the eve of the Baghdad invasion, a new combination of media had reinvented the *witness* as one who is able to connect and share perspectives with others—globally, and often simultaneously—beyond the borders of our individual cultures and geographies.

Shadows from Another Place: San Francisco <-> Baghdad

This powerful sensation of collapsed distances on the night of the U.S. invasion of Baghdad forged a common ground. In the series of web-based projects, *Shadows from Another Place* (2004),[13] I use this experience as a template to reframe common, familiar, everyday spaces as contested sites—sites that help us to investigate and critique the impact of distant events on our local places. *San Francisco <-> Baghdad*, the first project in the series, examines the relative impact of the U.S. invasion of Baghdad by overlaying the sites of bombs and missiles in Baghdad onto a map of San Francisco, documenting each mirrored site with photographs, maps, and GPS coordinates—the same technologies the U.S. military used to target initial sites in Baghdad.

Small geocaches are embedded at each San Francisco site for people with GPS devices to find.[14] The caches held copies of "The Iraq War-Roll Call of the U.S. Dead: Day by Day, Death by Death" by Warren Harkavy,[15] a compilation of all U.S. service personnel who died in the war between May 1, 2003 and March 19, 2004,[16] including their names, home city and state, age, dates of death, and details on how they died.[17] Bridging between the loss of one life and many, Harkavy's compilation approached each loss as singular, intimate, and profound, as both individual and collective. He allowed us to imagine the impact of loss in both granular and global scale: loss within families, local communities, and the nation, and how all are "unmade" through each single death.[18]

San Francisco <-> Baghdad juxtaposes two unrelated cities to visualize the impact of the invasion that took place in one location upon the other. Designed as a website using GPS coordinates and GPS devices to connect the two cities, the shadowed targets of bombs and missiles bridge physical and virtual spaces. Accessible via laptops and other portable devices that allow Flash, the work employs a spatial version of cognitive dissonance through the invasion seen in local terms, with local implications.

Spatial Dissonance

To get hold of something by means of its likeness. . . . A palpable, sensuous, connection between the body of the perceiver and the perceived . . . the nature of their interrelationship remains obscure and fertile ground for wild imagining—once one is jerked out of the complacencies of common sense-habits.

—*Michael Taussig*[19]

Cognitive dissonance describes a state of mind that arises when two contradictory ideas must be held in mind—for example, when information that is presented stands in conflict with strongly held beliefs. Some theories suggest that we attempt to move away from this state of contradiction by turning away from the new information presented to return to the safety and familiarity of beliefs we previously held. This conflict can also apply to the ways we think about (and practice) our relationship to space and place.

Regardless of whether the change is permanent or temporary, dissonance creates a rupture of—or a departure from—what is expected. Applying dissonance as a strategy has been used in many avant-garde practices. For example, the Surrealists' *exquisite corpse,* a method for creating compositions or drawings by having each person contribute in succession a portion without full knowledge of what has come before, challenged representational conventions of the body by drawing on both imagination and chance to introduce surprising corporeal components and configurations. The Situationists' 1955 revised map of Paris used *dérive,* or drift, to radically reconfigure La Ville-Lumière/The City of Light, constructing a map of the city based on the wanderer's experience of place rather than its conventionally designated geography.[20] Such interventions defamiliarize and sever the conventional relationships to that which is familiar, whether it be language, objects, or places.[21]

The value of such ruptures became the focus of research conducted by psychology professor Charlan Nemeth from U.C. Berkeley who concluded that "no role playing technique stimulates divergent thinking as does authentic dissent."[22] Nemeth's experiment involved introducing a dissenting voice within an experimental group of people who were told to identify the color seen on projected slides. A research assistant was planted in the group and was instructed to periodically call out the incorrect color (e.g., yellow for red).

> After a few minutes, the group was then asked to free-associate on these same colors. The results were impressive: Groups in the "dissent condition"—these were the people exposed to inaccurate descriptions—came up with much more original associations. Instead of saying that "blue" reminded them of "sky," or that "green" made them think of "grass," they were able to expand their loom of associations, so that "blue" might trigger thoughts of "Miles Davis" and "smurfs" and "pie." The obvious answer had stopped being their only answer.[23]

With locative and mobile media, the readily available virtual information "up there" allows new possibilities for configuring experiences in the physical, public space "down here" that can become an opportunity to reshape experiences in which viewers see things differently on the ground.[24] This tactic relates to *San Francisco <-> Baghdad*, where familiar, benign locations became virtual target sites, mapped in relation to actual target sites. It also characterizes the following three projects I will discuss, where relocating, to scale, the Gulf Oil Spill or a portion of the wall in the West Bank anywhere in the world, or making the Berlin Wall reappear *in situ* remakes public space through the combination of digital information with everyday physical surroundings. These projects thus create spatial dissonance: environments in which one spatially experiences uncanny contradictions, which can open up to new narrative views.

The Gulf Oil Spill

Paul Rademacher's *The Gulf Oil Spill* (2010) overlays the spill in the Gulf of Mexico to scale on disparate, otherwise untouched geographic locations in order to bring the equivalent impact of the spill home.[25] BP's Deepwater Horizon oil spill began in April 2010 and continued for three months until the spill was capped. The final estimate of the volume of oil spilled into the Gulf of Mexico was in the neighborhood of about 4.9 million barrels or 205.8 million gallons (776 million liters).[26] The very enormity of the spill dwarfed the capacity of conventional forms of news reporting to effectively convey scale and impact. This inability to bridge the gap between the event and its consequences was Rademacher's point of departure.

Rademacher's *The Gulf Oil Spill* is a mashup, combining data from various sources into one web location.[27] Rademacher used Google Earth's API and its 3D visualization capacity to overlay the spill onto any location in the world a viewer selects.[28] Participants type in the name of a city, and Google Earth "flies" them directly to that location, where they see the spill superimposed on that area, to scale.

The Gulf Oil Spill visualizes the impossible, the "what if" consequences of the environmental disaster translated through individual associations and connections to place. Viewers can sit in a physical location and see the impact of the spill around them with an uncanny immediacy of the emergent effects upon the surrounding, albeit untouched landscape.[29] Incompatibility becomes a new spatial logic that appears in the form of a disruptively powerful graphic linking environmental uncertainty to an otherwise unrelated place.

The Berlin Wall

The Berlin Wall by Marc Rene Gárdeya, an augmented reality, locative, and mobile media experience, casts a similar spatial tension by resurrecting the presence of the Berlin Wall in the same location it once stood.[30] Using a mobile phone, GPS system, and Layar (a free downloadable browser available for Android, iPhone and, most recently, Blackberry platforms), people standing at the wall's original

Figure 10.1 Image of *The Berlin Wall* project running on an iPhone. The project uses augmented reality to layer the Berlin Wall onto the site where it once stood. © Marc Rene Gárdeya. Image used by permission.

site can see the Berlin Wall on their cell phone screen, overlaid on the physical location before them (see Figure 10.1).[31] In a horizontal pan with a cell phone, the wall appears roughly to scale in the place it once stood, between the time of its construction in 1961 and its deconstruction in 1989, when the East German government opened access for citizens to West Berlin and West Germany.

Augmented reality (AR), a term coined by Tom Caudell and David Mizell in 1991, combines virtual and real-world environments, where the former enhances or augments the experience and presence of the latter. Existing in real time, the combination of physical and virtual fuses new spaces of real and imagined.[32] The augmented reality version showing a portion of the ninety-six mile wall appears like a specter still haunting the previous boundary of the city. *The Berlin Wall* makes the past visible again, bridging between now and then, for those whose lives were shaped by this structure and for those who lives were not. AR creates a presence that the body can respond to, opening all viewers to a powerful visceral comprehension of the wall's presence and authority, which, for twenty-eight years, constituted the boundary between the two worlds of East and West Berlin.

TheWall-TheWorld

TheWall-TheWorld (2011), a project in the series that I created, *Shadows from Another Place*, explores the impact of a fifteen-mile segment of the security fence in the West Bank while allowing participants to traverse the security barrier, both in its site of origin and, at the same time, in any city he or she chooses.[33] Accessing the work via its website, a participant types in the name of a city and Google Earth travels to that location. On the left side of the screen, the security wall appears in the West Bank; on the right side of the screen, the wall is overlaid onto the viewer's selected location. The participant navigates and explores the impact in both areas simultaneously.

Known by many adjectives including the *barrier wall*, *separation fence*, *security fence*, and *separation wall*, the West Bank security wall has been a contentious project since Israel began construction in 2002.[34] It is a sinuous concrete structure that winds from north to south, east to west, of a height that varies from eighteen to twenty-one feet. Originally proposed as a solution to the onslaught of public attacks by suicide bombers in buses, cafes, and other crowded public areas that riddled Israel in the ten years prior to breaking ground on the West Bank security wall, the structure now runs about 400 miles in length, within a country of about 270 miles from north to south. In spite of differences of cultures, histories, local economies, or politics, the West Bank wall radically alters daily life, both in its place of origin and in any site on which its shadow falls.

The Wall-The World utilizes the Web and Google Earth to imagine the impact of the structure in local terms, on local ground. Accessible via devices compatible with Google Earth's website plugin, users can explore the impact of the structure onscreen in the West Bank, and *in situ* in viewer-selected locations, changing what is familiar into "something that provokes disquiet because of its absolute proximity."[35] Drawing from the aforementioned work of Paul Rademacher,[36] and working with Canadian programmer Christopher Zimmerman, *The Wall-The World* bridges there and here, enabling a simultaneous bilocational view where each turn and twist occurs in parallel, on each respective ground. "Unable to visit my sister in Maryland," emailed one colleague beta-tester. "I travel three hours instead of a half-hour each way to get to and from work," said another.

The Transborder Immigrant Tool

> *Can't we rethink our sense of place? Is it not possible for a sense of place to be progressive; not self-closing and defensive, but outward-looking?*
> —*Doreen Massey*[37]

Places do not have "boundaries." According to Doreen Massey, they are always infusions of elsewhere. For instance, my neighborhood in San Francisco takes its shape and character from the Korean owner of the corner store, the cafe owner from Jordan, the cheese shop owner from Lebanon, the Filipino family that owns the frozen yogurt store (they sell a fabulous *lugao*-rice congee), my neighbors from Ireland, Sweden, Indiana, Vancouver, and New York. Massey writes that the definition of place is not usefully determined by the didactic inside/local/us and outside/global/them. Indeed, she contends, such a model can problematize difference and separation and lead to "certain forms of nationalism, sentimentalized recovering of sanitized 'heritages,' and outright antagonism to newcomers and 'outsiders.'"[38]

The Transborder Immigrant Tool brings attention to such conflicts taking place daily along the border between the U.S. and Mexico. Exacerbated by transborder economics and by the politics of the drug trade, the border has become a highly contentious territory, separated by a physical and technologically guarded wall.[39] San Diego, California, lies about fifteen miles from the California-Mexico border crossing at Tijuana, Mexico. This area is steeped in a history and culture infused by its geographic proximity and proliferating tensions relating to the U.S.-Mexico international border, where the conflict between "penetrability and vulnerability"[40] is enacted daily. South of the San Diego-Tijuana crossing and to the east is largely desert. Extreme temperatures of heat in some areas and cold in others make crossing dangerous and, too often, fatal for those attempting to make the journey. This extended territory is marked by a fence that runs about 600 miles and that spans, at the time of this writing, about 30% of the entire 2,000-mile border between the United States and Mexico.

The Transborder Immigrant Tool is a collaboration among five artists and writers: Micha Cardenas, Amy Sara Carroll, Ricardo Dominguez, Elle Mehrmand, and Brett Stalbaum.[41] Many of them live and work in San Diego. With roots in conceptual art and earlier activist projects relating to the Electronic Disturbance Theatre in the 1990s, *The Transborder Immigrant Tool* emerged out of discussions on how to use inexpensive and available consumer platforms to address and solve current pressing issues. The artist collective designed the tool from the ground up as a humanitarian response arising from what they saw as an urgent need to create a space of safety and "hospitality." Using off-the-shelf cell phones, the artists developed an application designed to lead travellers to existing water safety stations during the last mile of their journey through the desert (see Figure 10.2). The artists aim to develop content, verify data and maps, and foster a system of distribution and training in collaboration with border agencies and humanitarian workers.

The Transborder Immigrant Tool has evoked tremendous controversy and has been the subject of many critical reviews, some of which are chronicled on the *Transborder Immigrant Tool* website. According to Amy Sara Carroll, "Anytime it's been on media coverage . . . or sometimes if we do presentations, we get hate mail and death threats."[42] Ricardo Dominguez was put on temporary suspension from his tenure-track teaching position at the University of California, San Diego, during a university investigation of the project.

Brett Stalbaum distinguished between the intended design of the tool and common misperceptions. "When people think of GPS," explained Stalbaum, "it suggests a turn-by-turn metaphor. So when they hear on the news that this is a project that will 'give GPS to illegals,' I often think to myself that what people hear is that we are giving them something like a Garmin or a Tomtom that's going to help them go through the desert and help them arrive directly at a workplace to take peoples' jobs." The tool, he emphasized, is designed as "a last-mile design to help people who are suffering with difficulties due to exhaustion, fatigue and dehydration, . . . to find an emergency safety site."[43]

Figure 10.2 A billboard for the *Transborder Immigrant Tool* project. The project used off-the-shelf cell phones to help those crossing the U.S.-Mexico border find water stations in the desert, as well as access poetry during their journey. © Brett Stalbaum. Image used by permission.

The tool features both bread and roses[44]—safety information as well as poetry, delivered in Spanish and other languages.[45] "People ask, why do they need poetry on this?" says Carroll. "The aesthetic matters. One of the things we notice time and again was the dehumanization of migrants. . . . By intervening and insisting on offering the gesture of poetry is also to insist on humanity for the crosser."[46]

In addition to reminding people of the crossers' humanity, including poetry is a radical act, for it is a radical form that refuses to remain within the boundaries of standard, conventional language. Poetry is not restricted by grammatical laws of exactitude and can carry affect and sentiments uncontained by conventions of written and conversational exchanges. A poem, like a narrative, creates its own space not unlike the transitional spaces of crossings from Mexico to the United States—full of risk and danger lying outside of prescribed boundaries and borders.

Doreen Massey's description of place as a process relates directly to the circumstances along the U.S.-Mexican border where the politics of national borders give rise to spatial enactment of conflict and struggle on a daily basis. *The Transborder Immigrant Tool* creates a lens through which this contested geographic space is made visible and where conflicting narratives fight for dominance. The tool does not aim to resolve the conflict; rather it introduces and reminds people of *hospitality*, a compassionate reaching out as an action of inclusion that has been a nationally identifying gesture embedded deeply within narratives of U.S. history. These narratives acquire heightened significance within the context of the complex border politics and overarching political resonances. *The Transborder Immigrant Tool* spatializes the polemics that characterize border issues, and makes visible the cost of these conflicts in terms of ethics, humanity, and the costs of human lives.

Empathy, Narrative, and Neuroplasticity

[The] planet itself has become everyone's backyard.

—*Jeremy Rifken*[47]

Current medical imaging technologies and research are putting states of affect on a scientific map, literally mapping the reactions of our brains in states of empathy and compassion.[48] According to Dr. Richard Davidson, a research psychologist from the University of Wisconsin, the brain is an organ built to respond to experiences, and these experiences produce more changes in the brain than behavior or mental interventions, "more changes than medications or any other means."[49] Dr. Davidson's work is in a field he helped to shape, that of *neuroplasticity*, which focuses on the capacity of the brain to rewire itself. Davidson has explored this specifically in relation to the study of structural changes within the brain as it responds to experiences such as meditation. "We can make a choice between allowing the forces to continue to impact our brains willy-nilly," Davidson states, "or we can take a more active responsibility in shaping our brain in ways to promote more positive experiences."[50]

At the same time, emerging location-based and mobile technologies are constructing new geographies and territories formed through new interconnections and lived experiences of proximity that reshape the daily spaces in which we live. If current research on neuroplasticity is correct, perhaps augmented reality and other location-based experiences can potentially have deep physiological and neurological impact well beyond that of entertainment and spectacle, leading to new bridges between ourselves and others, whose lives and circumstances exist well outside of our own. Moreover, as we rewrite these spaces with new locative and mobile tools, Davidson's current research suggests that we, in turn, may also be rewriting *ourselves*, as these new experiences have the potential to change our internal, as well as our external, spaces.

Only our imagination limits what is possible in these newly forming territories brought into existence through new wireless technologies, interconnectivity, and location-aware systems. What shape our experiences will take in light of these emerging technologies and modes of interconnectivity is ultimately still an open question.

Narrative assists us in speaking and writing our way toward some greater understanding of the spatially radical and the rapid changes taking place where there is no central or overarching discourse to work our way through. Whether used as a strategy or a practice, narrative is the translation of these new geospatial experiences into a form that can be understood, conveyed, and "assimilable to structures of meaning," as Hayden White has noted.[51] These ideas fit with an important quote from writer and artist George Perec: "[T]he earth is a form of writing, a *geography* of which we had forgotten that we ourselves are the authors."[52]

Acknowledgments

The author gratefully acknowledges Stephanie Ellis, J. David Frankel, Carol Gigliotti, and Jan Peacock for their generous contributions to this article by way of comments and suggestions.

Notes

1. Rita Raley, *Tactical Media* (Minneapolis, MN: University of Minnesota Press, 2009), 25.
2. See http://34n118w.net/34N/.
3. 'Scape the Hood featured *Project Artaud*, a 37-year-old artist-run studio and housing collaborative; *Land & History*, revealing early ecological and cultural history prior to the overlay of the city (http://www.locative-media.org/projects/C89/); and the lively Saturday-only community-run *Mission Village Flea Market*. See http://www.locative-media.org/projects/C83.
4. See http://murmurtoronto.ca/.
5. As Michel de Certeau wrote, "Like those birds that lay their eggs only in other species' nests, memory produces in a place that does not belong to it." Michel de Certeau, *The Practice of Everyday Life* (Los Angeles, CA: University of California Press, 2002), 86.
6. Doreen Massey, *Space, Place, and Gender* (Minneapolis, MN: University of Minnesota Press, 1994), 147.
7. Jeremy Rifken, The Empathic Civilization: The Race to Global Consciousness in a World in Crisis (New York: Penguin, 2009), 425.
8. "Unrest in the Middle East and Africa—Country by Country," *CNN World*, March 9, 2011, http://www.cnn.com/2011/WORLD/meast/02/23/mideast.africa.unrest/index.html.
9. Susan Sontag, *Regarding the Pain of Others* (New York: Picador, 2004), 103.
10. André Lemos, "Locative Media in Brazil," *WI: Journal of Mobile Media* (Summer, 2009), http://wi.hexagram.ca/?p=60.
11. Hayden White, "The Value of Narrativity in the Representation of Reality," in *On Narrative*, ed. W.J.T. Mitchell (Chicago: University of Chicago Press, 1981), 1.
12. Ibid.
13. See http://shadowsfromanotherplace.net.
14. Geocaching, a worldwide treasure hunt that began in 2000, involves planting and finding caches—small containers or objects located by GPS coordinates listed on a centralized geocaching website. Cashes are now estimated to be over 1.5 million worldwide. See http://www.geocaching.com.

15. Ward Harkavy, "Day by Day, Death by Death" *The Village Voice*, March 16, 2004, http://www.villagevoice.com/2004-03-16/news/day-by-day-death-by-death/. The compilation of deaths is no longer available on this site; however, it can be fully downloaded from http://shadowsfromanotherplace.net. It has also been reprinted at http://www.globalsecurity.org/org/news/2004/040422-death-chronology.htm.

16. The significance of the two dates are as follows: On May 1st, 2003, President George W. Bush declared, "Major combat operations in Iraq have ended. In the battle of Iraq, the United States and our allies have prevailed." On March 19, 2004, President Bush gave the address, "One Year After Operation Iraqi Freedom," Washington, D.C., http://www.presidentialrhetoric.com/speeches/03.19.04.html.

17. Two examples from "Death by Death": "A private first class is killed when his convoy is hit by a homemade bomb and small-artillery [Stephen E. Wyatt, 19, Kilgore TX]; A specialist and a private first class are killed when an Iraqi garbage truck swerves out of control, rolls over, and lands atop their Hummer. [Douglas J. Weismantie, 28 Pittsburgh PA, Jose Casanova, 23, El Monte CA]." Harkavay's list suggests Homer's similarly detailed descriptions of death in the *Illiad*, both for fallen Trojan and Greek soldiers.

18. Elaine Scarry powerfully conveys the profound consequences of the loss of lives in wars and deaths, what she describes as the "the emptying of the nation" as it resides within each wounded or dying body. The specifics of loss in terms of knowledge, skills, memories, within communities, "all are deconstructed along with the tissue itself, the sentient source and site of all learning." Elaine Scarry, *The Body in Pain: The Making and Unmaking of the World* (New York: Oxford University Press, 1985), 122–123.

19. Michael Taussing, *Mimesis and Alterity: A Particular History of the Senses* (New York: Routledge, 1992), 21.

20. Guy Debord, "Psychogeographic Guide of Paris," ed. the Bauhaus Imaginiste, 1952, http://imaginarymuseum.org/LPG/Mapsitu1.htm.

21. For example, see defamiliarization strategies within Surrealism, Fluxus, and Conceptual Art; Freud's writing on the uncanny, exploring sensations an unfamiliar presence within familiar spaces; or writing by Viktor Shklovsky, an early twentieth-century literary critic, on "ostranenie," or "estrangement," as a way to "impart the sensation of things as they are perceived and not as they are known," Shklovsky, "Art as Technique," in *Modern Criticism and Theory: A Reader*, ed. David Lodge (London: Longmans, 1988), 12.

22. Carlan Nemeth and Jack A. Goncalo, "Rogues and Heroes: Finding Value in Dissent," in *Rebels in Groups: Dissent, Deviance, Difference and Defiance*, ed. Jolanda Jetten and Matthew J. Hornsey (Oxford: Wiley-Blackwell, 2011).

23. Jason Lehrer, "Twitter Strangers," *The Frontal Cortex*, http://scienceblogs.com/cortex/2010/07/20/twitter-strangers/.

24. Lemos, "Locative Media in Brazil."

25. See http://paulrademacher.com/oilspill/.

26. Maureen Hoch, "New Estimate Puts Gulf Oil Leak at 205 Million Gallons," *PBS NewsHour*, August 2, 2010, http://www.pbs.org/newshour/rundown/2010/08/new-estimate-puts-oil-leak-at-49-million-barrels.html.

27. A recent development, mashups combine multiple data sources into a single website. They are made possible thanks to application programming interfaces (API) first introduced in 2005 by Paul Rademacher in a site called HousingMaps.org. Rademacher brought together Bay Area real estate data and geospatial data to create an always current snapshot of the Bay Area's housing market. Rademacher initiated the idea that "anyone could create a map and put data on it," which was then "pretty foreign." Google Maps released their first web-based API in 2005, allowing data to be shared

across applications, giving rise to a generation of websites featuring both automatically updating content and collective community-contributed data, like Photobucket and Flickr. Rademacher estimates there may now be up to 400,000 API sites, which indicates "a huge need for personalized maps." Paul Rademacher, telephone interview with the author, January 21, 2011.

28. For information on Google Earth's API, see http://code.google.com/apis/earth.

29. Mobile access requires compatibility with Google Earth's API on Windows or Mac. At the time of this writing, Android, iPhone, and Palm are not supported.

30. See http://www.hoppala-agency.com/article/berlin-wall-3d/ and http://site.layar.com/company/blog/the-berlin-wall-is-back/.

31. First released in July 2009, Layar is an application for content development and a viewing browser. At the time of this writing, Layar has become the platform for a wide range of new augmented reality releases for mobile devices, from utilitarian and commercial projects to games and art. Recent examples include: *Historic Market Street* (http://www.layar.com/layers/sanfranciscoquake1906/), which juxtaposes the 1905 pre-earthquake view of the Miles brothers' film, "A Trip down Market Street" with the present location; *Recovery* (http://sunlightlabs.com/blog/2009/recoverygov-contracts-your-phone/), which geolocates and spatially maps the federal government recovery funds to institutional and business recipients; *The Uninvited Guests in the Museum of Modern Art* (http://sndrv.nl/moma) by Sander Veenhof and Mark Skwarek, which is perhaps the first augmented reality guerilla intervention with 3D virtual artworks geolocated within MOMA.

32. For a prescient view of locative media and augmented reality, see the CNN interview of William Gibson by the late Robert Hilferty at http://www.youtube.com/watch?v=GXaU_FLaSzo.

33. See http://thewalltheworld.net.

34. For a current listing of names, see http://en.wikipedia.org/wiki/Israeli_West_Bank_barrier#Names_of_the_barrier.

35. Anthony Vidlar, *The Architectural Uncanny: Essays in the Modern Unhomely* (Cambridge, MA: MIT Press), 222.

36. Thanks to Paul Rademacher for permission to adapt his API code and make necessary changes for the *The Wall-The World* project.

37. Doreen Massey, *Space, Place and Gender* (Minneapolis, MN: University of Minnesota Press, 1994), 2.

38. Ibid., 147.

39. See http://post.thing.net/node/1642.

40. Massey, 155.

41. Contributing artists: Micha Cárdenas (Artist/Performer/Theorist/Lecturer), Amy Sara Carroll (Poet/Assistant Professor of Latina/o Studies, Program in American Culture and English Department, University of Michigan), Ricardo Dominguez (Artist/Professor, Department of Visual Arts, University of California, San Diego and Co-Founder of the Electronic Disturbance Theater), Elle Mehrmand (Performance/New Media Artist/Musician), and Brett Stalbaum (Artist/Researcher/Programmer/Lecturer, Deptartment of Visual Arts, University of California, San Diego).

42. Kinsee Morlan, "After the Storm," *San Diego City Beat*, September 8, 2010, http://www.sdcitybeat.com/sandiego/article-8159-after-the-storm.html.

43. Brett Stalbaum, telephone interview with author, December 12, 2010.

44. "Our lives shall not be sweated from birth until life closes; Hearts starve as well as bodies; bread and roses, bread and roses." Excerpt from the poem, "Bread and Roses," by

James Oppenheim, published in *The American Magazine*, December 1910. This poem has been part of labor, human rights, and feminist actions since its early association with the 1912 textile strike in Lawrence, Massachusetts, also known as the Bread and Roses Strike. Mimi Fariña set the poem to music in 1976.

45. Coordinated by contributing artist Elle Mehrmand.
46. Amy Sarah Carroll, telephone interview with author, December 12, 2010.
47. Rifken, *The Empathic Civilization*, 426.
48. "Although there has not been enough research on the difference in terms of brain function, we shouldn't lump them together. Empathy is typically understood as a mimicking or simulating the emotions of another person . . . in terms of pain. If another person is subject to a painful stimuli and we record the observer's brain activity . . . [and see] the pattern of activation in the brain of the observer that resembles what might show if he or she were subjected to the same painful stimulus. . . . In compassion, you see something totally different. Compassion does not involve the experience of the same emotion as another person. . . . Rather compassion involves the disposition to relieve suffering." Richard Davidson, telephone interview with the author, February 9, 2011.
49. Richard Davidson, "Transform Your Mind, Change Your Brain," *Google Tech Talk*, September 23, 2009, http://www.youtube.com/watch?v=7tRdDqXgsJ0.
50. Richard Davidson, interview by David Van Nuys, February 26, 2010, *Shrink Rap Radio*, http://www.shrinkrapradio.com/2010/02/26/231-%E2%80%93-the-meditating-brain-with-richard-davidson.
51. White, "The Value of Narrativity," xi.
52. George Perec, *The Species of Spaces* (New York: Penguin Classics, 1998), 79.

PART IV
Mobile Games

11

THE GEOCACHER AS PLACEMAKER

Remapping Reality through Location-Based Mobile Gameplay

Ben S. Bunting, Jr.

How do the examples in this chapter help us understand the practice of story-telling in the mobile media age?

By linking players' movements in the physical world to their accomplishments in virtual gameworlds, location-based mobile games (LBMGs) have quite liter-ally added a new dimension to in-game storytelling. Exploding the traditional boundaries of the TV screen and computer monitor, LBMGs allow a game's story to extend beyond the virtual. For example, during a gameplay session, the local Starbucks might become the site for a battle with an enemy wizard, or a lonely tree on the horizon might turn out to be the final resting place of a pair of star-crossed lovers murdered by a jealous prince. After the game is over, such resonances remain with the player, effectively mingling gameplay with everyday life. This meshing of the virtual and the physical is exemplified in the LBMG geocaching, and, specifically, the geocaching-based game *University of Death*. Ulti-mately, I argue that LBMGs represent the possibility for more engaging in-game narratives as well as more meaningful player-directed explorations of gameworlds by virtue of their ability to blur the line between the physical and the virtual.

Keywords

*   **Unmapping and Remapping:** Unmapping is the imaginative act of strip-ping a known place of its culturally determined "place-values" so as to make it explorable again, and potentially able to be remapped. Remapping is the act of inscribing new place-values onto an explored space. In the context of this essay, these acts are performed with the assistance of a location-aware interface during the play of a location-based mobile game.

- **Location-based mobile games:** These are games that take place in a hybrid gameworld that is a synthesis of physical and virtual space. Such hybridized gameplay is enabled by interfaces that use GPS technology to link the player's progress in the game to their position in and/or movement through physical space.
- **Geocaching:** A location-based mobile game in which players are provided with the GPS coordinates of a hidden container (a "cache") via a website or other means, and they then use a GPSr or other GPS-enabled mobile device to navigate to those coordinates and locate the cache. Once a player finds a particular cache, their achievement can be logged, both physically at the cache site in a pencil-and-paper logbook and virtually on websites such as Geocaching.com.

An Introduction: Pullman, Washington, June 2011

To geocache is to uncover an otherwise invisible layer of place. To close in on a cache's location only to find another person or group of people surreptitiously looking around while sneaking looks at a GPS receiver (GPSr) or mobile phone is to cross paths with fellow players who understand a shared language. Following GPS coordinates to a cache location can only get you so close, and within that last twenty or so feet there are subtle signs—ways of placing a cache common to many geocachers—that, with practice, you begin to see in the same way that a hunter sees the tracks of his prey. Your commute to work and your walk to the store are changed in small but irrevocable ways once you know that there is a cache behind the DO NOT ENTER sign or inside the bole of the biggest tree in the park.

My first cache—a box the size of an Altoids container with a miniature logbook and a golf pencil squeezed inside—was hidden behind an old, now-defunct public telephone kiosk along Wilson Road on the Washington State University campus. Like hundreds if not thousands of other students at the university, I walk past this spot nearly every day, and yet I am one of the very few who knows that there is a cache there, who stops now and then to make sure that it hasn't been vandalized or to read new entries in its logbook. This hidden layer of knowledge changes the way I relate to this place even when I'm not actively geocaching. Geocaching thus challenges me to look at familiar places in new ways, to find new value in old places, and to then use that value to redefine what I thought I knew about, say, an old telephone kiosk.

Once, Lindsey and I found a cache located quite literally fifty feet from the front door of an apartment in which I had once lived for three years. Following the GPS signal into what I had always imagined to be a rather unexceptional stand of trees, we instead found the entire rusted chassis and engine block of a 1920s-era automobile, with the cache hidden in the glove compartment. Clearly, the cache's creator was using the geocaching community to draw attention to this generally forgotten but amazing relic, something that I had never seen before despite having walked within twenty feet of it hundreds of times.

Similarly, during our first-ever visit to WSU's Tri-Cities campus, where I had recently been employed to teach for the upcoming academic year, we spent most of the afternoon geocaching.

One of the caches we found that day has since become one of my favorites: located in the desert scrub slightly off the campus's main road, it is enclosed in a small wooden box that can only be accessed by uncovering a trap door in the ground buried under a pile of rocks next to a skeletal tree. On that day, finding that particular cache and three others gave me the beginnings of a sense of place in a new city that might have otherwise taken me months to cultivate.

★★★

We began this particular day by setting ourselves the challenge of finding twenty caches in Pullman between breakfast and dinner, but as the day has worn on, we've slowly come to realize that we've bitten off more than we can chew. We've been at it for close to ten hours now, but the shadows are slanting, the sun is turning a ruddy orange, and we've only found nine caches so far. We decide to scramble to find one more cache before nightfall, though, partially for the joy of exploration and partially because ten sounds like a better "final score" than nine does.

Our search leads us to Paradise Street as it runs behind the downtown strip and then up a hill to the south along Spring Street, into a neighborhood that I'm passingly familiar with but haven't spent much time in. Like many of Pullman's more southerly neighborhoods, this one is almost forestlike, the sidewalks choked with old, stout trees, and the houses far back from the street, peeking timidly out from behind the foliage at lot-sized intervals. We follow the street for awhile, at times wandering and at times allowing ourselves to be guided by the arrow on the GPSr's screen. Despite the chill in the air imparted by the setting sun, it's still a pleasant enough evening for a walk that it takes a few minutes before I realize that we've actually been walking around and around a particular block, circling the cache location but never getting any closer to it.

The northern, southern, and western sides of the block are dotted with houses, and there's no clear point of ingress to be found anywhere. As we circle back around to the east side of the block, the desire to wrap things up before dark—when it becomes legitimately difficult to find well-hidden caches—overwhelms the appeal of freer, less-directed exploration, and I change the GPSr to "Navigation Mode." The mode locates us as heading south on Spring Street and suggests that we take a right on Jackson Street in five hundred feet. We continue walking south, keeping an eye out for a street on our right. Well before we reach the first such street, though, the GPSr beeps, warning us that we've somehow missed our turn. We double back, and after a bit of walking it beeps again, warning us that we've now passed the intersection while moving in the opposite direction. There's a "Jackson Street" to the east, but it doesn't continue through to the west, like it would have to for the GPSr's directions to make sense. Instead, there's just a wall of trees where the street is supposed to be.

Lindsey is the one who finally spots the path. It looks ancient, and is more the size of a deer trail than a human one. It turns off from the sidewalk and runs uphill into the trees in the exact direction that "Jackson Street" was supposed to run. It's odd: now that we've seen it, the path seems obvious, but we'd already walked past it twice while looking directly at it. It's not hard to imagine someone living in this neighborhood for years, driving down Spring Street every day on their way to work, and never knowing that this path was there. Of course, we follow it.

Almost immediately, we're under a thick canopy of deciduous trees in the full height of their summer leafing. It's darker here, and the ground, which isn't paved, is spongy despite the fact that it hasn't rained in days. The path quickly curves to the north, and the entrance to Spring Street disappears behind the trees. We proceed further up the muddy hill until we're suddenly surrounded on both sides by huge beds of wildflowers. It looks as if these were, at one point, human-planted beds that have since grown wildly out of control, and now they crowd the path so tightly that we have to walk one foot in front of the other, as if we're walking a tightrope, to avoid crushing them. The purples and blues of the flower petals clash strikingly with the greenery that otherwise encloses us, and we stop for a moment to take a few pictures and to admire the view.

Once we proceed past the flowerbeds we are, for a moment, surreally misplaced, thrust into an unexpected wilderness. The trees around us are arranged just so, in a way that blocks our view of the road to the east and of the houses and yards that otherwise surround us. For a moment, the only sounds are birdsong and the wind, and it's almost possible to believe that this "new" part of Pullman that we've "discovered" isn't part of Pullman at all. We stand still for a moment, unwilling to break the silence, both grinning like idiots. Then a car whirrs by on Spring Street, destroying the illusion, and we continue on up the slope, across what seems like it might be someone's driveway, and along the last bit of a westward-leading path that opens up into a park. Nobody else is around, so we spend a few minutes enjoying the peace and quiet, then grab the rather obviously placed cache that we came for. As night falls, we head back to better-known parts of the city, content in the knowledge that Pullman can still surprise us.

Location-Based Mobile Gaming and Hybrid Gameworlds

The U.S. government began allowing unrestricted popular access to the data broadcast by its network of GPS satellites in the year 2000. Since then, that data—first collected through handheld, dedicated GPSrs and more recently through GPS modules embedded in mobile phones, PDAs, tablets, and other such devices—has been used in a variety of ways to erode boundaries between the physical and the virtual, often in the name of creating engaging gameplay experiences. When combined with the portability of mobile devices, GPS technology makes it possible for us to play in "hybrid" gameworlds that link our successes in virtual games to our movement through the physical world.

The term "mobile gaming" could potentially encompass a wide variety of playful experiences within gameworlds that are hybridized to varying degrees. For my purposes here, Adriana de Souza e Silva and Daniel Sutko's definition of mobile gaming is both effective and efficient. In the introduction to their *Digital Cityscapes: Merging Digital and Urban Playspaces*, they explain that "There are two common characteristics to all [mobile] games that differentiate them from traditional video games and physical games: (1) they use the city space as the game board, and (2) they use mobile devices as interfaces for game play."[1] From within this model, de Souza e Silva and Larissa Hjorth proceed to define three subclassifications through their essay "Playful Urban Spaces: A Historical Approach to Mobile Games," dividing up the medium of mobile gaming based, essentially, on the degree to which individual games rely on a virtual dimension to function.

Of particular interest to me is de Souza e Silva and Hjorth's definition of location-based mobile games (LBMGs). LBMGs "allow the linking of information to places, and players to each other via location awareness. Although LBMGs might have an online component, the game takes place primarily in the physical space and on the cell phone screen, as players can see each other and/or virtual game elements on their mobile screen."[2] This melding of virtually delivered information and physical sensory experience allows players to engage in explorations not unlike those found in the virtual-only gameworlds of video games like *Minecraft* or *The Elder Scrolls V: Skyrim* while remaining grounded in the physical world.[3]

LBMGs achieve this melding by using location-aware technology to overlay virtually expressed place-values—for example, the location of a treasure chest or magical amulet—atop physical locations—for example, the local burger joint—and the result can be so compelling that the player might find it difficult to tell where the game ends and everyday life begins. Thus, the experience of playing an LBMG often becomes less about succeeding at or "beating" the game and more about the surprising ways in which the virtual game-layer enhances and alters the player's day-to-day experience of the physical world. As de Souza e Silva and Hjorth explain, "[The player's] movement through the city might be goal driven—that is, when a player goes out specifically to play the game—but it is generally spontaneous—by moving through the city in their usual routes to school or work, players are accessed by the game—a fact that turns their experiences of the city into an unexpected playful adventure."[4] By "accessing" players even when they are ostensibly outside of the gameworld, LBMGs are changing what it means to play, as well as where and when that play can take place.

Traditionally, games have either occurred inside rule-bound, temporally and spatially limited physical spaces (within "the magic circle" as it is called by Johan Huizinga in his 1955 *Homo Ludens: A Study of the Play-Element in Culture*) or rule-bound, temporally and spatially limited *virtual* spaces (Huizinga's magic circle as enforced by the screens and controllers or keyboards of console or PC gaming systems). The hybrid gameworlds enabled by LBMGs, however, challenge these temporal and spatial boundaries. I will briefly consider what this challenge means for digital gaming, first generally, and then more specifically in terms of in-game storytelling. Using the example of geocaching, this essay will illustrate how LBMGs represent the possibility for more engaging in-game narratives as well as more meaningful player-directed explorations of gameworlds by virtue of their ability to use location-based mobile technology to enable the player as a place maker whose actions within the game continue to resonate in the physical world well after the game ends.

Unmapping, Remapping, and Geocaching

In his seminal work *Space and Place: The Perspective of Experience*, social geographer Yi-Fu Tuan writes, "Place is security, space is freedom: we are attached to the one and long for the other,"[5] and yet it is increasingly the case that we have little direct influence on either, at least in the physical world. Outside of our own homes, apartments, and dorms, most places have already been given an overarching purpose, or place-value, by the culture at large. While the characteristics that set apart certain "local" places are highly valued (e.g., unique qualities of a city like New Orleans), more often than not, places have been largely subsumed by a culture-wide march toward greater homogeneity in the name of efficiency. Walmarts are built according to the same layout from New York City to San Francisco, and McDonalds serves identical cheeseburgers at each of its over 13,000 American restaurants. Similarly, it is difficult to imagine the existence of an unexplored space without others' place-values already inscribed upon it in a world where Google Street View can now show us even the South Pole in exacting detail. Yet filling unmapped space with one's personal place-values remains a compelling, if elusive, experience, and I believe that providing this experience for players is the most important function of LBMGs. These spatially hybrid games can allow their players to first create explorable space from meaning-laden place ("unmapping") and then to write their own, personalized place-values onto that space ("remapping"). Let's consider geocaching as an example of this process in action.

The premise of geocaching is simple enough: players are provided with the GPS coordinates of a hidden container (a "cache") via a website or other means, and they then use a GPSr or other GPS-enabled mobile device to navigate to those coordinates and locate the cache. Once a player finds a particular cache, their achievement can be logged, both physically at the cache site in a pencil-and-paper logbook and virtually on websites such as Geocaching.com. There are many variations on geocaching's formula, but across these variations the game's basic mechanic stays the same.

While geocachers are playing, the virtual game-layer presented to them by their mobile device—generally a Google Maps–like map of their immediate area overlaid with icons representing cache locations—supersedes their usual interpretation of the physical world around them (see Figure 11.1). What might normally be a street full of restaurants, gas stations, and convenience stores becomes instead a series of alleys and pedestrian walkways broken at regular intervals by inconsequential buildings.[6] As Alison Gazzard writes in her essay "Location, Location, Location: Collecting Space and Place in Mobile Media," through such gameplay, "[t]he same places are visited, but with a new meaning, through virtual spaces augmented onto the familiar and bringing a new light to old surroundings. The space is now explored in a new way through this augmentation and the added game element of collecting."[7] This "augmentation" allows the player to unmap

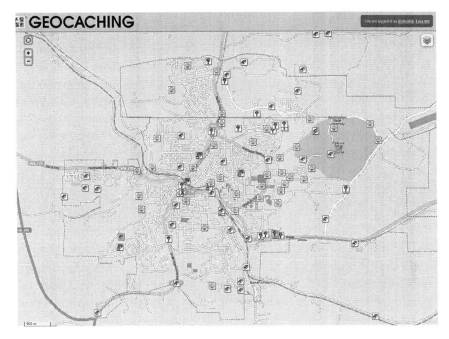

Figure 11.1 A screen capture of the geocaching interface, here showing the town of Pullman, Washington. The icons show geocache containers that have yet to be found by the user (the box icons), the geocaches already discovered (the happy-face icons), and various other caches like mystery caches and multisite caches.

known places, and the ludic pleasure of collecting (i.e., the joy received from engaging with the play elements of the game) motivates further exploration of the "new" spaces that result. Before the final "find" of the cache occurs, the player's focus is on the exploration of a known physical world imaginatively unmapped with the help of a mobile device that layers a virtual one atop it. Once the player's exploration has reached its logical conclusion, though, the game then allows the player to turn space back into place once more—*their* place.

With the finding of a cache, the gameworld and their journey through it continues to gain personal meaning, to be "remapped" by the player as a new place defined from their perspective. The meaning assigned to the map's points of interest by the game's virtual layer is reified by the presence of a physical cache, a resonance that strengthens the player's engagement with and belief in geocaching's hybrid gameworld.

In the aftermath of a find, the player's signing of the cache's logbook and/or their altering of other contents of the cache, as well as their efficacy—or lack thereof—in re-hiding it from the next potential geocacher all become physical manifestations of their personal interaction with a hybrid game-object, fodder for the generation of their own place-values that they will associate with the cache's location as well as alterations of the gameworld that will affect the experiences of the players who come to that location afterward. Virtually, when the player logs their find online, they are not only "leaving their mark," but they also have the opportunity to add to the geocaching community's store of information on that particular cache. Such information can include player logs, photographs, hints, tips, details about the cache's size and shape, and history about the area around the cache. In these ways, geocachers partake in and enable what Eric Gordon calls "network locality," a form of place making as sociocultural expression.[8]

In "Redefining the Local: The Distinction between Located Information and Local Knowledge in Location-Based Games," Gordon explains, "In the everyday practices of digital networks, there is increasing evidence that users desire to be located or locatable. This can be called *network locality*—the experience of inter-acting with located data within the perceived infinity of global access."[9] Gordon goes on to describe how information like that which geocachers post online to supplement their logging of a cache can not only effect the virtual instantiation of a place but also the physical, "real" one. By making their personal experiences of cache locations available to other players, then, geocachers not only have a chance to assign their own place-values to those locations but to also propagate those values through the Internet. Thus, these place-values can become an integral part of later players' experiences of the gameworld.

Gordon's "network locality" is an excellent way of describing how place making functions through geocaching. "The experience of network locality," he writes, "is premised upon the individual player's ability to control the rela-tionship between global access and local interaction."[10] In geocaching, this is a decision that is available to the player once he or she has uncovered the cache. Geocaching's ludic (or game-based) nature allows this control to be leveraged as remapping, or, as Gordon puts it, "When this practice is organized into a clearly demarcated game structure, network locality is potentially transformed into a context of local knowledge production."[11]

The most important expression of a geocacher's contribution to this project of "local knowledge production" is undoubtedly the creation of players' own caches. Any player who is registered on a geocaching website can place a cache at a location of his or her choosing in the physical world and then publish that cache's location online. In addition to the cache's coordinates, its creator can also post details about the cache if he or she so chooses. The world's current network of nearly two million geocaches was built entirely from such small, local acts of place making.

How Hybrid Gameworlds Are Changing Storytelling

Geocaching is a very simple yet powerful manifestation of LBMGs' ability to highlight the truth of Hjorth's claim that "place is more than just physical geo-graphic location ... places are constructed by an ongoing accumulation of stories, memories, and social practices."[12] Certainly, the physical experience of moving through a hybrid gameworld while finding caches helps the player to write new place-values over "old," known places, as do their contributions to "local knowledge production," made by the creation and sharing of new game content (either physically or virtually, or both). Yet, geocaching can also engage in storytelling by positioning the player as both audience and author.

I believe that, generally speaking, digital games can engage in two different types of storytelling.[13] The first type, what I call "narrative," hews closely to what we usually think of when we think of a game's "story." It is the linear—or at least primarily linear—arc of fiction that frames the player's progress through the game. The narrative of *Super Mario Bros.* is the player's quest to rescue the Princess. The narrative of *Final Fantasy VII* is the player's battle to defeat Sephiroth. The narrative of *Rome: Total War* is the player's effort to control the Roman Empire through war, diplomacy, and economics. Here, narrative's main function is not actually to tell a story per se, but to focus gameplay while maintaining the player's suspension of disbelief in the gameworld.

The second type of storytelling games engage in is what I call "game-story." As differentiated from the linear, agency-less narrative that often runs parallel to a player's experience in a gameworld, the game-story is the story of an individual's success or failure within the gameworld's rules. For example, unlike its narrative, the game-story of *Super Mario Bros.* is unique for every player and tells of their interactions with the gameworld's environment, characters, and obstacles as those interactions relate to the game's victory states and fail states. A player's game-story is the story of their place making within the game: how their actions change the contours—figuratively and sometimes literally—of the gameworld.

As game studies theorist Tadhg Kelly argues on his blog *What Games Are*, the drama that drives the appeal of traditional, narrative-based storytelling is actually impossible to engender using the format of the digital game, hence the oft-voiced though misdirected claim that "games can't tell stories." Kelly explains, "The inevitability and success of struggle in drama is built on the powerlessness of the audience. . . . Comedy, tragedy, and other kinds of drama flow from the empathy of watching things unfold without agency."[14] In a medium reliant on player agency—an agency that renders such drama impossible—Kelly believes that the focus of storytelling should be the gameworld itself. "Forget the person," he says. "The art of game design is all about the place."[15] In Kelly's "worldmaking" model of storytelling, the heart of the story is the struggle between player agency and the strictures of a rule-based gameworld: the game-story. "Writing" this game-story—playing the game—is a form of virtual place construction: the game maker programs the gameworld into existence, but the player's actions within that world are what actually evolve it beyond its original creation state into something interesting and uniquely reflective of each player's experiences.

Both narrative and game-story are rooted in the space and place of the gameworld. The narrative fictionalizes the game's rules so as to minimize the need for suspension of disbelief on the part of the player when interacting with the space of the game. The game-story, however, confirms for the player the value of spending time imparting his or her own place-values on the gameworld as a result of playing through the game. As might be expected, the rise of LBMGs affects both of these forms of story. Thanks to location-aware technology, game makers can now implicate a player's local geography and topography as well as nearby physical locations to heighten the effect of a game's narrative. Similarly, the game-story of a player's place making within the gameworld becomes even more compelling with the promise that meaning made during the game will persist afterward. To show more specifically how in-game storytelling can take advantage of the unique properties of an LBMG's hybrid gameworld, I will close by considering *University of Death*, a geocaching-based LBMG.

LBMG Storytelling and *University of Death*

Intrigued by the unique possibilities of storytelling via mobile gaming, Tim Hetland, Jacob Hughes, and I designed and implemented an LBMG of our own in the fall of 2009, a darkly humorous murder-mystery game, which we titled *University of Death (UoD)*.[16] As we believed geocaching to be an LBMG especially suited to empowering players as place makers within a hybrid gameworld for all the reasons that I enumerated above, *UoD* was conceived as a long-form geocaching "mission" of sorts: the player would move from cache to cache, uncovering new pieces of the game's narrative as they played.

UoD was set in Pullman, Washington—home to Washington State University, where we were all graduate students at the time—and as we walked the streets of the town and campus one night, imagining for the first time what *UoD*'s narrative might be about and what locations we could use for its narrative set pieces through the placement of caches, we began to realize just how evocative storytelling in a hybrid gameworld could be. For one, we noticed how effectively an LBMG's narrative can utilize a player's sensory experience of the physical world to heighten that player's belief in the fiction of the gameworld.

With this in mind, we chose to accentuate the game's murder-mystery theme by requiring the player to start by locating a cache hidden across the street from the Pullman Police Station. This first "start menu" cache required the player to choose one of three characters' roles to assume before continuing the narrative. The player's choice was reflected by the narrative as well as by the physical location that the player had to travel to next. For example, if the player chose to play as the main protagonist, a down-and-out detective, their next cache was located near a local bar and contained a narration of the player's recent, drunken exit from that bar. Thus, the hunt for this particular cache would have the player literally retracing the fictional detective's steps from his work at the police station, to the bar he frequents after hours, and then on to the location his drunken shambling led him next.

We also sought to reinforce the player's belief in *UoD*'s hybrid gameworld in a number of more subtle ways. First, we often included physical objects with some connection to the game's narrative inside the caches for the player to find. In one instance, the detective's search for his lost son turns up a cache that contains his son's favorite toy—mentioned earlier in the narrative—alongside the next clue from the boy's kidnapper. Second, many of the taunting recordings that the detective's nemesis leaves behind in the caches—essentially pieces of a spoken version of the game's narration—contained background audio that reflected the player's location. For example, as the player listened to a recording left near some railroad tracks, the kidnapper's voice would be suddenly overwhelmed by the *whoosh* of a train passing by in the background. Finally, we included references to various Pullman landmarks—both obvious and subtle—throughout the narrative intended to make the player constantly aware that the game they were playing and the narrative that they were "reading" by doing so were playing out in the physical world as well as on the screen of their location-aware mobile device: businesses within sight of cache locations were mentioned by name, street names were used to give directions, and so on.

Such resonances helped to dissolve the tension that often results from the traditional form of interacting with a virtual-only gameworld, wherein the player can only act upon that gameworld through the intermediary of an avatar. With *UoD*, we attempted to collapse the player and the avatar into one entity by making the imaginative distance between them as small as possible. Our intent was to draw the player into the fiction of *UoD*'s narrative by tying that narrative to the player's physical movement through the gameworld as closely as we could.

This player-avatar melding also enables place making through the player's "writing" of their game-story. Whereas traditional digital games would have the player make meaning in the gameworld only through a virtual proxy, LBMGs make it possible for players to interact directly with the physical world as part of the gameplay. The result is a situation in which the game can "access" the player—to use de Souza e Silva and Hjorth's term—outside the boundaries of the gameworld, encouraging the sort of remapping of known places that I described in my introductory anecdote. *UoD* was designed to facilitate such place making in a number of ways.

I've already described the most obvious of these in my section on geocaching: the simple act of tracking down and finding a geocache is a process of unmapping and then remapping, and *UoD* offered up this experience to players repeatedly. Depending on the character the player chooses to play in *UoD*, they had to find between five and eight geocaches before finishing the game. Hopefully motivated yet further by the game's narrative, any player that finished *UoD* would remember Pullman's Main Street bridge as the scene of a grisly murder and the Round Top hill on WSU's campus as the site of a showdown with a deranged killer. *UoD*, however, was meant to go beyond this basic remapping function of geocaching and allow the player to write a more detailed game-story onto the face of its hybrid gameworld.

The game's "start menu" cache gave the player a choice of personas that they could adopt for the rest of the game: the detective, the student journalist, and one of the killer's earlier victims (whose branch of the narrative played out in the gameworld's past). This decision was meant to set up the connection between player choice and the gameworld. Rather than serving a purely ludic purpose, the persona that the player chose actually affected what parts of the story they experienced, as well as the ways in which they would be expected to interact with the physical world for the rest of the game. The detective's path revealed the conclusion of the narrative, the victim's path shed light on the detective's motivations, and the student journalist's path cast aspersions on the detective's character. Taken together, all three paths told *UoD*'s full story, but each time a player played the game, they decided the shape of the narrative they would experience when they chose their character. Similarly, the type of puzzles and problems the player had to solve at each cache location was dictated by their character choice. The detective's path involved much logical puzzle solving and the piecing together of painstakingly gathered clues; the student journalist's path included historical research, undertaken partially in the university library; and the victim's path involved—as is appropriate for a victim—less agency and more of a sense of unseen forces moving the player toward their preordained fate.

In many ways, then, the player's experience of *UoD* was shaped by this first choice, but it was only one of many choices the player would have to make throughout the game. The narrative of *UoD* was made up of various branches— not unlike a *Choose Your Own Adventure* book—and though there were fifteen caches in the game, each character's path was made up of information garnered from, at most, half of those. Which caches the player visited depended ultimately on his or her choices. The choices the player made thus not only shaped how he or she experienced the narrative, but also how he or she moved physically through the gameworld and expressed the persona of detective, journalist, or victim. For example, at one point the player-detective was given the option of searching for a clue hidden in a public restroom. If the player chose not to pursue such a potentially uncomfortable course of action, he or she could have gone elsewhere and found a more accessible cache. Which clue the player found would influence how he or she interpreted the narrative's intentionally ambiguous endgame and the player's own part in it. Thus, the player's choices affected both the narrative and the course of his or her personal game-story.

With *UoD*, what began as a thought experiment succeeded as an interesting— if technologically simplistic—example of what is possible when digital storytelling is married to location-aware technology.[17] While geocaching is an LBMG that enables its players to unmap and then remap known places, it is my belief that such place making can (and should) function as a launch pad of sorts from which more ambitious narratives can be told, and personally unique, captivating gamestories can be written. On my walks around Pullman, I still find myself frequently "accessed" by *University of Death* when I think of Bryan Tower not just as an icon of the university skyline but also the site of a clandestine meeting between a young journalist and a hard-bitten detective, or when I remember that the water tower on the horizon overlooks the final resting place of a killer's last victim, a killer that I helped stop by unraveling a mystery that led me all over town one dark night. These resonances persist beyond the game for me, expanding the fiction's scope, turning it into something more than just fiction, reminding me of the existence of a hidden history that those who weren't *UoD* players will never know in the same way I do.

Notes

1. Adriana de Souza e Silva and Daniel Sutko, "Merging Digital and Urban Playscapes: An Introduction to the Field," in *Digital Cityscapes*, ed. Adriana de Souza e Silva and Daniel Sutko (New York: Peter Lang Publishing, 2009), 3.
2. Adriana de Souza e Silva and Larissa Hjorth, "Playful Urban Spaces: A Historical Approach to Mobile Games," *Simulation and Gaming* 40, no. 5 (2009): 614.
3. Though it could be argued that traditional video games are not *entirely* removed from physical space simply because their virtual gameworlds are only mediated by the borders of a screen and thus can be easily superseded by the demands of the "real world" at any time, I would argue that there is a distinct difference between a video game that seeks to draw the player's attention away from that "real world" and a mobile game that purposely merges with the physical world in order to create a hybrid gaming experience. Or, as Michiel de Lange has put it in "From Always-On to Always-There: Locative Media as Playful Technologies": "Digital games used to be largely set apart from the physical domain. Although digital games could be portable (e.g., PSP, Nintendo DS), involve bodily gestures (e.g., Wii), or be played at certain locations (e.g., in arcades), the play element of these games was confined to their own game spaces. . . . LBMGs are games whose outcome depends not only on the events on the screen but also on the player's positions in the physical world." See Michiel de Lange, "From Always-On to Always-There: Locative Media as Playful Technologies," in *Digital Cityscapes*, ed. Adriana de Souza e Silva and Daniel Sutko (New York: Peter Lang Publishing, 2009), 55–70.
4. De Souza e Silva and Hjorth, "Playful Urban Spaces," 618.
5. Yi-Fu Tuan, *Space and Place: The Perspective of Experience* (Minneapolis: University of Minnesota Press, 2008), 3.
6. Most caches are located in the spatial "seams" between known places. That is to say, geocaches are often found in alleys, parks, parking lots, etc., and are even frequently located outside the borders of cities, at interstate rest stops or state parks, for example. In fact, it is against the rules of the game to place caches inside buildings due to the difficulty of getting an accurate GPS signal indoors.
7. Alison Gazzard, "Location, Location, Location: Collecting Space and Place in Mobile Media," *Convergence: The International Journal of Research into New Media Technologies* 17, no. 4 (2011), http://con.sagepub.com/content/17/4/405.
8. Eric Gordon, "Redefining the Local: The Distinction Between Located Information and Local Knowledge in Location-Based Games," in *Digital Cityscapes: Merging Digital and Urban Playscapes*, ed. Adriana de Souza e Silva and Daniel Sutko (New York: Peter Lang Publishing, 2009), 22.

9. Ibid.
10. Ibid, 33.
11. Ibid.
12. Larissa Hjorth, "Mobile@Game Cultures: the Place of Urban Mobile Gaming," *Convergence: The International Journal of Research into New Media Technologies* 17, no. 4 (2011): 358, http://con.sagepub.com/content/17/4/357.
13. While there has been much heated debate in both academic and popular circles over the question of whether games can or cannot tell stories, for the sake of this essay I am going to operate on the assumption that they can. I am less interested in generating a model of in-game storytelling that will satisfy all critics than I am in generating a model that can illustrate clearly how LBMGs are changing what in-game storytelling is capable of at least attempting.
14. Tadgh Kelly, "Cars, Dolls and Video Games," http://whatgamesare.com/2011/02/cars-dolls-and-video-games-narrativism.html.
15. Tadhg Kelly, "Worldmakers," http://whatgamesare.com/2010/12/worldmakers-game-design.html.
16. Unfortunately, large portions of the game were repeatedly destroyed by vandals shortly after launch, and thus *UoD* was only playable in its entirety for a few months.
17. A number of local players even took *UoD*'s place making potential beyond the game proper by posting to the Geocaching website, where the first "start menu" cache is listed, and sharing their stories of playing and photos of a few particularly intense experiences.

12

PROXIMITY AND ALIENATION

Narratives of City, Self, and Other in the Locative Games of Blast Theory

Rowan Wilken

How do the examples in this chapter help us understand the practice of story-telling in the mobile media age?

This chapter looks at key instances where location-based mobile games have been used to make connections with complete strangers. The focus, in the first half of the chapter, is on how these issues have been developed in the locative gaming projects of the UK media art collective Blast Theory (particularly focused on *Uncle Roy All Around You* and *Rider Spoke*). The narrative elements of these locative games encourage or force players to interact with strangers. In so doing, players practice the community space of the city in a unique way: they reimagine the city as a space that—instead of alienating and isolating—encourages interpersonal connections with "the Other" (or those who are extremely different from us). These locative games thus also reveal that space-based game narratives can rei-magine ideas of community as that which is, in part, the ongoing interactions—through communication—with those who are different than the player while also allowing the player to occupy the place of the Other.

Keywords

- **Alienation:** Closely related to the term *estrangement*, alienation concerns the idea of something being separated from, or strange to, something else. Alien-ation forms a pivotal concept in Marxist philosophy (e.g., we are alienated from the products of our labor insofar as we experience these products as commodities). It is also used by sociologist Georg Simmel as a way of mak-ing sense of the direct impacts of modernization and industrialization on interpersonal experiences of urban life.

- **Other:** A term used to refer to a person that is different or distinct from oneself and from those one knows about. French philosopher Emmanuel Lévinas famously stated that the self, in both a psychological and a philosophical sense, is only possible through the recognition of the Other. The concept has been immensely important in feminist and postcolonial theory. While it has been used (perhaps most famously by the Palestinian literary theorist Edward Said) to highlight a negative reaction between Europeans and Anglo-Americans from those they have dominated, it can also reference the potential for positive encounters between self and Other, between peoples of different races, classes, and religions.
- **Proximity:** The fact or condition of being near or close. Proximity can refer to nearness in abstract relations, such as kinship, but the dominant meaning, and the sense in which the term is used here, now refers to nearness in space or time. For the sociologist Georg Simmel, what characterizes modern urban life is increased physical *proximity*, which tends to lead to a greater sense of *alienation* rather than increased social interaction.

Introduction

As I weave along the streets, stability is what I crave.
—*The Bats, "Steppin Out"[1]*

To raise the question of the nature of narrative is to invite reflection on the very nature of culture and, possibly, even on the nature of humanity itself.
—*Hayden White[2]*

This chapter is concerned with detailing key instances where location-based mobile media have been used to make (or encourage) connections with relative and complete strangers. The focus in the first half of the chapter is on how these issues have been developed in the narrative-based locative gaming projects of the UK media art collective Blast Theory. Particular attention will be given to *Uncle Roy All Around You* (2003) and *Rider Spoke* (2007), with further references to a number of others, including *Ulrike and Eamon Compliant* (2009) and *Day of the Figurines* (2006). In the second half of the chapter, these experimental projects of Blast Theory are read against key (poststructuralist) philosophical deliberations on community and difference in the work of Jean-Luc Nancy, Giorgio Agamben, and Alphonso Lingis.

That these projects are designed as games is important in this context. Locative games are significant in that they can lead to transformed understandings and experiences of place and everyday life: they serve to remind us that "places are constructed by an ongoing accumulation of stories, memories and social practices"; they encourage a questioning of the "too familiar" routines of daily life; and they expose us to "new ways of experiencing place, play and identity," and social interaction, as Larissa Hjorth has argued.[3]

Alienation and Urban Life

This investigation of the mobile phone as a device for connecting with others unfamiliar to us is set against a backdrop of a long tradition of conceiving of city life as profoundly alienating.[4] For instance, in the pioneering sociological work of Georg Simmel, large-scale urban development is seen to have wrought profound changes at the individual level that affect both individual psychological experience and how we interact with others. As Simmel famously writes, "[O]ne nowhere feels as lonely and lost as in the metropolitan crowd."[5] He goes on to write:

> The feeling of isolation is rarely as decisive and intense when one actually finds oneself physically alone, as when one is a stranger, without relations, among many physically close persons, at a "party," on a train, or in the traffic of a large city.[6]

Such situations, according to Simmel, constitute the very epitome of "loneliness in togetherness."[7]

Moreover, for Simmel, this uneasy mix of proximity and alienation as a result of the individual's close encounters with the mass (alienation *in* proximity), led to the internalization of a variety of strategies to manage encounters that had hitherto been unnecessary. So, for instance, following the rise of mass public transportation systems in the nineteenth century (such as the bus, train, and tramcar), there emerged a need for new ways of gazing at other urban dwellers for extended periods without speaking or communicating.[8] Erving Goffman coined the term "civil inattention" to describe this process.[9]

City life that is thus characterized by this kind of alienation is also evident in the later work of the American sociologist, Richard Sennett. According to Michael Bull, Sennett was writing of a New York before iPods and mobile phones, and describes it as a "place of indifference," of strangers passing by without any interaction.[10] Cities had become "places in which the urban subject fell silent."[11] As a result, Sennett argued, "there grew up a notion that strangers had no right to speak to each other, that each man possessed as a public right an invisible shield, a right to be left alone."[12]

In the context of this chapter, Simmel's account of these interactional processes is especially interesting for its emphasis on tensions between loneliness and togetherness, alienation and proximity. As Ole Jensen explains, "[T]he co-existence of nearness and remoteness" is considered by Simmel to be a key feature of human relationships.[13] Thus, the experience of urban life and of others is that, "while we think strangers are disconnected from us," in fact our experience of "strangeness means that he who also is far is actually near."[14]

What this suggests, in short, is that our experiences with and of strangers can be read two ways. Whereas for some critics, such as Sennett, city life is characterized by alienation, for others, such as Iris Marion Young, the city is understood as a space in which it is possible for an urban dweller to take pleasure "in being drawn out of oneself" by the diversity of people and locations in the city.[15] To approach the city in this way is to understand that other meanings, practices, and perspectives on the city are possible and can lead to opportunities for learning and new or different experiences.[16] According to this more positive, outward looking view, "the urban subject is open to encounters with difference/s that are not only 'tolerated,' but can be a source of pleasure."[17]

What of the role of technologies, such as various forms of mobile media, in this scenario? One of the persistent anxieties about, and charges against, mobile media is that they can have negative effects on social cohesion and engagement in the public sphere.[18] This perspective centers on the idea that use of these devices contributes to an understanding of "an individual as an isolated island in public,"[19] through what David Morley describes as a form of "psychic cocooning"[20] in which mobile users "can escape their immediate situation and interact with only like-minded persons."[21] For instance, in his book *Sound Moves*, Michael Bull describes modern mobile media, such as iPods and mobile phones, as "technologies of separation" and argues that they enable subjects to "retreat from urban space" by "neutralising it," thereby enabling the urban citizen to "remove themselves" from the "physicality" of urban relations.[22]

And, yet, just as I have noted two quite different and conflicting perspectives on urban life, it is important to be mindful of the many contradictions associated with mobile media and contemporary uses of them. As Michael Arnold argues, paradox and contradiction are at the center of our understanding and usage of mobile media technologies. In this sense, Arnold argues, they are very much "Janus-faced" technologies, "always and at once pointing in different directions": they facilitate independence as well as co-dependence, lead to a greater sense of vulnerability while also providing reassurance, facilitate social proximity at the same time as allowing greater geographical distance, blur the public and the private, and so on.[23]

In line with such reasoning, a central assumption in this chapter is that, just as mobile media can be used to reinforce existing social networks (connecting known with known), they also have the potential to open up new social and interactive possibilities (perhaps through connecting known with unknown, and stranger with stranger). Given this, it is valuable to ask how "innovations in mobile telephony" are, and might potentially be, "reconfiguring urban encounters"[24]—especially urban encounters with strangers. It is this precise question that I am interested in exploring here in relation to the narrative locative games of Blast Theory.

Narratives of City, Self, and Other in the Locative Media Works of Blast Theory

Blast Theory is an internationally recognized art group based in Brighton, United Kingdom. Led by Matt Adams, Ju Row Farr, and Nick Tandavanitj, and with a long-standing collaborative relationship with the Mixed Reality Lab at Nottingham

University, the group's work, in their own words, "explores interactivity and the social and political aspects of technology."[25] Many of their projects have sought to pose and explore "important questions about the meaning of interaction," both technological and interpersonal, and especially its limitations.[26] Many are also specifically focused around the use of mobile and locative media technologies.[27] Two of these projects are discussed in detail below.

Uncle Roy All Around You

The first of Blast Theory's narrative locative games to be examined here is *Uncle Roy All Around You* (2003). This project is significant in the present context for the way it makes questions of trust in strangers and confrontations between strangers a central component of the game play. It is a game that involves online and street players, as well as passersby and, at strategic moments in the game play, paid actors. The ostensive aim for street players of the game is for them to journey through the streets of a city (London in the first run of the game) in search of an elusive figure called Uncle Roy. Clues are provided to the players at various stages. Online players of the game can follow and interact with these street players, providing assistance or hindering their progress. As the game's developers explain, "[T]he core artistic theme of the work is trust in strangers—be they remote players, Uncle Roy or passersby."[28]

This issue of trust in strangers is explored in quite explicit ways at various strategic points, often in ways that "deliberately push the boundaries of interacting in public settings,"[29] and, at crucial moments, where game participants are asked to make "apparently risky decisions."[30] One of the key navigational tasks of the game is for players to locate Uncle Roy's office. Once located, players enter, and there they find a postcard lying on a desk on which is written the question, "When can you begin to trust a stranger?"[31] Players are asked to write their response to this question on the card; they are then told to take this card with them and leave the building. Once outside, they are instructed to climb into a waiting limousine; a stranger (a paid actor) also enters the car (see Figure 12.1). With the two passengers on board, the car pulls away from the curb and drives off.

> During the ride, the actor [the "stranger"] asks them [the game player] a sequence of questions about trust in strangers, and tells them that somewhere else in the game another player is answering these same questions. Finally, he [the actor/stranger] asks them whether they are willing to enter a year long contract to help this stranger if ever called upon. If they agree, he asks for their address and phone number, the car pulls up by a public postbox and the player is asked to post their postcard—addressed to Uncle Roy—to finally seal the contract.[32]

Figure 12.1 An image of the stranger who is encountered by players at the end of *Uncle Roy All Around You* by Blast Theory. The stranger asks the player if he or she is willing to enter a year-long contract with an unknown player, to be available if needed by that player. Image ©2003 Blast Theory.

What is striking about *Uncle Roy* is the way that it can be seen to engage with what Jacques Derrida has called "the foreigner question" and the challenge posed by "the law of absolute, unconditional hospitality."[33] Derrida's idea of unconditional hospitality to strangers means "that I open up my home and that I give not only to the foreigner . . . but to the absolute, unknown, anonymous other," without any expectation of them responding in kind.[34] For the participants of *Uncle Roy*, who were surveyed upon completion of the game, this call for hospitality as played out within the confines of the game invoked a range of feelings both negative (with some players describing feelings of uncertainty, mistrust, and, in at least one case, a heightened fear of strangers, whilst playing the game) and positive (with other participants reporting positive interactions with strangers).[35]

Rider Spoke

A mobile interactive work for cyclists, *Rider Spoke* debuted in London in October 2007. Participants of the game use a bike (either their own or one supplied to them) that is then fitted with a handlebar-mounted Nokia N800J, an earpiece, and a microphone.[36] Each rider is given an hour to explore the streets of London at night, "guided along the journey by the voice of Blast Theory co-founder Ju Row Farr."[37] The first spoken instruction to riders, delivered by Farr in a "calm and measured . . . style and tone reminiscent of a psychotherapist,"[38] asks them to seek out a quiet and appealing location where they can record into the device a name and a description of themselves. This recording—and its location—is then logged for other riders to listen to if they encounter that same location (see Figure 12.2). Following this, participants were, as Jason Farman explains,

> prompted to either "Hide," which allowed them to find a location related to one of Farr's prompts, such as "Find a place that reminds you of your father and record a story about it," or "Find others," which allowed users to "seek" other people's narratives located throughout the city.[39]

In some respects, *Rider Spoke* is the polar opposite of *Uncle Roy*: physical isolation[40] and quiet contemplation, rather than direct social interaction in a shared public space, are key; moreover, "there are no competitors, [and] the pace is decidedly slow to match Farr's soothing tone of voice."[41] These choices fit with a key aim of the project: commentary on the establishment and sustenance of interpersonal intimacy via mobile devices.[42]

Figure 12.2 A participant in Blast Theory's *Rider Spoke* listening to an audio story recorded (and geotagged) by another participant. Image © 2007 Blast Theory.

Despite these apparent differences, there are also clear discernible thematic consistencies between the two projects, particularly with respect to the central role of strangers in both. In *Rider Spoke*, the stranger is engaged in a number of ways.

The first and key form of interaction with strangers is through voice: "the piece asks participants to perform the tension between the voice and asynchronous forms of communication."[43] In Farman's analysis, he is specifically concerned with how, in *Rider Spoke*, the use of voice via mobile phones serves to "establish embodied connections and a sense of presence between interlocutors."[44] What this encouraged, in the words of one participant, was "a disconnected intimacy with a total stranger" through the sharing of recorded stories.[45] While the communicative process employed was intended to be asynchronous, the "sequential unfolding of the event"[46] became vital to the overall user experience. As *Rider Spoke*'s creators explain, as a participant listener-recorder, one cannot expect to give or listen to a secret told in confidence and then "provide something rigidly formal straight after."[47] Rather, the whole process encourages the swapping of confidences with strangers, with people who are otherwise unknown to you, because "anything less than another confidence of some kind would be seen as accountable."[48] Commitment to this "intimate stranger" is also asked of each player when, at the very conclusion of the experience, they are prompted by the narrator "to make and record a promise."[49]

Secondly, interactions with strangers—or, more precisely, the *figure* of the stranger—were also evoked through instructions such as that which asks riders to seek out a house or a flat with a window that could be looked through, one that they would like to enter, and to record a message explaining why.[50]

Thirdly, whilst *Rider Spoke* "sought to solicit 'a sense of isolation in an otherwise crowded city'"[51]—an aim which, in itself, presents a fascinating commentary on the work of Simmel, discussed earlier—two-way interactions with bystanders were clearly crucial to the overall experience of the work. At times, participants were cast as performers with bystanders serving as their spectators. At other times, the reverse occurred, "in that riders transformed bystanders into performers by presenting what they saw to others."[52] In this sense, *Rider Spoke* not only engages "the tension between the categories of presence and absence,"[53] but it also offers a powerful commentary on the tension between public and private as enacted in public space using a communication technology.

In the following section, I explore in greater detail the narrative structures of these (and other) Blast Theory works, before drawing out their implications for an understanding of these engagements with strangers and the Other.

Narrative Structures in Blast Theory's Locative Games

At one point in the "Introduction to the Structural Analysis of Narrative," Roland Barthes asks, "Who is the donor of the narrative?"[54] That is to say: who is the author, the main contributor, the driver of the narrative? These are deceptively difficult questions to answer when considering the narrative composition of Blast Theory's location-based games. On the one hand, in the provocative *Ulrike and Eamon Compliant* (2009), in which players are asked to identify with one of two former terrorists, the game follows a very detailed, prescribed narrative developed by Blast Theory that requires significant levels and forms of "compliance"[55] on the part of the participant for its success. *Day of the Figurines* (2006), in contrast, is a very different style of game: it is an SMS-based "pervasive game" that places players in a postapocalyptic imaginary town and encourages gameplay over a much longer time period with the intention that it will be integrated into participants' daily lives.[56] Nonetheless, like *Ulrike*, *Day of the Figurines* also follows a strongly prescribed narrative, albeit one that is complicated by multiple temporal narrative layerings.[57] On the other hand, *Uncle Roy* contains some prescribed elements, while *Rider Spoke* has "no background scenario or overarching metanarrative,"[58] and what is offered to participants by way of narrative fragments in both of these games is intended as scaffolding—or "stage directions"[59]—around which the larger narrative threads of the game are woven by players.

The difficulty in answering Barthes's question in relation to Blast Theory's work is further complicated by the extensive behind-the-scenes work that goes into each game in its very unfolding. Thus, while it is acknowledged that each Blast Theory project is a "*co-production* of players and behind the scenes staff,"[60] the role of the latter is significant in terms of its influence in managing the narrative fragments that are received by players in each game, such as text messages in *Rider Spoke* and *Day of the Figurines*, and how this information is filtered and then fed back into the gameplay—a process that is variously described as "recalibration,"[61] "orchestration,"[62] and "customisation"[63] of the game. It is a process that differs subtly but significantly from project to project, but is always performed with the overall objective of each game in mind: experimental sociality in the case of *Day of the Figurines*, for example, or communicative ambivalence, alienation, and encounters with strangers in the case of *Uncle Roy* and the closely related *I Like Frank* (2004).

In the context of this chapter, what is especially interesting about the narrative organization of many of Blast Theory's projects, especially *Uncle Roy* and *Rider Spoke* (but also others, like *Ulrike and Eamon Compliant* and *Day of the Figurines*), is the way that prescripting or cues—and "recalibration" or "orchestration"—of the narrative are developed in strategic ways that encourage or force encounters with strangers (the "Other" in the specific case of *Ulrike and Eamon Compliant*). Many of Blast Theory's narrative-based locative works set out to deliberately exploit the "play of possibilities," as Roland Barthes has termed it, for strategic purposes.[64] My particular interest here is in the significance of these narrative devices and how they, at crucial points, draw participants into interactions with relative or complete strangers, either in the form of passersby who are unwittingly enrolled in the action of the game, or in the form of paid actors who play key roles within the game.

Proximity and Alienation, Community and Otherness: Nancy, Agamben, and Lingis

In the final section to follow, I want to read these projects by Blast Theory against key (poststructuralist) philosophical deliberations on the notion of community and difference, specifically by Jean-Luc Nancy, Giorgio Agamben, and Alphonso Lingis. This serves a twofold purpose. On the one hand, these philosophical deliberations make explicit many underlying themes in the mobile media projects discussed above, as well as offering a robust critique of these projects. On the other hand, the experimental interactions with strangers explored in the work of Blast Theory provides a basis for responding to, and further reflecting on, the more abstract and equally speculative philosophical reflections on difference and otherness.

In turning to the work of these three philosophers, it is clear that while there are key philosophical differences distinguishing each thinker's body of work, there are also key points of convergence. One of these, and the area of principal concern here, is their responses to the concept of "community" and the need to radically rethink how this concept is to be, or could potentially be, reconceptualized. While each of the three thinkers employs his own distinct and preferred terminology—for instance, Nancy writes of a "workless community," Agamben of "coming community," and Lingis of "other community"—all are committed to rethinking the concept of community in ways that are unrestrictive, inherently unstable, and open to difference and otherness. Each approach to rethinking community in these terms has a bearing on the present discussion of mobile media and strangers and, therefore, each is examined in turn below.

One of the more striking departures from more traditional ways of conceiving of community is that developed by the French philosopher Jean-Luc Nancy in *The Inoperative Community*. In this book, Nancy is very suspicious of various attempts throughout Western history to conceive of community as a form of communion. For Nancy, community is not communion. This is because community as communion is constraining in that it suggests a "monolithic form or identity" that suppresses difference and promotes "exclusionary practices."[65]

According to Nancy's own reformulation of community, as Georges Van Den Abbeele explains, "community," such as it can be described using this term, is not a community of subjects, nor is it a "communion of individuals" in a sense that might suggest a "higher or greater totality (a State, a nation, a People, etc.)."[66] More particularly, community is not the product of work: "one does not produce it."[67] Rather, for Nancy, community is what is "'unworked."[68] He writes, "Such communities are described as 'workless' because its members are not brought together through a shared work, project, or set of interests, or lived experiences. Rather, it is the mutual recognition of the finitude or radical otherness of its members . . . that is the foundation of the workless community."[69] Moreover, community should not be thought of as a *thing* that can be actively created.[70] The idea that community is formed through bonding or commonality is problematic for Nancy. This is because community evades encapsulation. Any attempt to "capture" community will fail, as "community" cannot be fixed, actively produced, or reproduced, as "it differs with each 'occurrence/presentation.'"[71]

There would seem to be some clear similarities between Nancy's conception of community as "unworked" and certain aspects of the projects of Blast Theory discussed above. For example, Blast Theory's locative games share an interest in the temporary and in temporary "community" (or, in Nancy's terminology, in the "in-common" and "being-in-common")—especially as an "eruption or explosion of unimagined sociality," to use the architect Cedric Price's phrase.[72] Community, for Nancy, "necessarily takes place in what Blanchot has called 'unworking,' referring to that which, before or beyond the work, withdraws from the work," and which, because of this, "encounters interruption, fragmentation, suspension."[73]

However, a key difficulty in drawing comparisons between Nancy's philosophical formulations and the projects discussed above relates to the way that technology is used to enable but, more crucially, *maintain* various forms of social interaction. In each case, technology can be seen to provide a "scaffolding" of sorts, around and from which "community" might emerge. This runs counter to Nancy's conception of the "workless" community, which is against the idea of community as something that is "objectifiable and producible (in sites, persons, buildings, discourses, institutions, symbols: in short, in subjects)."[74]

This issue notwithstanding, what can be said about Blast Theory's projects is that they do "open up opportunities for potentially transformative encounters with 'The Other.'"[75] In *Uncle Roy All Around You*, such opportunities are a core to the experience of the game, as players interact with passersby, street players, those playing the game online, and, most dramatically, through the encounter at the end of the game with the stranger in the car, who asks a series of probing questions, including whether they are prepared to make a commitment to help a total stranger. The potential for "transformative encounters with 'The Other'" is even more explicit in *Ulrike and Eamon Compliant*, in which player-participants learn of and are encouraged to identify with one of two notorious former terrorists.

The Italian philosopher Giorgio Agamben's approach to thinking about community shares some of the same traits as the approach taken by Nancy, described above. Like Nancy, Agamben considers contemporary conceptions of belonging, togetherness, and community to be misguided and inadequate.[76] In response, Agamben sets out to establish "new articulations" or conceptualizations of community that escape from formulations anchored in, or oriented toward, exclusion and inclusion, violence and negativity, substance and identity.[77] Echoing Nancy's notion of a "workless community," Agamben argues that "a true community can only be a community that is not presupposed."[78] Rather, "true" community is one that remains open to the Other. In this sense, what he is proposing is still very much a "coming community": a community deferred, a community yet-to-come, a community of and for the future, a community *in potentia*.[79] Central to this future-oriented conception of community is the notion of "undecidability."[80] That is to say, those things that are to come are not "inevitabilities" but "(im)possibilities,"[81] and much depends on us: "the coming community *might* happen if and only if we do not let slip away certain opportunities and it *might not* happen if we do let them slip away."[82]

Central to this concept of a "coming community" is communication and the importance of communicating with the Other, with those who are in some way excluded. This lies at the heart of Agamben's critique of community. For Nancy, a central problematic element in existing conceptions of community is the notion of communion, or what he terms "fusion-into-oneness." For Agamben, a similar but slightly different problem is at stake: what is betrayed in, and obscured by, existing understandings of tradition and community is the role language plays in the formations of community.[83] Agamben's argument is that tradition is not about "belonging to this or that group, nation, soil, God, class, or municipality."[84] Rather, tradition "passes on the plain fact that we can speak and hence can be open to other speakers."[85] This emphasis on the potency of language, of communication, and of the ability to communicate *with others*, is a key feature of many Blast Theory projects. Central to *Rider Spoke*, for instance, is a communicative commitment to an "intimate stranger" in which riders are asked to perform their own personal acts of enunciation as well as submit to what Nick Couldry terms the "'obligation' to listen" to the enunciations of others.[86]

A similar set of concerns—otherness, difference, and the importance and potency of communication—motivates the work of the American philosopher Alphonso Lingis and are encapsulated in his notion of "other community." Lingis's "other community" has strong echoes with Nancy's notion of a "workless community" because, as Lingis argues, the other community "forms not in a work, but in the interruption of work and enterprises."[87] That is to say, it does not form through having, or in producing, something in common. Rather, it forms through "exposing oneself to the one with whom we have nothing in common."[88]

According to Lingis, "other community" manifests itself to us as an imperative to be open to otherness and difference. This imperative is worked out in ways that are thoroughly embodied and multisensorial. He writes:

> One exposes oneself to the other . . . not only with one's insights and one's ideas, that they may be contested, but one also exposes the nakedness of one's eyes, one's voice and one's silences, one's empty hands.[89]

Lingis suggests that, by turning to face another, you "expose yourself," you open yourself to "judgment, to need, to a desire of the other."[90] Thus, driving this multisensorial engagement with those around us is a belief, for Lingis, that "to recognize the other is to respect the other."[91]

Like Agamben, Lingis sees communication as crucial to any exposure to—and recognition and respect of—the Other. Communication is understood, here, in an expansive sense to include various technological prostheses *and* various "techniques of the body."[92] Lingis writes: "We communicate information with spoken utterances, by telephone, with tape recordings, in writing and with printing [. . . and] with body kinesics—with gestures, postures, facial expressions, ways of breathing, sighing, and touching one another."[93]

And yet, whatever the mode, communication, for Lingis, is always an attempt to work through confusion and interference.[94] A key challenge is to recognize that in order to communicate with another, "one first has to have terms with which one communicates with the successive moments of one's experience."[95] These theoretical considerations of language and its possibilities for "interchange" are clearly evident in many of Blast Theory's locative works, from *I Like Frank* and *Uncle Roy*, on to *Rider Spoke*. In the last of these, for instance, the gameplay is built around the combination of particular technological prostheses (bike, phone) and particular "techniques of the body" (riding, walking, speaking, listening) to encourage communicative interaction and interchange with others, both proximate (passersby) and distant (other players).

Conclusion

In this chapter I have examined the narrative games of Blast Theory, and the uses that they have made of location-based mobile media to prompt (and provoke) connections with relative and complete strangers. The desire for such interaction, I have argued, is deeply embedded in the narratives of each of these games and can be seen through the complex ways that these narratives are either established in advance of gameplay or managed throughout it. In the final part of the chapter, I argued that it is thus possible to read Blast Theory's work as exploring and testing new and future communicative terms of (and for) engagement between strangers. Each of their projects discussed in this chapter explore fleeting and unstable forms of social interaction (Nancy); each speaks to the future possibilities and potency of communication (Agamben); and each explores this issue of "exposure," recognition, and trust between strangers (Lingis) in ways that are simultaneously playful and thought-provoking.

In key respects, the game format of Blast Theory's projects is central to their success. Gameplay serves a vital mediating function. It provides an appropriate form for the exploration and expression by Blast Theory and Mixed Reality Lab of provocative (and at times controversial) experiences and themes, while at the same time permitting the maintenance of a playful distance in relation to these themes and issues.[96] The fact that location-based games tend to blur where the "magic circle of gameplay begins and ends"[97] can be a powerful mechanism for prompting players to further reflect on, and engage with, the themes and issues these projects raise. Equally, the playfulness that is inherent in the design of Blast Theory's narrative-based locative games enables both the player-participant and the "stranger" who encounters them (passersby, other players of each game) to gain their own "playful distance"—a process that the artist Krzysztof Wodiczko sees as crucial in fostering a "healthy curiosity" and, ideally, "communication and closer contact" between both parties.[98]

Therein lies the real force of Blast Theory's work: the deliberate and systematic creation of "uncomfortable interactions as part of powerful cultural experiences"[99] that challenge our understandings of distance and proximity, otherness and identification, and disconnection and connection.

Acknowledgments

This chapter is an output of the Australian Research Council (ARC) funded project, "The Cultural Economy of Locative Media" (DE120102114). I wish to thank Emily van der Nagel for her research assistance.

Notes

1. Robert Scott/The Bats, "Steppin Out," *The Guilty Office*, Mistletone Records, 2007. Reproduced with permission.
2. Hayden White, "The Value of Narrativity in the Representation of Reality," in *On Narrative*, ed. William J.T. Mitchell (Chicago: The University of Chicago Press, 1981), 1.
3. Larissa Hjorth, *Games and Gaming: An Introduction to New Media* (Oxford: Berg, 2011), 84, 89, 94.
4. For a very good overview of these debates, see Adriana de Souza e Silva and Jordan Frith, *Mobile Interfaces in Public Spaces* (New York: Routledge, 2012), 25–49.
5. George Simmel, quoted in *The Sociology of Georg Simmel*, ed. Kurt H. Wolff (New York: The Free Press, 1950), 418.
6. Ibid., 119.
7. Ibid., 119.
8. Ole B. Jensen, "'Facework,' Flow and the City: Simmel, Goffman, and Mobility in the Contemporary City," *Mobilities* 1, no. 2 (2006): 150.
9. Erving Goffman, *Behavior in Public Places: Notes on the Social Organization of Gatherings* (New York: The Free Press, 1963).
10. Michael Bull, *Sound Moves: iPod Culture and Urban Experience* (London: Routledge, 2007), 27.
11. Ibid., 27.
12. Cited in Bull, *Sound Moves*, 27.
13. Jensen, "'Facework'," 150.
14. Simmel in Wolff, *The Sociology*, lxiv, 445.
15. Alice Crawford, "Taking Social Software to the Streets: Mobile Cocooning and the (An-)Erotic City," *Journal of Urban Technology* 15, no. 3 (2008): 86.
16. Cited in Crawford, "Taking Social Software," 86.
17. Ibid.
18. See, for example, Sherry Turkle, *Alone Together: Why We Expect More from Technology and Less from Each Other* (New York: Basic Books, 2011).
19. Joachim R. Höflich, "Part of Two Frames: Mobile Communication and the Situational Arrangement of Communicative Behaviour," in *Mobile Democracy: Essays on Society, Self and Politics*, ed. Kristóf Nyíri (Vienna: Passagen Verlag, 2003), 50.

20. David Morley, "What's 'Home' Got to Do with It? Contradictory Dynamics in the Domestication of Technology and the Dislocation of Domesticity," *European Journal of Cultural Studies* 6, no. 4 (2003): 435–458.

21. Rich Ling, "The Social Juxtaposition of Mobile Telephone Conversations and Public Spaces" (paper presented at the Conference on the Social Consequences of Mobile Telephones, July 2002, Chunchon, Korea), section 5, para. 4.

22. Bull, *Sound Moves*, 28.

23. Michael Arnold, "On the Phenomenology of Technology: The 'Janus-Faces' of Mobile Phones," *Information and Organization* 13 (2003): 234.

24. Mimi Sheller and John Urry, "Introduction: Mobile Cities, Urban Mobilities," in *Mobile Technologies of the City*, ed. Mimi Sheller and John Urry (London: Routledge, 2006), 4.

25. "About Blast Theory," Blast Theory, http://www.blasttheory.co.uk/bt/about.html.

26. Ibid.

27. For a discussion of the significance of Blast Theory's work within contemporary media arts, see Darren Tofts, "Century of Change? Media Arts Then and Now," *Hyperrhiz: New Media Cultures* 8 (2011), http://www.hyperrhiz.net/hyperrhiz08/36-essays/110-century-of-change-media-arts-then-and-now.

28. Steve Benford et al., "*Uncle Roy All Around You*: Implicating the City in a Location-Based Performance" (2004): section 2, para. 1.

29. Steve Benford, "Pushing the Boundaries of Interaction in Public," *Interactions*, (July/August 2005): 58.

30. Steve Benford et al., "Uncomfortable Interactions" (paper presented at CHI'12, May 5–10, 2012, Austin, Texas), section 3, para. 14.

31. A similar provocation was included in their earlier 2004 project, *I Like Frank*, where, upon completion of the game, participants were asked, "Do you feel any closer to the people on the street around you?" Quoted in Samara Mitchell, "Are you real? Am I?" *RealTime* 60 (2004), http://www.realtimearts.net/article.php?id=7404.

32. Benford et al., "Uncle Roy," section 2, para. 16.

33. Jacques Derrida and Anne Dufourmantelle, *Of Hospitality*, trans. Rachel Bowlby (Stanford, CA: Stanford University Press, 2000).

34. Ibid., 25.

35. Benford et al., "Uncle Roy"; Steve Benford et al., "The Design and Experience of the Location-Based Performance *Uncle Roy All Around You*," *Leonardo Electronic Almanac* 14, no. 3/4 (2006), http://www.leoalmanac.org/wp-content/uploads/2012/07/The-Design-And-Experience-Of-The-Location-Based-Performance-Uncle-Roy-All-Around-You-Vol-14-No-3-July-2006-Leonardo-Electronic-Almanac.pdf.

36. Jason Farman, *Mobile Interface Theory* (New York: Routledge, 2012), 103.

37. Ibid., 104.

38. Alan Chamberlain et al., "Locating Experience: Touring a Pervasive Performance," *Personal and Ubiquitous Computing* 15, no. 7 (2011): 719.

39. Farman, *Mobile Interface Theory*, 104.

40. The choice of technology is revealing here: GPS technology was deemed too precise in determining participant location, and was discarded in favor of the less location-precise process of triangulation—or "finger-printing"—by wifi and mobile phone towers. See: Gabriella Giannachi et al., "Blast Theory's *Rider Spoke*, Its Documentation and the Making of Its Replay Archive," *Contemporary Theatre Review* 20, no. 3 (2010): 357.

41. Farman, *Mobile Interface Theory*, 105.

42. Ibid.

43. Ibid.

44. Ibid.

45. Alan Chamberlain et al., "Locating Experience," 722.
46. Ibid., 724.
47. Ibid.
48. Ibid., 724–725.
49. Ibid., 720.
50. Ibid.
51. Gabriella Giannachi et al., "Blast Theory's *Rider Spoke*," 357.
52. Ibid.
53. Farman, *Mobile Interface Theory*, 108.
54. Roland Barthes, "Introduction to the Structural Analysis of Narratives," in *Image Music Text*, trans. Stephen Heath (London: Fontana, 1977), 110.
55. Peter Tolmie et al., "'Act Natural': Instructions, Compliance and Accountability in Ambulatory Experiences" (paper presented at CHI'12, May 5–10, 2012, Austin, Texas).
56. Matt Adams, Steve Benford, and Gabriella Giannachi, "Pervasive Presence: Blast Theory's *Day of the Figurines*," *Contemporary Theatre Review* 18, no. 2 (2008): 219–257.
57. Steve Benford and Gabriella Giannachi, "Temporal Convergence in Shared Networked Narratives: The Case of Blast Theory's *Day of the Figurines*," *Leonardo* 42, no. 5 (2009): 443–448.
58. Gabriella Giannachi et al., "Blast Theory's *Rider Spoke*," 357.
59. Matt Adams et al., "Pervasive Presence," 232.
60. Andy Crabtree et al., "The Cooperative Work of Gaming: Orchestrating a Mobile SMS Game," *Computer Supported Cooperative Work* 16 (2007): 168, emphasis in original.
61. Alan Chamberlain et al., "Locating Experience," 721.
62. Crabtree et al., "The Cooperative Work of Gaming," 168.
63. Ibid., 174.
64. Barthes, "Introduction," 97.
65. Michele A. Willson, *Technically Together: Rethinking Community within Techno-Society* (New York: Peter Lang, 2006), 149.
66. Georges Van Den Abbeele, "Introduction," in *Community at Loose Ends*, ed. Miami Theory Collective (Minneapolis: University of Minnesota Press, 1991), xiv.
67. Jean-Luc Nancy, *The Inoperative Community*, trans. Peter Connor, Lisa Garbus, Michael Holland, and Simona Sawhney (Minneapolis: University of Minnesota Press, 1991), 31.
68. Nancy, *The Inoperative Community*, 31.
69. Pamela M. Lee, "On the Holes of History: Gordon Matta-Clark's Work in Paris," *October* 85 (Summer, 1998): 68, note 5.
70. Willson, *Technically Together*, 149.
71. Ibid., 150.
72. Quoted in Mary Lou Lobsinger, "Cybernetic Theory and the Architecture of Performance: Cedric Price's Fun Palace," in *Anxious Modernisms: Experimentation in Postwar Architectural Culture*, ed. Sarah Williams Goldhagen and Réjean Legault (Montreal, Canada: Canadian Centre for Architecture/MIT Press, 2000), 128.
73. Nancy, *The Inoperative Community*, 31.
74. Ibid.
75. Crawford, "Taking Social Software," 87.
76. René ten Bos, "Giorgio Agamben and the Community without Identity," *The Sociological Review* 53, no. s1 (2005): 20.
77. Ibid., 20.
78. Giorgio Agamben, *Potentialities: Collected Essays in Philosophy*, trans. Daniel Heller-Roazen (Stanford: Stanford University Press, 1999), 47.

79. Giorgio Agamben, *The Coming Community*, trans. Michael Hardt (Minneapolis: University of Minnesota Press, 1993).

80. For discussion of this concept of the "undecidable" in relation to Nancy's thinking, see, François Raffoul and David Pettigrew, "Translators' Introduction" to *The Creation of the World, or, Globalization*, by Jean-Luc Nancy, trans. François Raffoul and David Pettigrew (Albany, NY: State University of New York Press, 2007), 1–26.

81. ten Bos, "Giorgio Agamben," 21.

82. Ibid.

83. Ibid., 26.

84. Ibid., 27.

85. Ibid.

86. Nick Couldry, "Rethinking the Politics of Voice," *Continuum: Journal of Media & Cultural Studies* 23, no. 4 (2009): 580.

87. Lingis, *The Community*, 10.

88. Ibid.

89. Ibid., 11.

90. Lingis in Mary Zournazi, "Foreign Bodies: Interview with Alphonso Lingis (1996)," in *Encounters with Alphonso Lingis*, ed. Alexander E. Hooke and Wolfgang W. Fuchs (Lanham, Maryland: Lexington Books, 2003), 89.

91. Lingis, *The Community*, 23.

92. See Marcel Mauss, "Techniques of the Body," *Economy and Society* 21, no. 1 (1973): 70–88.

93. Lingis, *The Community*, 69.

94. Ibid., 70.

95. Ibid., 77.

96. Krzysztof Wodiczko, *Critical Vehicles: Writings, Projects, Interviews* (Cambridge, MA: MIT Press, 1999), 9.

97. Hjorth, 41.

98. Wodiczko, 8–9.

99. Steve Benford et al., "Uncomfortable Interactions," section 1, para. 1.

13

PLAYING STORIES ON THE WORLDBOARD

How Game-Based Storytelling Changes in the World of Mobile Connectivity

Bryan Alexander

How do the examples in this chapter help us understand the practice of storytelling in the mobile media age?

By looking at how storygames have been adapted for mobile devices, this chapter points to the practice of these games as being largely determined by the platform's affordances (such as GPS capabilities) as well as the various social uses that have become integrated with the device. Mobile storygames differ from games played on a console at home (as storygames on a mobile device can be played in small pieces throughout the day) and thus the kinds of narratives that are experienced have had to adapt to this mode of gameplay. As the game spaces and temporal aspects change, so do the expectations for reader involvement. Mobile devices are used for capturing the world around us, and this ability is increasingly being incorporated into the ways readers/players interact with storygames. The participants can now use their location, the images they capture on their phones, and their social network as elements of the storygame. What has emerged is thus an augmented reality for games using mobile media, one in which the physical landscape interacts with constantly transforming data to tell stories in unique ways.

Keywords

- **Storygame:** A cultural artifact that combines elements of play with those of stories. The narrative incorporates gameplay procedures and reward systems, having participants engage the story in tandem with playing the game. These storygames adapt the narrative to the platform and utilize the medium-specificity of devices like mobile media.
- **Augmented reality (AR):** While this typically refers to the mobile device's ability to associate digital content with specific locations in the physical world

through a visual overlay, it can also be understood broadly as the interplay between data and a physical place. It is thus best considered in a continuum ranging from "light AR," in which digital content is small in memory and display terms like text and vector-based images, to "heavy AR," which uses large databases and dynamic visual overlays to create an interactive display that simultaneously integrates the physical landscape and information about that location.

• **Interstitial storygaming**: This mode of storygame combines mobile digital content with strong narrative content and is capable of being played in short bursts of time. It is often understood as "breathing life" into the dead or unused moments throughout a day. Interstitial storygames can therefore be played while waiting for a subway or standing in line at the store.

Introduction

Mobile devices have become rich, exciting, and broadly accessible platforms for gaming. Digital games have been popular applications for mobile phones and personal digital assistants (PDAs) for over a decade. Handheld devices whose main purpose was gameplay date back to the later twentieth century, with influential successes such as the Game Boy and PlayStation Portable (PSP). Perhaps the persistence of portable digital gaming stems from the cultural memory of analog antecedents: the portable chess set, a Pokemon hand, or the humble pack of playing cards. Recall, too, that a deck of cards is not a single game, but a platform for many games. Beyond historical memory, convenience is also a factor for this modern version of mobile gaming, as players have greater access to digital games throughout the day than they would with larger computers (laptops, desktops).

While mobile gaming has boomed, a parallel renaissance has taken place in the form of digital storytelling.[1] Users around the world have created short, auto-biographical video narratives, ranging from national initiatives sponsored by the BBC to the individual work of passionate creators. As with mobile devices, digital storytelling has been going on since the late twentieth century, dating back to the first uses of computation for narrative purposes. The first examples include narratives shared by UseNet and email, and then were succeeded by stories expressed via the early Web, followed by social media, and mobile devices.

The intersection between these two recent developments in mobility and gaming is the subject of this chapter. It is a complex process, unfolding across several levels at the present time: competing industries (entertainment, telephony, consumer electronics); divergent cultural factors, especially at the international level; and changes in the larger computing environment as we (perhaps) transition away from the era of the "personal computer" (PC). I argue that we can grapple with this complexity by isolating the development of mobile gaming as a new narrative medium. This should be understood broadly to better think through its emergent ramifications.

First, the history and current practice of storytelling organizes itself into a different form when translated into the mobile world, especially under the impact of its specific *material* affordances: always-on connectivity, gaming's ludic nature, augmented reality, and so forth. Additionally, some of the physical features characterizing leading smartphones—accelerometers and touch-screen interfaces—allow tangible interaction with game-story content through gestures: shaking, tilting, caressing, and bumping. Second, at a *socioeconomic* level, the deeply social aspect of mobile life drives different forms of audience behavior than we experience with Xbox-style consoles. The ability to easily capture, manipulate, and share content continues the so-called "prosumer" revolution of media democratization. Moreover, the intertwining of mobile storytelling game experience with everyday life calls into question art's boundaries and the "fourth wall" of performance (the breaking of this fourth wall that artificially separates the audience from the actors/art ultimately forces the audience to engage the performance as participants rather than spectators). For instance, players of *Zombies, Run!* play right through public spaces, chasing or eluding enemies invisible to the populations within which the game is played.[2] Live-action role-playing games (LARPs), once marginal events, might become the mainstream template for the social impact of mobile storygames.[3] This suggests a *cultural* shift: public and private spaces transform to some degree when inhabited by mobile storygames that are partially constructed by their players and consumers.

Third, the shapes of handheld stories change *formally*. For instance, the relative scarcity of multitasking on handheld devices supports deeply immersive, yet narrowly focused stories. This contrasts enormously with multitasking-friendly devices (laptop, netbook, or desktop computers) or large media platforms (game consoles). The latter's screen breadth, complex display styles, powerful hardware, and "infinite canvas"[4] for display lead to multithreaded story consumption. In one web browser on a PC, users can Google a story's setting background in one tab, Facebook about a beloved character in another, while running Google Earth in a parallel window to track game events, as a friend chats in a third window, and unrelated music pours from a fourth. But smaller screens on often-underpowered devices constrain the story experience, leading us at times away from broad immersion and instead toward a single, informationally narrow experience.

As the space of story experience changes, so does the temporal dimension. One sits before an Xbox prepared for a story of long duration, but lifting a phone from a pocket elicits a very different expectation. We are accustomed to brief moments of access on smartphones and other handhelds, consulting them in crowded social spaces, during a conversation's lull, flicked open while driving (dangerously!).[5] This habitual expectation can lead users to prepare to consume small chunks of story content on the go, rewarding specific game-story formats: episodes, exercises, micro-missions instead of full missions, and side quests rather than epic ones. We should expect these diverse pressures to shape new modes of storytelling, and we will examine several here.

Capture and Consume

It is well known to users, if not fully understood by policy, that mobile devices of all sorts are vehicles for multimedia capture. Featurephones, and especially smartphones, enable us to both create and consume content at an accelerating pace. The post–PC world, understood to not exclude but include laptops and desktops along with more mobile devices, boosts content interaction opportunities. We should therefore expect the media realm to intersect ever more productively with social media (e.g., we record audio and then republish it as a podcast or to sites like Freesound). Watching a video clip, either as an entire story or as part of one, we key in a comment to the site, bookmark it via Diigo, or share it through Pinterest. Physical information feeds into these interactions through automatic geolocation or user-driven spatial identification (e.g., check-ins, queries for local game players). The physical world has begun to change under the impact of this technology-enabled behavioral change, as a second (digital) social layer adheres to the face-to-face world.

This sharing aspect of mobile usage plays a key role in the gaming world. Players have collaboratively constructed a large world of secondary social media around games. From YouTube to the blogosphere to game wiki sites, we can peruse reviews of games, discussions of their merits, guides to play, cheat codes, and even videos of games played straight through (the "Let's Play" genre). This body of content can be seen as a vast network of distributed game criticism. As mobile devices increase our opportunity to create, share, and experience media, we should expect this networked secondary world to grow, playing a supplemental role in storygaming. It is certainly easier for us to capture game content, either as players or participants, but it is more significant that we have many more opportunities to consume, contribute to, amend, and respond to secondary game media. Think of Googling a game walkthrough while literally walking through the physical environment where it is played, or using one handheld device to scope out alternative endings for a story being played on another handheld device.

The social stratum for storygaming on mobile devices has already emerged. *Hitchery* offers a good example.[6] The game requires players to create cartoonish avatars of themselves, which is already an established practice in gaming and social media. *Hitchery* goes further in that gameplay requires another player to download that avatar to their Android phone or iPhone. The second player's phone displays the first's avatar superimposed on the camera view display; the avatar thus "hitches a ride" on the phone. The hitchhiker-carrying player, whose phone is dubbed a "bus" for the game, has the chance of winning both reactions from the avatar's creator and points from the game for carrying the character to various destinations. The affordances of mobile phone hardware, noted above, impact this game in two ways. First, the *Hitchery* program lets "bus" drivers take photos of their cartoon hitchers in physical locations by superimposing the avatar onto whatever background their phone's camera captures. Naturally, these imbricated photos can be shared back to the hitcher's creator and to the world. The avatar's creator can, of course, consume these travelogue snapshots via smartphone at any time. Second, hitcher journeys are described not only through photos but also by GPS data generated by the device's movements through the landscape. The phone's location awareness and tracking features thus contribute to the story's content.

In an obvious sense, *Hitchery* is a mobile game, as it includes players, artificial rules, and a reward system; but just as obviously, it also works as a storytelling engine. After all, players can send their game *characters* on voyages, which are created by digital media and imagination. These avatars have at least a rudimentary identity, given their association with their creators, their initial profile, and their reaction to successive environments. Not all hitchers are real people, as some are storygame fictions ("robot hitchers"; in traditional gaming these are non-player characters, or NPCs). The combination of characters, settings, and passage through time describes, among other things, a narrative. Its integration within a smartphone-based game yields an exemplary storygame.

Beyond the social matrix of *Hitchery*-style mobile storygameplay, we can identify another way that mobile devices change stories: the mutation of audience experience by the multiplication of chances to play. Put simply, it is easier to play *The Mystery of the Colonel's Ghost* on one's Kindle Fire during the interstices of a day than it is to fire up *Skyrim* on a living room Xbox.[7] Waiting in line, traveling on a train, taking a break from work, or simply being in the bathroom now constitute potential storygame time. Many readers of this chapter have probably played *Angry Birds* or *Plants vs. Zombies* in those settings. When we contrast this kind of short-term media consumption with the long sessions required for the hundred-hour gameplay of games such as *Mass Effect 3*, it becomes apparent that game producers may shape mobile content toward these truncated game times. Mobile games have thus far tended to be play snacks (rather than meals) that are consumed at various moments throughout the day.

Joseph Esposito makes a similar point about a changed media diet in developing his concept of "interstitial writing." These are stories we read while "waiting for a plane, a doctor, or for a meeting to begin. That's a huge number of minutes in any day; a good portion of our lives is wasted while we are waiting for the main course to arrive.... How about the 10-minute crack? Five minutes? Think of your own day: How often are you simply waiting, doing nothing?"[8] Stories consumed this way will tend toward compressed length: "More likely short items will be strung together in an anthology; the thesis of the anthology ('brief bursts about the new administration'; '101 short poems about transistors and current') will suffuse each item with a sense of being part of a whole."[9]

Featurephones have long been fertile ground for this kind of experience, as users peered through those small screens into poems, pithy sayings, and passages from religious texts, to name a few. Esposito thinks mobile content will tend toward the self-contained, unlike the hyperlinked nature of web content. He writes, "[I]t is improbable that item A will lead serially to item B, to item C, and so forth.

It would simply be hard to gather the narrative in our minds if it were written in this way. More likely each episode will have a beginning and an end—and then cut to another episode, which may be built around a different time or place or another character. All the pieces get assembled in our minds, five minutes at a time."[10] Although Esposito is focused on nonludic texts, we can readily extend these observations to mobile gaming. Shorter storygames may well be the norm, brief vignettes rather than novels. Alternatively, discrete and condensed levels within a game (e.g. stages of a quest, locations on a map) may serve a similar function of getting the player in and done quickly. We can think of this as interstitial gaming or interstitial storygaming.

To get to that form, some games are repurposed or reimagined from other—sometimes nondigital—platforms. An increasing number of older, story-based games have appeared on mobile phones, reaching as far back as role-playing classics *Monkey Island* (1990) and *Beneath a Steel Sky* (1994). Fantasy role-playing games have appeared, most of which owe enormous amounts to a fairly derivative tradition. They are not usually ports, but are clearly variations on well known, beloved themes: *Chaos Rings*, *Hybrid: Eternal Whisper*, *Ravensword*, and *Xenonia*. First-person shooters, those staples of AAA console games, have started to appear in truncated form on smaller, mobile screens with the publication of *Max Payne* (2001) as the otherwise largely unaltered *Max Payne Mobile* (2012) for iOS and Android.[11] At a very different level, the Frotz interactive fiction (IF) reader, workhouse for a storytelling game form dating back to the early 1980s, can be used on handhelds.[12]

Along with Frotz, the PortableQuest website and app lets users replay the classic interactive fiction *Zork* on a Kindle, or in a phone screen just one hundred pixels wide.[13] PortableQuest (PQ) provides a good example of interstitial game play. A user can pull out a phone or Kindle, accessing the PQ interface in seconds. The hoary *Zork* opening screen appears:

West of House
You are standing in an open field west of a white house, with a boarded front
    door. You could circle the house to the north or south.
There is a small mailbox here.

A simple prompt follows. Users can then key in *Zork*'s basic commands, such as "open mailbox" or "go north." In return, the game presents a textual description of how the situation changed as a result of the player's action ("The little door swings open, and there is a letter inside the mailbox") followed by another prompt. The mobile game's keyboard limitations (small size and/or autocorrect) are mitigated by the simplicity of these sometimes abbreviated commands ("e" for "east"). PQ rapidly returns text describing the results of your commands, and the game proceeds. Tunnels are discovered, monsters encountered, and the plot develops. The game can then be saved, allowing the player to put away their phone or Kindle. The game resumes during the next interstitial moment, letting the user refresh his or her memory with commands "inventory" (to reveal what the character holds) and "look" (to repeat a description of the immediate setting).

Zork is not an episodic story, but neither is it one requiring deep and persistent attention. The genre's familiarity lets users rapidly enter, leave, and reenter play again. Its puzzles carve out spaces from the broader narrative, suspending plot for an instrumental scene. In this way, the PQ version of *Zork* resembles the *Myst* series of games (1993ff), and we should be unsurprised to recall that *Myst* was ported to a variety of handheld devices, including PlayStation Portable and iPhone.

Another example of this trend is the resurrection of *Choose Your Own Adventure* stories as iPhone apps. These classic children's books are often cited as print hypertexts, requiring readers/players to make frequent narrative decisions, embodied as physically turning to specific pages.[14] The simple mechanism works well in digital spaces and allows for new features: "Instead of turning to a particular page to make a choice, the U-Ventures apps allow the reader to tap the screen and enjoy, with sound, light and other special effects—music and alien voices, for example—added to the titles, as well as new variations and endings dreamed up by Packard. Enhancements include readers having to remember code words and type them in to affect the course of the story."[15] In this case, the storygame becomes more gamelike both in terms of game-associated multimedia and in functionality. In a similar fashion, the *Gamebook* and *Fighting Fantasy* series build on this paradigm, but "[i]nstead of simply choosing between two forks in a book and turning to that page, they have you roll dice to determine the outcome of the story," thus adding the in-game function of randomness for event outcomes.[16]

U-Ventures has been explicit about adopting the Esposito model of faster, shorter media experiences: "Packard is particularly excited about 'very fast-paced segments,' which would have taken up too much space in a printed book. There's no such problem in cyberland, and we take advantage of that."[17] Besides formal compression and increased secondary social media, we have seen storygames use mobile devices' other hardware affordances. For example, the *Ruben and Lullaby* app uses a phone's accelerometer to shape the storyline, the course of an argument between two lovers. The game presents bits of the story, then pauses, allowing the user to advance the story by touching the screen or shaking the phone. These physical movements can alter a digital character's posture or mood. Drawings display the effects, especially representations of the lovers' faces. Sound further develops this, as the storygame's music alters to express various conversational and emotional registers. The argument's outcome, and that of the relationship, is literally in the player's hands.[18]

Furthermore, adventure stories can be linked to the physical world. *Wherigo* is a platform for experiencing interactive fiction on GPS-equipped mobile phones, but one where players advance stories by interacting with the offline world. A *Wherigo* story frames itself by displaying initial multimedia content, followed by a task to accomplish—walk to a certain location, for example. Once done, the next multimedia piece of the story displays, advancing the plot, along with a prompt for the following action. Virtual items accumulate in the classic adventure game inventory; players can obtain or use them by moving in the offline world, or by in-game actions.[19] Stories, or "cartridges" in the *Wherigo* scheme, are open to genre and content. The *Wherigo* site suggests these categories: "Walking tour of city sights. Neighborhood scavenger hunt. Innovative marketing proposal. Pub crawl for your friends. Interactive fictional adventure. Alternate reality game."[20] *Wherigo* lets stories add to the world, in a sense augmenting reality.

Augmented Reality

Taking this digital-physical connection a step further, mobile storygames increasingly have access to augmented reality (AR) technologies, which connect virtual content to the physical world. Users can experience a story by playing it through a space, where game features are tied to specific locations. Players can unlock game content by interacting with the physical world, as the playing field maps onto literal fields. Such storygames represent a break from the older, predigital mobile gaming space, which was always abstracted from the immediate; for example, the content of a game of cribbage, portable Battleship, or Hearts is not transformed based on where the players are. First developed in the 1990s, AR suggested gamelike design from its earliest days. When J.D. Spohrer described medium- and large-scale AR projects in 1999, the results read now like virtual reality or in-game mapping tools: "[I]magine being able to enter an airport and see a virtual red carpet leading you right to your gate, look at the ground and see property lines or underground buried cables, walk along a nature trail and see virtual signs near plants and rocks, or simply look at the night sky and see the outlines of the constellations."[21]

Beyond the technical implementation, AR has also broken new conceptual ground in how we think about public space, communication, and social organization. As Nathan Jurgenson argues, the combination of mobile with social technologies empowers popular expressions of dissent like those seen in the Arab Spring or the Occupy movement in the United States. The interconnection of digital content accessed locally through mobile devices, used for local purposes, then shared globally, lets us think of AR as a sociopolitical technology, as an "augmenting" technology. This approach lets us see clearly the ways such digital-physical, global-local combinations enable communication, "occurring both on and offline to be far more participatory than ever before. . . . With social media, *people can see the difference they are making*. They are not just passively consuming dissent but are more actively involved with creating it."[22] That deep, emergent type of AR engagement is predicated on powerful interactions of users with others, and users with multimedia content; that kind of involvement contextualizes and underpins the ways we engage with mobile storygames.

As of this writing, AR has progressed to the level of production, if not maturity. Consumers are increasingly accustomed to various levels of connecting digital content to the physical world, be it through mapping services, restaurant recommendations, or hardware. The practice of capturing images and data for augmented reality applications has begun appearing in the mainstream. For example, the GE Smartgrid AR demo combines images from the user experience with preexisting, popup animations. The user prints out a single sheet of paper, and then holds it up before their computer's camera. A 3D digital environment unfolds on the screen, superimposed on video imagery captured before the screen. The user's face and immediate environment, captured by laptop camera, appear intertwined with an interactive, three-dimensional cartoon scene. Such is the way that the AR poetry book, *Between Page and Screen* by Amaranth Borsuk and Brad Bouse, works. Readers hold the book up to the laptop camera and the AR markers transform into interactive pieces of poetic dialog between two characters, P and S (for Page and Screen). In a way, AR projects like this reverse the aforementioned capture dynamic. Instead of players capturing content, the game captures players as content.[23]

Current AR services depend on some combination of hardware and software, depending on configuration and complexity: phone (smart- or feature-), object markers (QR codes), web services, printers (for popup AR), GPS, and others that may well appear before this chapter sees publication. The rising facial recognition industry might take the uses of AR as an engine for storytelling still further. Linking people to their social media profile could improve audience collaboration. Tools like Recognizr or Twitter360 should help people who don't know each other in person find each other more quickly. In games that blend story with real life, such as LARPS, players could identify each other—and game masters—more quickly.[24] Facial recognition check-in might be a way to enter a game.

AR's physical-digital involvement has shown some benefits for media experience and may become the matrix for new storygame projects. The *Tales of Things* project gives us one glimpse into how this can play out. *Tales* is a combination of web service and QR codes. Users add QR codes to objects they (putatively) own. They add content to those codes, including audio, text, image, or hyperlinks to web videos hosted on the *Tales* site.[25] For example, one might *Tale* an acoustic guitar, appending a link to a YouTube video of someone playing the instrument. Other users can read that code with handheld devices, consume the discovered information, and then draw inferences about the resulting links. They can also add new codes, letting a potential story accrete.

The project describes itself in very story-oriented terms: "Wouldn't it be great to link any object directly to a 'video memory' or an article of text describing its history or background?" It has as-yet unrealized game potential, starting from the scavenger hunt model. Imagine a game where players have to find objects whose *Tales* tags lead them to other objects.[26] *Tales* has already been used for public performance art. An Oxfam project set up a room full of *Tales*-marked items, some of which also included RFID chips connected to a public address system. Users could listen to items' stories privately, or else trip the chip-PA service and have the story played to the entire space: "It was a very public story as though suddenly someone touched an object and a whole store was woken up by this tale about where these objects had come from. What was amazing was that people wanted the damn objects. You could see them holding almost something as though it was in someone's living room, and it changed the entire atmosphere of the shop. Everyone was fascinated."[27] Once again a mobile storytelling project alters public space. We also see a similar case with another *Tales* project that used that system to elicit patron conversations about objects in the Grant Museum at the University College London (detailed in Chapter 19 of this collection, "Enhancing Museum Narratives: Tales of Things and UCL's Grant Museum.") Such projects work as story platforms; as games, they are just starting to be explored. We should anticipate seeing that potential realized, perhaps along LARP lines.

A similar mobile storytelling project took place in the Maine town of Biddeford. This project staged audio stories at key downtown locations. Residents recorded narratives about "heart spots," where they found personal or community meaning: benches where one kissed a true love for the first time, or the location of a favorite shop. Visitors and other residents can explore these spots by physically experiencing the area.[28] This project, facilitated by Barbara Ganley, builds on the similar Toronto-area *[murmur]* project.[29] In both projects, the audience is mobile, connected to the narrative through handheld devices.

Recently, such "narrative archaeology" stories have included more elements of game play. *Mad City Mystery* was a murder-mystery game staged across a Midwestern city. Play involved investigation of clues in environmental and political domains, which included actors playing story roles:

> Students must provide the police examiner (played by a real person) enough data to open an investigation into the causes of the death. In the process players use their handhelds to talk with virtual characters to learn life histories, access documents describing chemicals, conduct simulated tests for PCBs, TCE, and mercury, and must piece together an argument about the cause of the death. These students think Ivan may have been poisoned. Are they right?[30]

Mad City Mystery's use of AR is on the low end of the spectrum, relying on GPS and mapping technologies as a means of "augmenting" the physical landscape. Lev Manovich describes this as an interaction with "augmented space," which—in *Mad City Mystery*—"is the physical space overlaid with dynamically changing information. This information is likely to be in multimedia form and it is often localized for each user."[31] The ability to base a storygame on these technologies points to a range of possibilities for narrative, ludic AR.

One of the most innovative AR storygames is *Zombies, Run!*, which was mentioned briefly at the beginning of this chapter. The game's genre is a familiar one, with a lone protagonist trying to survive in the aftermath of a catastrophic zombie rising. The game's description reads, "You're Runner 5. Hundreds of lives are counting on you. You've got to help your base rebuild from the ruins of civilization by collecting critical supplies while avoiding roving zombie hordes. Can you save them and learn the truth about the zombie apocalypse?"[32]

The storyline involves a protagonist—the player—literally racing out from a safe base (home) to accumulate supplies, while dodging the ravenous undead. *Zombies, Run!* sends instructions from smartphone to player/runner, gridding out a local gamespace on top of the real world. When a zombie attack is announced, the player must sprint to survive, and will sometimes get killed in the event of running too slowly or in the wrong direction. The game warns the player to take care with the physical world, not confusing it with the game's. Those instructions are part of a continuous audio track, which includes other content items intended to further establish the story's world: orders from commanders, narratives of panic, mood-setting music, and, of course, the moans of the enemy. The game also displays a visual mini-game, a schematic of the player's base along with supplies successfully obtained, other characters (NPCs), and the current zombie threat. The player must allocate items strategically throughout the base.

We can use *Zombies, Run!* to summarize our discussion thus far. *Zombies, Run!* combines story and game in a mobile device. It can be consumed in short doses, with individual missions being played through a player's daily running routine. The storygame uses the affordances of device hardware: GPS tracking of location and multimedia output. It changes social spaces by using a light form of AR to map a digital storygame onto physical reality, as a neighborhood jogger suddenly swerves across a road or sprints down an alley for mysterious reasons. It connects with social media, as players can share their mission results through Twitter.

These storygames exemplify a new form of digital storytelling, one with fascinating implications for how we connect games, technology, and story. They also manifest some of the critical cyber-cultural tendencies of our times. Mobile storygames tend to embrace the social, carrying forward the Web 2.0 movement. The presence of user-created content and low-cost products suggests the Internet's culture of DIY practice will persist. However, the splintering of the digital world into distinct, deeply separated siloes (the Android-Google one, Apple's, Microsoft's) in which mobile devices do not have seamless "handshakes" with each other to share data, implies that storygames will schism into distinct experiences. Perhaps each platform will acquire a reputation for a different type of story. Until (and unless) HTML5 enables a return to the universal design capacities of the World Wide Web, we should observe this divergence closely.

Moreover, current debates about the transformation of privacy under the impact of ever-increasing means of capture may have resonance for these mobile storygames. Concerns about the possible uses (and abuses) of game-captured data, anxieties about the ever-increasing intrusion of digital interaction on daily life, could drive criticism of storygames on mobile devices. Indeed, as this genre develops, played in the interstices of daily life, we should anticipate multiple cultural responses to these games. Their social status will indeed evolve, perhaps drifting toward the art-for-art's-sake mode of contemporary interactive fiction, or perhaps migrating into the big leagues of AAA game producers.

At the same time, we should expect developments within the genre based on its record thus far. As I've noted here, mobile storygames tend to make use of the mobile platforms' hardware and software affordances. As those platforms evolve and new ones appear, mobile storygaming will take on new forms. The tendency of returning to old games to repurpose or republish them could uncover new fields of play and additional types of stories. The secondary field of social media supplementing these storygames may prove a fertile ground for research into how these new forms are played, and what kinds of stories are created and experienced.

Notes

1. The term arose in the 1990s from the work of a Californian nonprofit, the Center for Digital Storytelling (CDS), which developed a pedagogy for the popular production of short videos. For background, see Bryan Alexander, *The New Digital Storytelling: Creating Narratives with New Media* (Santa Barbara, CA: Praeger, 2011), especially chapters 1–3.
2. See https://www.zombiesrungame.com/.
3. See *Pervasive Games: Theory and Design*, ed. Markus Montola, Jaakko Stenros, and Annika Waern (Boston: Morgan Kaufmann, 2009).
4. Scott McCloud, Reinventing Comics: How Imagination and Technology Are Revolutionizing an Art Form (New York: Paradox Press, 2000).
5. Ilkka Arminen terms this as the "Lazarus effect," in which the mobile device is understood as "breathing life into 'wasted,' 'dead' moments." See Ilkka Arminen, "New Reasons for Mobile Communication: Intensification of Time-Space Geography in the Mobile Era," in *The Reconstruction of Space and Time*, ed. Rich Ling and Scott W. Campbell (New Brunswick, NJ: Transaction Press, 2009), 92.
6. See http://hitchery.com/.
7. See http://www.colonellight.org/.
8. In his article on interstitial publishing, Joseph Esposito insists on phones for this kind of story instead of e-readers or tablets. See Joseph J. Esposito, "Interstitial Publishing: A New Market from Wasted Time," *O'Reilly Radar*, December 12 2008, http://radar.oreilly.com/2008/12/interstitial-publishing.html.
9. Ibid.
10. Ibid.
11. See http://itunes.apple.com/us/app/max-payne-mobile/id512142109?mt=8&ign-mpt=uo%3D4.
12. The classic work on IF remains Nick Montfort, *Twisty Little Passages* (Cambridge, MA: The MIT Press, 2003).
13. See http://www.portablequest.com/.
14. Bryan Alexander, *The New Digital Storytelling*, 17–28.

15. "Want to choose your own adventure? There's a books app for that," *The Guardian*, August 1 2010, http://www.guardian.co.uk/books/2010/aug/01/choose-your-own-adventure-iphone-app.

16. Eli Hodapp, "The 'Fighting Fantasy,' 'Gamebook Adventures' and 'Sorcery!' Series—Now with Even More Installments," *Touch Arcade*, August 20, 2010, http://toucharcade.com/2010/08/20/the-fighting-fantasy-gamebook-adventures-and-sorcery-series-now-with-even-more-installments/.

17. "Want to choose your own adventure?" *The Guardian*.

18. See http://itunes.apple.com/us/app/ruben-lullaby/id302028937?mt=8.

19. See http://www.wherigo.com/. I am indebted to Jason Farman for drawing my attention to this storygame platform.

20. See http://www.wherigo.com/about.aspx.

21. James C. Spohrer, "Information in Places," *IBM Systems Journal* 38, no. 4 (December 1999): 602–628.

22. Nathan Jurgenson, "When Atoms Meet Bits: Social Media, the Mobile Web and Augmented Revolution," *Future Internet* 4, no. 1 (2012): 83–91.

23. See http://ge.ecomagination.com/smartgrid.

24. Concerning LARPs and storytelling, see *Pervasive Games*, ed. Montola et al.

25. For good examples of audio from the project, see Ari Daniel Shapiro, "Tales of Things," *The World*, August 31, 2010, http://www.theworld.org/2010/08/tales-of-things/.

26. See http://talesofthings.com/.

27. Shapiro, "Tales of Things."

28. Barbara Ganley, interview with the author, July-August 2010. See http://www.heartofbiddeford.org.

29. See http://www.murmurtoronto.ca/.

30. See http://spotlight.macfound.org/btr/entry/mad_city_mystery/.

31. For further discussion of this kind of augmentation, see Lev Manovich, "The Poetics of Augmented Space," *Visual Communication* 5, no. 2 (2006): 219–240.

14

"I HEARD IT FAINTLY WHISPERING"

Mobile Technology and Nonlocative Transmedia Practices

Marc Ruppel

How do the examples in this chapter help us understand the practice of story-telling in the mobile media age?

Mobile technologies are often used to create highly immersive, location-dependent narratives; more uniquely, though, transmedia fictions using mobile devices often-times don't require the audience to go anywhere at all. This means that mobile technologies are sometimes employed in *nonlocative* or *nonmobile* contexts, where someone might use a mobile device but isn't required to go anywhere in particular for it to contribute to the fictional world. This chapter considers the creative and interpretive consequences of this type of mobile technological use, one that nonetheless results in narratives containing an often complex intermingling between the real world and the fictional world of the narrative. In such a context, mobile technologies become instructively embedded in the fictional content of nonmobile media. Regardless of the specifics of their integration, it is argued here that mobile technologies help us to extend our perception of a narrative in ways that have little to do with physical portability and everything to do with metaphors of mobility and sensory extension. In doing so, they also point to the creative potential for restricting our senses in a way that is wholly unique to contemporary expressions.

Keywords

- **Nonlocative transmedia fiction:** The creation of an expansive fictional world that takes place across multiple media forms, one of which is the mobile phone. Here, the use of mobile media in these transmedia fictions does not utilize the site-specific, location-aware capabilities of the device. Instead, the device remains stationary and contributes to both the fictional and functional elements of the story (by being a technology used within the story and also one that is used by the participants to further the narrative through actions such as sending/receiving text messages, making phone calls, accessing websites, to name a few).

- **Alternate reality game (ARG):** A genre of transmedia fiction in which audiences and the technologies they use are incorporated into the fiction as characters and objects in their own right. Narrative elements are distributed through a range of media and often require that players collaborate in order to solve puzzles and advance the story. They can take place across extended periods of time and blend interactions in the physical world and the narratives that emerge across media forms.
- **Object-orientation:** The process through which objects are incorporated into a fictional world in a way that structures our use of them in the real world. The objects here are lively, integral parts of the narrative, in a similar way to the characters within the story. The objects also link the digital space of the story to the physical space of the participants.

> *"I heard it faintly whispering. . . . I had to go where I could talk to it."*
>
> —*Hana Gitelman, aka "Wireless"*

Introduction

Perhaps the most widespread mode of mobile narrative creation is the inclusion of mobile technologies as key components of transmedia design, where hardware like cell phones and laptops sit comfortably next to media like print novels, celluloid films, and console video games in constructing massively complex, connected, and, importantly, materially diverse fictional worlds. In arrangements such as this, narrative exists as a multisited and multimodal construct, where meaning and interpretation are always "stereoscoped" by the constant presence of multiple winding and weaving narrative pathways. Because transmedia design allows for the integration of multiple (often materially incompatible) sites of meaning some level of connection is needed between them to prevent incoherence. These fictions consequently often form extremely complex networks of meaning. This chapter will examine how the networked meaning of transmedia expression is impacted by three distinct modes of mobile integration: the placement of mobile technology in nonmobile media such as films or graphic novels (*embedded* approach); the creation of in-between spaces where meaning is created through the coordinated use of mobile technology and another, nonmobile site (*simultaneous* approach); or the 'flattening' of multiple media platforms into a single format for use on a mobile device (*convergent* approach).[1]

The contexts presented here, though, are somewhat unorthodox: rather than examine the spaces and places where the more common location-based practices of mobile use are engaged by transmedia practice, we will look instead at what might be more loosely and paradoxically termed 'stationary' mobile engagements, where the audience isn't necessarily required to move anywhere at all. In other words, this chapter seeks to locate what use there is for mobile technologies in (transmedia) narrative if these devices don't at least partially ask us to take to the "city streets."[2] Before examining this idea further, however, I want to first define and differentiate between a mobile narrative and a transmedia fiction, and list some common situations where mobile technology and transmedia meanings become intertwined.

Transmedia Fiction and Common Practices of Mobile Integration

Unlike mono-medium fiction, where a narrative is developed across a book *or* a film *or* a graphic novel, in *transmedia fiction* a narrative is developed across multiple platforms, often simultaneously (for another analysis of transmedia fiction, see chapter 4 of this book, "The Affordances and Constraints of Mobile Locative Narratives"). A narrative might begin as a book or a film, but it might end in a video game, a website, or even in a phone call with a character from the story. Following Christy Dena,[3] the term transmedia fiction—as opposed to transmedia "storytelling"—is used to highlight that it is not simply stories that are created here but rather entire worlds and universes, complete with functional objects, locations that can be explored, and multiple modes of interaction, including games and social networking.[4] The process of creating transmedia fiction is a *practice* where multiple authors, producers, and other creative entities outline, design, and distribute multiple ways of engaging with a fictional world, each of which play an important part in helping us form larger meanings.[5]

In many cases, transmedia fictions incorporate mobile technologies as crucial elements that help to realize their respective worlds. Here, transmedia practitioners often exploit what Scott W. Ruston calls the "forward-looking features" of mobile devices: interactivity, mobility, and location awareness.[6] According to Ruston, each of these features combines in different ways to produce three corresponding categories of mobile entertainment: spatial annotation projects (where a location or object is "tagged" by users with text, audio, imagery, or video and is accessed via PDA or smartphone GPS capabilities), location-based games (where the "real world" is used as a game board with a rule-based, goal-oriented narrative structure as its backbone; examples include projects like *PacManhattan*, in which players treated the Manhattan grid as a giant Pac Man board), and mobile narrative experiences (which weave together "fiction and locale, real world and storyworld").[7] In each category, audiences are compelled to shift between or temporarily inhabit both an actual, embodied experience of a particular place and any (fictional) content that might be digitally augmented or accessed from that space.

Most transmedia fictions tend to lean toward creating "mobile narrative experiences" in realizing place-based content. For instance, in alternate reality games (ARG), a genre of transmedia practice that incorporates audiences as participants in the fictional world of the story, mobile devices often enact location-based engagements that either draw from or feed into other sites. In *The Dark Knight* ARG and *The Art of the Heist,* for example, players were called upon via fictional websites to decode encrypted GPS information and then follow these trails to live events where, presumably, they would receive further information about the plot. Relatedly, in *Breathe With Me: London,* a transmedia murder mystery which incorporated live performances, web content, and scavenger hunts set in London, players were sometimes asked to use the popular website *GPS Mission* (slogan: "The World Is Your Playground") in order to locate and follow checkpoints that would lead them through a series of missions. One mission in particular had players walking in the dark, guided presumably by only the light of the screens of their GPS-enabled mobile devices as they moved through an old warehouse district, looking for a token that would give them access to the next stage of play.

In less space-specific uses, what I refer to here as nonlocative practices, smartphones and other web-enabled devices can be used to receive and send text messages and emails to fictional characters, to call characters' voicemails and, in some cases, to speak with them, either via voice recognition software or with live actors. They are also commonly used to stream videos or play video games related to the property. But is there anything really "new" about nonlocative transmedia experiences? As early as the 1980s, for example, media theorist and producer Janet Murray was involved in designing systems where online fictional experiences were augmented with working phone numbers, some of which led to voicemail systems startlingly similar to what we now see with many transmedia fictions and ARGs.[8] In this sense, nonlocative transmedia mobile practices like these aren't necessarily groundbreaking. Indeed, one could easily use a service like Google Voice to send and receive both these phone calls and text messages, and skip using a mobile phone entirely. In addressing the unique nature of mobile technology, John Kelly makes the simple yet important point that "the only advantage mobile devices have is the fact that they are portable."[9] In other words, many of the functions of mobile technology already exist (or can be duplicated) by other technologies such as televisions, the desktop computers, or landline phones.

So, is there anything specifically "mobile" about the use of mobile technologies in nonlocative practices? If we often don't actually go anywhere when we use these devices in transmedia contexts, then what's the point? It's possible that the answer to these questions lies in an unspoken—yet wholly pronounced—trait of mobile technology: its ability to provide a technological context for the (fictional) extension of our senses. In this context, we are encouraged to combine multiple sources of narrative information across separate media platforms, such as when we use our cell phones to send a text message to a fictional character whose contact information is provided on a television show. However, rather than being free and imminently "portable," as the name suggests, mobile media as it exists in transmedia practice are instead often first bound or "embedded" to fictional information present in other, less interactive media. It is here in these embedded contexts where we can begin to see the way that mobile technology is used as a substitute for movement even when we are standing still.

The Effects and Affects of Transmedia Mobile Embedding

> *Run.*
>
> —*Text message sent to a character's mobile phone in Heroes*

The pervasiveness of mobile technology's embededness in other media is so established that we often take it for granted. On the one hand, unless we are explicitly meant to do so, very rarely do we stop to notice the significance of a cell phone in a film, a laptop sketched in a graphic novel, or a portable MP3 player discovered by a player in a video game, as their use in these contexts is often rendered as natural as our own. On the other hand, fictional embedding in transmedia practice means that in order to create a more believable world, these same mobile objects are "linked" to the characters and events of the narrative.[10] The result of this embedding and linking is the creation of a pronounced *object-orientation* within that world, where we expect or, at least, suspect that these mobile objects we see in platforms like a television show or a video game will be useable and accessible to us. To put this differently, in order for a mobile technology to *function* as space to expand a transmedia fiction, it often must first be *fiction* in another site.

Here, it's worth distinguishing between two co-occurring (and competing) uses of these devices: on one hand, mobile devices such as cell phones, laptops, and portable gaming systems exist as hardware, as objects or props, that work toward populating a believable fictional world and, at times, interaction. On the other hand, though, they are used as sites to distribute and channel (narrative) content on their own in a way that exists outside of the fiction. This is a distinctive placement of mobile technology: it is neither used for isolated, mono-medium expressions (i.e., those without reference to other media where the story is expanded), nor as an object without any fictional correspondence (such as a video game that isn't playable to the characters of the fictional world it is set within). In other words, in transmedia fictions we learn *what* to expect of a given mobile technology and *how* to expect it by seeing how it is used in another, nonmobile site.

Context Sensitivity

Some examples should help to clarify these points. For instance, in NBC's *Heroes* (2005–2009), one of the largest transmedia fictions to emerge recently (it's composed of no fewer than 350 unique sites ranging from television episodes to graphic novels to online, interactive web stories), mobile technologies are used extensively by both the characters themselves and the audiences who wish to learn more about them. Early on in the *Heroes 360° Experience* and *Heroes Evolutions* both ARGs that took place in the *Heroes* universe, audiences had the opportunity to opt in to receive phone calls and text messages from a character named Wireless who, not-so-incidentally, has the power to intercept and decode wireless transmissions, making her a literal embodiment of the capabilities of mobile technology. Once they opted in, participants began to receive text messages which, much like their embedded use, beckon us to expand our view of the events of the storyworld from a perspective bound to information shared via mobile device. A message sent on April 10, 2007, for example, reads, "With all the information I hear, it's sometimes hard to tell where reality ends and imagination begins, but I'm convinced there's 'more than meets the eye.'" Other text messages compel us simply to "Learn more" (November 19, 2007 message) or "Don't believe everything you see" (April 28, 2009 message). Each message also contains links to other sites and, in some cases, audio and video files. At other times, the embedded use of mobile phones and the audience's functional use are meant to be seen as identical. On February 9, 2009, for instance, in a television episode titled "Trust and Blood," a character named Claire receives a text message from a shadowy figure named Rebel that says:

THERE IS HOPE. YOU CAN STILL FIGHT BACK.

That same day, thousands of participants in the *Heroes* ARG also received a text containing the same message. Those who watched the episode would understand the dual meanings of the message, where both the audience and the fictional character are incorporated into the same plot. It is only through the fictionalization of functional usage such as this that we can make such equations, as the content received makes little sense without a derived context to root it in. But what happens when the gap between two sites—one mobile, one not—is not as defined as it was in the examples thus far but is, instead, structured so as to encourage *simultaneous* use of a mobile device and another media platform?

Simultaneous Use

While the embedded integration of mobile technologies shows how a device's use can be instructively fictionalized in transmedia frameworks, the majority of the connections audiences make between analog and digital sites are experienced in staggered succession, occasionally making it impossible to engage with two or more sites simultaneously.[11] One can somewhat easily imagine reading a book like Mark Danielewski's *House of Leaves*[12] while listening to the audio of Poe's album *Haunted*,[13] a complimentary album that gives transmedia-like sound and voice to key aspects of the novel, such as the creaking of the house's walls, or the groans of the demon that is thought to live there. It is much more difficult to reconcile the strategies how we might, for example, engage in related transmedia experiences where each platform is designed to be dealt with on its own. How, for example, could we possibly play the video game *Assassin's Creed* while also watching Laurent Bernier's short film *Assassin's Creed: Ascendance* and reading Oliver Bowden's novel *Assassin's Creed: Renaissance* without switching our attention from one site to another?

The difficulty of this sort of interpretation is found in what Durk Talsma, et al.[14] refer to as the *split-attention effect*. According to the principles of the split-attention effect, "attending to an . . . auditory stream does not affect the processing capacity of the visual stimuli as much as attending to another visual source would," and, more generally, any two modes that rely on the same senses (two audio sources, for instance) are similarly difficult to reconcile.[15] In other words, we have a hard time paying attention to images when other images occupy our vision, or sounds when other sounds penetrate our ears. When we use sound *and* image together, though, we can process them quite well. Simultaneous transmedia experiences, then, can only truly occur when the senses through which they function are made to work complimentarily and without interfering overlaps.

Fourth Wall Studio's *Eagle Eye: Free Fall (EE: FF)* is a transmedia fiction that forces us to do just this: engage both mobile phone and computer screen simultaneously. Working as an extensional site to DJ Caruso's (2008) *Eagle Eye*, a film about a sentient computer program named ARIIA that exploits mobile networks to gain control of its users, in *EE: FF* we can choose to work with ARIIA and, via our own mobile phones, become a pawn in its game. What's interesting about *EE: FF*, however, isn't necessarily the way that it connects to the film (at the end of *EE: FF*, we watch as the main characters of the film are drawn into the events), but rather the way that it reveals and restricts the information we have available to us. Here, our contact with the fictional world and our comprehension of its events are structured almost entirely by the interplay between our own functional mobile phone use and a fictional embedded use positioned on a computer screen.

We begin *EE: FF* by visiting the website, www.eaglefreefall.com,[16] entering our information, and noting a warning that the lives of the characters "will depend on what [we] do." After agreeing to these terms, the screen crackles, dissolves, breaks into code, and a simple black window opens on the screen with the following message:

> Initiating contact. . . .
> Who we are is not important. What we need is.
> We are calling you at XXX-XXX-XXXX.
> The password is LIAR.

Almost immediately after this message appears, the player's phone rings. On the other end of the line is a woman's voice (the voice of ARIIA) which bluntly asks for the password. Upon supplying it, she informs us that if we follow directions, we will live. We are then told to "read our screen and do exactly as instructed," and are informed that our task is to find someone named Phil Maurro. After receiving a series of tiled images that show Maurro at various locations across a city—in a taxi cab, sipping coffee, placing a call at a phone booth, walking through a garage—we hack into a government tracking system and in locating Maurro's car, the screen shifts to a GPS-like map that then shows him speeding across the city, seemingly aware he is being pursued. Two more windows then pop up—one showing the speed of Phil's car, the other relaying the following message: "Accessing Phil's camera phone and vehicle systems. You will have to convince him to turn the car around. We are calling you."

From this point on, *EE: FF* becomes a game of juggling incompatible interfaces: we must monitor Maurro's speed, speak to both him and the unknown woman via the phone in our hands, and attempt to make sense of the video feed from the camera phone, which cuts between a frantic Maurro and the blurred walls of thruway tunnel (see Figure 14.1). Our perception of both the fictional and functional world, then, is effectively split: pressed to our ear is a device that relays aural information in whatever environment we inhabit, while on the screen we see the blurred interior of a highway tunnel framed by the passenger door and windows of Maurro's car. In order for this engagement to make sense, we must also reconcile the two competing channels, one of which—the audio from the cell phone—is also similarly layered as a three-way call, containing both the voice of Maurro and ARRIA.

The act of interpretation here, then, is heavily dependent on our ability to switch, sometimes rapidly, between phone and screen. Importantly, however, nothing we hear or say into the phone is broadcast from our computer speakers. Rather, aside from some ambient noise, the aural information coming from

Figure 14.1 Screenshot from *Eagle Eye: Free Fall*, where an embedded camera phone becomes a mobile focalizer within the fiction. Image courtesy of Fourth Wall Studios, 2008.

our computer is almost muted: using the camera phone video feed, we can see Maurro speaking and watch as he swerves erratically, pounding the steering wheel as he does so, but we cannot *hear* what he is saying or the brakes screeching. In other words, the information needed to complete the scene is *restricted* in a way that doesn't just promote the use of multiple media platforms but also necessitates a balance between phone and screen. After failing to convince Maurro to turn around (it's likely impossible to get him to do so), the car's acceleration is forced and its airbag deployed by ARIIA, sending it careening out of control and killing Maurro instantly. Yet even so, our vision continues. Lying on the pavement near the wreck is the still functional camera phone, through which we see cars passing over while the sound of their motors is heard through the phone we hold in our hands. The phone is no longer tied to a character, yet it is still our sole view of the fictional world. Eventually, the police show up, find the phone, trace it, and call us. We escape, barely, but are told by ARIIA, "You are now our tool, to be deployed when and as we wish," a line that suggests we are the equivalent of the technologies we use.

In another Fourth Wall Studios production,[17] *www.unnexclusive.com,* we must similarly work through a restriction or channeling of information. Tied to NBC's short-lived TV show *Kings* (2009), we are now placed in the role of a TV producer who must prepare a star reporter for an interview with an informant. After accessing the website and entering our information, a man in a trench coat walks out from the shadows and, pointing to his cell phone, mutters a few words we cannot hear. The phone, it seems, is our only mode of contact with the reporter, who points at his own mobile phone as if to suggest that this will be the only way to communicate with him. Almost directly after our phone rings and we answer it, the reporter turns his back to us, walks off again into the shadows (see Figure 14.2), and stays there, making it impossible for us to make out any gestures or lip movements he might make. Much like *EE: FF,* we are quite literally coerced into using our phones by a restriction of content, one that once again forces a split-attention engagement with phone and the screen in a manner that provides both interaction and immediacy. In this sense, they are a literalization of the filtering of information, which Kelly calls the "assisting interactions"[18] of mobile technology, the sum total of which results in a shifting sense of perspective in the fictional world.

Convergent Use

In a recent commercial aired on primetime TV, a teenage girl is shown walking out of school and into a large, open concrete yard, a red lunch tray in her hands. Seated all around her are her fellow students, each clad in the same dull uniform, each sitting listlessly at metal picnic tables eating his or her lunch. The girl looks around and, dejectedly, she moves across the yard towards an empty table, presumably to eat her lunch alone. Approaching the table, though, she finds an iPhone sitting on another

Figure 14.2 The reporter turns his back, encouraging mobile phone use in the audience in the www.unnexclusive.com project. Image courtesy of Fourth Wall Studios, 2009.

tray, its screen showing what looks like a book cover with the words "Cathy's Book: If found, please call (650) 266–8233." She looks around again and, with no one noticing, swipes her finger across the device. As soon as she does so, the world around her begins to transform: students who once ignored her now gaze at her as hand-drawn characters cut from paper, images and sounds cascade from the device and fill the sky, and a woman's voice whispers to the girl that "I know it all sounds crazy, but I'm leaving you the proof in case I don't come back." Smiling now, the girl is shown framed by the sun, staring at her transformed surroundings.

It's not just a book—it's me.

— Cathy Vickers, *Cathy's Book* app commercial

The description above is taken from the commercial for *Cathy's Book: Part 1,* an application developed for use on touchscreen Apple mobile devices such as the iPad, iPod Touch, and iPhone. Created by Running Press (a name that in itself suggests mobility), the *Cathy's Book* apps are adaptations of the book trilogy of the same name (Parts 1, 2, and 3 of the app all work with the first book in the series). Produced by Sean Stewart, Jordan Weisman, and Cathy Brigg, *Cathy's Book* (the print book) was a successful and inventive novel that incorporated several aspects of transmedia design into its narrative.[19] Bundled with the book is an evidence envelope containing a wide array of intrafictional objects ranging from folded restaurant napkins with phone numbers scrawled on them, death certificates, business cards, old newspaper clippings, maps, and even coins. Each of these artifacts is in some way related to either the book itself or another site outside of the book, where websites and phone voicemail systems are often only locatable through the items in the packet.

Throughout *Cathy's Book* (the print book), there is a pronounced emphasis on the tangibility of such engagements. Here, we might notice the differences in texture of the cardstocks and papers used for the artifacts in the packet, the lengthy descriptions from Cathy herself of what it feels like to touch them, and the fact that the book itself is meant to be viewed as a fictional object belonging to Cathy—her "lost" journal. Examples like this reflect the concept of object-orientation introduced earlier—only here we can actually hold many of the objects Cathy mentions in the book. This makes it all the more peculiar, then, that *Cathy's Book* has been so successful as an app. In some ways, this makes a degree of sense: no longer does someone have to reach from the book to the bundled artifacts to a keyboard to the Web in order to make sense of the story. Now, these same artifacts, phone numbers, and URLs are embedded within the (hyper) text of the book. With the swipe of a finger, we can call the numbers, browse the websites, and view the objects on the same screen, all without having to lug a book and a laptop around. Additionally, what were once Cathy's static drawings are now often kinetically animated, set to music, and bursting with graphical effects (see Figure 14.3). Even so, we are confronted with another version of the question that has lingered within this whole chapter: if something like *Cathy's Book* existed (and was successful) as a book, then is anything gained by adapting it to mobile technologies other than portability?

While the *Cathy's Book* apps lose much by way of the tangibility of the fictional object-artifacts, what they gain is an assertion of the relationship between how we perceive the world and mobility. Unlike the print book, the *Cathy's Book* apps allow for an integrated, seamless experience of both the text itself and links

Figure 14.3 The *Cathy's Book* app commercial. Image courtesy of Running Press Publications, 2010.

outside of it.[20] Here, for example, Cathy's references to historical events often contain hyperlinks to external sites, such as *Wikipedia*, where more information can be found. Several such links, however, do much more than provide extrafictional/contextual information for the audience: they provide instead a view of the real world as seen from the perspective of Cathy's fictional world. Take, for instance, the following passage:

> After school, I took the BART into the city and then a bus to *Haight-Ashbury*. My ArtGirl costume was OK camouflage for mingling with the Haight's tat-and-piercing crowd. I was wearing my Guess What You're Missing outfit: fitted black leather jacket, low-rider jeans and boots that went Stomp, Stomp, Stomp up the hill to Victor's Uncle's house.[21]

When we tap on the words "Haight-Ashbury," we are taken to a Google Maps street view of the area, one where the camera rotates 360°, showing us the whole block as it does so. Importantly, the passage that embeds this link is highly evocative and sensory in nature. We read descriptions of what Cathy is wearing and the sound of her boots stomping on the pavement before tapping the link. Later on, other links are embedded amidst passages that describe the smell coming from nearby restaurants, the "roar" of background conversations, and the sight of steam billowing out from a doorway on a cold night. While each of these descriptions suggests much on its own, the strategic placement of links within them yields a profoundly transformed fictional world, one that inverts the engagements of simultaneous use. Instead of split-attention integration, with the *Cathy's Book* apps there is no "in-between," no threshold space between two or more separate sites that we must negotiate in order to make sense of the narrative. Rather, *everything* in the *Cathy's Book* apps is already constructed so as to encourage a fictional perception of even real world locations.

Importantly, the fact that the *Cathy's Book* apps are not available for use with desktop or even laptop computers but only the most *portable* of devices also suggests another dimension to the experiences we have with them. Rather than just reading the text, tapping the link, and superimposing the fictional elements over the real world, if geography allows, we might also *wander* these same locations ourselves. The result of this is the creation of what theorist Adriana de Souza e Silva refers to as a "hybrid space," a transformation of "our experience of space by enfolding remote contexts inside the present context."[22] Unlike location-aware mobile experiences, though, where our device alerts us to the presence of geotagged content as we walk through a physical space, in projects like the *Cathy's Book* apps, we imaginatively tag the locations ourselves, giving them meanings that they otherwise would not contain. In doing so, we profoundly transform both real and fiction. Much like the other examples in this chapter, as we project ourselves through the lens of mobile technologies, our perspective becomes incorporated with the devices themselves.

Conclusions: Escaping the Permanent Present

The shift from location-based to location-agnostic, "stationary" mobile narratives is enabled partially by equating mobile technology to "seeing": we can see beyond ourselves through a combination of the right technology and a fictional world built to incorporate it. Part of the power and pleasure that comes from the integration of mobile technology in transmedia practice is that these devices are such a huge part of our daily lives. In co-opting them for fictional purposes, the narrative intervenes with its own unpredictable logic, one that draws from our present use of mobile technology for its own needs. Such an understanding reveals the dynamic nature of mobile technology as a purely semiotic metaphor in its own right—we associate movement, knowledge, and extended perception with mobile technology even when we do not have the means to engage it.

Each of the examples looked at in this chapter, however, represent a "current" usage of mobile technology, meaning that transmedia integration of mobile technologies is always a "now," rather than a "then" or "what if?" proposition. This means that while we will continue to see mobile embeddings, split-attention negotiations, and single device convergences, what we *won't* see are potentially new modes of conceiving of mobile technology, those that challenge the contexts of contemporary use by integrating such practices into unfamiliar and challenging fictions. Here, mobile use might be *restricted* in a way that evokes lost technological artifacts or even a usage that could have, but didn't, manifest. This is, to be sure, a strange place to imagine, one where we might ask our devices to (at least pretend to) do more or, conversely, less than they are capable. But it is a place worth considering, as it allows us to question both the assumptions we make about the devices we use as well as the ways in which these devices, regardless of their functions, work toward filtering our perception of *any* event, fictional or otherwise. We will, no doubt, continue to see more integrative uses of mobile technology in transmedia contexts, uses that do much toward engendering narrative complexity: more location-aware engagements, more pronounced object-orientations, perhaps even a one-to-one correspondence between what happens in embedded fictional use and in "real-world" extensional functional use. But because this is such an easy thing to imagine, it might be worthwhile to do the opposite—to envision that difficult place where mobile devices function in a manner completely different that we expect them to, where the everyday use that defines transmedia mobile design is itself called into question, leaving behind a space of pure imagination and possibility where fiction helps to redefine function.

Notes

1. These modes correspond to what Christy Dena sees as the main frameworks of transmedia fiction: a collection of mono-medium stories (a franchise), a collection of media that tells one story (expansive approach). See Christy Dena, *Transmedia Practice: Theorising the Practice of Expressing a Fictional World across Distinct Media and Environments* (Ph.D. dissertation, University of Sydney, 2011).

2. Steve Benford, et al., "The Frame of the Game: Blurring the Boundary between Fiction and Reality in Mobile Experiences," in *Proceedings of the SIGCHI Conference on Human Factors in Computing Systems* (CHI '06), ed. Rebecca Grinter, Thomas Rodden, Paul Aoki, Ed Cutrell, Robin Jeffries, and Gary Olson (New York, NY: ACM, 2006), 427.

3. Dena, *Transmedia Practice*.

4. Marc Ruppel, "Peripheries," in *Visualizing Transmedia Fiction: Links, Paths, Peripheries* (Ph.D. dissertation, University of Maryland, 2011). While audiences are often given access to such knowledge in extrafictional sites such as property encyclopedias, universe-level information usually exists first and foremost as purposefully un- or underdefined information that allows for imaginative projection. Such information is often included in transmedia "bibles," documents that detail, among other things, the background information undergirding a particular fiction. Usually, much of this information remains unseen by the audience.

5. These connections can be located partially through what I call "migratory cues," spaces in a transmedia fiction where contact between two or more sites is inevitable, and where our previous knowledge of a story is "cued" and combined with new content and contexts. See Marc Ruppel, "You Are Then, This Is Now: Technology, Nostalgia and Consumer Identity at CES 2007," *The Journal of Social Identities* 15, no. 4 (2009): 537–555.

6. Scott W. Ruston. "Storyworlds on the Move: Mobile Media and Their Implications for Narrative," *StoryWorlds: A Journal of Narrative Studies* 2 (2010): 103.

7. Ibid.

8. Janet Murray, *Hamlet on the Holodeck* (Cambridge, MA: The MIT Press, 1997), 110.

9. John Kelly, "Design Strategies for Future Wireless Content" in *Mobile Media: Content and Service for Wireless Communication*, ed. Jo Groebel et al. (London: Lawrence Erlbaum Associates, 2006), 74.

10. Dena, *Transmedia Practices*, 203.

11. Marc Ruppel, "Narrative Convergence, Cross-Sited Productions and the Archival Dilemma," *Convergence: The International Journal of Research into New Media Technologies* 15, no. 3 (August 2009): 295.

12. Mark Danielewski, *House of Leaves* (New York: Pantheon Books, 2000).

13. POE, *Haunted*, CD (London: Atlantic Records, 2000).

14. Durk Talsma et al., "Attentional Capacity for Processing Concurrent Stimuli Is Larger across Sensory Modalities than within a Modality," *Psychophysiology* 43 (2006): 541–549.

15. Ibid., 547.

16. Sadly, *EE: FF* is seemingly no longer being maintained. The disappearance of transmedia sites is a very real and quite tangible dilemma impeding its research. The websites constructed for ARGs, for example, often collapse in "404 Page Not Found" errors mere days after they are engaged. A system for transferring, storing, and maintaining the various digital sites of a transmedia project is desperately needed at this point; otherwise the concept of "replayability" will be an impossible one in such contexts.

17. Much like video game studies are increasingly moving beyond "close play" and moving toward analyses of game graphics engines (such as the Epic's Unreal 3 engine) as a means of understanding them, both *Eagle Eye: Free Fall* and *www.unnexclusive.com* are also built on the same engine, Fourth Wall Studio's proprietary RIDES technology. As such, we might expect certain similarities to appear with regard to our interactions, but I argue that such parallels are ultimately subjugated to the larger affectual resonance of mobile focalization.

18. John Kelly, "Design Strategies for Future Wireless Content," in *Mobile Media: Content and Service for Wireless Communication*, ed. Jo Groebel et al. (London: Lawrence Erlbaum Associates, 2006), 74.

19. Sean Stewart, Jordan Weisman, and Cathy Brigg, *Cathy's Book* (Philadelphia: Running Press, 2006).

20. Of course, a convergent experience such as this very much pushes the limits of what can and should be considered transmedia fiction, as all of its sites exist digitally. However, the varying modalities needed to negotiate the narrative of *Cathy's Book*—from aural to interactive to kinetic text—and also the distinctions present between the "book" itself and the sites existing outside of it (permission needs to be granted in order to visit a webpage, for example) also provide the cross-modal diversity needed for a minimally defined transmedia experience.

21. Stewart, Weisman, and Brigg, *Cathy's Book*, 16.

22. Adriana de Souza e Silva, "From Cyber to Hybrid: Mobile Technologies as Interfaces of Hybrid Spaces," *Space & Culture* 9, no. 3 (2006): 263.

PART V

Narrative Interfaces

15

NARRATIVE FICTION AND MOBILE MEDIA AFTER THE TEXT-MESSAGE NOVEL

Gerard Goggin and Caroline Hamilton

How do the examples in this chapter help us understand the practice of story-telling in the mobile media age?

This chapter situates the new stories, fictions, and formats for writing, reading, producing, and distributing narratives within the history of various reading platforms. We look at the increasingly strong relationship between narrative and mobile devices, stretching back to the design of e-readers for mobile devices and the emergence of narratives based on the capacities of cell phones (such as text-messaging stories and Japanese cell phones). We discuss the way that mobile media have been incorporated in ingenious ways into new kinds of situated, locational, cross-media, multimodal literary, artistic, and activist narrative practices. By looking at these emerging mobile storytelling projects through a historical lens (even looking back to the emergence of the novel), this chapter argues for a broader understanding of the practice of discontinuous reading. Engaging stories on platforms that are intimately connected with other media forms, the act of reading can extend beyond the linear, enclosed models of reading that characterize certain texts. As exemplified in e-readers, smartphones, and tablets, there is an opportunity for a much more intense encounter with narratives, and we foresee a much deeper engagement with narrative dynamics from a wider range of producers, consumers, co-creators and distributors.

Keywords

- **Narrative ecology:** The notion that narratives do not exist within the bounds of the medium through which they are conveyed. Instead, narratives exist in a much larger (and thickening) ecology of media (from print books to e-books, from oral storytelling to text messages) and societal influences (including the relationship between author, reader, and collaborative texts).

• **Decentralized narrative:** A narrative work that does not have an organizing "center" and can thus be experienced out of sequence. These kinds of works do not rely on a narrative arc or narrow narrative trajectory and are thus aligned with the category of nonlinear narratives. These works favor diversity (instead of unity) of style from section to section.

Introduction

Mobile media are changing the way we interact and communicate, and the way we tell stories. From the changing nature of the work of journalists in the newsroom to the collaborative art of computer game creation or the personal stories told each day on blogs and social networks, narratives are now created and consumed in an ever-expanding range of modes, informed and enabled by the principles of networked mobile and online communication. The global ubiquity and popularity of mobile communication among media users has given scholars the opportunity to explore how audiences are using mobile phones to construct their own stories as an alternative to those produced commercially. Today's mobile phone users have been the subject of many media analyses documenting the creation of amateur movies, games, or novels, along with other personal, autobiographical narratives that take advantage of the phone's multimedia tools such as a built-in camera, microphone, and global location positioning. Thus today there exists a teeming universe of storytelling efforts experimenting with narrative and mobile media. As yet, however, there has been little investigation of how conventional fictional formats such as the novel are responding to the affordances of networked mobile devices and the new possibilities for narrativity they offer. This is surprising, given the commonplace idea that the changes could be radical indeed, as Rebecca Young, for instance, has suggested when she writes, "New media technologies are changing the way we work, the way we view the world, and thus the way tell stories. . . . Narrative is fracturing and reordering as time, space and point-of-view are becoming increasingly modular and variable."[1] To set the scene for understanding recent developments in narrative fiction for contemporary mobile media—especially smartphones and tablets—it is important to appreciate the emergence of new narrative forms with earlier mobile platforms.

While there are a lot of ways of telling stories using mobile media and networked communication, in this essay our interest lies in exploring the effect of digital mobile communication networks on the narrative modes of fiction. To develop our argument, this chapter is divided into three parts. Firstly, we review early experiments with narrative in cellular mobile telephony, their cultures of use, and innovations. Secondly, we turn to a rather different history, that of the development of e-readers—distant relatives of contemporary mobile e-books—from the 1970s onward. We contrast these e-books with the wave of mobile narratives associated with the emergence of mobile cultures catalyzed by second-generation and third-generation networks. Thirdly, we look at the development of narrative fiction specifically for mobile reading devices, such as smartphones and tablets. We examine how these new narrative platforms respond to the successes and failures of these early experiments, particularly with regard to the delivery and development of networked narratives, and the new opportunities afforded by enthusiastic user participation in mobile media networks.

Early Mobile Narratives

Mobile phones were commercially introduced in Japan and the United States in the late 1970s, designed for vehicular use, with the first handheld mobile introduced in 1983, and the first generation of analogue mobile phones saw little obvious implications for new kinds of narrative practice. Of course, the telephone had long played an important role as a device in narrative, especially in novels, cinema, and television, as well as being used in a rich vein of telephone art. In addition, the introduction of the mobile phone—especially once it became light enough (due to miniaturization and digitization) not to require the kind of bulky equipment that for some time limited it to the realm of vehicular-based telephony—added a new cultural technology to other earlier portable technologies, including cameras, radios, and, notably, books.[2] While socially and culturally significant in many other ways, the arrival of portable voice telephony did not immediately result in narrative experimentation or innovation of an easily recognizable kind. When mobile phones did begin to attract attention for their literary fictions, it was due in large part to the phenomenon of text-message novels.

Something of an afterthought included in the second generation digital mobile Global System for Mobile Communications (GSM) standard,[3] the first use of text messaging occurred in 1992.[4] Since the end of the 1990s, text messaging has become increasingly popular—especially among youth cultures.[5] SMS triggered a wave of user, design, and provider innovation centering on text communications.[6] This cultural and linguistic blossoming was what seeded the cell-phone novel.[7] Working within the character limitations of SMS, epistolary, episodic, serialized, and other fictions were created by a continuum of amateur to professional writers (which is discussed in detail in the next chapter of this book, "Stories of the Mobile: Women, Micro-Narratives, and Mobile Novels in Japan"). Japan was a pioneer of the cell-phone novel (or the *keitai shōsetsu*), with the most organized and salient publishing industry centering on cell-phone novels. It appears that experiments with cell-phone fiction commenced in Japan as early as 2000. Cell-phone novels serve as one of the most obvious predecessors to the e-book applications used today on smartphones and tablet computers. Further, according some accounts at least, there is a medium-specificity to the cell-phone novel, as Kyoung-hwa Yonnie Kim suggests:

> While *keitai shōsetsu* shares many of the cultural displays of interactive lit-
> erature in cyberspace ... the phenomenon seems remarkably dependent on
> the material feature of "*keitai* as a thing," and results in an obsessive prefer-
> ence for *keitai* and the physical circumstances around its consumption. In
> terms of the remediation of email rather than literature, *keitai shōsetsu* is a
> cultural mechanism to build and maintain "literary activities" in everyday
> experiences using mobile media.[8]

As well as the epistolary precedents,[9] to put mobile messaging narratives in context, it is necessary to reprise the history of electronic texts, books, and reading.

Electronic Books versus Mobile Narratives

Electronic books have been in sustained development since the early 1970s. In his
famous 1972 essay, which described the prototype of the now iconic Dynabook
device, Alan C. Kay postulated that "'Books' can now be 'instantiated' instead
of bought or checked out. . . . A combination of this 'carry anywhere' device
and a global information utility such as the ARPA network or two-way cable
TV, will bring the libraries and schools (not to mention stores and billboards) of
the world to the home."[10] The Dynabook was never realized as an operational
device, let alone a commercial proposition, though it bears more than a passing
resemblance to Apple's iPad and other tablet computers of the 2000s.[11] Around
the time Kay conceived the Dynabook, Project Gutenberg, the first producer of
electronic books (what were then thought of as texts), was established in 1971 by
Michael Hart at the University of Illinois. Hart based Project Gutenberg on the
premise that

> anything that can be entered into a computer can be reproduced indefi-
> nitely . . . what Michael [Hart] termed "Replicator Technology." The con-
> cept of Replicator Technology is simple; once a book or any other item
> (including pictures, sounds, and even 3-D items) can be stored in a com-
> puter, then any number of copies can and will be available. Everyone in
> the world, or even not in this world (given satellite transmission) can have
> a copy of a book that has been entered into a computer. . . . The Project
> Gutenberg Etexts should cost so little that no one will really care how
> much they cost. They should be a general size that fits on the standard
> media of the time.[12]

Project Gutenberg advanced the notion that printed "books" could now become
electronic files or texts available for near-instant and very cheap transmission.
It was only later, at the turn of the century, that the concept of the e-book as a
distinct format and as a consumer item took hold. As Terje Hillseund explains:

Before the term e-book came around in the late 1990s it was not unusual to talk about electronic books in terms of files collected in the Gutenberg Project or books formatted on compact discs. [From 2001] the term e-book refers to digital objects specially made to be read with reading applications operating on either a handheld device or a personal computer.[13]

The "first e-book reader generation" included the Sony Data Discman (1990), the Franklin Bookman (1995), as well as the early Rocket e-book (1998) and Soft-Book (1998). The second-generation—with "modem capabilities, greater memory, better screen resolution, and a more robust selection of available titles"[14]—included the SoftBook Reader 1998, Librius Millennium device (1998), and the Everybook Dedicated Reader (1998). Sony launched its Sony Librie e-reader in 2005—pioneering the use of Ink technology for its screen.

Although the parallels between e-books, e-readers, and the mobile phone seem obvious to users in the era of feature- and smartphones, the affinities between these two portable cultural technologies took some time to coalesce. While, as we have observed, much more research about the rise of SMS novels is needed to precisely understand this phenomenon, it would appear that this was a parallel development to what was occurring in the much longer established e-book and e-reader domain. These two distinct streams did finally coalesce in the epoch of the smartphone (something clearly pioneered by the Japanese iMode approach to the mobile Internet).

With the establishment of second- and third-generation digital mobile phone technologies and the associated user cultures surrounding them, these devices became a site for inspiring creative experimentation with narrative formats and modes. Mobile phones also became important cultural technologies in the "narrative" turn, which saw (and continues to see) narrative deployed across a wide range of settings—whether personal or community narrative, narrative in tourism or cultural institutions such as museums, narrative in therapy, in mobile learning, or in the kinds of mobile-generated narratives involved in "vernacular creativity," "user-generated content," and "convergent culture."[15] These kinds of dynamic, collaborative, and situated narratives amount to an important new mode of storytelling that can be considered unique to mobile media. These practices were not the predicted outcomes of the development of mobile technologies, nor has their narrative potential fully unfolded. Yet it is clear that mobile media are playing a highly significant and quite specific role in the generation of new modes of narrativity.[16] For instance, Rita Raley, reflecting on locative mobile narratives, proposes that a "critical approach to the study of mobile narrative needs to account not only for the participant's relation to the work, but also for her relation to the work-as-environment and the environment-as-work."[17] Further, we would suggest, as much as mobile communication has made personal interactions more apparently public, mobile media thicken the narrative environment: more voices, more stories, an increased range of options for beginnings, middles, and ends—what we would characterize as a thickening of narrative ecologies.[18]

Elsewhere, reflecting on developments in narratives that work across different media forms (books, movies, games, merchandising), theorists now speak of storyworlds. We could see mobiles as often forming one element in such rich, complex storyworlds, sometimes clearly distinguishable—but other times forming a unique, inseparable part of a distributed narrative across technologies, platforms, and devices.[19] This fits well with Raley's argument that these narratives belong to a larger media ecology:

> When we participate in an SMS project or performance, we are making, using, decoding linguistic signs, but we are "not reading" in the sense that these activities are not necessarily given priority over seeing, listening, touching, and bodily movement . . . [suggesting that] printed books are one part of a broader media ecology but not distinctive in and of themselves; rather, they are part of a discourse network in which a work can be a book, anime series, video, or game.[20]

Scott W. Ruston expands this argument when he writes, "[G]iven the close association between mobile media and location, mobile-media projects can provide a bridge between real world and storyworld that features both intense interactivity and robust immersivity."[21] Ruston proposes something that he dubs "Mobile Narrative Experiences," projects that pivot on a "mobile media device, such as cell phone, laptop, or PDA, as the primary interface for accessing a story, and participants access that story while moving through space."[22] For Ruston, the "core narrative" is authored by the project creators, with "participants' engagement" creating an "additional narrative trajectory," intersections that allow this kind of mobile narrative to "highlight the recursive and multilayered nature of narrative itself."[23] Prototypes for mobile narratives abound, and, whether widely adopted, or not, they serve an important purpose, as a counterpoint to what have become the accepted narrative forms associated with mobile platforms. Thus in his discussion of the StoryTrek system for authoring and reading locative narratives, Brian Greenspan argues, "While it is unlikely that such locative narratives will soon replace eBooks and audio books or alter decontextualized reading practices, they do point the way out of the locative's emphasis on the here-and-now, and toward more embodied, dynamic, collective and multiply contextualized applications."[24] Further, in his authoritative account of contemporary mobile media narratives that depend on the histories of particular locations, Jason Farman contends that we can see how these manage to "transform this individual [mobile] interface into a site of community engagement and crowdsourced histories through various modes of storytelling," thus demonstrating "the ways that narratives are all site-specific and all sites depend on narratives."[25]

Books in Space

Thus far, we have charted the ways in which narratives first developed through mobile phones, and the very interesting set of developments associated with experiments to digitize the already mobile media format that is the novel. What made the decisive difference in catalyzing the possibilities of the e-reader was the advent of a new phase of development in the mobile Internet. This new phase is best characterized by the rise of smartphones such as the iPhone, various Android devices, and a range of tablet computers (a popular consumer market revivified with the advent of Apple's iPad). Users can now avail themselves of highly portable devices that offer ever-present connections to online networks for Internet browsing, email, location services, video, photo, and music in addition to regular telecommunications services such as voice and text-message services.

Importantly, these new networked devices were quickly embraced by audiences for reading novels, short stories, comics, and other fiction formats despite the fact that in the early phase of the smartphone's public marketing campaign little attention was directed to its capabilities as a device for reading e-books.[26] Until very recently, most e-books produced by the "big six" multinational publishers (Hachette Book Group, HarperCollins, MacMillan, Penguin, Random House, and Simon and Schuster) remained facsimiles of their printed counterparts. If you download a digital copy of a bestseller like *The Girl with the Dragon Tattoo* to read on a dedicated e-reading device, a multifunction phone, tablet, or a personal computer, you will find a product that is, at least to the naked eye, indistinguishable from its paper counterpart. In adapting novels composed for printed publication to the screen, the role of the printed, physical text in guiding design has been central. Even though the rapid (re)emergence of e-readers signifies a turning point in reading practices, there is a lag in new conceptualizations of the e-reader, as the dominant approach still seems to stake the success of the device on its capacity to imitate the layout and the reading experience of paper books.[27]

The production of books for devices that people use to email, call, play games, and tweet has important as yet ill-defined consequences for how narratives are created and consumed. By virtue of the potential to add novel reading to the list of things we are able to do within the space of a single device, those traditionally involved in the production of works of fiction (such as writers, editors, and publishers) are now beginning to collaborate with technology designers to produce digital alternatives to printed works of fiction. In particular, smaller publishers, entrepreneurial writers, and software developers are the ones bucking this trend, directing their energies into collaborating to produce "enhanced" e-books which explore opportunities for increased expressiveness and flexibility that are offered by networked mobile media. Debate rages on what "enhanced" exactly means, as in this advocacy from the firm eBook Architects:

> Some other eBook companies might try to tell you that endnotes that
> link both directions or linked subject indexes are enhancements to eB-
> ooks . . . we do not consider those to be "enhancements" because we see
> them as integral to the very concept of an eBook. eBooks should not just
> be flat digital versions of print books. . . . Enhancements are extras that most
> eBooks do not have.[28]

So, for instance, some enhanced e-books take the form of mobile phone apps that
replicate some of the design and aesthetic features of the printed novel but build
a suite of complementary multimedia around the primary material, taking advantage of the new forms of storytelling that mobile media and digital networks
have popularized. Like the many creative experiments with multimedia narratives
on third-generation phones that blend text with image or sound, or offer immersive, location-based, interactive narrative experiences, some contemporary digital
books give readers narratives augmented and supplemented with tools to support
their reading (wikis, dictionaries, primary sources), social networks where readers can share notes, bookmarks, reading metadata, and information about author
tours, new releases, back lists, and supplementary multimedia.

These new features can subtly change the way fiction is experienced and the
kinds of meanings that can be drawn from it. With mobile reading, the distinctions drawn between inside the story and outside the story take on a new kind of
fluidity. This makes all the activities adjacent to reading—researching the context,
reading reviews, buying complementary books, discussing your enjoyment—
much more contiguous, and woven, with the act of reading. Or perhaps the "act"
of reading is much more profoundly, and visibly, to be understood as a product
of the multifarious practices of mobile, networked consumption. This obviously
has great appeal to online book retailers who hope to capitalize on spur-of-the-
moment reading purchases. The growth of e-reading on mobile media has also
focused attention on the importance of intersecting networks of narrative that
take place whenever people read.

This potential to turn the focused habit of novel reading into another act of
browsing has been the cause of considerable popular discussion and concern.[29] A
digital book's network capability opens up portals away from the primary narrative: the means for distraction from the work of reading is packaged into the
book itself. Mobile reading positions the narrative in a new context, not simply
complemented by surrounding texts but instead, narrative delivered via networks
becomes part of the greater flow of information. For critics like Sven Birkerts, this
dispersed, nonhierarchical system proves a fundamental challenge to the novel:

> [I]f it happens that in a few decades—maybe less—we move wholesale
> into a world where information and texts are called on to the screen by
> the touch of a button, and libraries survive as information centres rather
> than as repositories of printed books, we will not simply have replaced one

delivery system with another. We will also have modified our imagination of history, our understanding of the causal and associative relationships of ideas and their creators. We may gain an extraordinary dots-per-square inch level of access to detail, but in the process we will lose much of our sense of the woven narrative consistency of the story.[30]

In this hyperbolic scenario, there is no longer a cohering of the story or the characters in a historical order or imagination; instead all is retrieved in isolation from its contexts. By making everything connected to everything else, information is radically flattened. Readers cannot situate their experience of particular characters or events in relation to the progress of the novel as a whole, or to the writer's body of work.

Putting the mobile device, its affordances, and narrative associations and investments into perspective, it is important to remember, however, that distraction and decontextualization are not new challenges to narrative. Indeed since the advent of the form, novelists have been experimenting with narrative voice, time, and context to communicate the complications of communication. Laurence Sterne's *The Life and Opinions of Tristram Shandy* (1759–1767) is often cited as early evidence of the novelist's interest in exploring an epistolary, nonlinear narrative. Julio Cortázar's *Hopscotch* (1963), Italo Calvino's *If On a Winter's Night a Traveler* (1979), and Vladimir Nabokov's *Pale Fire* (1962) are among the most well-known examples from the mid-twentieth century. More recently, contemporary authors have made the obvious response to the popularity of digital technology such as smartphones in our everyday lives, using their formats and affordances for creative inspiration. The prize-winning novel by Jennifer Egan, *A Visit from the Goon Squad* (2010), attracted the attention of critics for its inventive incorporation of the PowerPoint slide format as a narrative device. In a chapter of her novel told from the point of view of a young girl compiling a school assignment, Egan uses slides to convey a condensed account of domestic family life.[31] Beyond this much-discussed chapter, Egan's novel resonates with themes involving the passage of time, attention, distraction, and perception or point of view. Described by the author as a "decentralized narrative," each chapter differs in tone and form, making it possible to understand the book as thirteen short stories or as one large interconnected narrative. As the author explained in an interview: "It's so decentralized that it doesn't quite fit what I think we think of as novels being right now. And I don't really care about the term. It doesn't fit into a category comfortably. . . . I didn't really worry about an arc, because again, that feels more like traditional fiction."[32] Instead, in *A Visit from the Goon Squad*, characters provide the narrative links, recurring in the stories, sometimes occupying central, sometimes peripheral roles. Glimpsing these characters at different stages in their lives and from different perspectives, the reader is able to draw his or her own connections regarding cause and effect, and in doing so the dimensions of the book as "a novel" emerge.

As well as the printed novel, there is *The Goon Squad* app (produced by development team PopLeaf), which allows readers to arrange the chapters in any sequence or put them in chronological order. The digital version of the novel foregrounds the reader's ability to make connections between cause and effect, refracting characters, and making sense of the narrative. In this way the digital narrative experience is always unique in comparison to its printed counterpart. And, unlike the bound-and-printed copy, the narrative potential of the author's use of PowerPoint genuinely comes into its own on the mobile screen. On a mobile device, the chapter can be presented in color, in landscape orientation, and in the slideshow mode familiar to PowerPoint users. To be sure, many of these techniques draw from the legacy of the great novelists of the nineteenth century, such as Charles Dickens and William Thackeray, and from the formal experiments of the twentieth century's modernists and postmodernists. However, Egan's narrative is also intended to replicate the experience of storytelling in the current contextless digital landscape that troubles unenhanced critics like Birkerts. As Egan put it, "I was interested in how the present feels when you keep pulling someone out of it."[33]

In distinction to earlier experiments with narratives on digital platforms, particularly hypertext fiction of the sort popular in the 1990s,[34] novels formatted for mobile media extend (rather than upend) conventional modes of storytelling, authorship, and media production. Working in collaboration with the publishing industry, developers have produced networked narratives that incorporate the text, soundtracks, audio readings, video interviews, rough drafts, automatically updating reviews and news feeds, and supplementary historical or cultural information.[35] Other features of these narratives demonstrate particular sympathy for the interests and experiences of mobile readers by providing increased levels of narrative control and continuity: synchronous switch between text and audio storytelling, night mode for reading in dark spaces or on limited battery life, geolocation tagging, social bookmarking, and the capability of changing type settings and size. Thus, a novel read on an e-reading device or app no longer constitutes a single "portal" or platform into the fictional realm; instead readers can skip from one platform to the other according to their requirements (from reading a novel in-browser from the cloud to a dedicated e-reader app). The same single story can also be enjoyed in many different modes: readers can read text, listen to audio of the text, do both at once, or watch video of the author or an actor reciting text.

Many enhancements of the narrative space not only give readers increased flexibility and control of story space, but they also flag the value of the author to the reader in guiding meaning making, both within the story proper, and in the many narratives that circulate around the story space that contribute to what Roland Barthes famously described as the reader's "pleasure of the text."[36] For example, the 2010 novel by Australian musician and author Nick Cave, *The Death of Bunny Munro*, released for download to iPad and iPhone by Enhanced Editions, includes a range of additional features designed to take advantage of the multimedia capacities of these devices and Cave's status as a multimedia artist.[37] In addition to the written text, readers can choose to activate a soundtrack produced by Cave (in collaboration with his musical partner, Warren Ellis) to accompany the narrative, or switch on video or audio of Cave reading the story synchronized with the text. This last feature allows readers to move between the author's reading and their own at the tap of the screen (or enjoy both at once). Such innovations gently shift the sense of reading as a private, silent, and singular activity, and respond thoughtfully to the needs of mobile readers: one can remain enmeshed in the narrative even when one is called upon to cease reading and begin another activity that requires visual attention (disembarking from a bus, cooking, exercising, and so on). The experience of half-reading, half-listening to a book alters the narrative experience: memories of the text will be colored by how the reader takes it in, passage by passage, moment by moment. As the creator of the app explained, this is "[n]ot just digitizing the text, but digitizing the whole experience."[38]

Cannily, this edition of the novel also harnesses the multiple narratives that exist around the primary text—in particular those drawing on Cave's position as a well-known musician, composer of film scores, and poet of gothic sensibility. As Barthes and other scholars of reading practice have noted, the narratives of authorship that exist outside the text inform how readers make meaning.[39] In the case of Cave's book, the seamless integration of narratives of authorship (in the form of multimedia enhancements) into the reader's encounter with the novel serves also to enhance the role of the author as the director of narrative meaning.[40] Having Cave serve as author, composer, and narrator in the audio and video tracks, and allowing readers to move seamlessly between his telling of the tale and their own reading, creates a slippage between the much-celebrated creator and his readers (many of whom will also be fans of Cave's other work). This unusual narrative dynamic gives the novel a different texture: the integration of narratives beyond the written word (sound, video) and beyond the fiction (Cave's celebrity as a musician) makes the novel not just a multimedia narrative, but also a multimodal one.

Conclusion: The Never-Ending Story of Digital Narrative

The use of locative, mobile technologies within the domain of digital storytelling is an ever-evolving practice, fundamentally open to narrative shifts from writers, readers, designers, and interfaces alike. It is a narrative without a conclusion. The histories we have sought to reconstruct in this chapter chart out the unexpected emergence of mobile narratives. Whether it be in the SMS novels of Japan, China, and elsewhere, or the hydra-headed storytelling explosion associated with 2G and 3G mobile platforms, these examples of innovation in digital storytelling demonstrate how important the familiarity and functionality of the mobile phone has been in shaping contemporary narrative. It is important to note that these narrative experiments, catalyzed by mobiles, unfolded alongside a largely unrelated parallel track of industrial development of the "standalone" e-reader that preceded the cellular mobile phenomenon. While the bulk of those devices remain unadventurous, there are now many innovative enhanced editions, apps, and uses of tablet-based storytelling as complex nodes in a wider, recursive, locatable, recombinant, social, mobile media universe. These latest developments in mobile narrative suggest that we need to rechannel the vague nostalgia about the loss of earlier narrative experience into a serious enquiry into the mobile as a new turning point in the media and cultural histories of the book.

By virtue of our expanded ability to do so many different things within the space of a single device, scholars of media theory and practice are turning their attention to the ways that narrative is responding to the nature of networked communication.[41] A novel read digitally no longer requires a single access point into the fictional realm but instead provides multiple portals into this space. Readers can skip from one platform to the other according to their requirements (in-browser on laptop direct from the cloud to e-reader or downloaded app); they can read text, listen to audio, do both at once, or watch video, visualize, or imagine (or "bring to life") the story. Before a book reaches a reader, it is necessarily incomplete: writers rely upon readers to build and negotiate the story space in order to make meaning. To credit e-readers with "engaging" readers in "interactive" narratives is to miss the fundamental function of reading and disregard the centrality of the *human* reader to the narrative process.

Indeed, the biggest change for literature when made electronically present (cloud-based, accessible on this or that device, encountered in differing forms and extractions, quoted and misquoted) is that it is separated from the traditional contexts that authors and readers have typically relied upon to find their place in relation to story. With a digital novel, the author's words reach the reader in the same sequence they always have, but what alters is the material experience of the text in relation to narrative events. Yet, as we have suggested, narratives associated with mobile media devices entail new contexts, especially those instantiated by the dynamics of location.

Ultimately the constraints and metaphors inherited from print media are both powerful and limiting. When it comes to the changes taking place in the format of the novel, and the digital storytelling it represents, it is important to grasp that it is, as Peter Stallybrass observes, "a brilliantly perverse interlude in the long history of discontinuous reading."[42] The novel developed as a form despite the fact that the codex was designed centuries earlier for the nonfiction, indexical reading required by lawyers and businessmen. These words remind us of our tendency to think of technologies like mobile media as things to do with our recent digital culture, forgetting that the book is itself a technology with associated forms of media that has evolved over the course of many hundreds of years to tell stories in a variety of distinct and complex modes.

Notes

1. Rebecca Young, "The Digital Diorama: Reinventing Narrative for New Media," in *Image, Text and Sound: The Yet Unseen: Rendering Stories*, ed. Pauline Anastasiou and Karen Trist (Melbourne: RMIT Publishing, 2004), 15.
2. See: Paul Levinson, *Cellphone: The Story of the World's Most Mobile Medium and How It Has Transformed Everything!* (New York, NY: Palgrave Macmillan, 2004); Gerard Goggin, *Cell Phone Culture: Mobile Technology in Everyday Life* (London and New York: Routledge, 2006). On books as a predecessor form of "mobile interface," see Adriana de Souza e Silva and Jordan Frith, *Mobile Interfaces in Public Spaces: Locational Privacy, Control, and Urban Sociability* (London and New York: Routledge, 2012).
3. Friedhelm Hillebrand, ed., *GSM and UMTS: The Creation of Global Mobile Communication* (Chichester, UK: John Wiley, 2001). On SMS and MMS, see Gwenaël Le Bodic, *Mobile Messaging Technologies and Services: SMS, EMS and MMS* (Chichester, UK: John Wiley, 2005).
4. Friedhelm Hillebrand, ed., *Short Message Service (SMS): The Creation of Personal Global Text Messaging* (Chichester, UK: John Wiley, 2010), 126.
5. Eija-Liisa Kasesniemi, *Mobile Messages: Young People and a New Communication Culture* (Tampere: Tampere University Press, 2003).
6. Richard Harper, Leysia Palen, and Alex Taylor, eds., *The Inside Text: Social, Cultural and Design Perspectives on SMS* (Dordrecht: Springer, 2005).
7. David Crystal, *Txtng: The Gr8 Db8* (Oxford: Oxford University Press, 2008).
8. Kyoung-hwa Yonnie Kim, "The Landscape of *Keitai Shôsetsu*: Mobile Phones as a Literary Medium among Japanese Youth," *Continuum* 26, no. 3 (2012): 475–485.
9. Esther Milne, *Letters, Postcards, Email: Technologies of Presence* (New York: Routledge, 2010).
10. Alan C. Kay, "A Personal Computer for Children of All Ages," *National Conference Proceedings of Association of Computing Machinery*, 1972, http://www.mprove.de/diplom/gui/Kay72a.pdf.
11. On Alan C. Kay, see John Maxwell, *Tracing the Dynabook: A Study of Technocultural Transformations* (Ph.D. thesis, University of British Columbia, 2006), http://thinkubator.ccsp.sfu.ca/Dynabook.
12. Michael Hart, "The History and Philosophy of Project Gutenberg," http://www.gutenberg.org/wiki/Gutenberg:The_History_and_Philosophy_of_Project_Gutenberg_by_Michael_Hart. See also: Marie Lebert, *Project Gutenberg (1971–2008)*, http://www.gutenberg.org/ebooks/31632.
13. Terje Hillesund, "Will E-books Change the World?" *First Monday* 10 (2001), http://www.firstmonday.dk/ojs/index.php/fm/article/view/891/800.
14. Nancy K. Herther, "The e-book Reader is Not the Future of Books," *Searcher* 8 (2008).
15. Here we indicate the ongoing debate and discussion about cultural participation, narrative, and digital media, covered from a wide range of standpoints, including: Bryan Alexander, *The New Digital Storytelling: Creating Narratives with New Media* (Santa Barbara, CA: Praeger, 2011); Axel Bruns, *Blogs, Wikipedia, Second Life, and Beyond: From Production to Produsage* (New York: Peter Lang, 2008); Jean Burgess and Joshua Green, *YouTube: Online Video and Participatory Culture* (Cambridge, UK: Polity, 2009); Tim Edensor, Deborah Leslie, Steve Millington, and Norma Rantisi, eds., *Spaces of Vernacular Creativity: Rethinking the Cultural Economy* (New York: Routledge, 2010); Hajo

Grief, Larissa Hjorth, Amparo Lasén, and Claire Lobet-Maris, eds., *Cultures of Participation: Media Practices, Politics and Literacy* (Frankfurt: Peter Lang, 2011); John Hartley and Kelly McWilliam, eds., *Story Circle: Digital Storytelling around the World* (Chichester, UK: Wiley-Blackwell, 2009); Henry Jenkins, *Convergence Culture: Where Old and New Media Collide* (New York: New York University Press, 2006).

16. Ruth Page, ed., *New Perspectives on Narrative and Multimodality* (New York: Routledge, 2010).

17. Rita Raley, "Walk This Way: Mobile Narrative as Composed Experience," *Beyond the Screen: Transformations of Literary Structures, Interfaces and Genres*, ed. Jörgen Schäfer and Peter Gendolla (Bielefeld: Transcript Verlag/Transaction, 2010), 213.

18. For a kindred approach to thick narrative spaces, see Johanna Brewer and Paul Dourish, "Storied Spaces: Cultural Accounts of Mobility, Technology, and Environmental Knowing," *International Journal of Human Computer Studies*, 66 (2008): 963–976.

19. For instance, see Christy Dena, *Transmedia Practice: Theorising the Practice of Expressing a Fictional World across Distinct Media and Environments* (Ph.D. dissertation, University of Sydney, 2009), http://www.christydena.com/academic-2/phd/.

20. Rita Raley, "Mobile Media Poetics," *Proceeding of the Digital Arts and Culture Conference 2009, After Media: Embodiment and Context* (University of California, Irvine, December 12-15, 2009), http://escholarship.org/uc/item/01x5v98g.

21. Scott W. Ruston, "Storyworlds on the Move: Mobile Media and Their Implications for Narrative," *Storyworlds: A Journal of Narrative Studies* 2 (2010): 103.

22. Ibid., 103.

23. Ibid., 111. Cf. Rita Raley, "On Locative Narrative," *Genre* 41 (2008): 123–147; and Eric Kabisch, "Mobile After-Media: Trajectories and Points of Departure," *Digital Creativity* 21 (2010): 51–59.

24. Brian Greenspan, "The New Place of Reading: Locative Media and the Future of Narrative," *Digital Humanities Quarterly* 5, no. 3 (2011), http://www.digitalhumanities.org/dhq/vol/5/3/000103/000103.html.

25. Jason Farman, *Mobile Interface Theory: Embodied Space and Locative Media* (New York: Routledge, 2012), 130.

26. See Gerard Goggin, "Reading with the iPhone," in *Moving Data: The iPhone and My Media*, ed. Pelle Snickars and Patrick Vonderau (New York: Columbia University Press, 2011), 195–210.

27. For a discussion of the reluctance of publishers in Europe to embrace the "disruptive innovation" of digital formats, see Bozena Izabela Mierzejewska, "Disruptive Innovations in Book Publishing: Threat or Opportunity?" *International Journal of the Book*, 7 (2010): 51–60.

28. "Enhanced eBooks," eBook Architects, http://ebookarchitects.com/conversions/enhanced.php.

29. The most prominent recent discussion of the distracted reading habits caused by digital texts is Nicholas Carr, "Is Google Making Us Stupid?" *The Atlantic*, July/August 2008, http://www.theatlantic.com/magazine/archive/2008/07/is-google-making-us-stupid/306868/, and his companion book *The Shallows: What the Internet Is Doing to Our Brains* (New York: W.W. Norton, 2010).

30. Sven Birkerts, "Resisting the Kindle," *The Atlantic*, March 2009, http://www.theatlantic.com/magazine/archive/2009/03/resisting-the-kindle/7345/.

31. The UK *Guardian* newspaper republished this chapter of Egan's novel on its website, describing it as a short story for children. An interesting example of the way in which

the multimedia, multimodal narrative can change genres as it travels among different readers. See "Extract: *A Visit from the Goon Squad* by Jennifer Egan," *Guardian*, April 8 2011, http://www.guardian.co.uk/childrens-books-site/interactive/2011/apr/08/extract-visit-from-the-goon-squad-jennifer-egan.

32. Egan, quoted in Edan Lepucki, "Novelist of the Future: A Profile of Jennifer Egan", *The Millions*, July 12 2010, http://www.themillions.com/2010/07/novelist-of-the-future-a-profile-of-jennifer-egan.html.

33. Egan, quoted in Edan Lepucki, "Novelist of the Future."

34. Michael Joyce, *Of Two Minds: Hypertext Pedagogy and Poetics* (Ann Arbor, MI: University of Michigan Press, 1995); Jay David Bolter, *Writing Space: Computers, Hypertext, and the Remediation of Print*, 2nd edition. (Mahwah, NJ: Lawrence Erlbaum Associates, 2001); George P. Landow, *Hypertext 3.0: Critical Theory and New Media in an Era of Globalization*, 3rd edition. (Baltimore, MD: Johns Hopkins University Press, 2006).

35. It is worth acknowledging that the "enhanced" book is not strictly new in some respects. Any student would be familiar with the myriad annotated editions in existence to assist with the study of great works of literature, moments in history, and so on. Many trade paperbacks in contemporary literature also now come with reader's guides, book club discussion suggestions, editors introductions, and instructions for accessing further material from the publisher's website.

36. Roland Barthes, *The Pleasure of the Text*, trans. Richard Miller (New York: Hill and Wang, 1975).

37. Nick Cave, *The Death of Bunny Munro* (Edinburgh: Canongate, 2010); iPad App edition, November 10, 2010, downloaded from http://itunes.apple.com.

38. Peter Collingridge. "The Digital Innovators: Peter Collingridge of Enhanced Editions," *Publishing Perspectives*, http://publishingperspectives.com/2010/08/the-digital-innovators-peter-collingridge-of-enhanced-editions/.

39. See, for example, Roland Barthes, *The Pleasure of the Text* and *Image, Music, Text*, trans. Stephen Heath (New York: Hill and Wang, 1978) and Gerard Genette, *Paratexts: Thresholds of Interpretation* (Cambridge: Cambridge University Press, 1997). For a more contemporary account of multimedia paratexts in popular media culture, see Jonathan Gray, *Show Sold Separately: Promos, Spoilers and Other Media Paratexts* (New York: NYU Press, 2010).

40. Nick Cave, lead singer of a number of bands, has worked on the soundtrack of films like *The Road* and *The Assassination of Jesse James by the Coward Robert Ford*. As an author, he wrote the 1989 *And the Ass Saw the Angel*, and the screenplay for the 2005 film *The Proposition* (dir. John Hillcoat). In this audiobook, *The Death of Bunny Munro*, the Australian artist merges his interests in music and literature.

41. For the theoretical perspective on changes to narrative in network communications culture, see Lev Manovich, *The Language of New Media* (Cambridge, MA: The MIT Press, 2001). For a practical take, see Mark S. Meadows, *Pause & Effect: The Art of Interactive Narrative* (Indianapolis, IN: New Riders, 2003). For an approach that blends practical case study with recent theory, see Ruston, "Storyworlds on the Move: Mobile Media and Their Implications for Narrative," *StoryWorlds: A Journal of Narrative Studies* 2 (2010): 101–120.

42. Peter Stallybrass, "Books and Scrolls: Navigating the Bible," in *Books and Readers in Early Modern England*, ed. Jennifer Andersen and Elizabeth Sauer (Philadelphia: University of Pennsylvania Press, 2002), 47.

16

STORIES OF THE MOBILE

Women, Micro-Narratives, and Mobile Novels in Japan

Larissa Hjorth

> *How do the examples in this chapter help us understand the practice of story-telling in the mobile media age?*

Drawing on case studies of mobile phone novels in Japan, *keitai shōsetsu*, sales of which far exceed the sale of print text books in the West, this chapter looks at the role that user-created content plays in the creation of these cell-phone novels. In Japan, these mobile-phone novels are read, written, and commented on by thousands on their daily train rides to and from work. By employing user-created content, the readers/writers of these "micro-narratives" reflect a sense of place that is not just a geographic, spatial notion but also is a social, political, and emotional space. These cell-phone novels, the majority of which are written by women and for women, demonstrate how mobile media is undoubtedly transforming what it means to be creative and intimate while circumnavigating public and private spaces and places. Through *keitai shōsetsu*, women can bring intimate and private stories into public spaces, proffering new ways to experience storytelling in public places.

Keywords

*   **Keitai shōsetsu:** The Japanese term translated as "mobile-phone novels," these stories are written for, and often on, a mobile phone.
*   **Micro-narratives:** The compressed narrative style of mobile media, characterized by compressed expression, temporality, and space. While a cell-phone novel might be quite lengthy (or be distributed over an extended period of time), the narrative portions in micro-narratives like these are brief and compact and are thus designed for creation and consumption on this medium.

- **User-created content (UCC):** Online content that is created and distributed by the site's users. UCC generally heralds in the end of the "age of the professional" because anyone can be an author and distributor of content.

Introduction

Machiko often spent her daily two-hour train rides to and from work reading novels on her mobile phone (*keitai* in Japanese). Called *keitai shōsetsu*, these "mobile-phone novels" are written for, and often on, a *keitai*. For Machiko, there were many reasons why she loved the *keitai shōsetsu*. She loved the way in which the stories were written, compressed, and colloquial like a mobile email. She loved the way in which the stories were delivered in small episodes, easily consumed and responded to while in transit. She loved the content of the stories, often about womens' domestic lives. She loved the way in which the stories could be edited, commented upon, and changed. She loved the way in which there was often an ongoing relationship and dialogue between writers and readers. She also loved the way in which she could respond to the writer and the story by adding comments—so much so that even one of her favorite writers incorporated one of her suggestions in the amendments of a story.

With the uneven rise of mobile media—increasingly in the form of smartphones—we are also seeing the way in which we conceptualize and practice creativity, intimacy, and media literacy changing. In particular, mobile media—as a series of platforms, frames, and contexts—provides specific aesthetic, conceptual, and social features that allow for micro-narratives like *keitai shōsetsu* to flourish. The ability to quickly capture, upload, and share everyday practices—or what has been called the three *S*s by Mizuko Ito and Daisuke Okabe: storing, sharing, and saving—of mobile media is undoubtedly transforming what it means to be creative and intimate while circumnavigating public and private spaces and places.[1] Given this phenomenon, the impact of mobile media on the way in which storytelling and public reading is narrated and negotiated through and by public spaces is shifting. One key example of this transformation can be found in the case of *keitai shōsetsu* in Tokyo, Japan.

In the opening example of this chapter, we are presented with a typical *keitai shōsetsu* reader, Machiko. As we see, her reasons for being an avid reader were many. Much of these reasons revolved around Machiko's affinity for a new type of participatory media in which readers can be editors and so too can writers can become readers.[2] Specifically, Machiko's outlines a role of the reader that blurs traditional reader/writer paradigms and instead adopts a dynamic, participatory, and collaborative relationship. Through the mobile and ubiquitous nature of the *keitai*, Japan's love of the novel and other printed matter like *manga* (comics), has taken a new form: *keitai shōsetsu*. Two decades ago, Japanese trains were filled with readers of the millions of options of printed matter offered in Japan. With the introduction of the mobile Internet in the form of iMode in 1999, this love of the written word took another form/context/frame, the *keitai*. Adapted for, and often on, the *keitai*, *keitai shōsetsu* heralded a new appreciation of the printed word through the mobile, digital screen. Its networked capacities meant that unlike traditional printed matter, it could be easily changed, adapted, and revised in negotiation with the reader.

Indeed, *keitai shōsetsu* can be viewed as the precursor to the ubiquity of the iPad, Kindle, and tablets that ushered in a new appreciation of the literary in the West. Initiated in Japan around 2000, *keitai shōsetsu* has blossomed into a dynamic area for participatory media, which in turn has reenergized more traditional media like film and *manga*. For example, one of the most popular examples of the *keitai shōsetsu*, *Koizara*, was successfully adapted into a multimillion-dollar film. Part of the success of *keitai shōsetsu* can be attributed to a variety of factors: Japan's *keitai* market where mobile phone screens are big; long commutes on public transport are the norm; the specific characteristics of Japanese language; and the long tradition of the "personal, pedestrian and portable"[3] as part of everyday life. As a medium, it has been embraced by young women, as both readers and writers, for its ability to provide new avenues and contexts for expression around previously tacit and private practices (i.e., domesticity).[4]

The *keitai shōsetsu* phenomenon began with the founding of one of Japan's most pivotal sites on the mobile Internet, *Maho No Airando* (*maho* meaning "magic"), in 1999, which was made up of user-created content (UCC). Although *keitai shōsetsu* were initially written by professionals, by the mid-2000s, everyday users had begun to be inspired to write and distribute their own *keitai shōsetsu*. Predominantly written *by* women *for* women, this mode of new media highlights the significance of remediation[5]—many of the successful *keitai shōsetsu* (millions are produced yearly) are adapted into older media such as film, *manga*, and *anime*. The rise of the *keitai shōsetsu*—short stories written for the *keitai* that, in some cases, are translated into other forms of media such as films and *manga*—is a great example of the power of UCC in Japan. This practice can be seen as an extension of earlier gendered tropes of Japanese new media that was dubbed in the 1980s the "Anomalous Female Teenage Handwriting" phenomenon.[6] Characterized by "*kawaii*" (cute) transformations of the Japanese alphabet, *hiragana*,[7] this emerging genre of new media writing soon dominated mobile communication from the pager onward, thus heralding what has been called the "highschool girl pager revolution," whereby female UCC hijacked technologies industry had aimed at businessmen ("salarymen").[8]

According to Kyoung-hwa Yonnie Kim, *keitai shōsetsu* needs to be understood as "refashioning emails rather than literature."[9] Often young people move between emails and *keitai shōsetsu* as both genres and modes of address evoke a similar type of intimacy. Here, it is important to recognize that in Japan, the phone has long been the dominant mode for accessing the Internet, and thus mobile Internet emails are akin to SMS (short messaging service) in other cultural contexts.

In addition, *keitai shōsetsu* can also be seen as an extension of literary traditions evoked by arguably one of the first novels in the world (written in 1000 AD), *The Tale of Genji*. Drawing on *haiku*, letters, and love sonnets, "Murasaki Shikibu's" (not her real name; it is thought to be Fujiwara Takako) *the Tale of Genji* deployed *hiragana* to tell both the male and female side of the numerous lovers of the playboy "Genji."[10]

The popularity of cell-phone novels has been adapted and adopted elsewhere, with locations such as China, Taiwan, and Africa developing their own versions. In China—where for many working-class migrants the mobile phone is their only portal to the Internet—deploying new media like mobile phones and blogging for political means has become an important rite of passage.[11] In Africa, the democratic possibilities of the mobile phone as a multimedia device were harnessed in 2007 with the youth cult cell-phone novel, *Kontax*.[12] In most cases across the world, cell-phone novels have been highly successful with young people as a remediated form of the traditional paperback. The compressed, mobile, and intimate nature of the cell phone has provided many with an accessible way to connect different stories and subjectivities in a fleeting moment. Moreover, the nature of cell-phone novels as stories that are often shaped in consultation with readers (especially by experienced cell-phone authors) makes them a prime example of new reader-writer relationships.

In this chapter, I explore one in the many traditions informing the development and success of the *keitai shōsetsu* in Japan. Through this investigation, we can gain a sense of why this unique form of participatory media has been so successful in Japan and less so elsewhere. With the recent rise in smartphone and tablet consumption in many countries across the world, it is interesting to reflect upon whether the *keitai shōsetsu* culture can be replicated and localized elsewhere. In particular, this chapter explores the role of gendered, remediated media in Japan and how this informs *keitai shōsetsu* cultures. Firstly, I will contextualize the role of mobile media in providing a space for women, place, and domestication. Then I will discuss the specific relationship between *kawaii* (cute) culture, media practices, and young women in Japan. This will be concluded with a general discussion of *keitai shōsetsu* as a gendered and remediated form of mobile media UCC.

Mobile Homes: Place, Women, Domestication, and *Keitai Shōsetsu*

In the various methods for studying mobile media, it is not by accident that these media have been analyzed under the lens of domestic life.[13] The approach was developed by Roger Silverstone for domestic media like TV and then adapted by Rich Ling and Leslie Haddon for the context of mobile media. As an extension of domesticated technologies (e.g., television and radio) and their attendant, Raymond Williams's "mobile privatization,"[14] mobile technologies encapsulate some of the paradoxes of what it means to experience place and "home" today. As notions of mobility continue to gather speed and complexity across a variety of realms—geographic, socio-economic, technological—it is the mobile phone that has often been the harbinger for debates around these shifts. Underscoring "mobile privatization" is the rearticulation of domesticity beyond a simple physical place; domesticated technologies from the TV onward have sought to blur boundaries between the lived/imagined, global/local, and inside/outside. In particular, mobile technologies have been important vehicles in extending co-present practices of place. Place can be lived and imagined whilst both being here and there, home and away. This co-present sense of place is encapsulated by the role of domesticated technologies in configuring a sense of home.[15]

While domestication may have moved out of the home—literally, in the case of the mobile phone—emotional and psychological ties to the home as a symbol of family, belonging, and identity continue to grow. In this way, physical and geographic movements away from home—that can be associated with dislocation and loneliness—can be subsided ("put on hold") by the deployment of co-present domestic technologies like mobile phones. As David Morley observes, domestic technologies such as the mobile phone help to relocate domestic ties elsewhere.[16] Mobile technologies allow us to be tethered to the home: we are free to roam geographically from the physical space of the home, but the mobile phone helps us to remain constantly connected. But this electronic anchor is not without a series of paradoxes. The mobile phone sets us "free" to roam geographically, but its always-on function means that we are seemingly always available. This "wireless leash"[17] or "free but on a leash"[18] syndrome creates new types of outsourcing and full-timeness of domestic labor as noted by Misa Matsuda's notion of the mobile phone in Japan (keitai) as "mum in the pocket."[19] While previous domestic technologies like the TV functioned within the physical space of home to reinforce psychological notions of domesticity, mobile technologies allow these relocated domestic ties to be played out outside the physical space of the home. In the case of someone who is part of a diaspora, mobile technologies have helped to keep family connections strong despite physical dislocation.[20]

The paradoxes around mobile media and its relationship to place, and especially the domestic, are amplified in the case of keitai shōsetsu. Many of the stories focus upon the domestic sphere to set the picture for private and intimate women's stories. Through the portal of the keitai, readers can engage and collaborate with the readers and their texts. Often read in transitory, "third spaces" like trains, keitai shōsetsu are a great example of how mobile media tethers us psychologically and emotionally to a sense of home and the domestic while often on the run.

Written predominately by women for women, keitai shōsetsu are creative and intimate forms of mobile media that encapsulate the aesthetic, social, and psychological characters of the media. They illustrate the ways in which divides between the professional and amateur are changing and blurring through such expressions as UCC. They highlight the ways in which various forms of "vernacular creativity"—or, everyday creative practices that are often produced by amateurs rather than professionals—are imbued by gendered practices that operate around both the domestic and public.[21] Through *keitai shōsetsu* women can bring intimate and private stories into the public space, proffering new ways to experience storytelling in public places. *Keitai shōsetsu* are indicative of the intimate publics that are mobile media today. Stories of domesticity can be shared within the intimate public of the mobile phone. In this way, they are vehicles for gender performativity—that is, the ways in which gender is constructed and maintained through a series of localized gendered activities and regulations[22]—and subversion.

Herein lies the paradox for *keitai shōsetsu*: on the one hand, they reinforce gender stereotypes around women and domesticity with stories often locating women back within the home, while, on the other hand, they provide ways in which women's stories about domesticity—a neglected area in publishing—can be valorized by being written and read. In particular, we see how mobile intimacy, in the form of stories about the home and private life, can help to give voice to women through everyday media. We also see how gendered generational differences play out through the genres and types of stories told; many of the younger writers are interested in sensational stories, while more mature writers are interested in exploring the banalities of life. As feminist scholar Meaghan Morris reminds us, banality is the site in which power is naturalized and thus an important area for analysis.[23]

Keitai shōsetsu also highlight the specific role the "personal" has in Japan, especially around personal technologies like mobile phones and the Sony Walkman from the 1970s until now.[24] *Keitai shōsetsu* are interactive, discursive, personal, and immediate micro-narratives proffering readers quick, casual immersions of storytelling that cater to the multitasking and interpretability of contemporary work and life patterns. In short, they are encapsulated micro-narratives.

Through the intimate, personal nature of mobile media, we see the rehearsing of earlier forms of epistolary traditions—specifically women's fiction with its literacy devices such as letter writing. UCC is a great example of evoking the intimate through its economies such as vernacular creativity. The key feature of *keitai shōsetsu* is that it clearly links to older forms of Japanese media practice and highlights the role of women and gendered types of creativity in such media as *manga* and *anime* (animation) traditions.

One of the key features of *keitai shōsetsu* is that they tend to follow a diary-like, confessional, autobiographical model, very much reflecting Lauren Berlant's observation of the growing "publicness of intimacy"[25] being forged through the highly personalized and intimate media, the *keitai*. While this UCC phenomenon seems to herald the significance of new forms of creativity within ubiquitous media, we must ask what types of gendered labor practices are being played out. Is this a vehicle for reinforcing gender stereotypes about drama and literature? Or can this phenomenon be viewed as part of a broader process of empowerment and gendered performativity subversion that can be mapped back to literary transgressions such as the rise of "kitten writing"[26] in which women used *kawaii* (cute) culture (e.g., Hello Kitty) to create new vernacular forms of language? I would argue that the new media presented by *keitai shōsetsu* is a remediation of various forms of older gendered practices such as kitten writing, just as it is a vehicle for mixing old and new media genres and traditions such as *haiku* and *manga*.

The relationship between old and new media is clear in the case of *keitai shōsetsu* whereby a cyclical remediation is at play; the new medium is mapped onto the old storytelling media, and, in many ways, reshapes the old. Themes of domesticity and intimacy, as well as the rhetorical devices like letter writing, are deployed by *keitai shōsetsu*. This is then translated and adapted back into older media like films and comics. Here we see that *keitai shōsetsu* provides a lynchpin between the old and new media practices, as well as providing a new and dynamic context for rethinking writer and reader relationships and reshaping the public through mobile and intimate storytelling.

Moreover, *keitai shōsetsu* highlight the gendered contestations around work and leisure, public and private spaces. Far from evoking an "imagined" generalized audience like twentieth-century mass media, *keitai shōsetsu* epitomize participatory and collaborative media. By evoking a type of intimate public, *keitai shōsetsu* embrace the personal, vernacular, and conversational through their interfaces, platform, and story content. While conspicuously gendered in terms of content, authors, and readers, *keitai shōsetsu* also engage with Japan's long history of gendered forms of media practice.

In order to understand *keitai shōsetsu*—as part of broader UCC practices—we need to acknowledge the pivotal role played by in women in Japan. As I have noted elsewhere, younger women have been key in the rampant uptake and adaption of mobile media.[27] This gendered UCC phenomenon reflects more broadly the changing relationships between gender, labor, and technology ushered in via mobile media.[28] One way to explore this evolution of gendered and mobile UCC is to contextualize it into terms of women's literary subcultures like kitten writing.

Gendered Mobilities: The Rise of *Kawaii* Culture

The rise of the *keitai* from business tool to social accessory parallels the demise of the national symbol, the *oyaji* (salaryman), and the expanding power of young female users—epitomized by the female high school girl (*gyaru* or *shōjo*) user. Consumers, particularly young females, have played an integral role in both the growth and adaptation of *keitai* cultures; so much so that the emergence of new tropes of female empowered consumers deploying participatory media—or producing users that Axel Bruns calls "produsers"[29] or Alvin Toffler calls "prosumers"[30]—are indivisible from the *keitai* phenomenon, which, in turn, has been integral within emerging forms of Japanese technoculture.

It is impossible to understand the rise of *keitai* cultures as synonymous with the burgeoning female UCC without comprehending the pivotal role *kawaii* culture played at both techno-national[31] imagined community[32] and, more importantly, *imaging* communities levels. I use the term "imaging communities" to argue that through the vernacular creative processes of mobile media, users are able to *represent* their notions of place through UCC to *reflect* imagining communities.[33] Through mapping this relationship, we can gain greater acuity on emerging gendered mobile intimacies, labor, and capital. *Kawaii* culture has helped to embed mobile media within forms of localized gendered intimacy, and has thus provided both the backdrop and vehicle for the rise of female produsers.

According to Sharon Kinsella's groundbreaking research, *kawaii* culture arose as a youth subculture in the 1970s as a means of self-expression and rearticulation, and as a reaction to the overarching traditions that were perceived as oppressive. Young adults preferred to stay childlike rather than join the ranks of the corrupt adults.[34] This phenomenon highlighted the way in which "childhood" as a construct is conceived and practiced in locations such as Japan, with its premature adulthood, in contrast to the West.[35] Practices such as "kitten writing" are examples of youths subverting Japanese concepts by intentionally misspelling words and Japanese characters like *hiragana* in acts of political neologism.[36]

Kitten writing can be seen as earlier examples of *emoji* (emoticons) before it was institutionalized by industry as part of built-in *keitai* customization.[37] Under this light, the emergence of kitten writing with personal technologies in the 1970s is no accident; indeed, it highlights that the rise of industry-driven customization has been accompanied by the emergence of UCC personalization. In this way, kitten writing can be read as part of a tradition of female, UCC personalization practices that have sought to align the personal with the interpersonal. *Kawaii* culture's role in customization articulates a type of social glue to the co-present online space of the *keitai*. It transforms the technology into a socio-technology, bringing the role of the socio-cultural to the forefront of the technology.

Through *keitai* UCC, especially *kawaii* UCC, we can see many examples of female users finding inroads into creative activities. Thanks to UCC–oriented organizations such as maho-island, these users can be empowered on various levels—sharing and collaborating on stories as well as potentially making a career, and gaining professional recognition in the form of book publishing or film contracts. Far from *keitai* cultures eroding the significance of older, remediated media such as *manga* and film, they are providing new material for and interest in adapting stories by everyday users. The tendency of customization to be cute—or what Brian McVeigh called "technocute"—has taken various guises and turns in the rise of gendered new media in Japan.[38] It has been an important part in women gaining access and feeling comfortable with the emerging technocultures. Far from reinforcing stereotypes about gender, kitten writing has helped many young women lay claim to the *keitai* and turn it into a multimedia device for self-expression. The fact that kitten writing is now part of the mobile technologies' gender scripting (i.e., the *keitai* now comes with increasingly varieties of *emoji*) highlights how the UCC feminized practices have not only a long tradition—they have become institutionalized.

Conclusion: Locating the Mobile

The success of *keitai shōsetsu* can be attributed to many factors such as the long commuting time in Tokyo, the fact that mobile technologies are the dominant portal for the Internet, and the history of the portable in Japanese culture. What is particularly fascinating is the role *keitai shōsetsu* plays in understanding emergent gendered, remediated UCC practices in Tokyo. In this chapter, I have focused upon the *keitai shōsetsu* as part of women's literary and new media practices.

Keitai shōsetsu can be seen as part of the kitten-writing phenomenon that began in Japan in the 1970s—accompanying the birth and rise of personal technologies. Kitten writing has always fused the creative with the emotional and social, playfully merging Japanese alphabets such as *katagana* with the logographic in order to personalize a media-communication space. In this way, *keitai shōsetsu* extends two traditions: the gendering of *keitai* culture as well as the gendering of Japanese language. For these two reasons and more, it is hard to ignore the role of *keitai shōsetsu* as not only evoking the personal but also linking it a political currency in which gender is mobilized as a form of performativity and potential subversion. It highlights the way in which mobile media can be mobilized to harness both new and old forms of storytelling in innovative ways to foster emergent, remediated forms of writer-reader paradigms. *Keitai shōsetsu*—as indicative of UCC—represents the new forms of narrating in, and of, intimate publics today. The *keitai shōsetsu* provides an interesting lens to think through new gendered forms of UCC labor. These novels inspire users to become writers as well as being part of a broader trend toward the professionalization of UCC, particularly through its adaptation and translation into other media such as films.

Due to its success in Japan, *keitai shōsetsu* has attracted its fair share of fans and has simultaneously drawn criticism about its role in the transformation of traditional media literacy. Some of the criticism is a result of not understanding *keitai shōsetsu* as a remediation of earlier literary traditions. As noted earlier, the *keitai shōsetsu* draw on many traditions that are as gendered as they are localized. For this chapter, I have focused upon one of these traditions through *kawaii* cultures. Just as there are millions of *keitai shōsetsu*, there are multiple epistolary genealogies that inform this exciting phenomenon.

Last year, there were over one million *keitai shōsetsu* in circulation, and five of the top ten printed novels last year in Japan were adapted *keitai shōsetsu*. The new forms of media literacy and expression being fostered by *keitai shōsetsu* are providing new paradigms for author and reader relationships that are predominantly orchestrated by women for women. One can't help but wonder: if Jane Austen were alive today, would she be writing *keitai shōsetsu*? Unquestionably, the intimate, personal nature of mobile media provides a platform for rehearsing earlier epistolary traditions of women's fiction with its literacy devices such as letter writing. This is but one story of gendered UCC and the way in which mobile media remediates older traditions, platforms, media, and content.

Notes

1. See Mizuko Ito and Daisuke Okabe, "Intimate Connections: Contextualizing Japanese Youth and Mobile Messaging," in *The Inside Text: Social, Cultural and Design Perspectives on SMS*, ed. Richard Harper, Leysia Palen, and Alex Taylor (Dordrecht: Springer, 2006), 127–146; Mizuko Ito and Daisuke Okabe, "Everyday Contexts of Camera Phone Use: Steps Towards Technosocial Ethnographic Frameworks", in *Mobile Communication in Everyday Life: An Ethnographic View*, ed. Joseph Höflich and Maren Hartmann (Berlin: Frank & Timme, 2006), 79–102.
2. See Henry Jenkins for a general discussion of participatory media. Henry Jenkins, *Fans, Bloggers, and Gamers: Essays on Participatory Culture* (New York: NYU Press, 2006).
3. Mizuko Ito, "Introduction: Personal, Portable, Pedestrian," in *Personal, Portable, Pedestrian: Mobile Phones in Japanese Life*, ed. Mizuko Ito, Daisuke Okabe, and Misa Matsuda (Cambridge, MA: The MIT Press, 2005), 1–16.
4. Larissa Hjorth, *Mobile Media in the Asia-Pacific: The Art of Being Mobile* (London: Routledge, 2009); Larissa Hjorth, "Cartographies of the Mobile: The Personal as Political," *Communication, Policy & Culture* 42, no. 2 (2009a): 24–44.
5. Jay David Bolter and Richard Grusin, *Remediation: Understanding New Media* (Cambridge, MA: The MIT Press, 1999).
6. Sharon Kinsella, "Cuties in Japan," in *Women, Media and Consumption in Japan*, ed. L. Skov and B. Moeran (Surrey, UK: Curzon Press, 1995), 220–254.
7. Invented by Buddhist priest known as Kûkai (AD 774–835), *hiragana*, as a phonetic version of *Kanji*, was taught to women, as it was seen as simpler in comparison to *Kanji*. At this time, women spoke Japanese and wrote *hiragana*, hence why *hiragana* got defined as "women's language."
8. See Kenichi Fujimoto, "The Third-Stage Paradigm: Territory Machine from the Girls' Pager Revolution to Mobile Aesthetics," in *Personal, Portable, Pedestrian: Mobile Phones in Japanese Life*, ed. Mizuko Ito, Daisuke Okabe, and Misa Matsuda (Cambridge, MA: The MIT Press, 2005), 77–102; Misa Matsuda, "Discourses of *Keitai* in Japan," in *Personal, Portable, Pedestrian: Mobile Phones in Japanese Life*, ed. Mizuko Ito, Daisuke Okabe, and Misa Matsuda (Cambridge, MA: The MIT Press, 2005), 19–40; Misa Matsuda, "Japanese Mobile Youth in the 2000s," in *Youth, Society and Mobile Media in Asia,* ed. Stephanie H. Donald, Theresa D. Anderson, and Damien Spry (New York: Routledge, 2010), 31–42.
9. Young-hwa Yonnie Kim, "The Landscape of *Keitai shōsetsu*: Mobile Phones as a Literary Medium among Japanese Youth," *Continuum: Journal of Media & Cultural Studies* 26, no. 3 (2012): 1–11.
10. Hjorth, "Cartographies of the Mobile."
11. See Jack Qiu, *Working Class Network Society* (Cambridge, MA: The MIT Press, 2009); Wanning Sun, *Maid in China: Media, Morality, and the Cultural Politics of Boundaries: Media, Mobility, and a New Semiotic of Power* (New York: Routledge, 2008).
12. Dave Lee, "Mobile Novels Switch on S. Africa," *BBC News*, October 28, 2009, http://news.bbc.co.uk/2/hi/technology/8329537.stm.
13. Larissa Hjorth, "Domesticating New Media: A Discussion on Locating Mobile Media," in *Mobile Technologies: From Telecommunication to Media*, ed. Gerard Goggin and Larissa Hjorth (London: Routledge, 2009), 143–159.
14. See Raymond Williams, *Television: Technology and Cultural Form* (London: Fontana, 1974); David Morley, "What's 'Home' Got to Do with It?" *European Journal of Cultural Studies* 6, no. 4 (2003): 435–458.
15. Ibid.

16. Ibid.
17. Jack Qiu, "Wireless Working-Class ICTs and the Chinese Informational City," Special Issue of *The Journal of Urban Technology* 3 (2008): 57–77.
18. Michael Arnold, "On the Phenomenology of Technology; the 'Janus-Faces' of Mobile Phones," *Information and Organization* 13 (2003): 231–256.
19. Misa Matsuda, "Mobile Media and the Transformation of the Family," in *Mobile Technologies: From Telecommunications to Media*, eds. Gerard Goggin and Larissa Hjorth (New York, NY: Routledge, 2009), 62–72.
20. Deirdre McKay, "Sending Dollars Shows Feeling: Emotions and Economies in Filipino Migration," *Mobilities* 2, no. 2 (2007): 175–194.
21. Jean Burgess, *Vernacular Creativity and New Media* (Ph.D. Dissertation, Queensland University of Technology, 2007), http://eprints.qut.edu.au/16378/.
22. Judith Butler, *Gender Trouble* (London: Routledge, 1991).
23. Meaghan Morris, "Banality in Cultural Studies," *Discourse* 10, no. 2 (1988): 3–29.
24. Mizuko Ito, "Introduction: Personal, Portable, Pedestrian."
25. Lauren Berlant, "Intimacy: A Special Issue" in *Intimacy*, ed. Lauren Berlant (Chicago: University of Chicago Press, 2000).
26. Sharon Kinsella, "Cuties in Japan."
27. See: Larissa Hjorth, "Kawaii@keitai," in *Japanese Cybercultures*, ed. Nanette Gottlieb and Mark McLelland (New York: Routledge, 2003), 50–59; Larissa Hjorth, "'Pop' and 'Ma': The Landscape of Japanese Commodity Characters and Subjectivity," in *Mobile Cultures: New Media in Queer Asia*, ed. Fran Martin, Audrey Yue, and Chris Berry (Durham, NC: Duke University Press, 2003), 158–179.
28. See Leopoldina Fortunati, "Gender and the Mobile Phone," in *Mobile Technologies: From Telecommunications to Media*, ed. Gerard Goggin and Larissa Hjorth (New York: Routledge, 2009), 23–34; Judy Wajcman, Michael Bittman, and Jude Brown, "Intimate Connections: The Impact of the Mobile Phone on Work Life Boundaries," in *Mobile Technologies: From Telecommunications to Media*, ed. Gerard Goggin and Larissa Hjorth (New York: Routledge, 2009), 9–22.
29. Axel Bruns, "Introduction," *Uses of Blogs*, ed. Axel Bruns and Joanne Jacobs (New York: Peter Lang, 2006).
30. Alvin Toffler, *The Third Wave* (New York: William Morrow and Co., 1980).
31. Joseph Nye, *Soft Power: The Means to Success in World Politics* (New York: PublicAffairs, 2005).
32. Benedict Anderson argued that the rise of the nation-state could be mapped through the birth and rise of the printing press, whereby vernacular diminished and boundaries became more fixed. However, in today's intimate publics, the vernacular is emphasized. Benedict Anderson, *Imagined Communities: Reflections on the Origin and Spread of Nationalism* (London: Verso, 1983).
33. Hjorth, *Mobile Media in the Asia-Pacific*.
34. Kinsella, "Cuties in Japan."
35. See Philippe Ariés, *Centuries of Childhood: A Social History of Family Life*, trans. R. Baldick (New York: Knopf, 1962); Mary White, *The Material Child: Coming of Age in Japan and America* (New York: Free Press, 1993).
36. Kinsella, "Cuties in Japan."
37. Hjorth, "Kawaii@keitai."
38. Brian McVeigh, "How Hello Kitty Commodifies the Cute, Cool and Camp: 'Consumutopia' versus 'Control' in Japan," *Journal of Material Culture* 5, no. 2 (2000): 291–312.

17

TELLING THEIR STORIES THROUGH IPAD ART

Narratives of Adults with Intellectual Disabilities

Jennifer Chatsick, Rhonda McEwen, and Anne Zbitnew

How do the examples in this chapter help us understand the practice of storytelling in the mobile media age?

The Visual Storytelling Club in Toronto, a group of college students with intellectual disabilities, uses iPads as devices for nonlinear storytelling. Guided by various prompts and scenarios, the students draw responses from their own lives, drawing their stories as a means to work around limited literacy skills and difficulties in expressing themselves verbally (either as a result of verbal/speech/language impairments, shyness, or social anxiety in new settings or situations). Interestingly, the creation of visual stories was remarkably different when using an iPad versus other media such as marker and paper or even a desktop computer. The perceived affordances of the iPad, or the functions and opportunities it seems to offer, greatly impact the students' interactions with this medium as they create their visual stories. A part of the artist is constituted in the telling, and the medium is entangled in the tale. Thus, we conjecture that these types of devices begin to blur the boundaries between the tool and the stories told.

Keywords

- **Nonlinear storytelling:** The genre of storytelling that is characterized by narrative elements that are out of chronological sequence, made up of seemingly unrelated pieces, and is often interrupted and folds back onto itself at a later time.
- **Device acuity:** The keen sensitivity of a touch-screen device that allows for interaction on a very fine scale. The device's acuity—or "sharp perceptiveness"—can lead to the acuity of personal expression, as it allows for detailed interactions that best represent the participant's intended actions.

- **Medium-specific analysis:** The study of a medium's unique characteristics that set it apart from other media forms. This approach acknowledges that the ways in which content is conveyed (through what technologies, in what contexts, through which material means) will always be affected by the medium. Thus, a medium's content should not be studied independently of the medium through which it is distributed.

Introduction

Imagine a group of college students getting together after classes to discuss their day: how they got to campus, what they ate for lunch, new assignments and tests, and plans for the evening. The students learn about and get to know each other during this reciprocal exchange, discovering a mutual love for a particular film or sports team, finding common interests in fashion and food, and sharing common (or contesting divergent) beliefs and experiences. A discussion about favorite soccer teams might lead to a discussion about travel to one of the major soccer-playing countries, and this may segue to a chat about learned phrases from a foreign-language. As the conversation is interrupted and shifts back and forth among the students, animated and intense dialogues are generated, and individual ideas are linked together, forming a set of unique, shared, personal, and nonlinear stories. In this way, nonlinear storytelling represents a narrative genre that defies traditional literary structures.[1]

While the scenario above may seem very familiar to any group of students, the students described here are young adults with moderate intellectual disabilities who are involved in an extracurricular art initiative called the Visual Storytelling Club (VSC) at a college in Toronto, Canada. Given that many of these students have difficulties in recalling words or verbally articulating ideas, instead of using words as the building blocks of their stories, the students focus on using images to construct their narratives. They acquire images from sources on the Internet, from magazines, or create them by drawing or painting, and through digital photography and Photoshop. In taking this approach, the VSC pedagogy supports the development of visual literacy—that is, the use of visuals for the purpose of communication, thinking, learning, constructing meaning, creative expression, and aesthetic enjoyment.[2]

Visual Storytelling: Using Images to Create Nonlinear Narratives

In the VSC, students engage in several exercises to develop their skills in visual storytelling. For example, in an exercise called a "Day in the Life," the facilitator poses a series of questions such as, "What did you eat for breakfast?" "What are you wearing?" or "What is your favorite book/film/TV show?" The students answer these questions using downloaded online images. The goal of this exercise is to teach students how to use images to present a mental construct and how to format images effectively so that the completed piece can be shared with, and understood by, others. The resulting interactive conversations encourage even more developed dialogue (verbal and/or visual). This leads to expansive and creative nonlinear narratives that explain some of the emotions and challenges of life through the language of visual media. For students who are introverted, nonverbal, or have speech difficulties, these conversations are often the first times that they have communicated to this degree with their peers and classmates.

Some students in the VSC have mobility or visual impairments, so using a mouse and a desktop computer can be difficult. One student had to climb on to the desk and view the monitor from a distance of a few inches at a 90-degree angle in order to see the screen. Inspired by this and similar observations, we designed and conducted a research project to explore student experiences of using media to create nonlinear narratives. We focused on the use of a) paper and markers, b) desktop computers, and c) touch tablet technologies (specifically the iPad)[3] as different media platforms for communication and storytelling for students with intellectual disabilities. The project took place at Humber College Institute of Technology and Advanced Learning in Toronto, Ontario, in March 2011. This was a collaborative effort between Humber College ITAL and the University of Toronto. The research participants were students in Humber's Community Integration through Cooperative Education (CICE) program who were participating in the VSC.

The CICE program is a two-year certificate program specifically designed to provide a college experience for adults, who are nineteen years of age or older, with moderate intellectual disabilities. CICE students typically have limited literacy skills and may have difficulty expressing themselves verbally either as a result of verbal/speech/language impairments, shyness, or social anxiety in new settings or situations. As is often the case for young persons with disabilities, many students have been sheltered by parents or guardians, and attendance at college may be the first time they are able to practice being self-directed in their own lives.

Among this group of students, working with technologies in the classroom is also a fairly new experience. The first time a digital camera was used in the VSC, many students were too nervous to use or even hold the camera. One very anxious student told a facilitator that he was not allowed to ever use the family camera because he might break it. With some guidance and instruction, this student eventually put the camera strap around his neck and relaxed into the act of capturing images.

Engaging Abilities and Social Interaction

For young adults with intellectual disabilities, social interaction and communication can be challenging. While there are studies that examine the use of visual arts for therapeutic outcomes,[4] there is little research pertaining to adults with intellectual disabilities using images for the social communication of storytelling.

While the individual and collaborative output of the VSC participants is made without language, the students create stories that are distinct and detailed using captured digital images, collage, drawing, and painting. These students are expressing themselves in narrative ways using these media. The students are not passive and dependent on others for their expression. When asked to describe "What is art?" some of the answers included: a way to express yourself and tell stories about how you feel; a way to deal with sadness by taking the idea out of your head and putting it onto the paper; and art is good for you!

The VSC provides an opportunity to explore alternative forms of expression and communication by using diverse media to connect and share life experiences with each other and to identify with the community at large. A VSC facilitator provides a framework, encouraging the students to explore various media and to create and use images to say something about their lives. The VSC fosters conversation and storytelling by, for example, using lighting and digital SLR cameras to capture portrait images that display mood and offer insight into the personality of the subject, using Photoshop to enhance and manipulate portrait images, and experimenting with art and communication through storytelling by working to create and share personal narratives and collaborative anecdotes. Each week, the students are inspired to respond visually to an exercise; examples include exercises to find an image for each letter in the alphabet or tell a story about yourself in a self-portrait format using collaged magazine images. In the VSC, the creative process is as valuable as the work produced, and self-expression, collaboration, and sharing can offer the opportunity for personal reflection, inspire individual and community transformation, and make a difference. The images serve as a beginning to a larger conversation that stops and starts and often continues week to week. Amy Mullin, a scholar of aesthetics and feminist theory, considers artistic self-expression as something that holds the potential to foster social interaction and communication. Mullin states, "Art can start an encounter with another, and it can destabilize our terms of reference governing that encounter. To this extent it may enhance the possibilities that will emerge from that encounter with changed beliefs and attitudes."[5]

The Visual Storytelling Club as a Research Project Site

Data for our research project were collected during three particular visual storytelling sessions where we included the iPad as one of the media used make art and to tell stories. We were interested in comparing more traditional media, such as paper and marker, with the use of electronic media. Because all of the research participants had participated in the VSC prior to the research, they were familiar with engaging with artistic projects under the guidance of a facilitator, but the art forms prior to the research had always been more traditional, involving paper and markers, pencil or paint, photography, collage, and desktop computers. For the project, twenty-five iPads were loaned to the VSC for three weeks and returned at the end of the third session. Students were familiar with the iPad from television advertisements or by seeing people in the general public using one, but few had used one prior to participating in the research project.

Knowing that the iPad was going to be one of the tools used to create art during this period, the students enthusiastically attended visual storytelling with a significant increase in turnout, and they were extremely vocal about how "cool" the iPads were. At the outset, participants required some assistance familiarizing themselves with the iPad by learning how to maneuver the device and use each application, how to draw and paint with their fingers, and how to save each file. Initial frustration over how to use the device was short lived as participants promptly began to draw and paint using three available applications: Drawcast, Art Rage, and ASKetch[6] to draw, paint, and sketch.

Findings and Observations

A VSC facilitator offered the participants various suggestions and scenarios, asking them to create a visual response. Each student was inspired to draw and paint from his or her own imagination with a heightened level of embodied response. Initial individual projects included: draw your hand, draw what you had for lunch, draw your favorite part of the day, and draw your idea of a spaceship. These exercises familiarized the students with the iPad and the apps and fostered a unique approach and individual creative style. The next series of exercises included drawing a self-portrait, drawing the person sitting beside you, and passing an iPad back and forth between pairs, with each person contributing a line or design to complete an image. In the latter collaborative exercise the participants became very socially engaged, turning in their chairs and holding up the iPad to show one another works in progress or completed images. The collective environment fostered teamwork and partnership as students collaborated and inspired each other in a room filled with lively, animated conversation. Next, the students interviewed and asked each other a series of questions: "What is your favorite color, food, animal, season, number, movie, book?" They then drew and saved their responses. These interviews revealed a great deal about the personal lives of the students, and each image added to the next, creating a nonlinear visual biography.

The vocal volume level in the room varied from exercise to exercise. When the facilitator asked the participants to draw "silence," the energy in the room became very still, and the participants fell absolutely silent while the images were created (see Figure 17.1).

In another drawing exercise, a facilitator told the group that "an elephant just walked into the room," and there was much whooping, laughing, movement, and animation in response as the participants used the iPad to draw an elephant (see Figure 17.2).

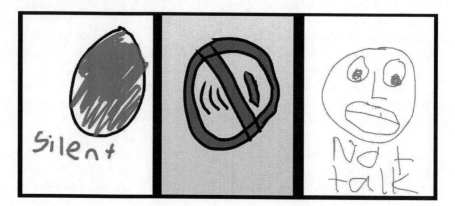

Figure 17.1 Screen captures of three of the images drawn by students on the iPad in response to the prompt, "Draw silence." Image courtesy of the authors reproduced with permission of the artists.

Figure 17.2 Screen captures of one of the images drawn by a student on the iPad in response to the statement, "An elephant just walked into the room." Image courtesy of the authors reproduced with permission of the artists.

CICE students are representative of Humber College students in that they come from diverse cultural and socioeconomic backgrounds, and many are bilingual or multilingual. Where they may differ from other college students is that they have often been sheltered socially. Prior to enrollment at Humber College ITAL, many CICE students had a very small circle of friends or may have only socialized mainly with family members outside of high school. Attending college can, in many cases, broaden a student's social circle and strengthen interest in developing friendships and romantic relationships. It is noteworthy that friendship and love were recurring themes found in the narratives of our research participants. For people with disabilities, sexuality and romance are often taboo subjects stemming from a social history of asexualizing this population.[7] Adults with intellectual disabilities may lack privacy, control over their own lives and choices, access to sex education, and may not have the means to communicate in order to express love, friendship, affection, and sexuality.[8] However, when offered an outlet for telling their own stories they were eager to create images depicting love (see Figure 17.3).

CICE staff, as well as VSC facilitators, reported that several students who developed and/or documented relationships with their peers—both romantic and platonic—while participating in the VSC became more open about discussing their relationships outside of the VSC. It appears as though the act of creating a visual nonlinear narrative of their feelings opened a door for them, making it easier to discuss who were the important people in their lives and what they wanted out of their relationships. Many students spoke to staff about their desire to get married, have a family, get a girlfriend or a boyfriend, make friends, meet new people, and also end relationships that did not seem to be working. Perhaps the experience of creating a visual narrative about their relationships and the value they place on love helped validate their experience for themselves as real and important.

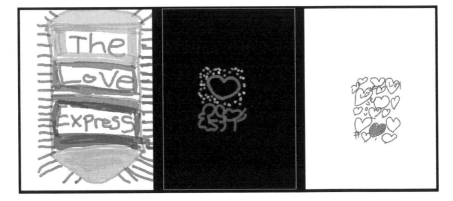

Figure 17.3 Screen captures of three of the images drawn by students on the iPad in response to the prompts about love. Image courtesy of the authors reproduced with permission of the artists.

Annabelle Nelson, Charles McClintock, and their colleagues studied the use of structured narrative storytelling with at-risk youth, concluding that collaborative storytelling exercises afforded positive peer-to-peer social bonding and impacted on positive self-image and confidence.[9] Similar to youth in this study, our participants can be categorized as devalued and marginalized, although the young adults in our study are marginalized primarily as a result of their intellectual disability rather than on the basis of their socioeconomic status. Our findings are similar to those of Nelson, McClintock, et al. in that participants bonded with one another throughout the process of engaging in storytelling. While our research participants used images rather than words, the results were comparable. We noticed a marked increase in social behavior as participants used the iPads for self-expression and collaboration. The social aspect of sharing narratives was an obvious benefit to the participants and likely influenced the narrative itself. Participants appeared to be joyfully sharing stories about themselves and eagerly learning about each other, transitioning from social isolation to an active social environment.

Positive relationships formed during the VSC tended to continue to develop outside of the club, often blossoming into deep and meaningful friendships. Shy, less verbal, and socially isolated participants were often observed chatting animatedly with fellow participants. The act of telling stories via art with the focus of sharing something about oneself seemed to create an environment that was safe and nurturing, allowing people to come out of their shells.

iPad Stories Compared to Stories Told Using Traditional Media

During the course of the research project, we observed some distinct differences when students used various media. Regarding sociality, the classroom was significantly quieter when students worked with markers and paper to construct their stories when compared to the noise levels when they used the iPads. In the case of using the iPads, students would chat with one another, turn around to share their work, or walk across the room to show their work to someone else. The artists were also more inclined to collaborate on iPad images as compared to paper-and-marker art, which suggests that socializing was a part of the story creation process.

We also noted that students tended to hold the paper vertically with their nondominant hand and draw with their dominant hand; however, when using the iPad, students would rotate the device repeatedly, changing its orientation throughout the process. We were also surprised by the amount of work produced and the speed in doing so when engaging in storytelling via the iPad when compared with other media. Students were quick to abandon a painting or drawing created on the iPad and move onto a new piece either by deleting the current one or saving it but rarely returning to complete it. In comparison, art created using more traditional tools, such as paper and markers, was very rarely discarded or abandoned. Participants were more inclined to work slowly and deliberately when using paper and markers and always signed their name to the work upon completion, whereas the majority of the iPad art images were unsigned by the artists.

Media Affordances: The Example of the iPad

In reviewing the findings, we asked the question, "Why did the student's experiences of telling stories via the iPads differ from his or her experiences when using traditional materials?" In other words, what was it about the devices that shaped experiences? From the data, we identified six opportunities (or "affordances") intrinsic to the devices, which appear to account for these differences. The iPad affordances were: acuity, scalability, portability, low-aspect, flexibility, and intangibility, and they are each described below.

Acuity: the touch-screen of the iPads provided students with the chance to use their hands directly on the medium, and this resulted in subtle detailing in the artwork that students could not readily reproduce using a marker or mouse. The iPad and similar touch devices make the creation of art more accessible to persons with fine motor skill problems, as these individuals may find holding a marker, pencil, or piece of charcoal difficult. The fine motor skills necessary to hold and manipulate these objects were problematic for many students in this project, thus the direct touch on the device surface, and the near real-time reaction of the surface to their hand movements, supported a wide variation of expression. In a way, this provided the students with a broader and more instinctive artistic "vocabulary" for their visual narratives.

Scalability: this refers to the pinch-to-zoom capability in the iPad that facilitates rapid resizing of text and images. When compared to using desktop computers, the scalability of the images on the iPad made the production of images more accessible for those participants in our study with visual impairments, as they were able to hold the device closer to their eyes and enlarge what they were painting or drawing. Certainly, these affordances do impact the narrative for someone who has visual challenges, making self-expression via these tools easier. The ability to zoom also allowed some students to experiment with creating art that required the audience to play with the size of the image as part of the "reading" of the narrative. An element of performance on the part of the audience was introduced as the artists encouraged this type of manipulation of images, a form of engagement that is often restricted in traditional art exhibitions.

Portability: the mobility of the devices, due to their lighter weights and hand-held forms, influenced the social engagement that permeated the production process of image creation. Students could lift and turn the devices in the air to show fellow students across the room what was on the screen. Also, there were many instances in which students would reach over and add something to another student's work in progress with a touch or two. The portability of the devices fostered an environment of participatory spirit and social engagement that we did not witness in the computer lab with the same group of students. It is interesting to note that while traditional art supplies like paper and markers are also very portable, the iPad has all of its art supplies securely tucked away inside in the form of applications. There is no danger of wrinkling your paper and no risk of losing your favorite colored marker with the iPad, making it arguably more readily portable than those traditional art supplies.

Low-aspect: the flatness of the iPads, meaning the close proximity of the device to the desktop, gave students opportunities to see each other in any direction. Labs with desktop computers are typically organized in rows with students assigned to a particular computer. In this configuration, students can communicate with those to their left or right; however, the size of the computers inhibits closer seating positions. In addition, the vertical monitor facing the user acts as both an obstacle to social interaction with those in front of or behind the user and also acts as an obstruction to sharing what is on the screen with a wider group.

Flexibility: this describes the multiple options presented to the user by both the physical device itself, and the many applications housed within the device. Students would turn, toggle, and spin the iPads during the course of their art making. As a consequence, the visual stories that they told on the iPad sometimes had multiple orientations, as they would start the piece in one direction and then turn the device and continue working in another. The device was perfectly suited to this form of adjustment. So too is paper; however, students never adjusted the direction of the paper while drawing, and they almost always placed the paper artwork in the "portrait" orientation and kept it there for the duration of the work. Perhaps there is an observed historical expectation of how paper art ought to be oriented that does not apply to the newer tablet device. In fact, the very nomenclature of orientation betrays a bias in the recommended way to use a page: for images of people, for a portrait, we use an aspect where the vertical length measurement is greater than that of the width. For images of scenery, or landscapes, we use the reverse aspect. Thus, when children are taught how to draw images of themselves or others, the practice is to use the portrait orientation.

This is compounded by the fact that in Western literate cultures, when writing (stories or otherwise), we are taught to use a portrait page orientation as well. This is even the default orientation for word processing software. However, for tablets such as the iPad, a key feature is the ability for the device to quickly change the on-screen content to match the direction in which the user has turned the device. It is easy to change directions, and most applications are designed to be used in either direction; hence, there is no inherent expectation on how it should be oriented. When asked why she was changing directions so often while using the iPad, one student remarked that the iPad was "so spinney and fun."

Intangibility: this affordance describes the digital content produced on devices like iPads and computers versus the art created on tangible materials such as paper. The digital artwork appeared to lack a kind of substantiveness, or tangibility, for students that may account for the rapid execution and the large volume of work done on the iPad. The rapidity with which the iPad images were executed and then abandoned or saved may also indicate that the students felt less of a connection to the story they were telling with the iPad. Building on Jill Mullin's research in her book, *Drawing Autism*, this may be an example of artists using their art to portray emotions when language may be unavailable, and this is often accompanied by a prodigious quantity of artwork produced by a single artist.[10]

Alternatively, students may spend more time with paper art and be more inclined to sign paper art as a result of being more familiar with this type of medium and the surrounding conventions. Therefore, their unfamiliarity with the iPad may have led to a desire to cycle quickly through the different applications to see what else could be created. The iPad seemed to become a sketchbook for ideas and images, offering an opportunity for sketching, reflection, revision, and development of a personal style. The iPad images were occasionally suspended, saved, and redrawn with more, less, or different detail on the following image. These image responses became part of the nonlinear narrative as defined by Werner Hammerstingl as, "processes of interruption, circular and unfinished references, and chronological anarchy."[11]

Conclusion

Are these mobile media tools or embedded artifacts in the process of telling stories? Sara B. Kajder states that "the technology was simply a delivery tool that ultimately provided a hook that tapped into students' existing visual and technological literacies."[12] In our case, the newness and cool factor of the iPad cannot be denied and may have functioned as a "hook." The iPad captured the interest of the participants and kept them engaged in the process of storytelling through visual art, but for our participants, it was more than a tool. It enabled participants to explore different art forms, encouraged socialization, and helped foster friendships.

Yet we hold a stronger belief that something else is at play. The affordances of the device appeared to become entangled with the very narrative processes in art making. Acuity, portability, intangibility, and flexibility do more than simply describe the characteristics of the device as they also describe the coming-to-being of the art and are a part of the stories told. A part of the artist is constituted in the telling, and the medium is entangled in the tale. Thus, we conjecture that these types of devices begin to blur the boundaries between the tool and the stories told.

Notes

1. Other examples of nonlinear narrative styles include *Choose Your Own Adventure* novels and, more recently, the incorporation of hypertext into writing.
2. Judy Baca and Roberts A. Branden, "The Delphi Study: A Proposed Method for Resolving Visual Literacy Uncertainties," in *Perceptions of Visual Literacy*, ed. Roberts A. Braden, Darrell G. Beauchamp, and Judy Clark Baca (Blacksburg, VA: International Visual Literacy Association, 1989): 65.

3. Apple iPads were used in this project for two reasons: a) Other tablet devices were not yet readily available in the market at the time of the study; and b) Apple Canada offered to loan the devices to the college for the duration of the study. We believe that the findings would be consistent for most tablet-type devices.

4. See Karen Caldwell, Kathleen T. Brinko, Rebecca Krenz, and Kristin Townsend, "Individuals with Intellectual Disabilities: Educators in Expressive Arts Therapy," *The Arts in Psychotherapy* 35, no. 2. (2008): 129–139; Stephen P. Demanchick, Nancy H. Cochran, and Jeff L. Cochran, "Person-Centered Play Therapy for Adults with Developmental Disabilities," *International Journal of Play Therapy* 12, no.1. (2003): 47–65.

5. Amy Mullin, "Art, Understanding, and Political Change," *Hypatia* 15, no. 3 (2000): 132.

6. The applications Drawcast and ASKetch were chosen because they were free, and Art Rage was recommended and featured on iTunes at the time of the research.

7. Winifred Kempton and Emily Kahn, "Sexuality and People with Intellectual Disabilities: A Historical Perspective," *Sexuality and Disability* 9, no. 2 (1991): 93–111.

8. Miriam Taylor Gomez, "The S Words: Sexuality, Sensuality, Sexual Expression and People with Intellectual Disability," *Sexuality and Disability* 30, no. 2 (2012): 237–245.

9. Annabelle Nelson, Charles McClintock, Anita Perez-Ferguson, Mary Nash Shawver, and Greg Thompson, "Storytelling Narratives: Social Bonding as Key for Youth at Risk," *Child Youth Care Forum* 37, no. 3 (2008): 127–137.

10. Jill Mullin, *Drawing Autism* (New York: Mark Batty Publishers, 2009).

11. Werner Hammerstingl, "Strategies in Visual Narrative," http://www.olinda.com/VC/lectures/Narrative.htm.

12. Sara B. Kajder, "Enter Here: Personal Narrative and Digital Storytelling," *English Journal* 93, no.3. (2004): 65.

PART VI

Memory, History, and Community

18

MOBILE MEDIA AFTER 9/11

The September 11 Memorial & Museum App

Alberto S. Galindo

How do the examples in this chapter help us understand the practice of story-telling in the mobile media age?

Tragedies like the 9/11 attacks are understood not only by witnessing the events but also by the ways these events are told and retold. When considering how such national traumas like 9/11 are told—through oral histories, photographs, visualizations like timelines, to name a few—how might the mobile phone as a narrative interface transform our relationship to these stories and these memorializations? Using the "Explore 9/11" app from the National September 11 Memorial & Museum as the main object of study, this chapter notes how the screen of the phone transforms our relationship to the screen as a story interface (as it is interacted with differently than television and film screens). The result is a narrative that exists across several spaces: the site-specific locations related to 9/11 experienced in tandem with images on the phone's screen, the audio space of the oral narratives that are unlocked when walking by certain locations, and the space of the archive of eyewitness accounts of the events (accessed through the phone's interface). An analysis of the app thus shows that acts of memorialization, especially when experienced through emerging storytelling interfaces like the mobile phone, must be read through the lens of narrative—narratives that simultaneously interrogate these traumas as intensely public and private, in the past and ever-evolving.

Keywords

- **Memorialization:** The act of preserving a history or memory. This can be done in many forms, including narratives, ceremonies, and the creation of a memorial site (such as a statue or the dedication of a public space).

The process of memorialization is often wrought with conflict because it tends to preserve a very specific perspective rather than encompassing a breadth of perspectives.

- **Hypermedia:** A type of media in which a text can easily lead into other forms of data and media, being experienced simultaneously or as a nonlinear journey. Hypermedia offer a kind of rhizome-like experience—spread out, without a core or center—in which one medium does not dominate over another.

- **Deterritorialization:** A term that arose from the work of theorists Gilles Deleuze and Felix Guattari, deterritorialization is the stripping away of the established structure, order, and familiarity of a place. This is typically followed by *reterritorialization*, or the establishment of new structures that define a place.

Introduction

Some critical approaches to post–9/11 cultural production called for the creation of new, dislocated spaces where a wide range of narratives could emerge.[1] This dislocation, in theory, and in the specific case of 9/11, would benefit narrative forms by taking them away from a strongly territorialized, overly nationalistic, and simple binary American discourse, and instead would allow for these narratives to be told from perspectives that were not normative and that would somehow challenge the main post–9/11 discourse. There has been a very strong literary criticism against these territorial narratives, mainly in fiction, for being unable to narrate 9/11 in any way that does not feel complicit with the immediate nationalistic and patriotic response created under the presidency of George W. Bush.[2] Perhaps questions about narrating 9/11 need to be raised not only in a variety of contexts or perspectives; but more specifically, these questions could be raised in relation to the form of the narrative itself. It seems that rather than putting the contents of a given 9/11–related text first, an approach to the form could provide a stimulating entry into post–9/11 cultural production. If the novel, for example, is not the best form for narrating 9/11 in this immediate aftermath, as Joyce Carol Oates claimed in 2005,[3] it could be useful to consider other forms of narrating 9/11, in this case, "Explore 9/11," an app designed for mobile devices.[4] If we follow Jacques Derrida's controversial point from 2003, when he stated that we do not know what 9/11 is, then his point is well taken, as "Explore 9/11" fully benefits from this "*unqualifiable*" condition, as Derrida described it, as this app tries to generate several narratives and hence several meanings of 9/11.[5]

"Explore 9/11" provides its users with a walking tour around the World Trade Center (WTC), firsthand accounts from witnesses presented via audio, a timeline, and an increasing photographic archive. It was released by the National September 11 Memorial & Museum on August 26, 2010, several days ahead of the ninth anniversary of the destruction and collapse of the World Trade Center as well as the other devastating events in Pennsylvania and at the Pentagon. Two aspects of the app are clear from this description: first, that "Explore 9/11" will try to navigate the historical, political, and spatial complexities of contemporary American and global history; second, that the app will also try to articulate a new vision for museums, memorials, and the act of memorializing. Therefore, by paying close attention to the multilayered narratives presented in "Explore 9/11," this chapter seeks to shed light on ways in which the aforementioned narratives intersect.

"Explore 9/11" operates as a polyphonic narrative, borrowing here Mikhail Bakhtin's term from *Problems of Dostoyevsky's Art*, where several points of entry and perspectives on 9/11 cross and overlap, making it rather unclear as to whether the app privileges any of the following components over the others: oral history app, museum and memorial companion, tourist's guide, remembrance device, or interactive tool. Keeping in mind that any of these aspects of "Explore 9/11" operate from a narrative standpoint as well as their respective narrative structures and techniques, this chapter looks at this app not as a case study, but rather as the pretext for larger reflections on narrative and storytelling, time as well as space, and processes of *memorialization*.[6] And finally, even though much has been written about the documentation of 9/11 on "old" media such as television and print, as well as "new" digital media, "Explore 9/11" relies on combining ways of narrating a historical, violent moment such as 9/11, and therefore provides a template for this kind of memorial work in the future.

"Explore 9/11" responds to the post–9/11 slogan, "If you see something, say something." The app itself is about the act of "exploring," be it as a concerned citizen, victim, tourist, or visitor, but exploring what others have "seen" of 9/11 and "said" about it before.[7] It fully relies on documented moments of "seeing" and "saying"; these documented contents are shared and commonplace for the many who witnessed the events. It could be argued that the app responds to the tradition of visual metaphors and visualizing technologies of the past, noting how mobile screens are quite different. Ingrid Richardson traces this difference in relation to mobile devices, which in turn allows her to conclude that mobile media screens require a completely different embodied relationship than previous screens do (such as film and television screens).[8] Therefore, the interest here is not whether to question any well-established facts such as the crashes, collapses, and deaths of 9/11, but the form in which this information is relayed through the app and screen of the mobile device. The contents of the app, mainly the first-person accounts and the images, of course shape the narrative form that the app needs to present this type of information, but this chapter argues that it is the form of the mobile app that generates the techniques used to narrate the events. That is, rather than hypothesizing that 9/11 as well as its related museum and memorial shape the app, this chapter will explore the ways in which the form of the app shapes its contents and, for such purposes, the form uses certain techniques to narrate these contents. With this in mind, this chapter pays attention to some studies on the novel, particularly the form of the novel, in studies by novelists such as E.M. Forster and Orhan Pamuk, as well as scholars such as Franco Moretti, where the form of the novel becomes the starting point for a reflection on its contents. Such stance on my part does not seek to treat 9/11 as if it were fiction, but rather these three works allow me to raise questions about the form in which "Explore 9/11" narrates 9/11. Therefore, previous inquiries into the form of narratives will prove useful in approaching the form of the app.

The website for Local Projects, the design team behind this app, describes itself as a "media design firm for museums and public spaces," and underlines the nature of "Explore 9/11" as a project on "collaborative storytelling" as well as mobile technology.[9] That is, this app is more interested in narratives and storytelling than in being a museum app, at least for the time being, which in part explains its vast difference from apps from other New York venues such as the American Museum of National History, the Brooklyn Museum, and MOMA, for example. The difference also stems from the fact that the 9/11 Museum had not even been built when the app was released (it was opened in 2012); it thus stood in comparison with actual, concrete museums that offered insights on their current collections and exhibits.

The concept of "Explore 9/11," in particular the notion of a mobile walking tour of a site that was destroyed and is currently under construction, drew quick, negative responses, as in the case of Jennifer Valentino-DeVries, who opened her review of the app for the *Wall Street Journal* by stating, "We were initially taken aback. There's a tendency to associate apps with fun, such that apps and 9/11 seem as though they should be diametrically opposed."[10] The concept of the touristic, educational, or memorial tour is not new, with more recent development such as virtual tours being offered, as in other New York–specific virtual visits, but in this particular case, the app opens the door for creating narratives of future constructions of what is yet to come.

On Storytelling

The home screen of "Explore 9/11" is composed of three main sections, named "Tour," "Explore," and "Timeline." At first glance, these three sections simply seem to be a narration of 9/11 in terms of time and space, mainly dividing the events in three major moments: the day of 9/11 itself, its immediate aftermath, and a projection of a future time to come. The task of this app, like many others, is to navigate time and space in the current present moment. But "Explore 9/11" does not seek to operate similarly to social networking media, which seek to document the time and location of individual or collective being; instead, it aims to take advantage of an interest in documenting time and space as much as possible. For these purposes, it relies on the specificity that time and space can provide, but always from the perspective of storytelling. If, as Walter Benjamin reminds us in "The Storyteller," the rise of the modern novel signaled a "symptom" of the decline of storytelling, 9/11 can be read as a kind of contemporary return to storytelling. As Benjamin presents it, storytelling is artisanal and "does not aim to convey the pure essence of the thing, like information or a report."[11] This simple description is very much present in "Explore 9/11."

The notion of storytelling is a key point of entry into 9/11, but more broadly into the construction of historical narratives through a mobile device. The cultural production of 9/11 in particular opens the door into a discussion about the ways in which storytelling, or oral history, can sometimes easily oscillate into a personal view of a historical account and myth making. Much has been said about the creative licenses and liberties taken when approaching a recent historical event such as 9/11. Regarding this issue of historical narratives on TV versus myth making, consider, for example, Mark Poindexter's conclusion to his analysis of the TV documentary, *The Path to 9/11*: "*The Path to 9/11*, however, is a spectacular piece of mythmaking, not of understanding or explanation, telling us more about ourselves as traumatized consumers of history than about the people who made it."[12] There are two particular sets of issues that "Explore 9/11" helps discuss in relation to contemporary history: 1) the development, construction, and uses of narratives of history for and through the mobile device app; and 2) the role of the app in shaping and informing contemporary history. That is, what we have here is both how the contents affect the narrative form—the form of the story—as well as how the form used in this kind of storytelling can mold the contents it puts forward.

As Franco Moretti demonstrated in *Atlas of the European Novel*, geography can become the key to certain kinds of narratives, where "*this* specific form needs *that* specific space . . . space is not the 'outside' of narrative, then, but an internal force, that shapes it from within."[13] The map in particular, seems to be of crucial importance to the narrative that "Explore 9/11" creates. The "Tour" section opens with straightforward instructions written under the "Play" button that opens the first audio account. These instructions state, "The tour begins at 20 Vesey Street. A Google map snapshot of the area links the different tour stops, with their respective audio and text transcript, and also includes written instructions such as, 'Walk towards WTC site. Cross Church St and stop by the park.'" The snapshots of the maps and the textual instructions can only be seen between stops; therefore, the maps serve as a narrative thread between them. These maps and instructions clearly serve visual and representational roles, as their sole purpose is to take the visitor from one place to another around Ground Zero. Map instructions, after all, create their own kind of direct narrative by using verbs in their respective imperative mood, as in the case of "walk" and "stop" quoted here. The narrative of the map seems to depend on these instructions and, of course, in following them in the order they were intended. It creates very clear expectations of anyone who uses the app, but the stops can be skipped when the user is not onsite by just tapping on any of the other stops of the tour.

That is, it is recommended for an onsite explorer to follow the map's narrative and instructions, but, hypothetically, one could create one's own tour. This notion of creating one's own narrative path could seem to be an alteration of the expected order of the tour, not only at the WTC site but also of any walking audio tours such as the ones at museums. The question to follow is, of course, "Does randomly choosing one's own stops affect in any way the narrative of the tour as put together by the app?" Such a question would go hand in hand with George Landow's theorization of hypermedia, where a text can easily lead into other forms of data and media. For Landow, hypermedia "denotes an information medium that links verbal and non-verbal information" and this kind of rhizome-like experience, is at the very core of "Explore 9/11."[14]

In this case, the experience of the tour seems to be the same even if the tour is completed in a different order. The recombination of the tour stops still put forward the same narrative, allowing the explorer two possibilities, whether to follow the tour, and hence the narrative, in order or at random, therefore keeping the meaning of the narrative still intact. The reason behind the standalone qualities of each stop solely depends on the narrative that each section puts together in a rather condensed way. It is crucial and to the benefit of the explorer that each stop in the tour be concise and direct. This allows for each stop to be self-contained and could even be experienced at different moments. In the case of "Explore 9/11," the names of the stops do follow a chronology: Impact, Collapse, Rescue, Evacuation, Recovery, Volunteerism, and We Remember. These terms underline the need for conciseness and respect for the spatial limits of the screen. The titles do not leave any space for doubt, and the mobile narrative depends on this directness. As seen here, the succinct and direct form of the app affects the way in which it narrates 9/11, while simultaneously the geography and the space almost require the app to organize its tour in a certain order, even if that order can be corrupted by the user.

Narrative Memorializations

"Explore 9/11" is not only a mobile historical narrative but a mobile memorial as well. It negotiates the need for direct and succinct language in information-heavy mobile apps, as noted earlier, with the conventions of memorials and *memorialization* processes. One of these conventions, in the specific case of 9/11, is the very description of the weather on that day, which can be found on the first tour stop. The screenshot of this first stop includes a photograph of one of the impacted towers with the "Play" button right in the middle of the photo. Once the user taps on the button, Bruno Dellinger's account begins, only on audio format and only audible with a headset, not on speakerphone. While the audio is playing, the user has two possibilities: looking at a timed slideshow of 9/11-related images onscreen, or looking toward the Ground Zero area in person.

Also, the user has the option to access a transcript of the audio by tapping on the small page icon on the top right of the screen, but this option would interrupt the two options previously mentioned. Dellinger, as a witness who was on the forty-seventh floor of the North Tower, starts by stating that, "the sky was so pure, the air was so crisp, everything was perfect, one of those New York days that you love and you remember." The convention invoked here is commonplace by now in first-person nonfictional accounts of September 11th and in fiction as well: the weather itself was perfect and memorable, which in turn makes the rest of the day memorable. The question here does not lie on whether this detailed account of the weather is accurate or not—indeed this day has been recorded as a clear, sunny day—but rather the way in which Dellinger's story is told. Dellinger's account and all the other stories included in "Explore 9/11" are first-person narratives that rely on the fact that these people were present in the area and, as such, can bear witness to some of the events on 9/11. Dellinger's testimony relies simultaneously on the arts of witnessing (what he saw and experienced) as well as storytelling (the way in which he tells what he saw and experienced). Storytelling, as Benjamin observed, became poorer in the aftermath of the First World War, and it is worth asking whether 9/11 and the wars that followed also put storytelling under duress and therefore required new ways of reformulating storytelling and witnessing of contemporary events for the mobile era. These personal accounts become doubly useful; they are oral histories and memorial narratives.

Valentino-DeVries, in her review of the app for the *Wall Street Journal*, underlines the importance of oral history by reminding the reader that the app "provides a look at history through the eyes of people touched by the event."[15] This notion of being "touched by the event," or bearing witness to it, highlights the collaborative storytelling sought by Local Projects in its design as well as the Museum & Memorial in its concept. By making storytelling, oral history, and memorializing into essential components of the app, it calls attention to both the role of storytelling in current mobile media practices as well as the role of mobile devices in the design, construction, and dissemination of storytelling. What becomes key here is the way in which the development of this app for a mobile device not only affects the construction of storytelling but also the effect that the combination of storytelling and a mobile device will bear upon the understanding of history and reality.

In the case of "Explore 9/11," there is a fine balance between the construction of a story through its narrative mechanisms and its simultaneous narration of real, historical events. This question on navigating the real, historical world and its relation to narrative techniques is very much present in Orhan Pamuk's introduction to *The Naïve and the Sentimentalist Novelist*. Pamuk mentions in passing that the reader of novels wants fiction to "sustain the illusion that it is actually real life."[16] This illusion is of much use here, especially as he further elaborates that the novel is contradictory in nature: we want it to be real, or as real as possible, but yet it is not. There is a contradiction, albeit of a different nature, within the very premise of "Explore 9/11" and other apps that seek to deal with contemporary history, politics, or memories, mainly because of the combination between the nature of their reliance on oral history and the by-now almost expected conventions of contemporary historical narratives.

"Explore 9/11" not only proposes a way to negotiate and incorporate storytelling and oral history with a mobile device; it also questions the role of the reader, spectator, and listener as their tasks easily interact and evolve, depending on the section of the app being used. The tour section requires the user to experience the app at least as a listener of the audio, a map navigator, and then as a spectator of either the slideshow or Ground Zero. The other possibility for the tour section is for the user to become a reader when taking advantage of the written transcript of the personal accounts. The "Explore" section provides photographs that are tagged by their location and can be seen either on the Google map or from a list that is organized based on the distance from the user. Because this section consists mostly of photographs and their captions, it makes the user into an observer rather than a listener or spectator like the tour section. The last and final section, the timeline, requires the user to read the timeline and its chronology, thereby making this section another possible task for the user as a reader. Therefore, it can be concluded that it is the tour section that presents the most possibilities for the user, namely the opportunity to be a reader, a spectator, and a listener.

This question of bridging the relationship between a user and a text is not new to mobile devices and their narratives. For Pamuk, for example, the title character in *Anna Karenina* embodies one of the main concerns for a reader of fiction: she does not want to *read* her novel on her famous return to St. Petersburg; she wants to *be in* the novel, to be part of it. For Benjamin, on the other hand, the key is not *being* in the narrative but rather being the listener, who retains the stories already heard and is able to repeat them in the future. Such concern is vital for an app such as "Explore 9/11" as well as other site-based, historical or memorial apps for two reasons: site-specificity and intimacy of experience. Site-specific apps such as "Explore 9/11" rely on the power, energy or, simply, the experience that the reader or "explorer" has throughout the space. This aspect underlines the conclusion made by the artists Camille Baker, Max Schleser, and Kasia Molga in their collective article on the aesthetics of mobile media art: "There is an unintended intimacy and affective nature of the device. Expressivity with the device constitutes a predilection for close-ups and a sense of immediacy—instant, realtime, 'being here now.'"[17] There is definitely a level of intimacy in "Explore 9/11," and it can be argued that it is more intended than not, if taking into account not only the subject matter of the app, but also the app's design, made specifically for this kind of mobile, individual and, hence, intimate device. Because, technically, there is no other space as the one used for the app's design, be it the WTC site or other memorials, the site itself becomes the primary driving force for the app's narrative and the reader's experience. The "Tour" section of "Explore 9/11" definitely follows this premise, as it is more an app about the WTC site than about 9/11 per se. The ways in which site-specific apps deal with their respective spaces are the subject of the next section, but within the realm of storytelling, it is indispensable to consider the role of the reader, as Pamuk does when he reads Anna's reaction to her own reading while on the train.

The comparison to Anna in *Anna Karenina* is not to say that there is a parallel between her reading of a fictional text and the user experience of a recent historical and nonfictional event. Rather, the comparison seeks to elaborate on the complexity of reading the WTC site walking tour, the images, the timeline, and the narratives that their interaction put together. At the very end of *Aspects of the Novel*, Forster concludes that "history develops, art stands still."[18] The writer is referring, of course, to the fact that the art of the novel, in its narrative core and goals, will basically remain the same, as new events will form history's course. Following Forster's argument, it could be argued that site-specific mobile apps as well as memorial-related ones will continue to evolve as new historical events take place, but they will still primarily rely on the art of storytelling and narrative and the indispensable role of the reader who engages with such narrative.

"Explore 9/11" relies on many of the narrative issues that Forster analyzed in nineteenth-century European novels, especially the practices of storytelling and memorialization as individual acts. Apps like this one, as well as their respective narratives, place their readers in a rather fascinating position because they make the stories of history and spaces become intensely personal, private, and possibly emotional. Keeping in mind that these apps are designed for individual-use gadgets, the storytelling therefore becomes an individual experience, very much like Anna on the train. The reader of site-specific apps becomes as close to the physical space as possible, which in turn makes the experience remain within the private sphere, even in public settings such as the WTC site. The storytelling in this case is directed only toward one "explorer," unlike a docent-led walking tour that is heard and experienced collectively; this individual and private aspect of the app does not privilege individual experience over a collective one but rather underlines the tensions present when experiencing mourning, grief, and *memorialization* in both collective and individual ways. That is, this app does not seek to provide one simple way to explore 9/11, but rather it offers ways to explore a variety of possibilities that address the individual and collective means that many have experienced and endured after such a complex combination of violent, historical events.

This app, like many other possible future memorial apps, brings the reader to the center of the narrative, or to at least experiencing it at its center, allowing for the complex experience of politics and history to take over while simultaneously allowing for a strong, intimate, and emotional connection. As Chris Matyszczyk concludes in his review of "Explore 9/11" for CNET, "No one can possibly find this iPhone app enjoyable. That's what makes it such a good idea."[19]

On Space

"Explore 9/11" relies on the Global Positioning System (GPS) to create the aspect of the app that varies the most, namely an archive of photographs solely based on the user's location, under the "Explore" section. Differently from the unchangeable, first-person accounts recorded and organized in the "Tour," "Explore" allows users to view 9/11–related images based on the user's current location. The photographs of the day of 9/11 itself are tagged based on the location where they were taken, which means, of course, that the images from the attacks are all in their respective areas of New York; Washington, D.C.; or Pennsylvania. This geographic tagging puts New York at the very center stage of the app, due to a larger portion of NYC–tagged images. This centralization of New York City underlines the significance of these events for the patriotic, national narrative, but it also highlights the weight of the space itself, the WTC site, as the focal space of such narrative.

Matyszczyk noted the importance of space as a condition of witnessing 9/11 and expressed this in his introduction to his blog post on "Explore 9/11" for CNET: "When it comes to 9/11, there are only two sorts of people. Those who were there and those who weren't." [20] "Explore 9/11," as a narrative, can do a twofold job: it territorializes and *deterritorializes*. If, on one hand, "Explore 9/11" does not fulfill the potential of deterritorializing the main narrative of 9/11 through its first-person accounts, it is able to generate a new territory through the visual narratives of the WTC space as created by the photographs. These images can be accessed in two ways, namely the photographs around one's own location or the images' tags. In the first case, the app generates a way of narrating the spaces and places of 9/11, according to one's location. Even within New York City, the images that pop up on the user's map will vary from Lower Manhattan to Chelsea, for example, when in fact the distance between the two neighborhoods does not amount to three miles. This visual narrative is solely based on the user's location, and the images can be chosen and viewed at the user's discretion. The visual narrative is new almost every time "Explore 9/11" is used, as the viewer can always choose a different order and because new images can be added to the app through the "Make History" section of the Memorial & Museum website. [21] This visual narrative has the potential to become an ongoing deterritorializing and reterritorializing enterprise, as the spaces of 9/11 lose and gain new meanings, be it the WTC site or, by metonymy, the rest of the country.

On the "Make History" section of the website, anyone can upload their 9/11–related images. This concept of the 9/11 Memorial & Museum as an open space is of extreme significance for the app, as the visual contents will be evolving and possibly expanding throughout time, which in turn will translate into a visual narrative that will be evolving and expanding as well. In that sense, the app works like any other interface that relies on users' updates; these are not updates to a user's personal narrative but rather a user's personal images that contribute to a larger, collaborative, and collective narrative. These individual and private contributions to a larger, collective, and public archive highlight a fascinating counterbalance between the public and private spheres as well as the roles of communities and its individuals. Furthermore, the mobile device in itself also emphasizes this counterbalance between private and public spheres, as it is a privately and (possibly) individually owned device used for public communication and the aforementioned public photo archive. As such, the potential for a nuanced and complex narrative of 9/11 is always possible. The images, as of now, heavily rely on and contribute to binary narratives, where heroes and victims become the center of a straightforward narrative, but as the archive expands, perhaps so will the scope of its narrative.

If the visual narratives in the "Explore" and "Timeline" sections have the clear potential for future expansion, the "Tour" section, with its audio testimonies and walking tour, remains unchanged for the time being, at least while the memorial and museum are under construction. The narrative put together between the testimonies and the tour is fixed in that sense. It creates a chronological account of that day and its aftermath through a combination of voices around the same set of historical events; the user will encounter the same walking tour and testimonies, with the added possibility of newer images, depending on their future upload or the user's locations. This potential for the growth of the visual narrative of a historical event is not an innovation in the media world, as online sites have worked with the concept of immediate and perhaps populist photographic documentation of world events; in fact, the images available on "Explore 9/11" are also accessible on the museum's site. The novelty or the potential of the app relies on bringing this concept of populist photographic documentation, where everyone is or can be a photographer, onto a mobile device through an app designed for the *memorialization* of a historical event. That is, this app and its memorial component serve as a rather large cloud where memorial images are collected, stored, and presented. Such a change in the process of *memorialization*, now through a mobile device, is a substantial contribution to the world of mobile narratives, in this case, mobile historical narratives as well as narratives about memorials.

On Time

Following a reading of space and memorialization in "Explore 9/11," it is necessary to approach the ways in which time is managed within the app. As mentioned, the 9/11–related images are organized in the app based on their location, whereas the "Timeline" option of the app presents the same images based on several timestamps, ranging from "Before 9/11" to specific times such as "8:46 AM—North Tower Hit." The specific timestamps, starting at "7:59 AM" until "11:02 AM Evacuation," is a narrative convention already in use in other 9/11 narratives such as *The 9/11 Commission Report*. The timestamp itself is already a popular convention in other types of mobile media, ranging from Twitter to Facebook updates. This need for time-specificity underlines an unending desire to stay current but also an interest in accuracy and geographic specificity. Timestamps allow for a simple way of organizing a narrative, whether it is one's personal history or a collective one, such as 9/11's. As mobile media narratives increase and evolve, it would be rather easy to speculate that the contents as well as the form will possibly change, but the use of specific, real, historical timestamps will not.

The "9/11 Memorial Walking Tour" that encompasses the entire tour section opens with an audio narration by Alice Greenwald, the Director of the National September 11 Memorial & Museum. Her first two sentences, in which she introduces herself and thanks the listener for downloading the app, are followed by two sentences that start with the subordinate clauses, "On September 11th, 2001" and "After learning of the other attacks." It is immediately clear from these narrative structures that there is a strong need for establishing time in this app. These narrative structures seek to set the clearest chronology possible and, in turn, give order to what can be perceived as the chaotic narrative of 9/11. Therefore, it is of crucial importance to mark the time and provide as much detail as possible in order to organize 9/11. To chronologize 9/11 becomes a narrative task, and therefore the app depends on its narrative structures—be it timestamps or subordinate time clauses—in order to be able to establish such chronology.

To conclude, "Explore 9/11" places the reader in a appealing position through its return to storytelling, use of past, present, and future notions of spaces and sites, and its embrace of chronologizing private yet collective time. In terms of current and future memorial and memorial apps, "Explore 9/11" demonstrates the need for multilayered, polyphonic narratives that will shape the form in which these narratives are presented, but also that these forms will also drive the ways in which history and storytelling are narrated through mobile devices. The proliferation of mobile narratives and apps will also require a more comprehensive and comparative approach to these kinds of narratives, and as "Explore 9/11" continues to evolve, the app will possibly continue to generate questions about history and aspects of the mobile form in contemporary cultural production.

Acknowledgments

I am very grateful to Jake Barton, founder and principal of Local Projects, the design firm behind the subject of this essay.

Notes

1. See Judith Butler, *Precarious Life: The Powers of Mourning and Violence* (London: Verso, 2004), 18.
2. Such criticism is eloquently articulated in Richard Gray's article and Michael Rothberg's response. See Richard Gray, "Open Doors, Closed Minds: American Prose Writing at a Time of Crisis," *American Literary History* 21, no. 1 (2009): 128–148; and Michael Rotherberg, "A Failure of the Imagination: Diagnosing the Post-9/11 Novel: A Response to Richard Gray," *American Literary History* 21, no. 1 (2009): 152–158.

3. Edward Wyatt, "After a Long Wait, Literary Novelists Address 9/11," *New York Times*, March 7, 2005, http://query.nytimes.com/gst/fullpage.html?res=9F04E1DC1E3DF9 34A35750C0A9639C8B63.

4. It is necessary to observe that even though access to devices such as iPhones, iPads, Androids, and especially iPods, have been on the rise, their use is bound by the cost of the devices as well as their service, which underlines socioeconomic issues that are outside the scope of this essay. It could also be argued and analyzed that the purchase of such devices can perhaps correspond to the patriotic act of spending, as proposed by President George W. Bush on September 20, 2001: "I ask your continued participation and confidence in the American economy. Terrorists attacked a symbol of American prosperity; they did not touch its source."

5. Jacques Derrida, *Philosophy in a Time of Terror: Dialogue with Jürgen Habermas and Jacques Derrida* (Chicago: University of Chicago Press, 2003), 85.

6. Memorializing 9/11 has taken a variety of narrative forms; among these there is an increasing number of digital memorial projects, including collective sites such as september11thmemorial.com, terroristattack.com, and CNN's *September 11: A Memorial*, as well as individual tribute pages on Facebook.

7. This component of "seeing" and "saying" continues to be developed by the Memorial & Museum through the Broadcastr, audio-only, 9/11 oral history app. See Karen Matthews, "New Broadcastr App Will Give Voice to 9/11 Oral Histories," January 17, 2011, http://www.huffingtonpost.com/2011/01/17/new-broadcastr-app-will-g_n_810008.html.

8. Ingrid Richardson, "Pocket Technospaces: The Bodily Incorporation of Mobile Media," *Continuum: Journal of Media & Cultural Studies* 21, no. 2 (2007): 208.

9. More information on Local Project's description of "Explore 9/11" can be found at http://localprojects.net/project/explore-911/.

10. Jennifer Valentino-DeVries, "App Watch: Museum Looks at 9/11 Through Photos, Stories," September 10, 2010, http://blogs.wsj.com/digits/2010/09/10/app-watch-museum-looks-at-911-through-photos-stories/ (accessed January 17, 2011).

11. Walter Benjamin, "The Storyteller: Reflections on the Works of Nikolai Leskov," *Illuminations* (New York: Harcourt, Brace & World, 1968), 91.

12. Mark Poindexter, "ABC's *The Path to 9/11*, Terror-Management Theory, and the American Monomyth," *Film & History: An Interdisciplinary Journal of Film and Television Studies* 38, no. 2 (2008): 65.

13. Franco Moretti, *Atlas of the European Novel: 1800–1900* (London: Verso, 1998), 70.

14. Landow proposes to read hypertext and hypermedia through the lens of multilinear, network-like interactions, which "Explore 9/11" exemplifies. George P. Landow, *Hypertext 3.0: Critical Theory and New Media in an Age of Globalization* (Baltimore: John Hopkins University Press, 2006), 3.

15. Valentino-DeVries, "App Watch: Museum Looks at 9/11 Through Photos, Stories."

16. Orhan Pamuk, *The Naïve and the Sentimentalist Novelist* (Cambridge, Massachusetts: Harvard University Press, 2010), 3.

17. Camille Baker, Max Schleser, and Kasia Molga, "Aesthetics of Mobile Media Art," *Journal of Media Practice* 10, no. 2 & 3 (2009): 119.

18. Forster, *Aspects of the Novel* (Orlando: Harcourt, 1985), 171–172.

19. Chris Matyszczyk, "9/11 iPhone App Examines, and Makes, History," *CNET*, http://news.cnet.com/8301-17852_3-20016160-71.html.

20. Ibid.

21. See http://makehistory.national911memorial.org/.

19

ENHANCING MUSEUM NARRATIVES

Tales of Things and UCL's Grant Museum

Claire Ross, Mark Carnall, Andrew Hudson-Smith, Claire Warwick, Melissa Terras, and Steven Gray

> *How do the examples in this chapter help us understand the practice of story-telling in the mobile media age?*

Written collectively by a group of academics, curators, and designers, this chapter looks at the utilization of mobile media for enhanced meaning making and narrative engagement in museums. Focusing on the collaborative project, titled QRator, this chapter analyzes the ways that QR codes have been incorporated into the Grant Museum as a means to increase the amount of information available about museum artifacts and, perhaps more importantly, involve the museum goers in discussing that content. Comparing the QRator project to other mobile museum projects, this chapter demonstrates the emerging trend to incorporate the "Internet of Things" into the experiences with historical objects. In the context of ubiquitous computing, in which devices are embedded into innumerable facets of daily life, objects can be connected with data in seamless and meaningful ways. This data can be contributed to, commented on, and altered by users as a means to bring historical objects to life and tie them into contemporary conversations about how objects become integral to the ways we practice modes of historicizing.

Keywords

- **Internet of Things:** A design concept in which every object is connected to the Internet through ubiquitous computing. Objects could become an integral element of the Internet through linking to it in a variety of ways, including RFID tags, dynamic barcodes, or microprocessors. Once these "smart objects" are seamlessly integrated into the Internet, they become active elements in the social contexts in which they operate.

- **QR code:** Short for "quick response" code, these 2D barcodes can encode a much broader range of data than traditional barcodes and can link out to almost any kind of media. The barcodes—which look like an arrangement of small black squares within a square grid—can be used to transmit text, link to a website, or install an app, and can be linked to a specific location.
- **QRator project:** A project that utilizes mobile media and QR codes to encourage museum visitors to interact with specific objects. Visitors offer their own interpretations and thoughts about museum objects, connecting their ideas to the broader conversations about these objects. These "narrative engagements," which stem out of personal preconceptions (and how those preconceptions may have been challenged in the museum) subsequently become part of the object's history through the interactive label generated by such interactions.

Introduction

Emergent mobile technologies offer museum professionals new ways of engaging visitors with their collections. Museums are powerful learning environments, and mobile technology can enable visitors to experience the narratives in museum objects and galleries and integrate them with their own personal reflections and interpretations. University College London's (UCL) QRator project is exploring how handheld mobile devices and interactive digital labels can create new models for public engagement, personal meaning making, and the construction of narrative opportunities inside museum spaces. The use of narrative in museums has long been recognized as a powerful communication technique to engage visitors and to explore the different kinds of learning and participation that result. Many museums make extensive use of narrative or storytelling as a learning, interpretive, and meaning making tool. It has been suggested that "[e]very museum visitor is a storyteller with authority. Every evocative object on exhibit is a mnemonic device. Every visitor interaction is story-making as visitors fit portions of our collections into personal frames of reference; most often in ways we neither intended nor anticipated."[1] Nevertheless, digital technologies—specifically mobile media—have been underutilized by museums to facilitate collaborative construction of narrative and meaning making.

Museums have undergone a fundamental shift from being primarily presenters of objects to being sites for experiences that offer visitors opportunities for individual meaning making and narrative creation. Many visitors expect (or want) to engage with a subject, physically as well as personally.[2] Visitors see interactive technology as an important stimulus for learning and engagement,[3] empowering users to construct their own narratives in response to museum exhibits. Beyond expected content synthesis, these immersive activities can stimulate learning. Engaged within this immersive environment, museum objects become rich sources of innovation and personal growth.[4] When visitors experience a museum that encourages individual narrative construction actively, these narratives are directed not toward the acquisition or receipt of the information being communicated by the museum but rather toward the construction of a very personal interpretation of museum objects and collections. The unpredictability of multiple narrative forms created by the use of mobile devices and interactive labels introduces new considerations to the process by which museums convey object and collection interpretation and opens up museums to offer a more engaging experience.

This chapter discusses the potential for mobile technologies to connect museums to audiences through co-creation of narratives, taking the QRator project as a case study. The QRator project aims to stress the necessity of engaging visitors actively in the creation of their own interpretations of museum collections through the integration of QR codes, iPhone, iPad, and Android apps into UCL's Grant Museum of Zoology. Although this chapter will concentrate on mobile technology created for a natural history museum, issues of meaning making and narrative creation through mobile technology are applicable to any discipline. The chapter begins with a focus on the development of mobile media in museums, followed by a discussion of the QRator project, which looks at the opportunities and challenges in utilizing mobile technology to enhance visitor meaning making and narrative construction. Finally, this chapter discusses the extent to which mobile technologies might be used purposefully to transform institutional cultures, practices, and relationships with visitors.

Mobile Media in Museums

Handheld technologies are becoming more embedded, ubiquitous, and networked, with enhanced capabilities for rich social interactions, context awareness, and connectivity. The ubiquity of mobile technologies has led to unprecedented changes in the provision of mobile museum resources, which are beginning to transform the experience of visiting museums. Mobile technologies and their uses within museum collections have until recently been explored primarily from a technical viewpoint, typically ignoring the larger impact these technologies can have.[5] Increasingly, museum professionals are considering the implications of mobile technologies on visitor experience and on ways of utilizing handheld technology for object interpretation and visitor engagement. However, there is yet to be a body of sustained critical thinking about the meanings and theoretical implications of the possibilities and transformations provided by mobile technologies in museums.

In the past decade, there has been a growing interest in exploring how digital and communication technologies can be developed to offer visitors a more personalized museum experience,[6] provide more flexible and tailored information, and facilitate interaction and discussion between visitors. Many museums are utilizing mobile technology to aid visitor orientation and wayfinding as well as to offer specific multimedia tours within the museum. The Tate Modern multimedia tours[7] use location tracking for personalized content delivery. Here, the handheld device includes background information, video, and still images that give additional context for the works on display, and offers visitors the opportunity to listen to an expert talk about details of the artwork. The British Museum has recently launched a multimedia guide that supports wayfinding and orientation without relying on location-aware technology.[8] The Exploratorium has undertaken numerous projects exploring mobile technology within the museum space.[9] The use of mobile technologies in museums has been focused around linear curatorial narratives, but there has been little incentive for visitors to create their own narratives. Only rarely have museum visitors been able to participate in narrative creation or sharing. Projects such as Bletchley Park Text encouraged museum visitors to construct narratives by sending text messages from specific exhibits; visitors could create a personalized webpage that linked their chosen topics in narrative threads.[10] Culture Shock, led by Tyne and Wear Museums, utilizes digital storytelling to make museum collections more relevant to the lives of people living in Northeast England.[11] The BBC's Capture Wales project encouraged community co-creation of narratives via a traveling multimedia facility and a number of narrative technique workshops.[12] However, these projects seem to hesitate in their approach to sharing individual narratives with other visitors within the museum.

In general, however, despite the growing interest in deploying mobile technology as interpretation devices in museums and galleries, and the substantial body of research concerned with visitor behavior, there is yet to be established a critical literacy for describing the functional link between the narrative experience and museum mobile technologies. There is preliminary evidence that handheld technology can increase engagement with museum collections[13] and with the physical museum surroundings,[14] as well as increasing visitor confidence, motivation, and involvement;[15] however, to date, no empirical studies of museums utilizing mobile technology have been undertaken to look specifically at visitor narrative construction.

The QRator project aims to stress the necessity of engaging visitors actively in the creation of their own interpretations of museum collections. The project is located within the emerging technical and cultural phenomenon known as "The Internet of Things"—the technical and cultural shift that is anticipated as society moves to a ubiquitous form of computing in which every object is "on" and connected in some way to the Internet. The project is based around technology developed at the Centre for Advanced Spatial Analysis at UCL and is an extension of the "Tales of Things" project, which has developed a "method for cataloguing physical objects online which could make museums and galleries a more interactive experience"[16] via means of two-dimensional barcodes known as QR codes (short for "quick response" code). The use of barcodes allows objects to be scanned and information retrieved in a quick and easy manner. The introduction of QR codes within QRator provides the opportunity to move the discussion of objects from the museum label onto users' mobile devices, allowing

Figure 19.1 A museum goer using the QRator project on an iPad, typing a response to one of the objects in the Grant Museum of Zoology at University College London. Image © UCL, The Grant Museum of Zoology and Matt Clayton.

the creation of a sustainable model for two-way public interaction in museum spaces (see Figure 19.1).

The Grant Museum: Enhancing Interpretation

UCL's Grant Museum of Zoology houses one of the country's oldest and most important natural history collections. It has a strong history as a teaching collection but also functions as a key gateway for the public to engage with academic issues in innovative ways. In 2003, the Grant Museum displays were reinterpreted as part of the Say It Again, Say It Differently project, which was aimed at helping museums to refresh their displays.[17] Reinterpretation resulted in bringing some sense of order to the Grant Museum; however, it was not possible to label every object in the dense museum displays. One of the goals for the project was to go beyond conveying facts about natural history to explore the many narrative threads of the objects in the museum. As Assistant Curator of the Grant Museum of Zoology, Jack Ashby, notes, "There is no centrally running theme through the museum—each specimen tells a different story, be it historical, mythological, museological, ecological or zoological."[18]

Additionally, the Grant Museum has been involved in a project with Collections Link, a network for sharing knowledge about museums practice, called Revisiting Collections.[19] Revisiting Collections explored methodologies for constructing narratives around objects and collections through working with focus groups. The narratives that resulted were made available in the museum through physical labels; the information was also attached to objects in collections databases. Focus groups and narrative workshops have limited scope for smaller museums, as it is time- and resource-consuming, and there are problems associated with biases from soliciting responses to objects directly in such focused sessions. The QRator project, through mobile devices, allows for "more honest" input from visitors, albeit responses that are still solicited but less steered by staff representing museums. The context is still shaped and framed by the objects and questions chosen by museum staff; however, museum visitors have the freedom to say as little or as much as they desire (or nothing at all).

One of the main problems of interpreting objects through object labels is that labels have to be condensed and succinct so as not to overwhelm the museum visitors with walls of text. As an example, a label for an elephant specimen in a natural history museum could discuss the conservation movement, elephant poaching, ivory jewelry, traditional medicines, elephants as religious icons, elephant behavior, extinction of mammoths, any one of the unique ways that elephants are adapted to their environment, the taxonomy of elephants, elephants as circus animals, elephants and memory, the evolution of elephants, elephants as a mode of transport, elephants and war, elephant folklore, elephant jokes, or elephants in popular culture. In a typical museum label, it will only be possible to construct a sentence on one or two of these themes. A favorite example at the Grant Museum is a label for a flying lemur specimen, which only serves to tell the visitor that a flying lemur is not a lemur and furthermore it cannot fly. Utilizing mobile media within the Grant Museum allows for greater depth of information as well as a greater flexibility in the kinds of content and information that can be linked to any particular object, including video, audio, images, and further links to other web content. Because visitors can opt to explore objects further, those who want to find out more can locate that information without overwhelming all visitors. Conventional museum labels only allow for one-way communication: as a consequence, there is insufficient space for cryptic labels or those that ask a question of a visitor to include explanations or allow a visitor to answer. The only way for a visitor to engage in this way would be to engage with museum staff. The QRator technology, however, allows for visitors to leave their own thoughts and comments on objects, which can be challenging to do seamlessly within museum spaces.

QR Codes and Constructing Collaborative Narratives

Visitor meaning making has been a dynamic research theme in museum studies for over a decade.[20] Both constructivist learning theory[21] and hermeneutic philosophy tell us that narrative is central to meaning making, and individuals actively construct meaning for themselves using their existing knowledge in interpreting new experiences.[22] The importance of narrative—and particularly narrative with multiple voices—[23] has become an influential element for constructivist interpretation in museums and should replace the traditional authoritative knowledge dissemination as the iconic mode for museums. Previous studies note the importance of visitor expectations in framing museum experiences.[24] Zahava Doering and Andrew J. Pekarik state that visitors bring their own "entrance narratives" to museums, providing a personal storyline informing their expectations and overall experience.[25] However, narratives and personal stories have had a much less prominent role in natural history or science museums, where the dominant mode of interpretation is a single-voiced authoritative explanation. Even the relatively uncomplicated interpretation of objects through object biography—rather than subject or personality biography—remains comparatively unexplored in museums and even more so in scientific museums.[26] Mobile technology can provide a platform to help to discover these internal stories and entrance narratives and share them with a wider audience, providing a broader, more personal interpretation of museum collections. We believe that through utilizing the strengths of digital storytelling—its ability to allow individuals to reflect and create their own meaning—[27] as well as being able to collect personal narratives of museum experiences, the use of mobile technologies in the Grant Museum can also contribute to the creation of interpretative communities and the sharing of multiple narratives.[28]

The QRator project offers opportunities for visitors to consume and create digital content, empowering members of the public to become the "curators." The project developed a custom UCL Museum iOS and Android application. QR codes were created for museum objects (and in some instances, entire interactive displays were created), linking the object to an online database that allowed the public to view "curated" information and, most notably, to send back their own interpretation using their mobile phone. The QRator project launched in March 2011 and is ongoing at the Grant Museum. A unique element of the QRator technology is the ability to "write" back to the QR codes. This allows members of the public to type in their thoughts and interpretation of the object and click "Send." Similar in nature to sending a text message, the system enables the Grant Museum to become a true forum for academic-public debate, using low-cost, readily available technology, enabling the public to collaborate and discuss object interpretations with museum curators and academic researchers. Visitors' narratives subsequently become part of the museum objects' history and ultimately the display itself, via the interactive label system, which will allow the display of comments and information directly next to the artifacts. This shift in focus from content delivery to narrative construction, it can be suggested, reflects an ongoing societal shift in digital media from static, centralized control to user-generated content and personalized learning. Personal narratives, interactive dialogues, and multiple interpretations saturate the Internet, and museums need to adapt to visitor expectations in order to fully enable rich meaning making experiences to take place.

The QRator project utilizes user-centered design principles by explicitly and actively including users in the development process from the beginning. When studying the users of digital technologies, it can be argued that *use in context* is an ideal method because there is a need to understand the real circumstances in which technology is used so that any problems can be identified.[29] Thus, to produce the mobile media that will be the most useful in a museum context, there is a need to understand the circumstances in which it will function. The project takes into account the concepts of users, narrative, space, object, and location, as well as the appropriate means of mediating the museum experience via a handheld mobile device. However, there are issues to take into consideration. If mobile engagement with museum interpretation can occur anywhere, then how can we track and record the learning and narrative creation processes? If learning and meaning making is interwoven with other everyday activities, then how can we tell when it occurs? If visitor meaning making is self-determined and self-organized, then how can we measure engagement outcomes? These are difficult questions with no simple answers, yet it is essential to address them if we are to provide evidence of the effectiveness of mobile media for visitor narrative construction and meaning making.

In order to address these questions, a small pilot study was undertaken to focus on the use of the mobile technology in context. Nine objects were chosen for a pilot project, utilizing Tales of Things. Tales of Things was chosen as the technology behind the QRator project due to previous implementations of the technology to explore the provenance of old objects and how the memories associated with these objects may impact social memories in the community. A case in point is the utilization of the system by Oxfam to explore and add value to donated goods within the charity sector.[30] The history of a household object often goes undocumented, tied up in personal and family narratives. Yet when an object is donated to a charity organization, these retail outlets become temporary museums. In the Oxfam context, the barcode label became the communicator of history with the ability to record new chapters in an object's life through a link to a smartphone. In short, Tales of Things is a bespoke technology allowing everyday objects to "talk" via the Internet of Things. QRator takes this a step further in a more traditional museum context whereby the objects represent different and interesting facets of museology. These included the museum's spotlight specimens: objects considered valuable in terms of their craftsmanship, history, and rarity; objects that either were not on display at all; or those that challenge the term "object" (such as the whole of the museum or transient features such as a display case for temporary exhibitions whose contents change periodically). Furthermore, some of these "objects" would not normally be labeled; thus, adding them to the Tales of Things library provides a novel way to access these otherwise publicly inaccessible objects.

The objects were deliberately chosen to explore the concepts surrounding the objects that could not adequately be highlighted by traditional, static museum hermeneutics. Museum labels often have a very strict word limit and cannot convey more than a single aspect, fact, or story about an object. It is important to note, however, that many of these narratives can be (and are) explored in a guided tour of the museum, but it is not possible for every visitor to receive a personal tour of the collection from an expert guide who knows the objects well. Many of these test objects were chosen to relay narratives as a proxy to staff-led tours with the added advantage of the capacity to record feedback and ask questions of visitors. Other objects were chosen because they are otherwise uninterpretable, either because they aren't "objects" in the normal sense of the word or because the narratives involved do not fit within the overarching narratives of the museum space. In the Grant Museum, the grander narrative is the evolutionary history of animal life on Earth. Discrete QR codes allow meta-narratives and cryptic narratives to emerge alongside the main narrative theme of the museum.

For example, the three legged skeleton of a quagga, a cast of *Archaeopteryx lithographica*, and the articulated skeleton of an anaconda were given QR codes to interpret multiple narratives of each specimen. The traditional labels for these objects situate them within the context of the taxonomic display. In the museum, the specimens represent the biological species and subspecies to which they are members. However, each of these specimens is also of interest outside of a strictly biological narrative framework. The quagga skeleton is arguably the rarest skeleton in the world and is mysteriously missing a leg and a shoulder blade. The museum has historical photographs of one of the other specimens—the anaconda skeleton—being prepared from a dead animal to an articulated skeleton. *Archaeopteryx* is one of the most important specimens in evolutionary biology; the Grant Museum's specimen is a plaster cast that is surrounded by a host of apocryphal historical stories.

Other specimens were labeled to allow a meta-analysis of the way in which museums work. A red deer skull had been labeled as "Bambi's Dad" by the museum conservator. Tales of Things was used for this specimen to highlight potential contentious interpretation in museums, questioning whether there is a place for humor or if such labeling is disrespectful. Another specimen, unidentifiable and sealed in wax, was put on display and labeled to emphasize the elements of detective work inherent in working in museums (as well as the difficulties associated with the ownership of cultural heritage and displaying uncertainty). Other objects, including an *Archaeopteryx*, a fluid preserved specimen of the extinct marsupial thylacine, and a nineteenth-century Blaschka glass model of a snail prompted questions around the problematic concepts such as authenticity, real and fake objects, the fallacy of empirically identifying organisms, and the sentimental and financial value of historical associations.

Lastly, the museum itself was tagged in the Tales of Things system in order to explore what is meant exactly by "the museum." "The Grant Museum" itself can be used to describe a series of geographical locations, including the museum, storerooms, and offices, but these locations can be changed. Does the identity of the Grant Museum reside in the building, in the objects housed in the building, in the combination of the two, or in the cultural practice of "the museum"? When objects were removed from the space in UCL's Darwin building, did it stop being "The Grant Museum"? What happened to "The Grant Museum" while objects were in storage? Did the room cease to be the Grant Museum when the last specimen left, when it closed to the public, or when the sign was taken down? The term can also be used to describe a collection of 68,000 objects. For legal purposes, the Grant Museum means something very particular. In other senses, the Grant Museum is more of a brand or identity. Labeling the museum as "an object" in a way that would be impossible to do with traditional labels was intended to provoke thoughts about how we define objects as well as enabling visitors to add tales from within the object itself.

It is possible to discover how visitors interact with and create narratives from the museum objects by analyzing the frequency of codes scanned and to study visitor feedback in the form of tales, further links, and other information that visitors leave on the Tales of Things site. Although this does not quite establish a dialogue with museum visitors, it does allow museum curators to ask questions of the visitor or use contentious objects to provoke a response. The QRator project found that utilizing contentious objects and asking provoking questions encouraged visitors' participation in collaborative narrative creation. In this way, mobile technology has the capability to support visitors' meaning making by framing and focusing their activities and interactions. During the trial period for the QRator project, the objects were available to be scanned *in situ* for a period of two weeks. This coincided almost exactly with the relocation of the Grant Museum of Zoology, allowing only a two-week period before the museum was closed to the public. In total, the nine Grant Museum objects added to the Tales of Things site had been viewed online 1,374 times, and a total of 34 scans occurred.

Once the QR codes were scanned, the visitors developed the narrative of the objects by adding their own interpretations. This reshaping of audience involvement and narrative construction centered on museum objects facilitates creative, independent analysis, promoting a personal connection with museum exhibition subject matter that has been suggested to be unparalleled in more traditional and passive approaches to museum interpretation.[31] Visitors to the museum felt the QR codes provided a more personalized experience compared to gallery books because they could see information more easily and because it added the crucial component of allowing them to use it while walking around the museum. Several visitors stated that using QR codes in the gallery enhanced their museum experience and made them spend more time in the museum. As noted, the narratives provided by the QRator project offered an understanding of some of the specimens that would have otherwise been difficult to grasp and appreciate.

From these the preliminary findings of this small pilot study, it was felt there was satisfactory user engagement to develop this concept further by utilizing QR code technology with situated iPads in the museum space itself, providing a platform for narrative creation. The Grant Museum now hosts iPads containing "Current Questions" for visitors to engage in, enabling the museum to be a place not simply for a passive experience but for conversation. Each object on Tales of Things has a unique identifier, which the iPad uses to access the object's information, QR code, and subsequent narratives left by visitors from the server. The QRator application is therefore a viewer for the Tales of Things website, allowing visitors to interact directly with existing narratives. The QRator project has thus far produced over 6,100 individual visitor narratives, focusing on the personal interpretation of the Grant museum's collections.[32] It is possible to suggest that this further extension of the QRator project denotes that visitor narrative construction via mobile media is making a valuable contribution to enhancing the museum experience.

Conclusion

Further research is underway with the aim of developing other methods for mobile devices to expand and augment public engagement inside natural history museum spaces. It is not sufficient that mobile technology enhance visitor narrative construction and the overall museum experience; "it needs to be demonstrated that these new technologies enhance museum experience."[33] We believe that by the end of the QRator project, we will be able to demonstrate that mobile technology can impact a visitor's experience of museums and his or her personal narrative creation.

Mobile media resources in museums have gone from being primarily utilized as audio guides that provide structured linear narratives to become quite diverse in functionality, offering a range of personalized content. John H. Falk and Lynn D. Dierking's contextual model of learning is a compelling framework to utilize when designing and developing such personalized content for museum narratives on mobile devices.[34] The key feature to this approach is the emphasis on context: in order to deliver narrative-rich mobile media, museums need to be aware of the personal, sociocultural, and physical contexts within which to enable museum goers to make meaning from their experience.

This chapter has aimed to introduce the concept of mobile technology in museums as a way to create narratives of museum visitors' experience and then share multiple narratives with an interpretive community. By offering opportunities for visitors to consume and create digital content, museums can take a proactive role in developing new narratives around museum collections, enabling direct experience of content production. This new co-creation of narratives has effective cultural outcomes; utilizing mobile media has enabled the Grant Museum to highlight visitors' active role in creating meaning of their own museum experience. Each visitor has his or her own agenda, identity, motivation, and interests, and will approach the museum with different perspectives. As a result, visitors find their own personal significance within museums and are now able to share it with other visitors. Visitors are empowered to create their own "digital stories," narratives constructed from their own interpretation of museum collections. However, museum mobile technology cannot be used in isolation. These tools are important, but of equal importance is their relationship to other forms of museum interpretation, and of course, the visitors themselves. It is vital to incorporate the views and previous experience of visitors when undertaking collaborative content and mobile technology development in museums. This research reinforces how complex museum experience is, as well as the difficulties of designing for narrative construction in a museum setting. This chapter offers insights into why, and in what ways, mobile media—specifically QR codes and digital collaboration interpretation technology—have the potential to enhance the personal and community narratives and meaning making of museum experiences.

Notes

1. Robert R. Archibald, "Touching on the Past," Missouri Historical Society, St. Louis, Missouri, (2006), http://www.nmu.edu/communicationsandmarketing/sites/Drupal CommunicationsAndMarketing/files/UserFiles/Files/Pre-Drupal/Horizons/2007/f07/bonus_article-touching_on_the_past.pdf.
2. Marinna Adams, Jessica Luke, and Theano Moussouri, "Interactivity: Moving Beyond Terminology," *Curator: The Museum Journal* 47 (2004): 155–170; see also John H. Falk and Lynn D. Dierking, *Learning from Museums: Visitor Experiences and the Making of Meaning* (New York: Alta Mira Press, 2000).
3. John H. Falk, et al. "A Multi-Institutional Study of Exhibition Interactives in Science Centers and Museums," unpublished evaluation report (Annapolis, MD: Institute for

Learning Innovation, 2002); see also Graham Black, *The Engaging Museum: Developing Museums for Visitor Involvement* (New York: Routledge, 2005).

4. Matthew Fisher and Beth A. Twiss-Garrity, "Remixing Exhibits: Constructing Participatory Narratives with On-Line Tools to Augment Museum Experiences," in *Museums and the Web 2007: Proceedings*, ed. Jennifer Trant and David Bearman (Toronto: Archives & Museum Informatics, 2007), http://www.archimuse.com/mw2007/papers/fisher/fisher.html.

5. F. Cameron, "Digital Futures I: Museum Collections, Digital Technologies, and the Cultural Construction of Knowledge," *Curator* 46, no 3 (2003): 325–340.

6. Geri Gay and Angela Spinazze, "Handscape: Exploring Potential Use Scenarios for Mobile Computing in Museums," *Cultivate Interactive* 8 (2002), http://www.cultivate-int.org/issue8/handscape/.

7. Nancy Proctor and Chris Tellis, "The State of the Art in Museums Handhelds in 2003," in *Proceedings of Museums and the Web 2003* (Toronto: Archives & Museums Informatics, 2003), http://www.archimuse.com/mw2003/papers/proctor/proctor.html.

8. Silvia Filippini-Fantoni, Sarah McDaid, and Matthew Cook, "Mobile Devices for Orientation and Way Finding: The Case of the British Museum Multimedia Guide," in *Museums and the Web 2007: Proceedings*, ed. Jennifer Trant and David Bearman (Toronto: Archives & Museum Informatics, 2007), http://conference.archimuse.com/mw2011/papers/mobile_devices_for_wayfinding.

9. Sherry Hsi, "The Electronic Guidebook: A Study of User Experiences Mediated by Nomadic Web Content in a Museum Setting," *Journal of Computer-Assisted Learning* 19, no. 3 (2003): 308–319.

10. Paul Mulholland, Trevor Collins, and Zdenkek Zdrahal, "Bletchley Park Text: Using Mobile and Semantic Web Technologies to Support the Post-Visit Use of Online Museum Resources," *Journal of Interactive Media in Education* (2005), http://jime.open.ac.uk/jime/article/view/2005-24.

11. Culture Shock, http://www.cultureshock.org.uk.

12. BBC, "Capture Wales," (2001-2008) http://www.bbc.co.uk/wales/arts/yourvideo/queries/capturewales.shtml.

13. See Proctor, Burton, and Tellis, "The State of the Art," and Hsi, "The Electronic Guidebook."

14. Laura Naismith, Mike Sharples, and Jeffrey Ting, "Evaluation of CAERUS: A Context Aware Mobile Guide," in *Proceedings of mLearn 2005* (Cape Town, South Africa, 2005): 112–115.

15. Ellie Burkett, "Using Handheld Computers to Stimulate Critical Studies in A-Level Art," *Becta* (2005), http://www.docstoc.com/docs/34589133/Using-Handheld-computers-to-stimulate-Critical-Studies-in-A-level-Art.

16. Jim Giles, "Barcodes Help Objects Tell Their Stories," *New Scientist*, April 17, 2010, http://www.newscientist.com/article/dn18766-barcodes-help-objects-tell-their-stories.html.

17. Alison Grey, Tim Gardom, and Catherine Booth, *Saying It Differently: A Handbook for Museums Refreshing Their Display* (London: London Museums Hub, 2006).

18. Ibid.

19. Collections Link, http://collectionslink.org.uk.

20. See Lois H. Silverman, "Visitor Meaning-Making in Museums for a New Age," *Curator: The Museum Journal* 38, no 3 (1995): 161–170; and Eilean Hooper-Greenhill, *Museums and the Interpretation of Visual Culture* (New York: Routledge, 2000).

21. George E. Hein, "The Constructivist Museum," *Journal of Education in Museums* 15, (1995) 1–10.
22. See Jerome Seymour Bruner, "Frames for Thinking: Ways of Making Meaning," in *Modes of Thought: Explorations in Culture and Cognition*, ed. David R. Olson and Nancy Torrance (Cambridge: Cambridge University Press, 1996), 93–105; Roger Shank, *Tell Me a Story: Narrative and Intelligence* (Evanston, IL: Northwestern University Press, 1990); Kieran Egan, "Narrative and Learning: A Voyage of Implications," in *Narrative in Teaching, Learning, and Research*, ed. Hunter McEwan and Kieran Egan (New York: Teachers College Press, 1995), 116–125; and Eilean Hooper-Greenhill and Theano Moussouri, *Making Meaning in Art Museums 1: Visitors' Interpretive Strategies at Wolverhampton Art Gallery* (Leicester: Research Centre for Museums and Galleries, 2001), http://www2.le.ac.uk/departments/museumstudies/rcmg/projects/making-meaning-in-art-museums-1/Making%20meaning%201.pdf.
23. Lisa Roberts, *From Knowledge to Narrative: Educators and the Changing Museum* (Washington, DC: Smithsonian Institution, 1997).
24. See John H. Falk, et al., "The Effect of Visitors' Agendas on Museum Learning," *Curator* 41, no. 2 (1998): 106–120; John H. Falk, "The Impact of Visit Motivation on Learning: Using Identity as a Construct to Understand the Visitor Experience," *Curator* 49, no. 2 (2006): 151–166; Gaea Leinhardt and Kevin Crowley, "Museum Learning as Conversational Elaboration: A Proposal to Capture, Code and Analyze Museum Talk," *Museum Learning Collaborative Technical Report* (Pittsburgh, 1998), http://earth.lrdc.pitt.edu/mlc-01.pdf.
25. Zahava Doering and Andrew J. Pekarik, "Questioning the Entrance Narrative," *Journal of Museum Education* 21, no. 3 (1996): 20–22.
26. Samuel J.M.M. Alberti, "Objects and the Museum," *Isis* 96 (2005): 559–571.
27. See Glynda A. Hull and Mira-Lisa Katz, "Crafting an Agentive Self: Case Studies of Digital Storytelling," *Research in the Teaching of English* 41, no. 1 (2006): 43–81; Kevin Walker, "Narrative and Mobile Learning in Practice and Theory," *II Kaleidoscope Workshop on Narrative Learning Environments* (Palermo, Italy, June 2006); and Scott Ruston and Jen Stein, "Narrative and Mobile Media," *MiT4: The Work of Stories* (Cambridge, MA, 2005), http://web.mit.edu/comm-forum/mit4/papers/Ruston%20Stein.pdf.
28. Stanley Fish, *Is There a Text in this Class? The Authority of Interpretive Communities* (Cambridge, MA: Harvard University Press, 1980).
29. Melissa Terras, Claire Warwick, and Claire Ross, "Building Useful Virtual Research Environments: The Need for User-Led Design," in *University Libraries and Digital Learning Environments*, ed. Penny Dale, Jill Beard, and Matt Holland (Surrey: Ashgate, 2011): 151–167.
30. Ralph Barthel et al., "Tales of Things—The Internet of 'Old' Things: Collecting Stories of Objects, Places and Spaces," presented at the *Second International Conference on the Internet of Things* (Tokyo, Japan, November 29-December 1, 2010).
31. See Silverman, "Visitor Meaning-Making" and Hooper-Greenhill, *Museums and the Interpretation of Visual Culture*.
32. See "QRator at the Grant," http://www.qrator.org/about-the-project/qrator-at-the-grant/.
33. Falk and Dierking, "Enhancing Visitor Interaction," 28.
34. Ibid.

20

MOBILIZING CITIES

Alternative Community Storytelling

Mark C. Marino

How do the examples in this chapter help us understand the practice of story-telling in the mobile media age?
When trying to portray the diversity of urban spaces, mobile phones open narratives to include more kinds of voices in a more complex portrait of social relations. This chapter examines examples of this emerging genre, specifically focusing on *Voces Móviles* (*VozMob*) and *The LA Flood Project*, each of which tell the stories of Los Angeles that typically go untold. *VozMob* is a journalism project that allows itinerant day laborers, or *jornaleros*, to report and publish the events they witness in the city. The *LA Flood Project* is a work of locative art that presents both real and imagined accounts of Angelenos who have encountered a crisis. Both of these projects use mobile phone technologies to complicate the very notion of "mobility" by calling attention to the ways economic, racial, and ethnic status facilitate or restrict movement whether in the forced movements caused by natural calamities or in the itinerant nature of *jornaleros*, whose constant movement is a sign of their marginal status. Together these projects show how mobile technologies act as media of inclusion by allowing a diversity of voices to speak about a city as the storytellers cross this heterogeneous urban landscape.

Keywords

- **Polyphonic narratives:** "Polyphony" was originally used in music to describe the use of two distinct melodies being sung in a song. In literature, it means the inclusion of many voices in a work of writing or storytelling. Polyphony in narrative assumes that the inclusion of "many voices" does so in a way in which no voice necessarily dominates over other voices: they all are given equal status.

- **Heteroglossia:** Used by philosopher and literary critic Mikhail Bakhtin (who also extensively discussed "polyphony"), this term signifies the many writing styles and modes of discourse that can appear within one particular narrative form, specifically used to analyze the novel. Bakhtin argued that heteroglossia signified that every utterance in language had to be interpreted by its context, and thus, "a word uttered in that place and at that time will have a meaning different than it would have under any other conditions."[1]

Introduction

Los Angeles is a city infatuated with its own image. The Hollywood movie industry loves to churn out films that depict the city, celebrating or sending up its vanities, shuttering its racial diversity or peeking at it through the slats of film noir. In the words of Michael Sorkin, "L.A. is probably the most mediated town in America, nearly unviewable save through the fictive scrim of its mythologizers."[2] Still, despite its singular role in the Southern California cultural economy, film seems too singular a medium to render the city. Or rather, studio films—produced through excessive capital, circulated to movie houses, locked in official versions— fail to serve the dynamic flow of a city. Along similar lines, codex books ultimately become agents of incorporation and unification despite their heteroglossia (i.e., their inclusion of many writing styles); they must contain the sprawl of enclaves and subjectivities within the confines of their twin covers. That structural limitation has led some to formal experimentation, as in the case of Mark Danielewski's Los Angeles-based novel *House of Leaves*, which among other novelties, tells the tale of a tattoo apprentice in the footnotes of a script for a Blair Witch–style horror movie. This formal experimentation is a sign that the older media forms are proving insufficient when considering the hyper-urban space, while the city has watched one of the most multivocal forms, the newspaper, sheds its columnists and its pages. Others turn to hypermedia forms, as in the case of M.D. Coverley's interactive narrative *Califia*, which traces the quests of three characters through maps, multimedia outlets, and a multiplicity of interfaces.

Like trying to catch the tide in a fishing net, new biographers of Los Angeles quickly discover that monophonic media do not do justice to the seventy-two cities or over 140 languages represented within the greater Los Angeles region, a region that is bound ultimately by Santa Barbara to the north, Riverside to the east, and San Diego/Tijuana to the south.[3] With the spine falling off the novels and movies reaching off the screen, the city seems to call out for new forms, forms that can transport, without transposing, more voices. Yet, how to even begin collecting those voices from almost 500 square miles of L.A. County (about twice the size of Washington, D.C.) from a population moving on buses, trains, and over 500 miles of freeway? How do we collect those voices that remain outside the studio gates? In such a context, the technology that unifies, that brings these voices together, is not the television set, the movie house, the radio, or the newspaper; instead, it is a technology that remaps the urban landscape, not with roads, but with coverage areas: the mobile phone.

Even before mobile phones became the dominant information technology, outpacing personal computers around the globe, the image of the Angeleno with a mobile phone, or more specifically a car phone, became iconic in film and television, not so much because of the power of that nascent technology but because of the city's obsession with mobility. Mobility is a complex equation in a city like Los Angeles. L.A. is the hub of immigration, famous for destroying its own public transportation infrastructure—clogging its once historic freeways with epic traffic snarls—while constricting the movement of its racialized citizens through neighborhood compacts and redlining. In such a space, mobility—to be able to decide where and when one moves—equals status. Nonetheless, in the mire of perpetual gridlock, the movie producer in the Mercedes will sit parked on a freeway while urban hipsters wheel through the city on fixies behind a Latino mayor who seeks to establish cicLAvia cycling festivals and to secure bike lanes. Meanwhile, within noisy hulks of MTA buses, the riders can pass invisibly. Mobile phones offer this diverse array of Angelenos the ability to stay connected to one another while crossing the city. As the number of mobile device subscriptions in America has reached 326 million, higher than the nation's population, there are now many more Angelenos with cell phones than with automobiles.[4]

If the Greater Los Angeles area was stitched together first by the need for access to water, then by rail and freeways, it is being reconfigured and reorganized by cell towers and mobile users. As the freeways are bounded by walls, entrances, and exists, the mobile-phone space is bounded by coverage area. However, the seeming freedom of movement within this system also comes with the technology to pinpoint location. If in the past, location of media use—particularly specific geographic location—has been an undertheorized component of media analysis, in the mobile moment, "geolocation" is a foregrounded element of the technology, as it both delimits and inspires occasions for use. As so-called "smartphones" proliferate, geolocation is becoming a central use of the medium, particularly in emerging activist and art practices.

Representation and Representatives

The chief affordance mobile telephones bring to narratives, fictional or factual, is the ability of a larger percentage of the community to represent themselves. Representation, as it turns out, is more than just a question of how something is portrayed for an audience. This point was made most presciently by Gayatri Chakravorty Spivak, who, in her oft-cited essay, "Can the Subaltern Speak?" draws a distinction between two kinds of representation: portraiture (*darstellen*) and political proxies (*vertreten*). In other words, representation can be how someone is depicted, or it can be how someone's political interests are managed.[5] Too often,

Spivak argued, the portrait, drawn by those in power, is used to determine the appropriate way to govern those who are without power. Consider the example of the undocumented immigrant who is often represented in the media and who is legislated against based on these media images rather than on his or her own accounts. In theory, the solution is to create the opportunity for the subaltern group to speak; however, Spivak's answer to her own question is, simply and reductively put, "No, the subaltern cannot speak." The power relations between the colonizing group and the colonized simply do not permit self-conscious representation.

Although no work could satisfy Spivak's criteria of self-representation, the two projects in this chapter attempt to interrupt the conventional media narratives through which many in the city are spoken about and, consequently, spoken for. They do so by attempting to strive for a "polyphony"[6] that puts a premium on voices that are, on the one hand, unfiltered and, on the other hand, not overridden by a framing voice, the way a journalist on a segment on a television news broadcast might frame the voices of those who are interviewed in the story. What preserves this polyphony, then, is that both of these mobile distributed narratives of the city do not synthesize the voices into one narrative but instead collect them in a database. It is the reader, not a narrator or editor, who collates and collects, sequences and sutures. Thus, the outcome is not a definitive story but instead a navigable database of tales. As artist and ethnographer Sharon Daniel puts it, the goal is "not to speak for" her subjects "but to bring them on as collaborators."[7] Ultimately, these narratives envision themselves as always partial, as contributing to, and at times reframing, the larger set of narrative portraits of shared spaces. These highly portable networked technologies facilitate the collection and circulation of mobile distributed narratives within a city that bursts the seams of traditional narrative forms.

The mobile narrative forms that follow present attempts to organize communal self-representation, featuring stories gathered. They share several traits: they are created by groups of contributors, they have not been put in linear form, they have not been contained by a central voice (other than an interface), and they are mediated by mobile telephones either in collection or transmission. At the same time, they are not produced independently. In each of the cases, a second party has developed the tools and infrastructure for collecting the stories and ultimately frames the narratives within the context of an interface (and also in the texts and videos promoting the pieces). What marks the departure from the anthology, documentary, or even museum exhibit—though they are the nearest progenitors—is the increased ability of the contributor to deliver his or her perspective, as well as an emphasis on the database over the path through it.

This chapter considers two projects: one, *Voces Móviles*, which gives voice to a largely overwritten yet undervoiced community in Los Angeles, and the other, *The LA Flood Project*, which maps voices, both real and imagined, onto the urban landscape. The two projects begin with Los Angeles for their operating environment;

however, rather than examining L.A. as it is produced by centrally controlled media (film, TV, radio, newspapers), these projects use mobile media to convey the stories that develop outside the system in the slippages, potholes, and gaps. These mobile-phone narratives create counter-narratives of the city, examining the impressions outside of the master narrative of the routine operation of civic laws.

VozMob-ilization [Add Francois Barr, Sasha Costanza-Chock]

In Los Angeles, *Voces Móviles* (*VozMob*) or *Mobile Voices*, seeks to give an itinerant population direct access to publication in the contemporary mode of blogging and social media. The project focuses on a populations that are critical to the L.A. construction industry, the day laborers (*jornaleros*) who move nomadically throughout the city seeking work. Often undocumented, these workers, participating in a gray market, make an impact on the local environment through their labor, but by definition will unlikely appear on the books, are rarely accounted for, and hence operate outside the political, social, and material economy of the city. *VozMob* seeks to make these *jornaleros* into *jornalistas*. It was initiated as a joint project between the Annenberg School for Communication and Journalism at the University of Southern California and el Instituto de Education Popular del Sur de California (Institute for Popular Education of Southern California: IDEP-SCA), along with Los Angeles Community Action Network (LACAN). IDEP-SCA, which has assumed operational control of the project, continues to develop and extend *VozMob* as "a platform for immigrant and/or low-wage workers in Los Angeles to create stories about their lives and communities directly from cell phones."[8] *VozMob* expands the notion of "citizen journalism" to include those not typically counted with the citizenry. In 2010, the project won a United Nations World Summit Award for promoting access to digital communication.[9]

VozMob relies on the ability of mobile phones to send text messages to email addresses, a function that predates contemporary smartphones. When using the system, *jornaleros* file reports using text, audio, or images (or some combination of the three) and send them through their phones to the site. The other half of this mobile communication circuit is the database-driven online communication system. This system, built on the open-source platform Drupal, receives the messages and strips out the various pieces of information (date, author, title, message) to post them on the site. The USC group continues to develop the *VozMob* platform, which is now available to be extended and modified (or forked) through the GitHub versioning system. As a result of this system, the messages from the *jornalistas* can be posted as soon as they are sent, giving these contributors direct publishing access. More importantly, unlike the newspaper model, the *jornaleros* can publish from anywhere in the city without touching base with the editors or physically returning to the site of publication. The lag between event and report evaporates along with the obstacles to representation.

However, according to Ben Stokes, a USC graduate student working on the project, not every group that expresses interest in the project is ready to accept the implications of live citizen journalism, of having the groups they represent publish directly to the Internet. The postings do not take the form of a polished newspaper article nor do they have a standardization of format to make them easy to repurpose in the news system.[10] However, these *jornaleros* do not merely report on their lives as day laborers; they also turn their attention toward the system of the city itself. *Mobile Voices* does not give voice to those who are merely highly mobile but mobilizes the voices of those who have not frequently been heard. As a marginalized and underrepresented population, those voices are not necessarily going to serve the public relations goals of the city.

In one post, titled "Police in action," a *VozMob* reporter comments on a scene in which two LAPD officers flank an African American male, legs spread, before a squad car.

> The police in Skid Row continue to do their thing, their illegal thing. Time to stop that illegal BS right now. Soon, soon, soon, soon.

Another post by "pam" bears the title, "POLICE: To protect the rich and to gentrify the poor." Other messages cover everything from official city news to cultural events, demonstrations, and even street performances. However, the photograph of the police officers in the "Police in action" post takes on a special significance because that photo was not by a professional journalist for a commercial news outlet but rather by an individual *jornalista* posting to a site for *jornaleros*. It cannot even be called citizen journalism because the reporter is not necessarily a "citizen." *VozMob* presents a communication environment that operates outside of the closed media sphere. The *jornalero* goes from having the rights of a dog to civic watchdog, and despite the passport to low status, the lack of documentation, the *jornalero* can produce and circulate documentation of the operations of the state.

The mobile phone is a decentralized narratological device for documenting the city. Unlike previous media forms, mobile phones have been successfully marketed across economic lines. At the same time, these same "accessible" technologies continue to mimic the personal computer in their functionality. More importantly, even before the advent of the smartphone, recording and data devices allowed owners to take photos, video, and audio of their surroundings. While laptops were more costly and less portable, cellular phones offered a technology that a transient labor population could rely on. They could be operated in locations across the city and could function on periodic access to global Internet networks. More often published as text than as audio, *Voices* symbolizes the expression of individual observations of the city from those who often have no voice.

The LA Flood Project

Launched in 2006, as the red tide of media coverage of Hurricane Katrina was receding, *The LA Flood Project*—a multimodal, locative media project—started with the premise of a fictional deluge that submerges the city of Los Angeles. As it has grown into a mobile-optimized website and a mobile-phone app (in development), the collaborators, known as LAinundacion, have developed three major components: oral histories, fictional narratives, and an emergency simulation. While the oral histories are spoken by Angelenos and focus on a variety of crises that have befallen the city, the fictional narratives and emergency simulation focus on an imaginary epic flood. As the site describes:

> The LA Flood Project is a Rashomon-style multi-POV locative narrative experience that unfolds across LA, spilling over our cast of characters and the participants who join the flood through their cell phones. The Flood dredges to the surface the unspoken laws and logic of the city. It reveals hidden boundaries even as it spills over them.

In this way, *The LA Flood Project* combines elements of lived and imagined histories brought together on two annotated Google maps.[11] Travelers can interact with the piece in variations of three basic modes. The first is to read the Twitter stream of the piece, either during particular enactments when it is performed in "real" time or by reading transcripts. The second is to navigate one of the two maps either while traveling though geographic space of Los Angeles or by clicking on the web interface. The third way people can interact with the piece is by contributing their own lived memory of an event (and eventually their own fictional account of experiencing the flood) using the map interface or Twitter.

These modes of interaction embody the conflicts over the city (and how it is represented) that Iain Chambers describes in *Migrancy, Culture, Identity*. He writes,

> Maps are full of references and indications, but they are not peopled. They project the changing disposition of space through historical time in a mixed geometry of political, economic, and cultural powers. . . . But that preliminary orientation hardly exhausts the reality in which we find ourselves. For the city's denuded streets, buildings, bridges, monuments, squares and roads are also the contested sites of historical memory and provide the contexts, cultures, stories, languages, experiences, desires and hopes that course through the urban body.[12]

The LA Flood Project attempts to repopulate that map, to annotate it with the grit and absences of the city, and then to wash away layers of human infrastructure. It is an act of decorating a Google map not with mere points of interest but with graphical pushpins that open up to textual and audio reimaginings of the spaces and voices of those who would suffer in an epic flood. As travelers move through the city in person or via the map, they can select a point of interest to open a bubble with text and an embedded video. In this way, *The LA Flood Project* becomes not just an act of speculative cartography but rather an attempt to give polyphony to a map.

To that end, *The LA Flood Project* owes a debt to several sister projects: The Global Poetic System, *Invisible Seattle*, and Hypercities. The Global Poetic System was a literature-centered mobile-phone application developed by Laura Bórras and Juan B. Gutiérrez for the E-Poetry 2009 conference. The project was designed to offer travelers the ability to navigate the city of Barcelona across a meta-layer that marked the literary works written about various locations. *Invisible Seattle*, developed by the artist-collective the Invisibles in several media forms in the early 1980s, became known as the novel written by the city of Seattle.[13] To create that work, the Invisibles engaged in a series of content collection projects, asking Seattleites questions (such as, "Where is the best place to get killed in Seattle?"), and then incorporated the answers into the novel. Hypercities is a mapping platform developed by Todd Presner and others at UCLA, modeled after his Hypercities Berlin. Hypercities offers layers of historical data on top of real-time and historical maps. More importantly, it represents a platform for collecting and situating information by layering it virtually on an urban space. One of the more recent projects on Hypercities presents the narratives of historic Filipinotown, an ethnic enclave in Los Angeles first officially recognized in 2002. Produced by the PDUB Collective, a "youth + civic engagement" organization, this project presents visitors with digital content about Historic Filipinotown (Hi Fi) in the form of audio, visuals, and text. As with all the Hypercities projects, the map is a central interface for accessing and indexing these stories. The PDUB collective redraws the map by creating the collection of historical documents located upon the map, which then becomes the basis for the live, navigable museum.

The LA Flood Project is a distributed mobile narrative that grows out of this tradition of collecting data about the city and mapping it onto the city, in this case pairing the Google maps API and other information channels. In so doing, it participates in a growing trend of mashing location-based information with other forms of Internet content. Sophia Liu and Leysia Palen have documented this growing trend in their article, "The New Cartographers," in which they discuss the convergence of media, including photo sharing and microblogging platforms, which have led to the rise of many collectively created maps, particularly in moments of crisis. Liu and Palen discuss contemporary crises that have given rise to these mashups including wildfires in Los Angeles, Earthquake maps, swine-flu tweets, and Iranian political protests. From Michael Goodchild, they find the neogeographer's slogan, "We are all experts in our own local communities."[14] *The LA Flood Project* reflects back on this emerging communal form of information mashup by using the practice for fictional exploration.

However, *The LA Flood Project* was designed to be used *in situ*, to be used by travelers of Los Angeles as they moved through the city. Building on one of the first locative media narratives, *34 North, 118 West, The LA Flood Project* layers content upon the geospatial coordinates of the city. In so doing, it seeks to transform the city through a meta-layer of creative data accessible through mobile devices, particularly phones. As the project description explains, "A flood has hit Los Angeles. It is spilling deeper across streets, yards, roads; a disaster is unfolding across the city and voices are being heard on cell phones from the epicenter and beyond." In the original demo of the project, those voices were accessed through a voice tree menu over telephone lines. The goal was to use a platform that provided maximum access. However, as smartphone platforms began their exponential proliferation, it quickly became apparent to the project team that applications such as mapping tools and browsers would soon be standard across phones. The current version of the project maintains the role of voices by embedding the map with videos that contain the audio content originally delivered over the phone.

Inspired by the Global Poetic System, *The LA Flood Project* was designed to offer an augmented experience of the city as people moved through it. For that reason, areas on the map are described at a level of detail that cannot be assumed merely by looking at map. Consider the intersection of Martin Luther King Blvd. and Denker in the Leimert Park area of Los Angeles:

> The intersection of Denker and King marks the intersection of justice and injustice. Of clean wash and dirty gas station lots. LAPD across from Celes King III Bail Bonds, finger printing, and notary public. And if that doesn't wash it all clean, please step up and meet the Congress of Racial Equality, one of the big four Civil Rights groups to rise up in the nation. CORE, King, Cops, Wash, and Gas. If you are dirty or running on empty, if you are on the right or wrong side of laws, just or unjust, this intersection will help you find your way. And when the waters come in, from all four directions, station managers look out through bulletproof glass and say: Let's see what happens next.

Or consider the description of an area of the campus of the University of Southern California:

> Just outside the glass doors of the faculty dining room, Town and Gown, a woman, bundled in sweaters, threadbare, pauses with her listing rolling cart, over-full with soda cans and other trash-can discoveries. She sits on the lip of a fountain, which is off today because of the calls for rain. Across from her, something she has passed a thousand times but never noticed, a metal ship above the doors of the building. And further up, adorning the

top, cement dolphins and sea horses. Is it just her imagination that she hears rushing water?

Both these segments demonstrate the ways in which the descriptions direct the eye of the traveler, just as a label might in a museum exhibit. Although a museum catalog might be available online, the placards are developed to complement a particular spatial configuration.

The LA Flood Project, like *VozMob*, depends on contemporary smartphones' ability to offer the assemblage of technologies such as GIS/GPS, recording technology, and content management systems. Like *VozMob*, *The LA Flood Project* collects stories from Angelenos; however, unlike *VozMob*'s work to expand the notion of L.A. through underrepresented informants, *The LA Flood Project* expands its coverage by enlisting authors to reflect creatively on the city by rewriting the landscape through a fictional, epic deluge. *The LA Flood Project* thus asks participants to look at the landscape around them through imaginary augmented reality goggles. Furthermore, while *VozMob* provides one stable location to house the narratives, maintaining in effect the free movement of its contributors, *The La Flood Project* seeks to locate those stories in space by annotating maps with their locations.

At its core, *The LA Flood Project* is a piece of locative narrative, in which the elements of the narrative have been annotated onto online maps of Los Angeles, accessible through both Google maps and the Hypercities platform. The project imagines the ways the city would be transformed in the wake of a flood of epic proportions. The narrative is delivered as descriptions of the way various places in Los Angeles are impacted by the flood in its beginning, middle, and end stages, and is also complemented by monologues from point-of-view characters who are also experiencing the flood. All of this information is organized around pushpin locations, with the characters represented, in the Google map, by blue swimmer icons. When interactors select one of these icons, they open an annotation with either text or video (or both), the video framework serving primarily to deliver audio performances of the monologues by actors.

Distributed narratives like *The LA Flood Project* present themselves as the products of a million little microphones in the hands of a self-reporting population. *The LA Flood Project* seeks polyphony through the use of actors and multiple authors as well as first-person accounts recorded and archived as audio and video. Oral histories were gathered by USC students in the fall 2010 semester, documenting experiences that Angelenos have had with crises. They collected reports of earthquakes, riots, fires, and even train crashes. However, these accounts did not become the word-for-word material of the project; instead, the project sought to enact the "ethnographic ventriloquism"[15] advocated by project-advisor and L.A. historian Norman Klein, a practice of interviewing subjects and then letting their words direct our words. The characters that emerged in the project did take inspiration from these interviews and, ultimately, ranged in ethnicity and socio-economic status. While some of the characters seem to grow out of Angeleno archetypes, such as a wealthy xenophobic white man from Mulholland Drive or an African American preacher, others fit in with contemporary issues, such as the character of the subprime mortgage broker. These monologues locate subjective experiences of the crisis in a body, a place, and time, as these characters live through the three stages of the flood in a particular area.

The flood becomes a way of framing the city, and even the characters use it metaphorically. The preacher Reverend Les R. Fretten, modeled after Cecil B. Murray, uses it as a sign from God and then later as an opportunity to highlight community action. In another monologue, 19-year-old Juan Dominguez, "an idealistic student, debating between majoring in Philosophy, or Poetics, or Creative Writing, since Poetics is not a major that exists in the burgundy and gold of a private university," assesses the desolation from atop a dorm. He reflects on "catastrophic thinking," singing, "I can see clearly now/the rain is here." For Dominguez, "catastrophic thinking" is a form of "social control," delivered to him in the form of headlines about wars and the sufferings of the poor. Then, assessing his own situation, he says:

> Luckily for me, Park Side Student Housing's roof top is high enough I am not going to drown just yet and the view . . . even though the world has become but a quiet lake now, with a few roof tops shining visibly in the horizon, and furniture, and objects, placidly drifting with their spines above the waters. I now know I should've gone Wednesday to hear that panel on the warming of the planet or the melting of it. Well, at least all this water will cool it a little.

These characters emerge from a collection of writers, populating the city not in service of an overall plot but following the model of mobility, in expression of authorship distributed across a landscape.

At the 2011 Festival of Books in Los Angeles, an *LA Flood Project* event focused on the effects of the flood at the host site of the main campus of the University of Southern California. For that demonstration, *The LA Flood Project* authors, now expanded to include several novelists and poets, wrote monologues and narrative pieces specifically for the campus. At the same time, it added two technologies to the piece: QR codes and Twitter. To help identify the narrated Flood locations, LAinundacion placed QR codes around campus as virtual trail marks, which acted as links to the project website. Adding QR codes to the project has two effects. On the one hand, it links the project more closely to mobile technologies. Second, it acknowledges the ties between the physical locations and the online maps, showing the continued need for physical markers. Sticker QR codes allowed the project team the ability to do what once was the purview of the city managers and property owners. Consider, for example, the metal placards leading up to the downtown Manhattan Branch of the New York Public Library. Each contains a quote from a text from the shelves of the library embossed on a copper plate and implanted into the sidewalk. Such a project would be far beyond the average citizen until they take out their smartphone, open a map application, such as Google Maps, and begin their own annotation of the space. Sticker QR codes offer a physical marker that such annotations exist.

The second technology added to *The LA Flood Project* was the microblogging platform Twitter. The material affordances and constraints of the user interface of mobile phones has led to the rapid expansion of Twitter, as the 140-character limit of the platform grows out of the restrictions on SMS of 160 characters. It thus evoked the rise of text messaging in mobile-phone culture. The difficulty in typing longer posts on the handheld devices has also fueled the rise of this technology, which supports and encourages brevity. *The LA Flood Project* has run its Twitter simulation twice so far, once during the Festival of Books and over the course of a week in October 2011, during which over sixty five Twitter users participated in the narrating of the flood. To participate in the simulation, Twitter used hashtags, unique strings of characters that follow the # symbol and help group posts together. More recently, hashtags have become part of the interface as many Twitter clients allow users to click on a hashtag an easily call forth all the tweets on a specific topic. At the Festival of Books, *The LA Flood Project* made use of two tags: #laflood to mark inclusion in the fictional flood project and #LATFOB the tag being used by the festival of books to delimit those tweets. As a result, *The LA Flood Project* was able to serve up its *War-of-the-Worlds* style flood simulation through parasitical means, by stowing away, as it were, on the official Festival of Books hashtag.

The Twitter narrative was made up of a collection of voices, some emanating from *The LA Flood Project* group of core writers, others from the participants joining in by using the hashtag. The main @LAFloodProject account offered updates on the events of the flood:

> @LAFloodProject Warning: Flash Floods likelihood increasing for parts of the Southland over the next eight hours. #laflood

The simulation had a *War-of-the-Worlds* effect at times, as @mjcreativespark, apparently unaware of the fictional frame, expressed concern about driving up from San Diego, where there wasn't a cloud in the sky. The characters from the point-of-view monologues also tweeted their experience, including @RevLesRFretten who offered shelter, "The Church is open for shelter from the storm but not the storm of your soul." When reader-participant @iseehawksinla retweeted a fictional post by the @USCParking account that "Parking Structure A is completely flooded," the university-operated account was quick to contradict. Again, *The LA Flood Project* operated as venue for online improv—also called netprov—as well as a play on contemporary media practices in situations of disaster.[16] During the weeklong simulation, participants, with names like @broseiden1, struggled for survival, sometimes fending for themselves, other times banding together. While some perished, others survived to reflect on their journey:

> @nickpm1 @Dancerprof such a powerful and inspirational experience, and in the end, we're all better for it Fri October 28

Conclusion

In a monologue set at the California African American Museum, Nzingha Clarke writes about the experience of a Senegalese security guard, Ousmane, who speaks of his silence when being rescued along with a museum curator, "sweet girl":

> I never say my story. I never say in Senegal, in my village, we are artists too. When the sweet girl asks me about school I talk learning English and accounting, but I don't say I wish I never come to America—too much talk and no touch and people looking through me—so I paint pictures to keep my village with me and my home, my little room, is sun and the faces of my people and everything I remember is on my walls. The sweet girl and the art in this museum—faces that look like me, but are not my face; stories I know that are not my story—and this, my museum, are living in Los Angeles.

Ousmane at once desires to present himself as upwardly mobile American immigrant (learning English and finding more lucrative employment) and as an African artist who can depict his culture without merely presenting his own story. Distributed mobile narrative projects like *VozMob* and *The LA Flood Project* seek to disrupt the simplified media narratives in the same way. In a continually mediated city like Los Angeles, with its tremendous geographic scope and diversity of population, mobile distributive narratives can avoid reducing the people in its stories to types. Instead, through polyphonic narratives, these projects capture as many voices as possible and tell stories that often go untold.

Notes

1. Mikhail Bakhtin, *The Dialogic Imagination: Four Essays*, ed. Michael Holquist (Austin, TX: University of Texas Press, 1981), 428.
2. Quoted in Mike Davis, *City of Quartz: Excavating the Future in Los Angeles* (New York: Verso, 1990), 20.
3. See Davis, *City of Quartz*.
4. CTIA Advocacy, "U.S. Wireless Quick Facts," http://www.ctia.org/advocacy/research/index.cfm/AID/10323.
5. Gayatri Chakravorty Spivak, "Can the Subaltern Speak?" in *Colonial Discourse and Post-Colonial Theory: A Reader*, ed. Patrick Williams and Laura Chrisman (New York: Columbia University Press, 1994), 66–111.

6. Here I invoke Bakhtin's term from *Problems of Dostoyevsky's Poetics*: in which polyphony names not just the multivocality of the novel but the multiplicity of discourse registers that a broad spectrum of voices brings. See Mikhail Bakhtin, *Problems of Dostoevsky's Poetics* (Minneapolis, MN: University Of Minnesota Press, 1984).
7. In "Public Secrets" and "Blood Sugar," Sharon Daniel's collaborations with designer Erik Loyer, the pair create novel interfaces to navigate nonsequentially the voices of contributors who offered their tales to the piece. Central to Daniel's practice is collecting and archiving the histories of women in prison or in needle exchange programs and presenting them even more prominently, arguably, than her own authorial voice. Quoted from Sharon Daniel, Presentation at the NEH Vectors Summer Institute, Institute for Multimedia Literacy (Los Angeles: University of Southern California, July 26, 2011).
8. See "About Vozmob," http://vozmob.net/en/about.
9. "Mobile Voices Wins UN Information Technology Award," *USC Annenberg News*, November 15, 2010, http://annenberg.usc.edu/News%20and%20Events/News/101115VozMobUN.aspx.
10. Ben Stokes, Interview with the author, July 30, 2011.
11. All told, *The LA Flood Project* uses Twitter, WordPress, YouTube, Google Maps, Drop Box, and UCLA's Hypercities platforms to deliver its content.
12. Iain Chambers, *Migrancy, Culture, Identity* (New York: Routledge, 1994), 611.
13. *Invisible Seattle: The Novel of Seattle, by Seattle* (Seattle: Function Industries Press, 1987).
14. Sophia B. Liu and Leysia Palen, "The New Cartographers: Crisis Map Mashups and the Emergence of Neogeographic Practice," *Cartography and Geographic Information Science* 37, no. 1 (2010): 88.
15. Klein's use of "ethnographic ventriloquism" was specific to this artistic project rather than a broader proposal for sound anthropological methodology.
16. Rob Wittig and I have developed this form of online improvisation for *The LA Flood Project* and subsequent projects. Later developed in Rob's dissertation, the first articulation appeared in a blog post by Marino and Wittig. See Mark C. Marino and Rob Wittig "Netprov—Networked Improv Literature," *Writer Response Theory*, http://writerresponsetheory.org/wordpress/2011/05/12/netprov-networked-improv-literature/.

ACKNOWLEDGMENTS

This book is perhaps the most collaborative project I have ever worked on; thus, there are many people to thank and acknowledge. First, I must thank each of the authors who contributed to this collection. They each put in an extensive amount of time conceiving of the ideas in the chapters, working with me on approaches that would fit with this collection, and then producing several revisions. Their patience and encouragement through the long process has been invaluable. I am incredibly proud of the work they have produced here and am honored that each of them has agreed to work with me to create a book of such caliber.

I am also extremely grateful for the people at Routledge for believing so strongly in this book and offering such strong support throughout this process. After working with Erica Wetter as my editor for *Mobile Interface Theory*, I was thrilled to get the chance to work on another book with her. She is such a phenomenal editor, and this work exists because of her vision and guidance. I am also grateful to Margo Irvin for all of her help, guidance, and encouragement as she helped shepherd the book through the publication process. As always, the production staff at Routledge is a fantastic group, and I am thankful for all of the skill and knowledge they bring to this process.

I would also like to thank my colleagues in the Department of American Studies at the University of Maryland. They have each gone above and beyond to support my research and offer wisdom and guidance, and they have believed in the importance of my work. I am grateful to be a part of such a collaborative and supportive department.

Finally, I would like to thank my family. My wife, Susan, has been so amazingly supportive, sacrificial, and encouraging throughout the process of working on this book. The majority of this book was worked on soon after the birth of my first child. Looking at the scope of this book in hindsight, it seems like an insurmountable thing to accomplish while spending most of my days raising our son. With the help of my wife and our family, we were able to complete this book. Again, I am tremendously proud of this collection and thankful to all who have been involved to help it move from the initial concept stage through production and distribution.

ABOUT THE CONTRIBUTORS

Bryan Alexander is a researcher, teacher, writer, speaker, futurist, and consultant working in the field of academia and technology. He is the senior fellow for the National Institute for Technology in Liberal Education (NITLE), where he focuses on emerging trends in the integration of inquiry, pedagogy, and technology and their potential application to higher education. His current research interests include the digital humanities, future studies, digital storytelling, social media, and information literacy. His 2011 book, *The New Digital Storytelling*, was published by Praeger. Alexander holds a Ph.D. from the University of Michigan and has taught English and information technology studies as faculty at Centenary College of Louisiana. He lives in Ripton, Vermont, where he homesteads in an off-the-grid direction with his family and many animals.

John F. Barber is a faculty member of the Creative Media & Digital Culture Program at Washington State University, Vancouver. His teaching and research focuses on digital archiving and curating, usability and interface design, and digital audio. His recent publications include, "Winged Words: On the Theory and Use of Internet Radio" in *Going Wireless: A Critical Exploration of Wireless and Mobile Technologies for Composition Teachers and Researchers* (Hampton Press, 2009). He is also noted for creating the preeminent resource regarding the life and works of American author Richard Brautigan: The Brautigan Bibliography and Archive (www.brautigan.net) and for his work with The Brautigan Library (www.thebrautiganlibrary.org).

Ben S. Bunting, Jr is an Assistant Professor of Humanities at the Oregon Institute of Technology. His areas of research include game studies, space/place theory, ecocriticism, urban exploration, and locative technology. He has published several book chapters and journal articles on these topics and is currently working on turning his interdisciplinary dissertation "Alternative Wildernesses: Finding Wildness in 21st Century America" into a book, as well as editing a collection on the idea of reading video gameworlds as "virtual wildernesses." He earned his Ph.D. from Washington State University in 2012.

Mark Carnall is the curator of the 67,000 specimens held in the Grant Museum of Zoology. He has previously worked and volunteered at local, national, and university natural history museums. Since arriving at the Grant Museum in 2004, he has been working to document and conserve the zoological and paleontological collections, as well as making the collections more available to audiences through the Internet and through public engagement work. He is also involved with the museums outreach and education program.

Jennifer Chatsick has worked as a literacy worker in several community-based adult literacy programs and has worked as an integration facilitator, supporting students with intellectual disabilities, in a college setting for ten years. Jennifer is currently working toward the completion of her BSW at Ryerson University.

Adriana de Souza e Silva is Associate Professor at the Department of Communication at North Carolina State University (NCSU), affiliated faculty at the Digital Games Research Center, and a faculty member of the Communication, Rhetoric and Digital Media (CRDM) program at NCSU. De Souza e Silva's research focuses on how mobile and locative interfaces shape people's interactions with public spaces and create new forms of sociability. She teaches classes on mobile technologies, location-based games, and Internet studies. De Souza e Silva is the co-editor (with Daniel M. Sutko) of *Digital Cityscapes—Merging Digital and Urban Playspaces* (Peter Lang, 2009), the co-author (with Eric Gordon) of *Net-Locality: Why Location Matters in a Networked World* (Blackwell, 2011), and the co-author (with Jordan Frith) of *Mobile Interfaces in Public Spaces: Control, Privacy, and Urban Sociability* (Routledge, 2012). She holds a Ph.D. in Communication and Culture from the Federal University of Rio de Janeiro, Brazil.

Jason Farman is Assistant Professor at University of Maryland, College Park, in the Department of American Studies, and a Distinguished Faculty Fellow in the Digital Cultures and Creativity Program. He is author of the book *Mobile Interface Theory: Embodied Space and Locative Media* (Routledge, 2012—winner of the 2012 Book of the Year Award from the Association of Internet Researchers), which focuses on how the worldwide adoption of mobile technologies is causing a reexamination of the core ideas about what it means to live our everyday lives: the practice of embodied space. He is currently working on a book project called *Technologies of Disconnection: A History of Mobile Media and Social Intimacy.* He has published scholarly articles on such topics as mobile technologies, Google maps, social media, videogames, digital storytelling, digital performance art, and surveillance. Farman has been a contributing author for *The Atlantic* and *The Chronicle of Higher Education*. He has also been interviewed on NPR's *Marketplace Tech Report*, and in *The Christian Science Monitor*, the *Baltimore Sun*, and *The Denver Post*, among others. He received his Ph.D. in Digital Media and Performance Studies from the University of California, Los Angeles.

Jordan Frith is Assistant Professor in the Department of Linguistics and Technical Communication at the University of North Texas. His research focuses on mobile technologies and social media. He is particularly interested in location-based social networks like Foursquare and how people use them to connect with others. His research also focuses on how people manage privacy when using social media and how mobile technologies affect the way people experience place. With Adriana de Souza e Silva, he has co-authored the forthcoming book, *Mobile Interfaces in Public Spaces: Locational Privacy, Control and Urban Sociability* (Routledge, 2012). He has published articles in journals such as *Mobilities* and *Communication, Culture and Critique*. He received his Ph.D. from the Communication, Rhetoric and Digital Media Program at North Carolina State University.

Alberto S. Galindo is a scholar focusing on U.S. Latino literature and culture. Currently, he is working on a series of essays centered on 9/11–related cultural production from the United States and Latin America. The project seeks to ask questions weighing different types of narratives such as novels and mobile-phone applications and their relationship to spaces such as New York City and the U.S.-Mexico border. The first essay from this project, "Contagion of Intellectual Traditions in Post-9/11 Novels," was published as part of a collection titled *Contagion: Heath, Fear, and Sovereignty* from the University of Washington Press (2012). This larger project is founded on his dissertation research titled "Atlas of AIDS: Culture, Circulation and AIDS in Latin America," (Princeton, 2006) which looked at HIV/AIDS as a historical and cultural event that altered the narratives of Latin American and Caribbean writers.

David Gauntlett is Professor of Media and Communications at the University of Westminster, where he co-directs the United Kingdom's leading center for media and communications research. He is the author of several books, including *Creative Explorations* (2007) and *Making Is Connecting* (2011). He has made several popular YouTube videos, and produces the website about media and identities, Theory.org.uk. He has conducted collaborative research with a number of the world's leading creative organizations, including LEGO, the BBC, the British Library, and Tate.

Gerard Goggin is Professor of Media and Communications at the University of Sydney. He is author of various books on mobiles, including *Politics of Mobile Social*

Media (with Kate Crawford); *Mobile Technology and Place* (with Rowan Wilken); *Global Mobile Media, Internationalizing Internet Studies* (with Mark McLelland); *Mobile Technologies: From Telecommunications to Media* (with Larissa Hjorth); and *Cell Phone Culture*. He holds a doctorate in English Literature from the University of Sydney.

Steven Gray is a research associate with the Centre for Advanced Spatial Analysis and a Ph.D. student at University College, London. He is currently working as part of a project that aims to provide a platform to meet the demand for powerful simulation tools by social scientists and public and private sector policymakers. Previously, Gray worked at the University of Glasgow as a research assistant with the Glasgow Interaction and Systems Group (GIST—Computing Science) as part of the EPSRC–funded Open Interface project. His current research interests include human computer interaction, mobile development, accessible web development with a focus on social media, web-based mapping, and ubiquitous computing.

Dene Grigar is Associate Professor and Director of The Creative Media & Digital Culture Program at Washington State University, Vancouver, who works in the area of electronic literature, emergent technology and cognition, and ephemera. She is the author of "Fallow Field: A Story in Two Parts" and "The Jungfrau Tapes: A Conversation with Diana Slattery about *The Glide Project*," both of which have appeared in the *Iowa Review Web*, and *When Ghosts Will Die* (with Canadian multimedia artist Steve Gibson), a piece that experiments with motion-tracking technology to produce networked multimedia narratives. Her most recent project is the "Fort Vancouver Mobile," a project funded by a 2011 NEH Start Up Grant that brings together a core team of eighteen scholars, digital storytellers, historians, and archaeologists to create location-aware nonfiction content for mobile phones to be used at the Fort Vancouver National Historic Site. Grigar is a curator of media art, specializing in electronic literature, and is currently developing exhibits for the Library of Congress, the Modern Language Association, and the Electronic Literature Organization.

Caroline Hamilton is Australian Endeavour Fellow researching in collaboration with the Institute for the Future of the Book and McKenzie Research Fellow in Publishing and Communications at the University of Melbourne. She is the author of *One Man Zeitgeist: Dave Eggers, Publishing and Publicity*. She holds a doctorate in English Literature from the University of Sydney.

Lone Koefoed Hansen is a researcher working in the interface between mobile media, urban space, and everyday performativity. She is Assistant Professor at Aarhus University (Denmark) in the Department of Aesthetic Studies and the Digital Design Program. Her Ph.D. focused on digital aesthetics and culture in the age of pervasive computing and mobile media, and she has published work in journals such as *Digital Creativity* and *International Journal of Performance Arts and Digital Media*, in books such as *Interface Criticism* (Aarhus University Press), and at conferences such as Digital Arts and Culture.

Larissa Hjorth is an artist, digital ethnographer, and senior lecturer in the Games Programs at RMIT University. Since 2000, Hjorth has been researching gendered customizing of mobile communication, gaming, and virtual communities in the Asia–Pacific—these studies are outlined in her book, *Mobile Media in the Asia–Pacific* (Routledge, 2008). Hjorth has published widely on the topic in national and international journals such as *Games and Culture Journal*, *Convergence*, *Journal of Intercultural Studies, Continuum, ACCESS, Fibreculture*, and *Southern Review*, as well as co-editing two Routledge anthologies, *Gaming Cultures and Place in the Asia–Pacific Region* (with Dean Chan, 2009) and *Mobile Technologies: From Telecommunication to Media* (with Gerard Goggin, 2009). In 2010 Hjorth released *Games & Gaming* textbook (Berg, 2011). Since 2009, Hjorth has been Australian Research Council discovery fellow with Michael Arnold, exploring the role of the local and social media in the Asia-Pacific region.

Andrew Hudson-Smith is Senior Research Fellow and Research Manager at the Centre for Advanced Spatial Analysis (CASA), University College, London. He is Editor-in-Chief of *Future Internet Journal*, an elected fellow of the Royal Society of Arts, and Course Founder and Director of the MRes in Advanced Spatial Analysis and Visualisation at UCL. He is author of the Digital Urban Blog, recently voted one of the "Top 5 Web 2.0 Blogs" by *PC Pro Magazine*: http://www.digitalurban.blogspot.com/. His work has featured widely in the media including, *Sky Television*, *The Times*, *The Guardian*, and most recently, *New Scientist*, BBC Radio 4, and BBC Radio 5.

Susan Kozel is a dancer, choreographer, and philosopher working at the convergence of performance and digital technologies. She is Professor of New Media with the MEDEA Collaborative Media Initiative at the University of Malmö, Sweden, and is the director of Mesh Performance Practices (http://www.meshperformance.org). She has published and performed widely. Her writing includes *Closer: Performance, Technologies, Phenomenology* (MIT Press 2007); a book in progress called *Social Choreographies: Corporeal Aesthetics with Mobile Media* (expected in 2013); and recent pieces on artistic research, ubiquitous computing, and bodily expression in electronic music. Her collaborative performances and installations include the *Technologies of Inner Spaces* series (*immanence*, 2005; *Other Stories*, 2007; and *The Yellow Memory*, 2009); *whisper[s] wearable computing*, 2002–2005; and *trajets*, 2000–2007. Current collaborations include experiments with social networking applications for improvised performance (*IntuiTweet*, 2009–2010) and (*Alone or Not*, 2011), and using augmented reality mobile-phone applications as a space for embedding movement in urban spaces.

Paula Levine is a visual artist focusing on experimental narrative and new forms of narrative spaces. Her research/art practice is in GPS technology, wireless, and remote devices. Levine has twenty years of experience in experimental documentary photography and video. Her current work looks at hidden dynamics as a way to develop new understandings about the nature of place. Her works have been shown in video festivals, galleries, and museums worldwide. Levine teaches in conceptual/information arts, an area focusing on digital art and experimental technologies in the Art Department at San Francisco State University.

Mark C. Marino is an associate professor (teaching) at the University of Southern California where he also directs the Humanities and Critical Code Studies (HaCCS) Lab. In addition to his work on *The LA Flood Project* as part of LAinundacion, he has written electronic fiction and drama, having worked on video games and as a consultant for Disney. He is Director of Communication for the Electronic Literature Organization and the editor of *Bunk Magazine*, an online humor 'zine. Most recently, he has collaborated on *10 PRINT CHR$(205.5+RND(1));: GOTO 10* (MIT, 2013), a book-length, critical code studies reading of a single line of code.

Rhonda McEwen is Assistant Professor at the Institute of Communication, Culture and Information Technology at the University of Toronto. She holds an MBA in IT from City University in London, United Kingdom; an MSc in Telecommunications from the University of Colorado; and a Ph.D. in Information from the University of Toronto. McEwen's research and teaching centers around information practices involving new media technologies, with an emphasis on mediated technologies for persons with sensory disabilities, mobile communication, social media design, and youth information practices. She has worked and researched digital communications media for fifteen years, both in companies providing services and in management consulting to those companies. McEwen is currently researching the use of iPod and iPad devices by nonverbal autistic children for communication and sociality in two Toronto school settings.

Brett Oppegaard, Ph.D., Assistant Professor of Communication at Washington State University, Vancouver, has developed a research expertise in net locality, or mobile place-based media. He and Dene Grigar earned a National Endowment for the Humanities Digital Start-Up Grant for an innovative mobile media partnership with the National Park Service. He now works in The Creative Media and Digital Culture program at WSU Vancouver, in partnership with The Edward R. Murrow College of Communication at WSU Pullman, and his research specialty of mobile media has led him to explore ways in which journalism and mediated interpretation can expand into scholarly place-based forms through locative media, augmented reality, and mixed reality.

Didem Ozkul is a Ph.D. candidate at the Communications and Media Research Institute at the University of Westminster. Her current research concerns people's use of mobile communication technologies in urban spaces, particularly focusing on spatial perception. For her research, she engages in creative methodologies (sketch maps) in order to explore and visualize the transformations in sense of place and whether mobile and locative media has an affect on those transformations. Details about her study can be found at www.mobilenodes.co.uk.

Jeff Ritchie is Associate Professor and Chair of the of Digital Communications Department at Lebanon Valley College and teaches courses in information design, narrative across media, writing for digital media, multimedia design and development, and video games. He received a B.A. in English and a B.S. in Marketing from Indiana University, an M.A. in English from the University of South Carolina, and a M.Ed. in Educational Media and Computers and a Ph.D. in English from Arizona State University. His current research focus is information design, digital media narratives, designing choice architectures, and the rhetoric of interactivity and space. He serves as Assistant Editor for *The International Digital Media and Arts Association (iDMAa) Journal* and sits on iDMAa's board.

Claire Ross is a research assistant in the Department of Information Studies, and for the Centre for Digital Humanities at University College, London. Her research focuses on user evaluation and user-centric design of social media applications, online museum collections, and cross-repository searching. Her specific research interests include usability studies, Web 2.0 applications, social media, museum e-learning, digital heritage, and digital repositories. She is also Chair of the Digital Learning Network for Museums, Libraries and Archives.

Marc Ruppel is Program Officer with the National Endowment for the Humanities. He completed his Ph.D. at the University of Maryland, College Park, where he wrote a dissertation that applies network visualization as a tool in understanding audience, media, and narrative in transmedia fictions. Ruppel has worked on projects ranging from the NSF–funded educational Alternate Reality Game *The Arcane Gallery of Gadgetry* (http://www.arcanegalleryofgadgetry.org/) to Reboot Stories' *Robot Heart Stories* (http://www.robotheartstories.com/), and has published several articles on transmedia practices in journals such as *Convergence: The International Journal of Research into New Media* and the *International Journal of Learning and Media*.

Mark Sample is Associate Professor in the Department of English at George Mason University, where is he also an affiliated faculty member with Mason's Honors College, its Cultural Studies program, and the Center for History and New Media. His teaching and research focuses on contemporary literature, new media, and video games. His examination of the representation of torture in video games appeared in *Game Studies*, and his critique of the digital humanities' approach to contemporary literature is a chapter in *Debates in the Digital Humanities* (University of Minnesota Press, 2012). Sample has work in *Hacking the Academy*, a crowdsourced scholarly book forthcoming in print by the digitalculturebooks imprint of the University of Michigan Press. Sample's most recent project is 10 PRINT CHR$(205.5+RND(1));: GOTO 10, a collaboratively written book about creative computing and the Commodore 64, which was published by MIT Press in 2013. He received an M.A. in Communication, Culture, and Technology from Georgetown University and his Ph.D. from the University of Pennsylvania.

Melissa Terras is Reader in Electronic Communication in the Department of Information Studies at University College, London, and is Deputy Director of the Centre for Digital Humanities at UCL. She is the Programme Director for the new M.A. in Digital Humanities at UCL. Her research is in the development of technological approaches that would allow new research within the humanities, including image processing, digitization, and usability. She is Secretary of the Association of Literary and Linguistic Computing, and is the General Editor of *Digital Humanities Quarterly*. She is Associate Director of the LinkSphere project and co-Investigator of the eScience and Ancient Documents project.

Claire Warwick is Reader in Digital Humanities in the Department of Information Studies at University College, London, and Director of the UCL Centre for Digital Humanities. She is also the Programme Director for the M.A. in Electronic Communication and Publishing, and Vice-Dean for Research for the Faculty of Arts and Humanities. Her research is in the area of digital humanities, particularly in the development and use of electronic texts and digital libraries. She is Associate Director of the LinkSphere project, and lead researcher of the User Experience group of the INKE project.

Rowan Wilken holds an Australian Research Council–funded Discovery Early Career Researcher Award (DECRA) in the Swinburne Institute for Social Research, Swinburne University of Technology, Melbourne, Australia. His present research interests include locative and mobile media, digital technologies and culture, domestic technology consumption, old and new media, and theories and practices of everyday life. He is the author of *Teletechnologies, Place, and Community* (Routledge, 2011) and co-editor (with Gerard Goggin) of *Mobile Technology and Place* (Routledge, 2012).

Anne Zbitnew is a lecturer and instructor at the Humber College Institute of Technology and Advanced Learning. She is an educator, a photographer, and a visual storyteller currently working on an undergraduate degree in Disability Studies at Ryerson University in Toronto.

INDEX